AF663529

Public Administration in the 21st Century

Public Administration in the 21st Century

Edited by

DR. NOORJAHAN BAVA
Professor of Political Science (Retd.)
University of Delhi and
Member, Executive Council
Indian Institute of Public Administration
New Delhi

KANISHKA PUBLISHERS, DISTRIBUTORS
NEW DELHI-110 002

KANISHKA PUBLISHERS, DISTRIBUTORS
4697/5-21 A, Ansari Road, Daryaganj
New Delhi-110 002
Phones : 2327 0497, 2328 8285
Fax : 011-2328 8285
E-mail: kanishka_publishing@yahoo.co.in

Public Administration in the 21st Century

First Published–2004
Edition–2010
ISBN: 978-81-7391-698-5

PRINTED IN INDIA

Published by Madan Sachdeva for Kanishka Publishers, Distributors, 4697/5-21A, Ansari Road, Daryaganj, New Delhi-110 002, Typeset by Sunshine Graphics, Delhi, and Printed at Rajdhani Printers, Delhi.

RAJ BHAVAN
BANGALORE

December 10, 2003

Message

I am happy to learn that the Indian Institute of Public Administration, with which I have been intimately associated for over four decades, is organizing a two-day National Conference on Public Administration in the 21st Century on December 12-13, 2003 as part of the Golden Jubilee Celebrations of the Institute.

I am also pleased to note that distinguished persons at the helm of India's higher education—Dr. Arun Nigavekar, Chairman University Grants Commission; Dr. V.R. Panchmukhi, Chairman, Indian Council of Social Science Research; and Shri Arun Bhatnagar, Secretary, Department of Personnel and Training, will be actively participating in the inaugural session, giving the benefit of their valuable perceptions and inputs.

Administration has increasingly become inter-disciplinary and para-disciplinary in character. Not only social sciences but even physical sciences necessitate intimate, close and continuous exchange and interaction. Knowledge has been called a seamless garment. All categories and branches of knowledge ultimately aim at the betterment of society in consonance with the requirements and compulsions of a fast changing society. It is only through the mutuality of understanding and support of different institutions and fields of knowledge that we can take meaningful view of the concepts of governance in the 21st century with its challenges, opportunities and possibilities. This only further underscores the relevance and significance of the scope and worth-whileness of the Conference that you propose to hold as well as the vital importance of inter-institutional coordination which your effort represents.

Much as I would like to personally attend the function, commitments in Bangalore prevent me from doing so. However, on this happy occasion in the annals of the IIPA, I convey my best wishes for the success of the Conference. My sincere appreciation goes to the Hon'ble Chairman of

UGC and ICCSR, and Secretary, DOPT for their strong academic and financial support of the Institute for this laudable purpose. I hope that such academic, collaborations grow from strength to strength, benefiting the partner institutions, academic community and the country at large.

T.N. Chaturvedi

(T.N. Chaturvedi)
Vice-President, IIPA,
Chairman, Golden Jubilee
High Powered Committee

Dr. P.L. Sanjeev Reddy
Director
Indian Institute of Public Administration
New Delhi.

Foreword

Public Administration at the present juncture is undergoing a paradigm shift. New challenges thrown up by the changes in socio-economic and political landscape and the seamless possibilities offered by the new technologies call for a wider and deeper understanding to make public administration capable of responding to these sea changes. The cutting edge issues of improving governance and making it responsible and responsive remain important. But they are beset with increasing problems of efficiency, commitment, motivation, resource constraints, conflicting pulls, and rising expectations of the citizens which need to be addressed upfront.

Efficient and effective governance requires institutions, delivery mechanisms and the framework of supportive rules, regulations and procedures to continuously evolve in harmony with each other and in tune with the changing milieu. Inertia, inefficiency and asymmetries in relevant institutions and their practices can frustrate the best of programmes and policies. Responsive and responsible administration is critical to the fulfillment of our avowed social, economic and administrative goals. Even when there is a growing pressure to gravitate towards market and civil society, the issues of distributive justice, rule of law, and social warrant necessitate a key role for public administration. A proper administrative framework with vibrant mechanisms and efficient systems need to be in place to ensure citizen centric administration.

IIPA being a premier institute for research and teaching of public administration in India, has over the last fifty years been actively involved in responding to the concerns of public administration in order to make it more meaningful and relevant to the changing needs of the society. As IIPA celebrates its Golden Jubilee, this responsibility becomes even more significant. To commemorate the occasion, a two-day National Conference was hosted to facilitate mature discussions on **'Public Administration in the 21st Century'**.

The Conference discussed various trends, challenges and reforms in public administration, new paradigms in public administration, human resource development and human rights issues, IT revolution and E-Governance, decentralization and development administration with a view to answer the societal needs. It is recognized that the dynamic discipline of public administration is overflowing with paradigmatic diversity, conflicting cross currents, and a continuing assault on all orthodoxies. We discerned a surge of interest in the normative dimensions of public administration making it a key player in the process of democratic governance. Looking at the richness of the deliberations and the quality of papers presented by reflective theoreticians and practitioners, it was considered worthwhile to put together the proceedings of the Conference and the papers presented in the shape of a volume.

The imperatives of public administration in the 21st century are new forms of governance with a wide range of active participants as old forms of public and private governance are proving ineffective and inadequate. The rigid modes of power concentration that mark the existing organizations would increasingly give way to more flexible and dynamic models. In the increasingly globalizing world, national governments seem destined to become only one of many decision-making modes on a vast network. Setting and achieving goals would require constantly changing constellation of collaborative efforts. Fostering shared values is a prerequisite for functionally efficient and eminently workable networking decision-making. To adapt to these changes, public and private organizations are required to regularly redistribute responsibilities depending on the nature of the tasks at hand rather than on the basis of rigid hierarchies. Success will depend on using the richest sources of knowledge about the specific problem and solution as per the contextual relevance. A radical diffusion of authority and acceptance of experimentation with its failures and breakthroughs appear to be key ingredients for realizing the benefits of unfolding profound changes.

This volume, with contributions from 'high end scholars' from across the country will hopefully catalyse a healthy debate on the manner in which public administration in this country needs to transform itself in the interest of citizens and thereby contribute to improving the quality of life, societal peace, harmony and progress in the emerging global knowledge society. The papers cover wide and variegated range such as modernising Public Administration, Public Policy model, Public Choice orientation, Reinventing Government, Good Governance, New Public Management and Strategic Management. Notwithstanding their distinctive identities these trends have interlinkages and intrinsic commonalities that make contemporary public administration richer and profounder.

The scholarly message of His Excellency Shri T.N. Chaturvedi, the then Vice-President, IIPA, who is currently the Chairman of the Executive Council of IIPA as well as the Governor of Karnataka and Kerala has set the right tone for the Conference triggering a healthy and seamless interdisciplinary interaction. I convey my gratitude to the late Shri S.B. Chavan, Chairman of IIPA, and Shri Chaturvediji for their sustained support and guidance for making the Golden Jubilee celebrations of IIPA a landmark event. I express my thanks to all the authors, speakers, sponsors, discussants/participants for making this Volume a storehouse of knowledge. My colleagues in the IIPA who provided necessary infrastructural support for successfully conducting the Conference deserve appreciation. I compliment and congratulate **Prof. Dr. Noorjahan Bava**, an active member of IIPA's Executive Council, for ably editing the Volume and imparting a fascinating shape to the wide ranging deliberations. The entire IIPA fraternity would feel amply rewarded if this publication can trigger a healthy and constructive debate on the issues of contemporary relevance and concern so well flagged in the Volume.

5.6.04

June 6, 2004

DR. P.L. SANJEEV REDDY
Director
Indian Institute of Public Administration
New Delhi.

Acknowledgements

This Volume marks the successful completion of Fifty Years of glorious existence and spectacular service rendered to the Nation in the field of Public Administration by the Indian Institute of Public Administration, founded by **Pt. Jawaharlal Nehru**, the First Prime Minister of India on March 29, 1954, based on the recommendations of **Prof. Dean Paul Appleby**, a consultant of the Ford Foundation.

With deep gratitude and sincere thanks the Editor **(Prof. Noorjahan Bava)** acknowledges on behalf of the late **Shri S.B. Chavan,** Chairman, Executive Council of the Indian Institute of Public Administration, **Hon'ble Shri T.N.Chaturvedi,** Chairman, High Power Committee on Golden Jubilee Celebrations and **Dr. P.L. Sanjeev Reddy,** Director of the IIPA, the receipt of the great financial help/grants-in-aid provided by the **Department of Personnel and Training, Ministry of Personnel, Public Grievances and Pensions, Government of India** and **Shri Bhaskar Chatterjee, IAS,** Director-General and Member-Secretary, **Indian Council of Social Science Research** without which the IIPA could not have hosted the two-day **Golden Jubilee National Conference on Public Administration in the 21st Century** on December 12-13, 2003 at New Delhi.

I am deeply indebted to **Prof. Arun Nigavekar,** Chairman, University Grants Commission for accepting our invitation and delivering the Inaugural Address at the Conference on December 12, 2003.

My sincere thanks go to late **Shri S.B. Chavan,** former Chairman and other members of the Executive Council of the Institute for approving my proposal, submitted in February 2003, to hold a National Conference on Public Administration in the 21st Century as part of the Golden Jubilee Celebrations of the IIPA and for nominating me as a Member to the High Power Committee to work out the modalities of the celebrations.

I sincerely thank Hon'ble **Shri T.N.Chaturvedi,** Chairman of the Golden Jubilee High Power Committee for appointing me as the Convenor of the National Conference on Public Administration in the 21st Century and as the Editor of the Golden Jubilee Volume comprising the proceedings and papers of the Conference. I also take this opportunity to offer my profound thanks to His Excellency **Shri T.N.Chaturvedi,** Governor of Karnataka for sending his gracious Message and Good Wishes for the success of the Conference.

My profound and sincere thanks to **Shri G.C.L. Joneja,** Vice-President and Chairman, Standing Committee of the Institute for presiding over the Inaugural Session and **Shri B.C. Mathur,** Hony. Treasurer of the IIPA for delivering the Valedictory Address.

I am deeply indebted to **Dr. Sanjeev Reddy,** Director, Indian Institute of Public Administration for all his enthusiastic and timely help, unstinting cooperation, support and resourcefulness without which I could not have organized and conducted the two-day National Conference with such a run-away success. In fact, the Golden Jubilee Conference was his show and I only provided the intellectual inputs and played an instrumental role as the Convenor of the Conference.

My special thanks to Dr. Reddy and his Office Staff for providing me secretarial assistance; for interacting/inviting dignitaries, generating resources for the Conference and extending comfortable stay and hospitality to all the delegates for four days, December 11-14th, 2003.

My sincere thanks are also due to **Dr. Naresh Kumar,** Registrar, Indian Institute of Public Administration for overseeing and coordinating the activities connected with the Conference.

My profound thanks go to **Shri T.K. Kaul,** Deputy Registrar (Academic Support) and **Dr. B.D. Singh,** Research Officer for all the good work done by them at two different stages. First, they zeroxed and circulated the entire set of the Conference papers amongst the delegates and dignitaries besides manning the Registration Desk and serving refreshments to participants on the two days of the Conference (December 12-13, 2003). At the second stage Mr. Kaul and his staff carried out an onerous job connected with the publication of the proceedings and papers of the Conference into the **Golden Jubilee Volume on Public Administration in the 21st Century.** After the Editor (Prof. Noorjahan Bava) edited all the papers and the transcripts, they ensured that the corrections made by the Editor were carried out carefully in the manuscripts and floppy diskettes. I thank them once again in putting the manuscripts–both the Hard Copy and the Soft Copy into shape prior to handing them over to the Publisher, Kanishka Publishers, Distributors, New Delhi.

I also thank **Dr. P. Bapaiah,** Deputy Registrar (Finance and Administration) and his staff for managing and keeping proper accounts of the grants given by the Department of Personnel and Training, Government of India and by the Indian Council of Social Science Research for the Conference and also for efficiently handling the work relating to the disbursement of the T.A. and Honorarium bills to the paper presenters, session chairmen and rapporteurs.

I wish to thank all the delegates from various universities in the country who braved the Delhi winter and came and presented their papers. My thanks are also due to **Prof. S.R. Maheshwari, Prof. S.P. Verma, Prof. V. Bhaskara Rao, Prof. Ramesh K. Arora, Prof. R.K. Sachdeva** and **Prof. Renuka Garg** for chairing and efficiently conducting the various Business Sessions of the Conference those two days. I also thank **Dr. Inderjeet Kaur, Dr. Radhanath Tripathi, Dr. Sangeeta Dhal** and **Dr. Durgesh Nandini** who acted as the Rapporteurs for the Conference.

Given my long association with the IIPA as its Life Member for more than 30 years, as Member of the Executive Council for four consecutive terms (16 years) since 1988 till date and as the proud participant of the prestigious IIIrd Advanced Professional Programme in Public Administration of the Institute in 1977-78 as the Delhi University and UGC Fellow, I would be happy if the readers treat this Golden Jubilee Volume as my humble tribute to this National Institution of Excellence.

I also thank Mr. Sunil Dutt, Publication Officer of IIPA and the Publishers for their effort of bring out the publication in record time.

PROF. NOORJAHAN BAVA
Member, Executive Council
Indian Institute of Public Administration
Convenor of the National Conference
and
Editor of the Volume

26.5.04
New Delhi.

Preface

As decided by the Executive Council, Indian Institute of Public Administration and its High Power Committee on Golden Jubilee Celebrations of the Institute, IIPA hosted a two-day **National Conference on Public Administration in the 21st Century** on December 12-13, 2003 as part of the Golden Jubilee celebrations with Prof. Noorjahan Bava, Member, E.C. IIPA as the Convenor. It was attended by a large number of dignitaries, academics, administrators and social activists. More than 40 Professors and Readers in Public Administration, Political Science and Management from various universities across India presented papers on different paradigms and emerging concerns of public administration in the twenty first century.

The Conference began with a Welcome Address by Dr. Sanjeev Reddy, Director, Indian Institute of Public Administration. He pointed out that the IIPA was founded by Pt. Jawaharlal Nehru in 1954 based on the recommendations of Dean Paul Appleby, Consultant, Ford Foundation for the avowed purpose of promoting the discipline and practice of Public Administration in the country through education, training, research, consultancy, seminars/conferences/workshops, and publication of books, documents and the Indian Journal of Public Administration. Dr. Reddy also observed that the Institute has been effectively discharging its role as one of the think tanks of the Government of India, Planning Commission, State Governments and Public Sector Undertakings during the past 50 years by providing valuable policy inputs besides promoting the development of the discipline of Public Administration. He also read out the Message from H.E. T.N. Chaturvedi, Governor of Karnataka and Vice-President of the IIPA for the success of the Conference.

In her Preliminary Remarks Prof. Noorjahan Bava, the Convenor mentioned that one of the major purposes of the National Conference was to offer a national forum to the public administration community in India to discuss the impact and implications of the landmark developments that have happened in the real world particularly since the later half of the 20th century on the study of Public Administration. She pointed out thus:

At the dawn of the 21st Century the study and practice of Public Administration stand at the cross roads. Current transitions and transformations have changed and are changing the approaches, methods, contours, substance and subject-matter of public administration. Great currents of metamorphosis have swept both the art and science of public administration due to the impact of many national, international and global developments that happened during the second half of the twentieth century. These include *inter alia* the nuclear weapons race and rivalry between the two Super-Powers- US and the former USSR, the Movement for Sustainable Development, Information Technology and Communication Revolutions, demise of the Soviet Union and the Communist Bloc, and the end of Cold War, the policy of Liberalization, Privatization and Globalization, the Feminist Movement, Ethics in Public Administration, Public Management Approach, and Post Modernism to mention just a few.

Following the paradigm shift in the policy of the Government of India (and the States) in favour of Privatization, Liberalization and Globalization since 1991, the landscape, machinery and procedures of Indian Administration have undergone a sea change. Debureaucratization, downsizing and rightsizing the government, reinventing the government, good governance, e-governance, divestiture of Public Sector enterprises, greater role for the civil society in governance and development-these are the buzz words one hears these days. Cross-border terrorism, insurgency (in the North-Eastern states), cultural nationalism, militant communalism, river water disputes between riparian states, growing judicial activism, a decade of coalition governments at the centre, are other developments that have led to far-reaching impacts on the Indian polity and administration.

The Conference was inaugurated by **Prof. Arun Nigavekar,** Chairman, University Grants Commission. **Shri P.L. Suvrathan,** IAS, Additional Secretary (AR), Ministry of Personnel, Public Grievances and Pensions graced the occasion by his presence. **Dr. V.R. Panchmukhi,** Chairman, Indian Council of Social Science Research who was a Guest of Honour could not make it in the last minute due to jet-lag. The inaugural session was presided over by **Shri G.C.L. Joneja,** Vice-President and Chairman, Standing Committee of the IIPA and **Shri B.C. Mathur,** the Hony. Treasurer, IIPA passed the Vote of Thanks.

There were Business Sessions on Good Governance, Globalization, IT and E-Governance, New Paradigms in Public Administration, Human Rights, Women's Empowerment, Decentralized Governance and Human Resource Development. Papers were presented and floor participation took place in each session.

Professors S.R. Maheshwari, S.P. Verma, V.Bhaskara Rao, Ramesh K. Arora, R.K. Sachdeva, and Renuka Garg presided over the Business Sessions.

A Key-Note Address was delivered by **Mr. Gerard Lemos,** Vice-Chair, British Council on some aspects of British Policy and Administration on December 13, 2003 at 11.30 A.M.

Dr. Inderjeet Kaur, Dr. Radhanath Tripathi, Dr. Durgesh Nandini and Dr. Sangeeta Dhal acted as the Rapporteurs.

The Valedictory Address was delivered by Shri B.C. Mathur, Hony. Treasurer, IIPA. **Dr. Sanjeev Reddy,** Director of the IIPA presided over the Session. With a Vote of Thanks by **Prof. Noorjahan Bava,** the Conference came to a successful end at 6 PM on Dec. 13, 2003.

The proceedings of the Conference form the content of Part I of the book. Part II of the book consists of the papers presented on the two days. In all 25 presentations were made at the Conference. These papers find their appropriate place under one of the sub-themes into which the contents of the book is structured, namely Public Administration: Trends, Challenges and Reforms; New Paradigms in PA; HRD/Human Rights; IT Revolution and E-Governance; Good Governance and Decentralized Governance and Development Administration.

In their paper "Emerging Trends in Public Administration", **Prof. S.Bhoopathi Rao and Dr. M. Lingaiah** draw the attention of the readers to the controversies surrounding the definition, status of the discipline and the core-periphery areas/focuses of public administration. After highlighting some of the competing models in the field and the challenges of the 21st century, they spell out some of the emerging trends in Public Administration. According to the authors, these include: wider appreciation of the multi-disciplinary, multi-paradigmatic nature of the subject, end to "dichotomy thinking", search for new theories and practices, increasing demand for P.A. education programmes and new agenda for crises management. The paper also contains some suggestions for improvement of the discipline.

Dr. Sujata Singh in her paper 'Internationalization of Public Administration: Overcoming Historical Barriers', examines the factors that hindered the evolution of Public Administration from becoming an international discipline. Whereas Business Administration has conquered international frontiers, PA has developed as two separate disciplines- one for the developed West and the other for developing countries. She traces the problem to the Post Would War II initiatives taken by the West. She concludes by warning public administrationists that the inexorable march of NPM is leading to P.A. loosing its turf to business administration.

Dr. V. Bhaskara Rao, In his paper "Public Administration in 21st Century" bemoans the declining role of the State and Public Administration in India and the assertion of the Market ever since the adoption new Economic Policy by the Union Government in 1991 under pressure form the World Bank and IMF. Under-the powerful influence of the LPG model, the democratic institutions of India are made to serve the interest of capitalism rather than democracy. Thus the market model of government in the form of New Public Management is threating to eliminate democracy as a guiding principle in Public Administration. Under this present "phenomenon of economic imperialism" citizens are treated as mere clients/customers, government is treated as nothing more than a business and public administration is separated from the public policy process. Thus it is a threat to democratic governance.

Prof. Harbans Pathak, in his paper: 'Civil Service Reforms: An Agenda for the 21st century' extols the values of independence, efficiency, integrity, impartiality, objectivity and accountability of the civil service as the indispensable characteristics of good governance. Arguing that the presence of these qualities is to create confidence of the citizenry in the civil service, he urges that nothing should be done by the political masters or by the bureaucrats to erode these values. Now that India has adopted the market model of governance under New Economic Policy, Structural Adjustment Programme, Liberalization, Privatization and Globalization, reforms (in the role and functions of the State, government and administration) are necessary and inevitable to ensure market friendly governance.

In her useful and informative paper on "Public Administration and Post Modernism" the learned author **Prof. Noorjahan Bava,** (also the Editor of this book) brings out the meaning of the concept of POMO, its content and consequences for public administration in a lucid manner. She pinpoints that as a social theory POMO debunks not only the well-established categories in the literature on public administration such as bureaucracy, politics-administration dichotomy, scientific management, hierarchical control etc. but also challenges the intellectual traditions and metanarratives found in modern thought such as scientism, reductionism, logical positivism in philosophy of science, canons of analytical logic in philosophy, instrumental rationalism, universalism, foundationalism, constitutionalism (liberalism) communitarianism, Marxism, structural-functionalism and systems theory.

She points out that it is vital to remember that POMO is not a simple philosophy or theory. For, the theoretical underpinnings of postmodernism lie in the heady mixture of many philosophical traditions i.e. phenomenology, constructivism, structuration theory and critical theory. The postmodern public administration-also known as the Discourse Alternative to the Orthodoxy in public administration represents the attempt to deconstruct 'Bureaucracy' because it is 'reified' and it does not capture the totality of the public sector activities, and should be substituted by the concept of 'public energy field' comprising the civil society, citizen groups, and the media. It redefines the term 'public' in terms of Hannah Arndt's conceptions of 'public sphere' and 'agonistic tension' and Habermass's concepts of 'public sphere' and 'Communicative Competence'.

In his interesting and useful paper on "New Public Management: Emerging Concerns" Prof. Ramesh K. Arora observes that eversince Public Administration attained identity as a discipline hundred years ago, there has been a constant confluence of Management Science and Public Administration. He thinks that if there is one 'paradigm' in the discipline of P.A., it is perhaps 'New Public Management'- the paradigm that emerged in the early 1990s as a result of the twin movements of re-inventing the government and good governance. His paper deals with what is NPM and its positive effects on the study and practice of Public Administration.

In her informative paper, the learned author **Dr. Asha Gupta** focuses on the paradigm shift from Public Administration to Public Management in the context of Globalization, and radical changes in the core values, structures and public service delivery system valorized by NPM in sharp contrast to the traditional values and assumptions of PA. It produces a culture that extols the role of the managers as heroes, profits as success and conspicuous consumption and social status as an end in itself. It is not concerned at all with values such as equity, social justice, needs, and service. On the contrary, the State/Government and P.A. are sought to be depoliticized and marketized, and in the process of 'reinventing the Govt.' the 'Citizens' are reduced to mere 'consumers'—an economic man concerned only with self interest, profit maximization, consumerism and materialism.

The author also deals with the opportunities and constraints faced by developing countries from the twin forces of globalization and IT and spells out some strategies to overcome political and economic hegemony of the developed countries.

One of few most enduring themes in the discourse on Public Administration namely, Politics-Administration Dichotomy is revisited by **Prof. C.V. Raghavulu** in his paper in the context of the new paradigm of New Public Management.

He recalls the genesis of the doctrine of politics-administration separation, and its corollary-the neutrality of civil service- at the hands of Woodrow Wilson, and Max Weber-of course for different reasons and their failure to meet the ground realities in modern states. The first modern thinker to burst the 'myth' of the politics-administration separation is Prof. Paul Appleby who asserts that bureaucracy plays an increasingly important role in the process of policy formulation. Under their profound influence the neo-classical and public choice theories proponents of NPM advocate rolling back of the State–a role involving "steering" rather then 'rowing' of the economy; and hold markets are superior to the public bureaucracy in improving aggregate welfare and economic efficiency. He warns that NPM would result in centralization of decision-making, diminution in the power, authority and number of civil servants and loss of standing.

Among the various strategies available to modern

organizations for achievement of their growth, prosperity and survival, Human Resource Development. (HRD) has been acknowledged as the most effective strategy all over the world. **Prof. Bharati Sharma** in her conceptual paper, on 'HRD Initiatives for Organizational Growth' presents in a very lucid manner the various components of the concept of HRD and its critical importance for the survival of any organization in the fast changing uncertain world.

Dr. Prem Saran, a senior IAS officer, an Indologist, Religious Anthropologist and advocate and practitioner of Yoga, has developed an eponymous model - "Human Resource Development Model for Leadership, Creativity and Stress Control" with government as a learning organization. The author claims many virtues for his model such as its cross-cultural/global outreach, a sound philosophical foundation rooted in ancient Indian-Hindu cum Buddhist techniques of meditation particularly- the Kundalini Visualization Yoga and the ultimate "sixth discipline" for operationilizing Peter Sengi's concept of fifth discipline for a learning organization. In the absence of concrete, hard, empirical evidence to back up, the claims remain hollow and lose their credibility.

One of the new paradigms that emerged in the 1980s is Human Rights. Neither the goal of good governance nor development can be achieved in any society without recognizing and implementing human rights-civil, political, economic and socio-cultural. The Democratic Republic of India is a signatory to the Universal Declaration of Human Rights as well as other conventions on human rights. To what extent human rights are recognized, respected and protected by the police is a very relevant issue for Indian democracy. The issue is becoming more and more serious with each passing day, given the increasing cases of custodial crimes/death in different states of India. What is the track record of the Delhi Police in this vital matter is portrayed by **Dr. Radhanath Tripathi** in his well-researched paper (based on his Ph.D. work) on "Police Administration and Custodial Crimes in Delhi in the Context of Human Rights".

In his interesting and useful study on 'Social Value Creation through Information and knowledge: Vision of the 21st Century' **Prof. R.K. Sachdeva** first defines what is social value creation and then explains how it can be achieved in organizations–

Government and private by harnessing the Information Technology. He also informs readers of the 10th Plan initiatives taken by the Government of India to develop the IT Sector to make India an IT superpower. The challenges and constraints involved in the development, operation and utilization of IT in government and private organizations are also very well brought home by the author.

In their useful study, 'Electronic Democracy: Concepts, Trends and Implications for India' **Dr. Y. Pardhasaradhi** and **Dr. J. Musalaiah** define E-Democracy as any democratic political system in which ICT is used to carry out the crucial functions of the democratic government such as supply of information, communication, interest articulation and aggregation, decision-making, deliberation and voting. The technological innovations that make these activities electronically possible include the use of increasingly sophisticated computer chips, lasers, fibre-optics, databases, public and commercial satellites etc. According to the authors, E-Democracy may take any one of the three forms: (*i*) Teledomocracy, (*ii*) Cyber democracy and (*iii*) Electronic democracy (Hagen). While both tele/cyber democracy strive to establish more forms of direct democracy within a political system through the use of ICT, E-D. aims at improving representative democracy. They go into advantages and disadvantages of E-Demo under five models: electronic bureaucracy model, information management model, populist model, civil society model and political campaigning model. In India only 1.65 per cent of the total population access the Internet and it impacts only 60 million people as against 64 per cent in Japan, 54 per cent in China.

Dr. Y. Pardhasaradhi etal in their very useful study on "Public Administration and ICT Paradigm" describe how the use of electronic information and communication technologies (ICT) in Government has given rise to the emergence of the new phenomenon of E-governance which is regarded as an essential tool of good governance. The study carried out on CARD and E-SEVA, the two projects launched by the A.P. Government lends evidence to the fact that E-governance has been found to facilitate efficiency, effectiveness, transparency, accountability, responsiveness and responsibility in the delivery of public services in an integrated manner by various govt. departments under 'one roof'; it improves the interface between government-citizen and government-civil society. It empowers the citizens through their participation in governance, and through information sharing. The authors inform the readers that the Information Communication Technology (ICT) has become the paradigm of PA in the 21st Century.

Prof. S.C. Arora's paper on 'Good Governance at the Grass roots level' accepts the Western-modern definition of the concept of good governance as that system of governance which is characterized by political and bureaucratic accountability, the rule of law, independence of the judiciary, freedom of expression and information, people's welfare-oriented government and administration and cooperation between the government and civil society organizations. He takes a close and hard book at the implementation 73rd and 74th Constitutional Amendments as the instruments for the establishment of good governance at the grassroots level in various states of India. He identifies a number of stumbling blocks that come in the way of the rural and urban local bodies and prevent them from functioning successfully as units of decentralized governance. He believes that the series of suggestions and reform measures that he has put forward, if seriously implemented, will ensure that the Panchati Raj institutions and municipal bodies can truly and effectively function as units of local self-government in the country.

In his paper on 'Good Governance for Sustainable Development: A Study of People's Institutions in Rural Andhra Pradesh', **Dr. T. Satyanarayan** takes a critical look at the functioning of people's institutions such as Panchayati Raj Institutions, Self Help Groups, Community based organizations etc. in AP in the context of good governance for sustainable development and brings out a number of shortcomings in their operations.

The extent to which a government can succeed in providing 'good governance' with efficiency, economy, financial self-sufficiency, accountability and transparency through mechanisms such as public (government)-private partnerships, state-civil society and market collaboration, active participation of citizens in public affairs, a dedicated and honest bureaucracy and strong political leadership armed with the will to solve the problems of the people in a corruption free environment is what portrayed in the case study of Surat Municipal Corporation by **Prof. Renuka**

Garg and Dr. Priti Garg in their paper on 'Delivering Social Services: A Case Study'. That the convergence and collaboration between the State, Market, Citizenry and Civil Society in pursuit of common purposes can work wonders is the most important lesson that one learns from this case study of Surat.

To achieve the goal of good governance an effective system for redressal of public grievances must be in place at all levels of the government. This is the message one gets from the paper 'Public Grievances Redressal System (PGRS) in India' by **Dr. Inderjeet Kaur.** It not only throws light on the evolution, structure and procedures of the PG mechanisms in the country but also the innovative measures taken by GOI to usher in E-Governance and web-based redressal of public grievances and on-line delivery of public services to the people.

In the context of the ongoing liberalization, privatization and globalization, process in India since 1991 and decentralized governance at the grass roots level due to 73rd and 74th Constitutional Amendments, 1993 **Prof. Marino Pinto** christens the twin developments as "Glocalisation" and studies the impact of these economic and political reforms in her interesting analysis entitled 'Glocalization in Mumbai'. Her study focuses on the problems of governance of Mumbai arising from the interactions and interrelationships between the Municipal Corporation of Greater Mumbai, Mumabi Metropolitan Regional Development Authority, Maharashtra Housing and Area Development Authority, Maharashtra Water Supply and Severage Board and Pollution Control Board.

Dr. B.V. Chalapathi, in his paper 'Urban Governance in Andhra Pradesh: An Appraisal' based on the micro study that he carried out in the Proddatur Municipality of Cuddapah District, the author avers that the challenges confronting municipal bodies as units of local self government in urban areas are many and varied. He has identified some of them such as problems relating to decision-making, lack of compliance with rules and regulations, lack of coordination, inadequate power for the chairperson of municipal bodies, lack of training, and problems relating to assessment and collection of property tax, the main source of income of these urban authorities. He perceives that greater devolution of power by the State Government, strong political will and commitment to democratic governance will pave the way for the successful functioning of local self-govt. in urban areas in the post-74th Amendment era.

In her interesting study on 'Gender Issues in Global Development,' **Dr. Lipi Mukhopadhyay** first raises the question: Why gender issues are important in the context of the on-going process of Globalization. She assumes that the issue needs to be looked at from socio-psychological perspectives: viz. need for equal rights and opportunity for women and men, negative impacts of gender-based occupational segregation on the social status and position of women and right of women to access fruits of development. The study concludes that only concerted efforts by the Government, with full participation and cooperation of NGOs and Civil Society groups can solve the problem of inequality and injustice of women arising form the globalization process.

No human society can truly develop without its women members' active and full participation and involvement in the processes of governance and socio-economic development. To leave women citizens out of the orbit of development is to invite definite failure of all development programmes, be that of the government or private sector or civil society. Included in this compendium of articles are "Empowerment of Women" by **Dr. Shiv Raj Singh** and "Women's Empowerment in the Panchayati Raj System: The Case of Orissa" by **Dr. Sangita Dhal.** Their findings, if accepted by public policy makers and administrators would lead to formulation of realistic policies on women's empowerment.

In a federal parliamentary democracy, such as India, Central-State relations in general and the role of public administration at the central, state and local levels in particular is of great interest not only to politicians, practising administrators and managers but also to teachers and scholars of political science and public administration. Article 356 of the Constitution of India which provides for President's Rule in any Sate of the Indian Union where Government of the State cannot he carried on in accordance with the provisions of the Constitution has become very controversial, in the light of the misuse and abuse of the power behind the Article by both the Congress and non-Congress Governments at the Centre. Since 1950 to 1999, President's Rule has been proclaimed 106 times in various states more for political vendetta than for Constitutional reasons. Prof. S.S. Tiwana in his very useful study on "Article 356 and Central-State Relations" refers to the misuse of this Article for political purposes, draws attention to the Sarkaria Commission recommendations on centre-state relations and the resolutions passed at the Srinagar Conclave of the Inter-State Council on the problem before spelling out the lines along which the Constitution needs to be amended in order to ensure cooperative federalism in India.

The centrality of the role of Education in national, individual, socio-economic and politico-cultural development of any society cannot be underestimated, least of all in a developing nation like India. In their interesting piece entitled "Higher Education in India: Policy Issues and Challenges" the two learned and experienced educational administrators—**Dr. Yasodha Shanmugasundaram and Dr. Vedagiri Shanmugasundaram** highlight Government's policies and its challenges on higher education. They focus on universities in generating knowledge and employment opportunities, promoting research, scientific/industrial inventions and human resource development.

It is my fervent hope that this anthology of essays on public administration will be found very useful by teachers, students, researchers administrators and managers. There is no doubt that this Golden Jubilee Volume is an important milestone in the annals of the Indian Institute of Public Administration which has been rendering yeoman service for the last 50 years to the promotion and development of the study and practice of Public Administration in the country.

New Delhi
29.4.2004

PROF. NOORJAHAN BAVA
EDITOR

Contents

PART II: PAPERS PRESENTED IN THE CONFERENCE

CHAPTER I: Public Administration: Trends, Challenges and Reforms

CHAPTER II: New Paradigms in Public Administration

CHAPTER III: Human Resource Development/Human Rights

List of Contributors

Prof. S.C. Arora, Department of Public Administration, Maharshi Dayanand University, Rohtak.

Dr. Asha Gupta, Reader, Department of Political Science, Bharati Mahila College, University of Delhi.

Dr. Bharati Sharma, Professor of Management (OB & HRD), Indian Institute of Public Administration, New Delhi.

Dr V. Bhaskara Rao, Former Professor of Public Administration, Kakatiya University, Warrangal, Andhra Pradesh; Prinicipal, Chaitanya P.G. College. Warrangal and Secretary cum Treasurer, New Public Administration Society.

Prof. S. Bhoopathi Rao, Head, Department of Public Administration, Osmania University, Hyderabad.

Dr. B.V. Chalapathi, Associate Professor and Head, Department of Political Science and Public Administration, Sri Venkateshwara University P.G. Centre, Cuddapah.

Prof. Harbans Pathak, Professor and Head, Department of Public Administration, Punjabi University, Patiala, India.

Dr. Inderjeet Kaur, Reader, Department of Political Science, Satyawati College, University of Delhi.

Dr. M. Lingaiah, Associate Professor, Department of Public Administration, Osmania University, Hyderabad.

Dr. Lipi Mukhopadhyay, Associate Professor in Behavioural Science, Indian Institute of Public Administration, New Delhi.

Dr. J. Musaliah, Assistant Professor of Political Science, Osmania University, Hyderabad, India.

Dr. Marina R. Pinto, Former Professor of Public Administrative, Department of Civics & Politics, University of Mumbai.

Prof. Noorjahan Bava, Professor (Retd.), Department of Political Science, University of Delhi and currently Member, Executive Council, Indian Institute of Public Administration and Convenor, IIPA Golden Jubilee National Conference on Public Administration in the 21st Century (December 12-13, 2003).

Dr. Y. Pardhasaradhi, Associate Professor, Department of Public Administration, Osmania University, Hyderabad, India.

Dr. Prem Saran, IAS, Commissioner, Administrative Reforms and Training, Government of Assam.

Dr. Priti Garg, Reader, Department of Public Administration, South Gujarat University, Surat.

Dr. Radhanath Tripathy, Lecturer, Department of Political Science, A.R.S.D. College, University of Delhi.

Prof. C.V. Raghavulu, former Vice-Chancellor, Nagarjuna University; Chairman, Centre for Development and Governance, Hyderabad.

Prof. Ramesh K. Arora, Former Professor and Head of Department of Public Administration, and Dean, Rajasthan University, Jaipur; Visiting Professor at HCM Rajasthan State Institute of Public Administration, Jaipur.

Dr. K.V. Ramesh Raju, Professor, Department of Public Administration, Osmania University, Hyderabad

Dr. Renuka Garg, Professor, Department of Business and Industrial Management, South Gujarat University, Surat.

Dr. R.K. Sachdeva, Professor of Management, Indian Institute of Public Administration, New Delhi.

Dr. Sangita Dhal, Lecturer, Department of Political Science SGTB Khalsa College, University of Delhi.

Dr. Y. Satyanarayana, Associate Professor of Public Administration, Kakatiya University P.G. College, Nirmal, Adilabad Dt., Andhra Pradesh.

Dr. Shiv Raj Singh, Chairman, Department of Public Administration, Himachal Pradesh University, Shimla.

Dr. Sujata Singh, Reader in Policy Sciences, Indian Institute of Public Administration, New Delhi.

Prof. T.S. Tiwana, Department of Public Administration, Punjabi University, Patiala, Punjab.

Dr. Vedagiri Shanmugasundaram, Director, Institute for Advanced Studies & Research, Chennai; Former Member, Executive Council, IIPA and former Vice-Chancellor, Manonmanian Sundaranar University.

Mr. T.K. Ventatamallu, Research Scholar, Department of Public Administration, Osmania University, Hyderabad.

Dr. (Mrs.) Yosodha Shanmugasundaram, Member, Executive Council, Indian Institute of Public Administration, and former Vice-Chancellor, Mother Teresa Women's University.

PART I

PROCEEDINGS OF THE CONFERENCE ON

Public Administration in the 21st Century

INAUGURAL SESSION
(12 December 2003 FN)

WELCOME ADDRESS

Dr. P.L. Sanjeev Reddy, Director, Indian Institute of Public Administration

With the permission of the Chair, I would like to extend a very hearty welcome to all of you, who have come all the way to attend this two-day Conference on "Public Administration in the Twenty-First Century".

My special welcome to Dr. Arun Nigavekar, Chairman, University Grants Commission, who has very kindly agreed to come here today to deliver the Inaugural Address. All of you are aware of the multi-dimensional achievements of Dr. Arun Nigavekar. Under his able stewardship, UGC celebrated this year as the Golden Jubilee Year. Luckily, IIPA and UGC happened to have the same father, the same parentage as Pandit Jawaharlal Nehru started both the institutions at about the same time. Naturally, both the institutions are now celebrating the Golden Jubilee Year. We have common missions and common visions and we share the same destiny by extending the frontiers of knowledge.

We, in the IIPA are interested in exploring the various options available in the field of public administration to serve the people, to serve society better. When public policy is already there, what is most relevant is its implementation through the functionaries by their motivation and capacity building. We have to see how close they are to the citizens, whether they are responsive, transparent, accountable and efficient, because these are some of the things, which are very very crucial, and I am sure this Conference will be addressing some of those issues.

My special welcome to the Chairman of the Session, Shri G.C. L. Joneja, who was former Chief Secretary to the Government of Orissa, a very seasoned administrator. We have invited him to be here, because from him we can know the changing contours of public administration over the years, because even before independence he was in service. He started in the IAS, and held very senior positions in Orissa.

My special welcome to Shri B.C. Mathur, one of the senior-most administrators, who joined the Indian Administrative Service in 1950. He has served with distinction in many Ministries including Supply and Personnel, and also in the CAT. He would be sharing his views with us in the course of the next two days.

I would also like to extend a special welcome to Prof. Noorjahan Bava, Member, Executive Council, IIPA who is the Convenor and the prime mover of this Conference. She has taken upon herself the sole responsibility of organizing this Conference and IIPA is only providing the back up for her.

I would like to extend a very warm welcome to all the outstation Professors, who have taken the trouble of coming here in this wintry morning to Delhi.

I am sure, the deliberations here would have a profound impact on the future road map for public administration. For this august audience, I need not dwell on the subject in detail. You all know the changing profile of public administration, the change in societies, the technological breakthrough that has taken place, which is non-linear and discontinuous, IT revolution, e-governance and so on. The new challenges that are now facing society are well known. There is decline in public decency and increase in corruption levels. Somebody estimated that today 3-1/2 trillion dollars is the value of corruption in public life.

The UNICEF Report points out that India is yet to catch up in terms of prevention of infant mortality, in terms of the weight of the child at birth time, general mortality rate, drop outs from schools and so on. We have to catch up on various counts.

If India is to be a superpower, as envisioned by his Excellency President of India, Dr. Abdul Kalam, what are the things to be done? We have a long way to go and public administration will provide an excellent opportunity for various functionaries, policy makers and legislators, and to the judiciary to interpret the policy in terms of the Constitution and the legal framework. All of these will provide us umpteen opportunities for a great academic discussion, which will have a profound bearing on the policy framework.

I would like to mention here that some eminent people have already come here like Prof. S.R. Maheswari, Prof. S.P. Verma, Prof. Ramesh K. Arora and Prof. V. Bhaskara Rao. We would like to extend a very warm welcome to them. In fact, I would like to mention at this stage that all of you have made our day.

IIPA is interested in developing new areas, new disciplines, especially in syllabus formation and content. In what way this particular discipline, which is of peculiar or particular relevance in modern times, can acquire a new paradigm, new complexion and new models, like public-private partnership for instance, accountability, citizen's charter and so on? So many various dimensions are coming here. So, in this context of technology driven public administration, value anchored public administration, how can we develop it in order to create an impact on the society and its quality of life? UN has already been saying that what is important is not GNP or per capita income, but the quality of life. In achieving this quality of life, in achieving higher and higher levels of growth and quality of life, how best public administration can play a part, we have to consider that in depth. In this background, the papers that we have received are extremely profound and impacting on these aspects. I am sure, you will have opportunity to really discuss all the issues and come up with your inputs and suggestions.

With these few words of welcome, I would like to request the Chairperson of this Session, Shri G.C.L. Joneja, who is the Chairman of the Standing Committee, one of the senior-most administrators, to kindly conduct the proceedings of this session.

CHAIRMAN'S REMARKS

Shri G.C.L. Joneja, Vice-President, IIPA

I would like to reinforce with my own welcome what the Director Dr. Sanjeev Reddy has already extended to you. It is a pity that Shri Arun Bhatnagar, Secretary, Personnel, could not join us because of a family problem. Dr. V.R. Panchmukhi may be able to join us a little later. At the moment, he is still recovering from the jet lag of his visit to Mexico. In fact, the short delay in starting the meeting was because we were expecting these gentlemen to be able to join us in time. I am glad that out of the galaxy of people, who would have spoken at the Inaugural session, luckily we have with us Dr. Arun Nigavekar, the Chairman of the UGC, who will deliver the Inaugural Address.

It is a very nice feeling that so many of you have thought it wise and proper to share our happiness in the commemoration of the 50th anniversary of the setting up of IIPA. As you would have seen from the papers circulated to you, this was the outcome of a report by Dr. Paul Appleby, on the initiative taken by our then Prime Minister, the late Shri Pandit Jawaharlal Nehru. In fact, his faith in the objectives and purposes for which the IIPA was set up was so great that he continued to preside over its functions and responsibilities till the end of his life, till 1964.

Shorn off various ostentations, in simple words, the mandate that he gave at that time was to bring awareness and importance of public administration. That was something, which was badly lacking at that time. I am not too sure if the right type of awareness has come about even till now.

The other important functions were training, consultancy and research. Under the dissemination programme, we not only have to undertake publications on various issues connected with public administration but also set up what may be considered one of the best libraries in the country on the subject.

Our Journal is very highly respected. One can take a certain measure of pride in the achievements of IIPA so far. But we have been having occasional reforms on our work, trying to put things right after every 5 to 10 years. But, at this stage, when changes have taken place in a very drastic manner, and continue to be taking place, it is a good landmark that we have to think afresh as to what we should be doing and have a new vision, even a new mandate for the IIPA.

At the same time, whatever the mandate, whatever the constraints in the modern times, the basic thing is that we have to train public servants in the Central and State Governments, which cannot be and should not be ignored. To adopt the private sector model in the IIPA would mean that people would have to spend, each individual would have to spend, about R.2 lakh or so to get even admission. That is not the spirit in which the IIPA was set up.

We have to provide public service, we have to ensure dissemination of public administration and bring about awareness of the right type. If you take the political side of public administration, again, I know that we have been able to get a firm hold on democratic principles and set up political democracy. But we are still experimenting so far as the political side is concerned. Now in the last few years we have been experimenting with the coalition system. The government is no longer formed by one important political party. Now we do not have two clear major political parties one in the government and the other in the opposition but a coalition system. It is not only at the central stage, but it is also at the state stage that it is becoming the order of the day, if one may say so. So, we are now experimenting that system.

On the functional side, on the economic side, we have taken to adopting a new system of giving up the idea of a controlled economy and getting on to the free market economy. But let us not forget that even a free market economy has got to be regulated. There is no getting away from that. Nowhere in the world the free market has been functioning as if free market has been let loose. There has to be some discipline and some regulation even there, and that has to be ensured.

These are some of the problems that we face today. We are at the crossroads. It is not merely the 50th anniversary stage, but it is also an important landmark in the country's progress, where we have got to see what IIPA can do in the matter.

This Conference has been convened at the initiative of the High Power Committee, set up by the Executive Council, for the celebration of the 50th Anniversary. The task of organizing and conducting this Conference was entrusted to Prof. Noorjahan Bava, a Member of the Executive Council. She has just recently retired from the Delhi University as Professor of Public Administration.

Friends, we have this task of looking at the problems, which we face now and what we would be facing hereafter, and trying to work out a new concept for our functioning and have a vision for it. Now it has to be a practical vision, not just a dreamland. Dreaming is good to the extent that it gives you inspiration to do things in a different way, in a better way and in an improved way. Technology will help, but even technology has to be controlled and guided. But we have to take full advantage of the technological developments and see to what extent they could help us in improving our functioning.

Friends, after we have heard a few preliminary remarks from Prof. Bava, who is organizing this Conference, we will hear the words of wisdom from our Chief Guest and colleague, Dr. Arun Nigavekar, Chairman of UGC, when he delivers the Inaugural Address. May I now call upon Prof. Noorjahan Bava, the Convenor of the Conference, to give us her Preliminary Remarks?

PRELIMINARY REMARKS

Prof. Noorjahan Bava (Convenor)

Mr. Chairman, Additional Secretary, Department of Personnel and Training, Government of India, Dr. Arun Nigavekar, Chairman, UGC, Dr. V.R. Panchmukhi, Chairman, ICSSR, (who would be joining us soon) Dr. P.L. Sanjeev Reddy, Director, IIPA, Shri Salim Haq, Director, DOPT, Shri G.C.L. Joneja, Chairman, Standing Committee and Vice-President of IIPA, Shri B.C. Mathur, Treasurer, IIPA, Shri U.C. Aggarwal, Editor, IJPA. Distinguished delegates, Hon'ble Guests, Faculty Members, Registrar and Librarian of IIPA, Ladies and Gentlemen!

As a Member of the Executive Council of IIPA and Convenor of this two-day National Conference on "Public Administration in the 21st Century", I deem it a great honour, privilege, prestige and pleasure to extend a very hearty and warm welcome to all of you.

Today, which is a red-letter day in the annals of the Indian Institute of Public Administration, on this happy and important occasion, we remember and salute Pandit Jawaharlal Nehru, the first Prime Minister of India and the founder President of IIPA till the end of his life. On the recommendation of Dr. Dean Paul H. Appleby, distinguished Professor of Public Administration and Consultant to Ford Foundation, this Institute was established and the Indian Journal of Public Administration was started. The then great political leaders, eminent administrators and academics signed the Memorandum and Rules of the Institute and registered the IIPA on the 13th March, 1954.

The purpose of this Conference is three-fold. Firstly, the Conference seeks to fulfil the grand purpose for which the IIPA was established, as mentioned in the Memorandum, namely, to promote the development of the study and practice of Public Administration in the country. Secondly, the Golden Jubilee

National Conference marks the 50th birth anniversary of the Institute and we celebrate the glorious existence and noble service rendered by the Institute to the country in the field of public administration over the last 50 years. Thirdly, on the dawn of the 21st century, the study and practice of public administration stand at the crossroads.

Great political events, developments and revolutions have taken place in the world during the later half of the 20th century, at the global, international, regional and national levels. These have brought about a great metamorphosis in the contour, approaches and paradigm of the discipline of public administration. Some of the most important events include the founding of the United Nations for peace and development in the world, the emergence of the developing nations, the super-power rivalry, the arms race, the cold war and its end with the demise of the Soviet Union and the Soviet Socialist Bloc, the triumph of democracy, the emergence of US as the sole super-power, Information, Communication and Computer Revolutions, Sustainable Development, Human Rights, and Feminist Movements and many more, to mention just a few.

Nearer home, in India, following the paradigm shift towards globalization, liberalization and privatization, the Government's policy since the 1990s has moved from a state-centric Nehruvian model of development and nation-building to the free market economy. The landscape, machinery and procedures of Indian administration have undergone a sea change. Cries of Good Governance, meaning de-bureaucratization, downsizing and right sizing of bureaucracy, reinventing government and greater level playing field to the civil society organizations rent the Indian sky and air.

To this day, I do not know of any national level conference or seminar that studied the impact of all these mind-boggling developments in a comprehensive manner on the intellectual field and practice of Public Administration, though there have been some seminars on some fragmented aspects. The purpose of this Conference is precisely to offer such a national forum to the public administration community in the country to take stock of these mega changes on the discipline and practice of public administration and to study the road map for the future directions of this subject. I hope this Conference will serve as a great learning experience to about 40 eminent Professors and Readers from more than 20 universities and colleges in the country, from Kanyakumari to Kashmir, from Gujarat to Assam, who are participating in this conference for this purpose.

I want to express my profound thanks to the Chairman of Indian Council of Social Science Research, Chairman of UGC and Secretary, Department of Personnel and Training, Ministry of Personnel, Public Grievances and Pensions for their moral and financial support to the IIPA, which enabled us to organize this Conference. Once again my warm welcome to all of you.

May I now request Dr. Sanjeev Reddy, Director, IIPA, to give a floral welcome to the Chief Guest?

MESSAGE FROM H.E. T.N. CHATURVEDI

Vice-President, IIPA and Governor of Karnataka

DIRECTOR: I have great pleasure in reading out the Message, which we have received from the Hon'ble Governor of Karnataka:

"I am happy to learn that the Indian Institute of Public Administration, with which I have been intimately associated for four decades, is organizing a two-day National Conference on 'Public Administration in the 21st century'. I am also pleased to note that Dr. Arun Nigavekar, Chairman, UGC, Dr. V.R. Panchmukhi, Chairman, ICSSR and Shri Arun Bhatnagar, Secretary, Department of Personnel and Training, would be actively participating in the Inaugural Address and giving us the benefit of their valuable perceptions and inputs.

Administration has increasingly become inter-disciplinary and para-disciplinary in character. Not only social sciences but even physical sciences necessitate intimate, close and continuous exchange and interaction. Knowledge has been called a seamless garment. All categories and branches of knowledge ultimately aim at the betterment of society in consonance with the requirements and compulsions of a fast changing society. It is only through the mutuality of understanding and support of different institutions and fields of knowledge that we can take meaningful view of the concepts of governance in the 21st century with its challenges, opportunities and possibilities. This only further underscores the relevance and significance of the scope and worthwhileness of the Conference that you propose to hold as well as the vital importance of inter-institutional coordination which your effort represents.

Much as I would like to personally attend the function, commitments in Bangalore prevent me from doing so. However, on the happy occasion in the annals of the IIPA, I convey my best wishes for the success of the conference. My sincere appreciation goes to the Chairman of the UGC and ICSSR and Secretary of DOPT for their strong academic and financial support to the Institute for this noble purpose. I hope that such academic collaborations will grow from strength to strength, benefiting the partner institutions, academic community and the country at large." It is signed "Shri T.N. Chaturvedi, Vice-President, IIPA, Chairman of the Golden Jubilee High Power Committee and the Hon'ble Governor of the State of Karnataka".

I have now great pleasure to extend floral welcome to the Chairman, UGC, to the Chairman of this session Shri G.C.L. Joneja and Shri B.C. Mathur, Treasurer of IIPA. (*Loud Cheers*)

May I now call upon Dr. Arun Nigavekar, Chairman, UGC, to let us have the benefit of his wisdom and guidance in his Inaugural Address?

INAUGURAL ADDRESS

Dr. Arun Nigavekar, Chairman, University Grants Commission

Shri Joneja, the Chairman of the Inaugural Session, Shri Mathur, Prof. Maheswari, my old friend from Pune Prof. Verma, Dr. Sanjeev Reddy, who is the Director of this institution, Prof. Noojahan Bava, who is the Convenor of this Conference, distinguished participants and friends!

Let me first congratulate IIPA for having rendered such wonderful work in the last five decades. As Dr. Sanjeev Reddy mentioned, both our organizations, IIPA as well as UGC, are in the Golden Jubilee year. We are having our Golden Jubilee on the 25th of this month and I think you have it on the 13th March next year.

Well, IIPA and UGC have been having close links and particularly we are using your guesthouse more often! Dr. Reddy has been discussing with me many new things that he wants to initiate. I think this is a good occasion, particularly the Golden Jubilee Year, to initiate those things. (*Loud Cheers*)

As you know, in the Indian higher education system, unfortunately, public administration is always mixed with political science discipline. I do not know where the history started, but in most of the universities it is the Department of Political Science and Public Administration. Even in Pune, where I was Professor in Physics, many other things and finally the Vice-Chancellor, I realized that right from the days of Dr. Garge, when he was there, this was a mixed system of Political Science and Public Administration, so much so, in many universities public administration is not recognized at all, and it is taken as an appendage of political science. That is the very unfortunate part.

Public Administration as an Interdisciplinary Subject

Public administration per se has now emerged as a discipline but it is an inter-disciplinary subject. I would like to say that it is not a subject where you can say it is a stand-alone type of subject, because it needs the blending of many different subjects from different disciplines.

Central and State Institutes of Training for Public Administrators

This is why you can see that most of the State Governments and also the Central Government have created independent institutions for training of public administrators. In fact, the closest analogy to the Government of India system is the American system, not in terms of efficiency and effectiveness, but in terms of hugeness and complexities.

Now quite a few things go on happening in parallel in both the nations. For example, right after independence, one of the decisions that the Government of India took, particularly in science subjects, is that it decided to establish independent research institutions. They felt that for the growth of the nation, for catching up with science and technology, it is necessary to create an independent structure for science research. It had its own impact. Now, after five decades, you can see the pure science discipline in most of the universities is in deathbed, because there was a parallel entity created, a very lucrative situation created. Most of the good faculty in the universities drifted to research laboratories and the universities were kept at their mercy.

A similar thing happened in administration. We created independent institutions for training of administrators. The same pretext was taken. It is a different thing, we need to do it differently. The education sector will not be able to meet it. So, it was created. Later on, in our country, there was a group of people, who started propagating that concept, may be a group of scientists or a group of administrators, they are different *avatars*. They go on talking about independence and the importance of keeping it separate from the educational structure.

Later on, we started realizing that unless there is deep understanding, particularly from the academic point of view, and

deep root is built into the basics of the discipline, the appendage of training does not help. So, it is the learning process that is important, the training process is something added to that. So, the same thing started happening. As it is happening in science and technology, it is happening in administration.

Administration As a Pillar of Government

Well, why I say that India is similar to US is because in US also the same thing has happened. In US the system has grown, the system has become enormous. I was going through a particular document, where it was indicated that the federal structure/the Federal Government are not aware of many institutions that are being run in US. They are on paper, the expenses are committed, the system is running, but they do not know where it is. This is what the audit report says, that there are a large number of institutions, which are running, but the government does not know where it is. You find them in the budget, you find them in the expenses, you find them operating, but the government does not know where they are.

I think we are facing the same situation in India, because India is a huge country. These are problems of hugeness, so many things go on happening and people really do not know about them and are not able to keep track of them.

This being the story, where do we start today is the basic question. Because it is true that there is no escape from administration, we call it as one of the pillars of the democratic system. ***Just like polity or judiciary, administration is one of the important pillars of government,*** if I may put it in a very generic sense. Of course, what we call the fourth pillar is the media, which represents the society, or rather supposed to reflect the society.

So, this has been the position for decades, right from the time of kings, and it is so even today. The structures have changed, but the need for government is always felt. Now the need for governance comes into the picture because the society, human society, always likes to behave in a certain organized manner. In fact, that is the difference between humans and animals. The humans are endowed with the process of thinking, humans are gifted and that is why they are different from the animal species. They try to rationalize things. But it has also the disadvantages, because the humans also behave in a very peculiar manner compared to animals, which is not expected. To give you an example or an indication, we do not find any animal specie killing identicals. We have never heard of a tiger killing another tiger or a dog killing another dog. In fact, it is a very interesting thing. But we find humans killing humans. This is the dichotomy.

Since we are endowed with more brain and more thinking power, we started abusing it. Rather than using it, we started abusing it for a bad thing and not using it for a good thing. So, to get over it, in our own wisdom, we started laying down certain rules, certain ways of operation. The entire family system emerged out of the social rule. The entire society structure came out of the behavioural pattern, which each one of us started defining.

Having established that, then there was the need to create a structure, which will set the rules, which will set the patterns, which will allow us to say, yes, this is the way it should operate. So, it is a self-derived system. Otherwise, why should one decide, okay, we will walk on the left side, why vehicles go in a particular direction? We have created this to create an order. Having created that sort of structure, it needs to be seen that it happens. That is where the administration came into the picture, because it is the policy to drive vehicles on the left side of the road. Who created it? We created it, because we want a certain discipline on the road, we do not want traffic to get jammed. We wanted vehicles to move in a particular manner. Everything that happens in the family is set because of some set of rules. Why do we decide to get up at a particular time and go for work at a particular time? We want some order in the system. So, our entire life, entire behaviour, is going by a certain mechanism that we created for ourselves. To see all that is happening, we need governance. We try to see that is happening. So, we have checks and balances.

When we talk of administration in the 21st century, when we are saying we have switched over from the 20th to the 21st century, we have all probably missed something bigger. It is not just a change of the century, it is the change of the millennium that we are seeing. We have gone from the second millennium to the third millennium. In fact, all of us are very lucky creatures. Very few people are able to see the change of the century, but very very few people are able to see the change of the millennium, the transition from one millennium to another millennium. So, when we are talking about the governance or administration in the 21st century or third millennium, one has to look into the entire thing that has happened till today and then try to see what is it that we want to do tomorrow.

It is very logical to say that I have not said any big words of wisdom in that. Everybody wants to have a look at what has happened, everybody wants to look at what we want. But one thing that has emerged is that there is the biggest and highest order of continuity. It is that continuity that I was talking earlier, the system created by the people and for the people, to run the system as a whole. That has not changed, and that is not going to change, unless you get a society of robots.

In a way, nowadays people are saying that humans are getting converted into robots. That is also behavioural change. If you see in the western world, people are so much put in boxes that they are more or less behaving like robots. We also say very often that our life is getting so much constrained, compartmentalized or truncated that we are locked into what we are doing, we do not understand other things in life and it has its own problem.

The western world has its own problem. We talk of moral turpitude, and lack of peace of mind; these are the words that we use. We say, that they have everything but they do not have peace of mind. They have materialistic advantage but that is not the end we are looking for.

Governance for Peace as a Core Value of Administration

So, these additional things, which are coming, these probably were not there in such magnitude in the 1970's and 1980's or in the earlier centuries, when life was very comfortable. Now that has become an important element in the governance of the country. I say this because *it is not only efficient administration, not only effective administration, it is an administration which strives to give peace of mind, it is an administration which propagates the comfort role for a living creature, that becomes a core entity in administration, in governance.*

This is the element, which we have been talking about, but we have never taken it at the center of the agenda. Today let me talk of administration. We talk of all things. We talk of using technology; we talk of efficiency; we talk of effectiveness; we talk about opening; and we talk of transparency, every aspect, which we feel, are essential in the technology-oriented world. They have been given emphasis. But we do not talk of governance for peace of mind.

In fact, when I was going through all the documents that are here, I once again realized that this is a component that we have lost. In fact, as the Chairperson of the UGC, I have been propagating the concept that it is also necessary that education for social transformation, which has been our agenda for the last five decades, will continue to remain the agenda for the 21st century.

Now we talk of education for economic development, because we are talking of knowledge-linked society, we are talking of knowledge-linked economy. We say that knowledge has become the unit of currency. Now it is not the dollar that is the unit of currency, it is knowledge that has become the unit of currency.

With all that development, we do not seem to have one thing that is needed, we do not have peace. So, education for peace, education for comfort of mind, education for moral balance is something, which I am trying to propagate, in the same manner, in the same capacity. I feel that governance for peace is also a theme that we need to discuss in depth.

When I am using the term peace, I am talking about the generic term, peace for the individual, peace for the family, peace for society, peace for the nation, peace for the globe or world as a whole. It is in that generic sense that I am talking about peace. So, if that is the theme that we have to look at, then what are the aspects that we need to concentrate on in the 21st century?

Computer and Communication Revolutions

Well, first things first. The 21st century has a new image that has emerged, because of certain science linked technological revolutions, which have come into the scene. In fact, those revolutions started sometime after the Second World War but we completed the revolution.

Humans created the machines. Machines created by humans hold information. Machines created by humans play that information. Machines created by humans retrieve the information as and when needed. Machines created by humans organize the information. That is why we talk of an artificial brain. The concept of artificial brain emerged out of these machines. The concept of an intelligent robot is a beautiful marriage of computers and science and technology and the development in mechanical power. That is one thing, which we have to bear in mind

But do not forget who created the machine. It is the humans. Who created a role for the machines? It is again the humans. Whether it is system software, which runs the machine, or whether it is application software, which allows us to use the machine in a particular manner, it is again the human entity.

Something more happened and it happened in a miraculous manner right after Edison sent the first telegraphic message in Morse code, which we talk about in terms of communication. It triggered the era of revolution in communication, in science and technology, which came because of satellites, later on through optic fibre connectivity, V-sat, all those things which we talk about. That created another revolution so that we were able to communicate anywhere, any place at any time, at any instant. So, we talk of this communication revolution. Today India is also directly involved in the communication revolution.

So, we had these two beautiful things. The revolution in computer science and technology was the earlier path before communication. In fact, this is the only significant time gap. Both were happening in parallel. The computer revolution took place a little faster, because the computers started getting stretched, with smaller and smaller computers, from macro to micro, putting in a large number of passive and active components in smaller and smaller areas, which were able to hold larger and larger amount of information. So, we started talking about Geiga, (?) Mega byte, Tera byte, all sorts of things. Not only that, it was able to do things faster and faster. So, we started talking of Microsecond, Nanosecond, Pico second and Tera second. So, it is a different direction. In one way, we are doing in astronomical figures for holding information, another way we are going to the other end of the spectrum of time for doing it faster and faster. So, these are the two ends of the time spectrum with computer and science and technology.

The other thing is the communication revolution that I talked about. Today, as you know, we are able to communicate much much faster because of these two things. Because of these two things, the human mind, as it is endowed with brilliance for the best way of doing things, they married the two things, computer science and technology with communication science and technology. That took us to what we are often fond of saying as the last word, information, communication and science and technology (ICT).

With this marriage of computers with information and communication technology, communication has another new dimension. Because it is not only that I am in a position to hold any information, it is not only that I am able to play with the information, it is not only that I am able to retrieve information, but I am also able to send it, I am able to communicate it. So, the entire governance is dependent on communication. ***It is communication, which controls governance.*** If there is no communication between you and me, what kind of governance am I talking about? I am sitting at some place; you are sitting at some other place. I am saying, "I want you to do this", but there is no communication. Then how can the other person comply with my orders? So, this communication, fastest communication, has given rise to a new depth and dimension to the entire area of governance and administration.

Information is Power

But there is something more that has happened, something more that is happening because of this more effective way of doing things. ***Information has become important and the core in governance.*** Why is the Commissioner, the Collector, Judge, Teacher or whosoever it is, more endowed than somebody else who is at the other end? Because he or she is holding the information or has access to that information. ***Access to information is power.*** If I know something, which you do not know, that means I have an advantage over you. So, the entire governance is linked with access to information. So, the access to information is another entity. Today that access to information is probably locked in the files, those yellow papers.

That is called secrecy. We talk of secrecy. We talk of intellectual property. Look, government also has got intellectual property. We do not understand it very vehemently, because we were always linking access to intellectual property certainly to technology. But what is technology? ***Technology is ultimately conversion of science into a useful tool.*** So, those who have got hold over science can control the technology. Those who know how to convert science into technology are the big people, who are talking about intellectual property rights (IPR).

In governance also it is equally true. We never thought of it. Because we do it day to day, we do it any number of times, we do not realize that. But there is also this part, which is significantly important. That is why people are now talking about the right to know. Why are people talking about the right to know? Why are people talking about access to information? Because it is known that having access to certain information has roots with governance.

If I have access to information and there is open transparency, then my importance is lost, because you know everything that I know. So, all the middle order linkage system collapses. I do not know whether you have seen *The Hindustan Times* of today, where they say that Web-based administration is getting more popular in a country like India also. People are using technology more and more even in rural areas. It has grown enormously today. Why? It is only because of this.

I will give you a very small example. In the last one year, the railways created infrastructure whereby you can book tickets by sitting at your home on any day and the ticket would be delivered at your house for a fees of Rs.20. It is a massive structure that they created. They started the computerized reservation a few years ago. See what sort of miracle has started happening. The middlemen have now realized that they have no role and this happened just in six months. Around a million bookings are being done every day. Now the Indian system is big and we have all big numbers. Earlier, they were not able to cope with that. Now with the introduction of this new system of booking, all other booking systems and the ills that go with those booking systems have become redundant. It is all because we have got the access to information. If I want to go from Bangalore to Chennai, by sitting in Delhi I know which train, I can book in that train and get the ticket at my home. It is simple access to information. So, that access to information and my effective use of it has changed my life and has changed governance. ***It is not only access to information, it is appropriate mechanism, methodology and framework for use of that access to information, which is another important aspect of governance.***

So, in the 21st century, when we are talking of governance, we will have to take into consideration all these various aspects and put them in a jigsaw puzzle to create the picture which is addressing the issues of today. ***It may be governance for efficiency is necessary and governance for effectiveness is absolutely essential. But governance, which is going to enhance the life styles in a different way for humans, becomes the core aspect of the 21st century.*** This is now possible because of the things that I talked of, because of the new things that have emerged, which hitherto was not happening.

So, tomorrow's public administration has to be endowed effectively with these additional technology-mediated governance, if I want to use the term that Dr. Sanjeev Reddy was using, without losing the core of the entity, that is humans, with the sheer objective of making governance a comfortable commodity for living creatures. That is where my concept of governance for peace starts coming up. If you want, you can use the term value system or moral aspect. This has become an important aspect of the 21st century. I have just placed this thought before you. I felt this dimension probably is at the core of public administration in the 21st century.

I would like to thank Dr. Sanjeev Reddy for inviting me here. I thank you for kindly listening to my thought process. I am very happy to inaugurate this National Conference. (*Loud Cheers*)

MR. CHAIRMAN: Thank you, Dr Arun Nigavekar. You have provided us a good base for deep thinking with a thought-provoking address. We hope that everyone who is present here will pass on this message and will be benefited by it. Now with all these developments, the human being is the core cannot be neglected and should not be neglected. It is a point very well taken. I am sure, in our discussions to follow later on, we will keep that in mind. I once again thank you for a very wonderful lecture.

VOTE OF THANKS

Shri B.C. Mathur, Treasurer, IIPA

Chairman Shri G.C.L. Joneja, Dr. Arun Nigavekar, Dr. Sanjeev Reddy, Prof. Noorjahan Bava and so many friends here at the moment that it is very difficult to take all the names here:

It is my very pleasant duty to propose a Vote of Thanks to all of you, particularly the Chairman of UGC, Dr. Arun Nigavekar, who has brought out some very relevant ideas for future government, especially the comfort zone and the idea of peace.

We are really discussing here for today and tomorrow e-governance, developing new modes of decentralized and democratic administration, study of good governance reports from all over the country, what is happening all over the world, so that we know what is exactly going on. In this endeavour, we have been helped by the Department of Personnel, especially the Department of Administrative Reforms, in a big way.

We have been seeing the change in administration. I remember, when I was the District Collector of Balasore, there was a cyclone, which happened about 48 years ago. We used pigeons to get information. Pigeons are still being used, I am told. People will laugh at the idea that we are still living in very ancient times. But I did use pigeons to get information about the position, because we could not go anywhere on account of the floods. It was impossible to move and reach other places. Yet, we wanted information and then decide what to do. So, we had to resort to pigeons.

Today we are living in a different world. As you said, the millennium changes we have seen. Having worked in government for over 50 years, we now see what is the impact of science and technology on our administrative system. How are we going to change the study and meaning of public administration and also the pitfalls that will follow?

We may have very great ideas and also a view of what is happening to the common man. But is he peaceful? Is he happy? Ultimately, that should be resolved. Good governance has to see that the people are satisfied; there are some ethical values; and not that we all become robots ourselves. Although we create all these things, the question arises we create them for what? The purpose should be very clear. All these things are very good. Getting information, receiving information, analyzing information, all that is very good. But, at the same time, at the back of it, how far are we creating a better life for ourselves and for our family?

Today we find that everybody is under tension. In my days, we used to go to office punctually, came back and at about 6 p.m. I was back at home. At 7 p.m. I used to go to the club and play billiards. Today it is just impossible. Once I told one of my uncles, who used to be a senior officer in the railways, that I have got a lot of work and I am coming back at 7 p.m. He told me, "either you are inefficient or you are trying to show off."

So, today things have changed. It is not just possible to follow what I did. Yet I am very proud of what we did. We did a lot of things. We met people. I was in the Orissa cadre. Since there were no bridges on the rivers, we had to go by boat. It was a good time. Because there were no bridges on the rivers, nobody came. So, we had a lot of time to talk to people. We met people all the time. I will not dwell on it further, because I have not come here to give a lecture on that.

My role here is only to thank all of you for having come here. You have already raised many of these points in the papers that have been submitted by you. I am sure, we will discuss those points. Some new points were brought in, which require very deep thought.

I am very grateful to Dr. Arun Nagavekar for having brought out these ideas, because these are not only thinking points but actually they are acting points. But unless we implement them, they are of no use. We have been very good at preparing notes or preparing programmes, but our implementation has been poor. Therefore, the ideas that have been brought out here, how do we implement those in actual life and in the study of public administration in various universities that will have to be considered.

I am very happy that a point was raised about the discipline of public administration in the various universities. IIPA has played a great role in that. We started our MDPA programme; we started various programmes in the universities. In the UPSC's Civil Service Examination today Public Administration is a very popular subject.

Therefore, the study of public administration is not just an appendage to the Department of Political Science. In some of the places it is a part of the Department of History. I know in some places it is a common Department of History and Political Science. So, today there is a need to see that there should be a greater role for the field of the study of public administration in the various universities. One of the ideas behind this Conference will be to see how far can we have in the various universities a Department of Public Administration exclusively seeing to the needs of public administration in the lives of the people. For e-governance it has become much more important. This is something like technology coming out of science. So, something has to be done in this direction.

I am again expressing my grateful thanks to all of you, who have come here, on my behalf and on behalf of the IIPA, with which I have been associated as a Member of the Executive Council for about 30 years now. Thank you very much indeed.

MR. CHAIRMAN: Ladies and Gentlemen, we now break for tea, which is being served outside this hall. Please join us for tea and then reassemble here for the next session.

(*The Inaugural Session then Concluded*)

BUSINESS SESSION-I

(12 December 2003 FN)

Good Governance and Public Administration

PROF. NOORJAHAN BAVA: Let us now begin the First Business Session. We are behind the schedule by about 30 minutes.

The Chairperson for this First Business Session is Prof. S.R. Maheshwari. I would be carrying coal to Newcastle if I make an attempt to introduce Prof. Maheshwari to the public administration community of this country. He is the doyen of the discipline of public administration. He is a very prolific writer. There is hardly any aspect of the study of public administration, which he has not touched in his volumes. He has produced a large number of books, including on local governments and even administrative theory, which are very useful to the student community in particular. If anybody asked for the names of books on Indian Public Administration, we always remembered his books. I have not counted how many books he has produced. But I can safely say that being a great intellectual leader in the field of public administration, he has made available a very large number of very good books to the public administration community.

Coming to the next facet of his personality, Prof. Maheshwari was appointed as Professor of Public Administration and Political Science in the Indian Institute of Public Administration, where he had long innings. He is one of the very distinguished Professors of this Institute. Today we are doing him proud by extending an invitation to him to preside over this session and we are really recognizing the importance of his contribution to the study of public administration and to the Institute in particular.

So, I am very thankful to Prof. Maheshwari for having accepted my invitation to chair this session. I also make a request that if he is free and if time permits, he may come over here and join us for the Valedictory Session tomorrow.

Now I request Prof. Maheshwari to preside over this session and conduct the proceedings till lunchtime, which will be at about 1.30 p.m. Our lunch break is from 1.30 p.m. to 2.30 p.m. Till then this session shall go on.

DIRECTOR (DR. P.L. SANJEEV REDDY): On behalf of the IIPA, I welcome Prof. Maheshwari with a bouquet of flowers. By honouring him, we are honouring ourselves.

REMARKS BY PROF. S.R. MAHESHWARI, CHAIRMAN, I BUSINESS SESSION

Dr. Sanjeev Reddy, Prof. Noorjahan Bava, Prof. Bhaskar Rao, Prof. S.P. Verma, Prof. Harbans Pathak and friends!

In fact, there are more friends here than my capacity to remember them and identify them. In the first place, I am very grateful to IIPA for conferring this honour on me to preside over the First Business Session of the National Conference on a momentous topic, namely, "Public Administration in the Twenty-First Century".

Prof. Bava, I really feel humbled by your magnanimous introduction. I am like all of you, a student of public administration. I have the satisfaction to see that the discipline is flourishing despite voice of gloom made by various scholars from time to time.

The theme of this session is "Public Administration in the Twenty-First Century". It is an exciting century for public administration, both as a field of intellectual enquiry and practice. It brings us with new paradigms, new approaches, new challenges and new issues. Any sound discussion of public administration of the twenty-first century would remain incomplete without an analysis of the shape of public administration in the past 20th century.

The 20th century, as you all know, saw the emergence and strengthening of positive governance in all countries of the world. Public administration, which is another term for public bureaucracy, was viewed as the new guard capable of solving all the problems of the society. Therefore, there was a relentless rise of public bureaucracy in the 20th century. Public bureaucracy was taking up new and novel tasks of governance and it was consequently expanding. Mankind looked upon public bureaucracy as a solution to all the problems.

In India, we mention the 1990s as the period of the reforms. The real problem began in the '80s. You can say that science began to march ahead even in the '70s. In the western world, the trend was visible in the '60s. Anyway, there was some weariness felt about the solutions and the villain was seen to be public bureaucracy. Because of the tardiness in the problem solving the economic health of the country deteriorated. India was going into the debt trap deeper and deeper. Public undertakings were running in losses. L.K. Jha Report was a grim reminder of the disease that gripped India at that time.

Therefore, a deeper analysis showed that what was discovered to be a solution was itself in a diseased position. As a result, public bureaucracy became the god that failed. The Government of India announced its New Economic Policy in 1991, announcing an era of commitment to Free Market, Liberalization and Globalization.

This was a U-turn for India. The Nehruvian model of development was abandoned and now India was seeing its salvation in free market economy, in economic liberalization, in globalization. Well, free market economy is a euphemism, which stands for market capitalism, a very significant word at this stage. The scholars, many of them trained economists, painted public bureaucracy this time in dark colour. Some of the names we already know. Niskanon was one of them, Carlson is another and Anthony Down yet another. These are among the more notable names, whose writings led to deep disillusionment with public bureaucracy. By the same token, they built a formidable case supportive of the public sector with its legacy of managerialism and its appurtenances.

The discipline of public administration could not remain unaffected as a result of the writings of these scholars and the discipline saw new theories, new paradigms in the form of Public Choice theory, in the form of New Public Management (NPM). The new public management adopts managerialism from the private sector, which is uncritical acceptance of managerialism. In other words, NPM marks the advent of the mercantile theory in public administration.

When I was just jotting down some of my thoughts for this morning presentation, I came across still another concept in public administration—the new concept is called new public service. We hear so much about the discipline of public administration. What about the practice of public administration? The feeling is growing that today we have too much of government, we should have less of it. At the same time, there is less of governance, we should have more of it. Friends, I do not have to remind you that there is a difference between government and governance. As somebody said, a wise king should be proud not of government but of governance. This quotation is given in the English Oxford Dictionary. At the same time, in the years to come, governance would dominate the horizon of public administration in India and many other countries and it would be the dominating theme, both on the part of theoreticians of public administration as well as the practitioners.

In order to know the practice of public administration, Indians will have to consult the Report of the Fifth Pay Commission chaired by Pandian. It is the most explicit, most coherent textbook on administrative reforms of the 21st century. Although the Fifth Pay Commission said that there should be another review of the civil service, including its pay structure, after 10 years, nothing has been done so far. Therefore, until another Pay Commission supersedes it, this is the most valid textbook.

What is the message of the Fifth Pay Commission? Offloading of functions; some of the functions should be stopped, some should be offloaded to non-government sectors of the society; there should be de-layering; there should be introduction of desk officer system; attention should be given to accountability and transparency; performance appraisal should be improved; citizen orientation should be instilled into the bureaucracy; the citizens' charter has to be introduced; quality improvement, and quality control. All these aspects have been covered in the Central Pay Commission Report of Pandian, and these must be understood very clearly.

Friends, I would conclude by making a reference to three other points, which I noticed in public administration. We are told that public administration is withdrawing, government is withdrawing. It is not withdrawing. It is changing the style of functioning, from "rowing to steering". Public administration would be engaged in the task of a 'facilitator' instead of engaging itself in the task of 'ruling'. The space to be vacated by administration or the State would be occupied by the Market and the Civil Society.

Now when the market starts stepping in, then the market will have to be watched very carefully, whether the market is observing the rules of the game or not. Therefore, India will see more of organizations like SEBI, Disinvestment Commission, Competition

Commission and the Telecom Regulatory Authority of India. In other words, India will be creating bodies like the independent Regulatory Commission of the United States of America. This development is welcome, but it is not without dangers and risks. When the regulator and the regulated meet, when they interact, there are dangers. The American study says the regulator becomes the regulated and the regulated becomes the regulator. The private sector organizations captured these watchdog organizations. As a result, corruption enters the scene and it is the greatest curse of India.

There is a second thing that has to be watched very carefully. Under pressure to downsize the public bureaucracy, the Ministries and Departments are today creating what they call autonomous organizations. Nobody knows how many of them exist in India. A broad survey would put the number at 500. I stopped at 500. I did not have the capacity to go on listing them. They get funds from the taxpayers. They have not yet received the attention of the scholars and academics of the country.

I have already told you that the space to be vacated by public administration is being occupied by the market and by the NGOs. Now the NGO is a negative definition, which is not very helpful. Public administration is generally concerned with the executive branch of the government but now we have to redefine its territory. NGOs are non-governmental, but public administration must start studying them, because they are engaged in the new activities of importance, meaning and sense to the society.

Friends, I would not like to take any more of your time. These are some of the thoughts that I thought I should share with you.

Prof. Noorjahan Bava has already stated that we would go on till 1.30 p.m., till lunch time. There are a number of very interesting papers to be presented. Then it is my duty to leave some time for questions also, is it not? Once the presentations are over, there would be questions. Would you like to ration time for the individual paper presentation?

Prof. S.C. Arora, Prof. Priti Garg, Dr. Inderjeet Kaur and Prof. Marina Pinto presented their papers and responded to the questions raised by Dr. Pardhasaradhi, Prof. V. Bhaskara Rao, Shri Binod Anand and Dr. Radhanath Tripathi.

(*First Business Session Concluded*)

BUSINESS SESSION-II

(12 December 2003 AN)

Globalization and Public Administration

PROF. NOORJAHAN BAVA: We are now starting the Second Business Session of this Conference. The topic of the Session is "Globalization and Public Administration" and Prof. S.P. Verma is chairing it. He is an all India figure, a well-known figure in the field of public administration. So, once again I am carrying coal to New Castle if I try to introduce Prof. Verma to this audience of eminent people on public administration.

He was a distinguished Professor of the Indian Institute of Public Administration. He made his mark here by introducing a number of innovations. He takes a lot of interest, not only in IIPA but also in the field of public administration. He founded the Department of Public Administration in various universities because of his zest for institution building. He started the Department of Public Administration in IGNOU way back in 1987, about 15 years ago. Though he retired from service, he is still continuing to take an active interest in the subject and is conducting courses in various universities. I am given to understand that in IGNOU they are now going to start post-graduate degree programme in public administration. It will be the first University in Delhi to have a separate department of public administration.

The third most interesting thing about him is that way back in the early '90s, some of us, who came here to attend the meetings in IIPA, felt the need to have a national forum for public administration. No doubt, the Indian Journal of Public Administration is running. But there is no organization for the teachers. So, a teaching organization for public administration was founded and the first issue of Public Administration came out soon. Like the Indian Political Science Association, there is the Indian

Public Administration Association. It brought out one issue. Then I do not know what happened, it went into some legal problems. Afterwards, we did not hear of any publication or any meeting. I am a Life Member and I have paid my full subscription. But I did not hear anything at all from them.

So, in the absence of any institutional forum for exchange of thoughts and ideas, a few people interested in the subject, like Prof. Bhaskar Rao, Prof. S.P. Verma, Prof. Mohit Bhattacharya, Prof. Inamdar from Pune and myself, decided that we would start an organization. That is how the Public Administration Society of India was founded. It is doing good work. We are bringing out, not any journal, but a News Letter. Prof. Bhaskar Rao is the Secretary. Prof. S.P. Verma was the Chairperson. Now for the last two years, Prof. Arvind Sharma from the North East University, Mizoram is the President and I am the Vice-President of that Association. There is some forum now and it is going to be registered. We have a good number of both Life and Ordinary Members.

So, Prof. Verma is very closely associated with teaching and research in public administration. He was also carrying out the responsibility of being the Editor of the Indian Journal of Public Administration of IIPA. The Executive Council of the IIPA appointed him as the Editor of this journal. It is a quarterly and every year there are four issues. He has edited the IJPA for four years. Now that we have some change of leadership, Shri U.C. Aggarwal has taken over the Editorship of the Journal. But Prof. Verma continues to take interest in inspiring young people and guiding them in the field of public administration.

Last but not the least, he is the Deputy Chairman of the Delhi Regional Branch of IIPA. IIPA has got both Regional and Local Branches. Almost every State, save a few, have got a Regional Branch and some Local Branches within the state, so that the purpose for which the Institute was founded could be fulfilled throughout the country through these channels of Regional and Local Branches. As far as the Delhi Regional Branch is concerned, I must say, I was the Founder Secretary, Shri Swaroop was the Treasure and H.E. Shri T.N. Chaturvedi, the present Governor of Karnataka was the Chairman. Prof. S.P. Verma is the Deputy Chairman of the Delhi Regional Branch. So, he is very busy presiding over the meetings, seminars and conferences of the Delhi

Regional Branch connected with the subject of public administration.

I am sure, by honouring Prof. Verma, we are in turn honouring the subject of public administration and also the Institute of Public Administration. If we put it the other way round, then also it is correct. So, I would now request Prof. Verma to preside over this session.

Before we start the presentation, on behalf of all of you, as a mark of honour to the Chairman, we are presenting him a bouquet. (*Loud Cheers*)

REMARKS OF PROF. S.P. VERMA, CHAIRMAN, II BUSINESS SESSION

Prof. Bava, Prof. Bhaskar Rao and all the other distinguished members present here. When Prof. Bava invited me to chair one of the sessions, I very readily agreed. You know there is a phrase "Barkis is willing"!

But whatever she said in her introduction about me bring to my mind many incidents of the past. Further, there are only two papers. I have some nostalgia. Being nostalgic, the whole scenario from the day I started my teaching career passes through my mind. If I were in an institution like IIPA and if we had enthusiastic organizers like Prof. Noorjahan Bava, I should be celebrating my golden jubilee, because I started my teaching career in July 1953. So, I have completed 50 years of teaching. I am still teaching, though not every day, but 3 to 4 days in a week I am on my feet. So, the whole panorama of the discipline appears in my mind.

I have seen the changes, which have been taking place in the field or in the discipline of public administration and political science. Originally, I have started with political science. But, thanks to Dr. M.P. Sharma, the first department of public administration was started. There is another interesting story here. If you are a good teacher, one day or the other people will recognize you. This has happened in my career at various stages.

In those days, Prof. Awasthi was teaching in a Government College in Nagpur, which was part of the erstwhile Central Provinces and Bihar. Then he got an overseas scholarship to do MBA in Harvard. In those days, Government sent some of the best professors, including those in IIM, on scholarship to Harvard. At that time, I had started my career in Jabalpur. Later, I was transferred to Nagpur. One day I got a message from Dr. M.P. Sharma. At that time, I had just two or three years of teaching experience while Dr. M.P. Sharma was already an established professor. His was the first book on public administration, which we knew in India. When I met him, he said: "Mr. Verma, you know, Prof. Awasthi has gone to USA?" I said, "yes". Then he asked, "Would you like to teach the paper that he was teaching?" I was taken aback, because Prof. Awasthi was my examiner in MA in international relations. So, it was a big honour to me.

It was much later that I discovered how Dr. M.P. Sharma got my name. I remembered, in my B.A., Political Science class, there used to be a very shy girl, sitting at the back, who never opened her mouth. She happened to be the daughter of Dr. M.P. Sharma. So, if you are a good teacher, your name travels.

That is how my introduction as a teacher in public administration started. People like Dr. S.P. Ranga Rao, who have themselves retired as Professors, they were in my class when I was a Lecturer. So, my story of public administration began, my journey began at that time. Then we had only two or three books on public administration and they were all that we were taught. It is only when as a Fullbright scholar that I went to USA that I came to know a little more about administration. So, the 1950s were spent in India and the early 1960s in USA. By this time, within the next decade, I have seen the changes that were taking place.

I had occasion to offer papers in American Government and Public Administration and learnt more and more. I saw how the institutes of public administration were established in various universities and how the Department of Public Administration started. I had the good fortune of meeting quite senior professors like Wendite. He was one of the earliest, who wrote "Enquiries Into Political Science". I had the good fortune to come in contact with people like Robert Dough and Bill Bright, who is still there in the Northern California University. That really cought me up. So, on my return to India, I had one goal, namely, to keep up the traditions of public administration.

You could see how high was the prestige of the name IIPA in those days. When I was offered a job in IIPA and I left my job in Madhya Pradesh, which was a government job that would have given me pension today. Here I did not get any pension, because

IIPA then did not have a pension scheme. They started it only in 1998. So, I chose, I made a deliberate choice to join IIPA.

I can share with you the information now that IIPA in those days had a set of people with very high calibre, senior professors like Prof. Jagannatham and Prof. Thorat, who made their name. They were not Professors simply confined to the classrooms of IIPA; they had wide access to and had interaction with the various universities.

During my stay in IIPA from 1966 to 1986, the two decades I spent there, I knew that for the discipline of public administration to develop, it was not enough to confine ourselves only to the officers who came here and did a programme for the Department of Personnel, but we have to strengthen the Department of Public Administration in the different universities.

So, I could say that I was fortunate that I could establish good rapport with various universities, starting from Shimla in Himachal Pradesh, to Warrangal, where our friend Dr Bhaskar Rao was there, to Hyderabad, Tirupati, Guntur, the South Indian Universities, in Surat, Jaipur and other places. I maintain this is what kept me going.

Now we are celebrating the Golden Jubilee of IIPA and remembering Dr Paul Appleby. I feel today that Dr Appleby's major plan, for which he wanted this Institute to function, was to be the forum where the Institute could bring together the practitioners of public administration with the academics. So long as Prof. Menon was there, there was a programme where he used to give fellowship to young teachers and some of them came here, people like Prof. Khanna, who became a Professor here. Prof. Maheswari was brought here as a fellow. That is something missing now.

I think in this Golden Jubilee Year, one of the first steps which we should take is to again bring a situation where IIPA is not an adjunct of the Government Department or a Ministry, or dealing itself only with the training of civil servants. Unless you strengthen the discipline by bringing in teachers of public administration, and establishing Visiting Fellowship, I think you will not be serving the discipline of public administration. I still have full faith and belief that so long as Prof. Bava is there in the Executive Council—I have ceased to be a Member of the Executive Council for the last one and a half years—we will continue to make efforts to see that this bond and link between IIPA and the Departments of Public

Administration in the various universities is not only strengthened, but also reinforced, because that is the only way that public administration can come to the fore.

Now when my friends tell me that I am a retired professor, I reply, no, I am not retired. I still go to the library and ask the librarian what is the latest book on the subject. So, I can say that I have seen the transformation from the British days of Angrezi Raj to the age of information technology. I have participated in e-governance. So, it has been a long long journey.

I remember as a schoolboy, when my father was a postmaster in a small place, when we had to go to the district headquarters, we had to cross a stream and I travelled in a bullock cart. So, I have passed through the bullock cart age to the jet age and even super jet age and I am still there. I hope I will still be there when it will take only two hours from Delhi to Melbourne or New York, because such rockets are coming, which will take us to those places in no time. This is the change we have witnessed.

That is why I say that the subject that you have selected for discussion is very appropriate. It is true that we should still do work with the municipal government, with vigilance, with redressal of grievances. These are all very relevant to the Indian people, who are still suffering. They are very important. But, as teachers, it is our responsibility to look ahead, to visualize what kind of society we are going to have in the year 2020, or 2030—I will not be there then but most of you will be there—what will be the nature of the society, what will be the kind of problems that the administration will face, what are the aids which the administration will have. This is the vast panorama that is opening before us. I can assure you that in the coming decades the changes are not going to be minimal, the changes are not going to be incremental, but the changes are going to be vast. While I was travelling in decades, you would be traveling in centuries, and that is a big change, which I look forward to.

I am very glad that this initiative has been taken by Prof. Bava and Professors and Lecturers in the Universities and departments will follow it up, which will subscribe substantially to the growth of this discipline.

So, no more of my autobiography. The first two presenters of this session, Prof. Bharati Sharma and Dr. Sujata Singh are not here. So, I call upon Dr. Lipi Mukhopadhyay to present her paper on "Gender Issues in Global Development". I have faced this gender problem earlier, as I told you. I was hoping to top the list in the University examination in my class but a girl beat me. In various fields girls have been topping. This is our experience. So, I never underrate any gender. I have always respect for them. I do not forget that in my house I am in a minority of one, because my wife and daughter are on one side and I have to submit to them!

After Dr. Lipi Mukhopadhyay and Dr. Asha Gupta presented their papers, they also responded to the questions raised by Prof. Harbans Pathak, Prof. V. Bhaskara Rao, Dr. Inderjeet Kaur and Mr. V. Radhakrishnan.

INTERVENTION BY PROF. NOORJAHAN BAVA: This Second Business Session addresses the issue of Globalization and Public Administration. Now various issues have been touched upon in this session. I would not go into all of them. I shall just confine my remarks, comments or intervention on two sub-themes of this Conference. One is the Gender issue and the other is Good Governance in the context of globalization.

The first one is gender issue. We are all aware that the feminist movement is a global movement. It is part of the global process. At least this is what we, the votaries of feminist movement, are trying to achieve, namely, that it becomes a global issue. Because the women all over the world, in the society, whether it is in the West or in the East, their status remains very low. As far as governance is concerned, the administration is concerned, even though in the social status there may be differences, those differences are one of degree, not of kind. So, by and large, the women are a suppressed lot. They are the marginal sections. In India we call them as weaker sections. We are physically weak. But we are healthy. We are as intelligent as men. Sometimes my husband tells me "you are more intelligent than me".

Basically, we are human beings. This is a fact. God has created only male and female gender. One object may be for the survival of humanity. Humanity should go on, mankind should go on. That is the only purpose of this distinction between male and female gender. In all other respects, the male and female species have equal rights, capabilities, skill and competence.

You have to provide them equal opportunities. They should have equal rights. Why deny them their right? We cannot talk of development at the macro or micro level by leaving women out from the orbit of development. Therefore, the gender issue is a global issue. The women all over the world, through civil society organizations, through non-governmental organizations, both the print and electronic media, they are fighting a war against their male citizens, against the patriarchal society, which suppresses them, dominates them and homogenizes them.

Therefore, in this context, in this age of democracy and development or good governance, I do not see any hope, any ray of hope or light of hope for good governance, by keeping women out of the processes of governance or development. So, it is very essential that they should have political participation, administrative participation, participation in economic and social activities. It is very very essential. The participation of women hinges upon their realization of their human rights. It is part of the human rights movement as well. The human rights movement and the feminist movement have coalesced. They are marching towards the realization of the same objective or goal, realization of first and foremost goal as human beings, as equal citizens, as equal members of the society. The day we achieve or realize this goal of social, political and economic equality, that is the day when we can really say we have achieved just development. It is my own interpretation.

MR. CHAIRMAN: Day before yesterday I saw one CNN interview of Mrs. Shirin Abidi of Iran. Here is an example of a Muslim lady who stands for certain principles. She is not afraid of the orthodox Mullahs. Look at the role she has played as a civil servant, lawyer, judge and human right activist. This is quite contrary to the stereotype picture, which we get that women all over the Muslim world are backward, they are exploited. She stood not only against the conservatism of the mullahs, but she stood against the mighty power of the state as a human rights activist. This shows that there are women as capable as men, if not better, given the opportunities. Look at the United Nations, look at various international organizations and see the top position women are holding. Then I was so happy to read in the newspapers today the story of the 13-year old girl from Bihar, who became a prodigy and she could show what education can do. What is more surprising is that up to the age of 11 she has not been sent to school. So, this is the kind of changes that we want to take place and they are going to take place before long.

PROF. NOORJAHAN BAVA: If I may switch on to a personal note on the gender issue. I am a Muslim, born in a Muslim family.

But I was very lucky to have very enlightened parents, who saw the importance of education and they educated me. They gave me freedom not to wear a burqa. But I am a humble Muslim. I do not want to miss my prayers. My faith is very firm. I am very secular in outlook. When it comes to my personal life, yes, I try to observe the duties of a Muslim. But the moment I step out of my house, I am in the public domain. I deal with hundreds of people, students, teachers, neighbours and others. They do not follow the same faith. But I have as good relations with them as I have with my own people at home. I am totally secular. I am for secularization of culture, political culture, and social culture. But when it comes to the personal domain, you have the right to freedom of religion. It is a matter of faith and you cannot compel any person to follow any particular faith.

My parents gave me total freedom of education. I gave the same freedom to my daughters. I gave them excellent opportunity and equal rights. Perhaps, if I had sons, I would have treated them the same way. I have taught them to be good hard working citizens. Now they are doing well in their lives and contribute to social good. I have practiced in my life what I am saying, preaching.

It is possible to live in peace, in harmony with people belonging to other religions. You must have respect and tolerance for other religions. It is very wrong for people to think that Islam is terrorism or Islam believes in terrorism. This is all because of a few terrorists. They have spoiled everything, even their own religion in the name of Islam. Islam means tolerance. That is the meaning.

The Prophet in his own lifetime, had shown greater tolerance for the Jews, and Christians. Their places of worship were protected. The followers of Prophet Mohammed were commanded to show respect to the dignity and womanhood of women as a whole, belonging to any religion, not to touch women or children in the case of war. He had treaties concluded, which respected the right to tolerance of religion and places of religious worship. All this has been forgotten by a handful of people, the terrorists who are politically motivated, who want to capture power. They have nothing to do with the tenets of Islam. They are not real Muslims; they are defaming religion. So, please do not think that this religion is bad. This religion will bring peace to the world. It has respect for other religions of the world. We have to live in communal peace and harmony.

The other issue on which I would like to comment as a teacher is New Public Management (NPM). A lot has been said and written about it. What is NPM? This needs to be re-defined. By NPM is meant that you give up the earlier approaches to the study and practice of public administration, what is called orthodox approach in public administration, the traditional approach that treats public administration as public bureaucracy, for example. You cannot think of public administration without public bureaucracy. Everything connected with public falls within the purview of public administration. Public interest is the core idea along with public bureaucracy. Public interest, public good and public properties are the three concepts around which the study of public administration revolves. It is the duty of the public administrators to protect and promote public interest, public goods and public property.

As the UGC Chairman was saying this morning, I do not know when this separation began where the linkages began. Public Law is a parent discipline. Public administration is rooted in public law as well as in Political Science. Like all children of all parents, they grow and develop wings and fly away when they grow up. They build their own nest, develop and start their own family. Like that, even the intellectual side of public administration has grown in that way. It has become inter-disciplinary; it is no longer an uni-disciplinary subject. However, every social science has to say something on public administration. We have to integrate it, because it is inter-disciplinary, multi-disciplinary. Our perspective has also to be inter-disciplinary. I know we, as political scientists look at a particular problem only from the political science angle. But we know as public administrationists what economics, sociology or psychology has to contribute to the problem.

The problem of identity crisis, which bothered the subject especially after the second world war, the problem of the status of the discipline of public administration, that crisis of identity has been resolved by the realization that it is inter-disciplinary, it is no longer uni-disciplinary.

MR. CHAIRMAN: Like other sciences, we are members of the extended family. It is necessary for us to remember that for our own existence. The other point is what Dr. Arun Nagavekar made this morning. Unlike the enlightened history, psychology or arithmetic, public administration is not a single discipline subject.

Actually, it is very important to know that it is multi-disciplinary and inter-disciplinary. Therefore, public administration cannot be equated with other social sciences. We have to recognize that public administration will not be public administration, if we do not draw the value systems from the rest of society.

What are the objectives, what all we have to study in public administration, we derive from social sciences, from our philosophy, and theology. Therefore, let us accept. Public Administration cannot be compressed into a single subject like history. That is where the real difficulty comes in. I think it is mentioned in one of the papers. No if you take the broader perspective and look at this problem, you talk of public administration as public management. Here there are designations, where people are designated as managers in public administration, like in business you have administrators. So, both business and administration have the same terms.

PROF. NOORJAHAN BAVA: Therefore, what is new is that the proponents of the management discipline want to change the nomenclature, the word public administration by calling it as new public management. Even degrees are offered like Masters in Public Management. Thus you are narrowing public administration to management.

MR. CHAIRMAN: Management is just one tool; it is one part of public administration.

PROF. NOORJAHAN BAVA: Henri Fayol in his concept or notion of administration says that management involves six processes, as Planning, Organization, Management, Command, Coordination and Control (which he spelt out). Then he found that these processes are common to each and every organization, including public administration. It is only in the English speaking countries that the word "administration" is used to denote management of government affairs while in all other organizations it is the term 'management' that is used.

Now the new concept for management science, (NPM) would like to see the development and growth of that study to cover everything, including public administration. So, it is nothing but old wine in new bottles. We have already been adopting management techniques. I have learnt all these methods in the Indian Institute of Public Administration, when I did the APPPA Programme way back in 1977-78. Our administrators are also following it. But IIPA is not following it in its own home; no performance budget, nothing; and it is still traditional. But we teach our administrators that we have to follow these management techniques. So, we have to ask this question, what is the gain here?

MR. CHAIRMAN: We tell them that it should be made applicable in their jobs. I need not add it to my discipline.

PROF. NOORJAHAN BAVA: I will now explain what is the harm in the adoption of this new term for public administration. There is a fundamental difference between public and private administration, which grew up over centuries. Now it is being forgotten. Management speaks for profit, for private administration. It is always associated with maximization of profit, whereas public administration exists for promotion of public interest, public purpose. Earlier public administration was not even a subject for business administration. If we bring in the concept of profit motive which is central to private business administration into Government, that means we are endorsing/accepting the nefarious act of bribing the administrators, encouraging the administrators to take and give bribe, and follow many other malpractices prevailing in the private sector.

MR. CHAIRMAN: Money has become God now.

PROF. NOORJAHAN BAVA: This is total distortion of the basic and fundamental difference in values/norms/objectives between public and private administration. As a student or teacher, in whatever capacity, I just cannot simply reconcile myself to this metamorphosis in the connotation of the term public administration. I rebel against the reference to the discipline as public management, I agree that we do have public sector enterprises, they are economic enterprises, and they have to be competitive, efficient, and also make profits. But that profit has to be ploughed back to the public in various ways; it does not go to the private pocket. But what happens to profits made in private sector companies? That money goes back to the pockets of Tatas, Birlas and others. We do not and can not do it in the Government sector. So, how can you just ignore this basic distinction between public and private administration? The public management approach defeats the noble purpose for which public administration exists—protection and promotion of public interest, public good, and public service.

Secondly, in public administration we speak for the people, as citizens of the country. Now in new public management, they have become customers, clients. That means that there is no need for the State at all. You need only private companies and they will solve all the problems.

There is the superior side of human nature, the concern for the community, concern for the country, concern for the weaker sections, the spirit of altruism for example. All these noble values are ignored in NPM. Now we have come back to the 19th century idea of liberation of the self, maximizing the benefits for the self, which is the rationality. Everything else has been forgotten. It is the resurgence of the earlier 19th century political theory of liberalization and utilitarianism.

PROF. V. BHASKARA RAO: As a part of the Golden Jubilee celebrations, IIPA has organized this Conference on the topic of "Public Administration in the Twenty-First Century". Since you are organizing this Conference on behalf of IIPA, are you holding this view as the Convener of the Conference of IIPA? Because there are guidelines of the Government of India.

PROF. NOORJAHAN BAVA: I am speaking as a Professor of Public Administration, as an academic, not in my capacity as the Convener. I am not here to give directions for the future development of the Institute. You are misunderstanding me. I am only organizing this Conference to have a public forum for you to express your views.

PROF. V. BHASKARA RAO: Now the Government of India are adopting the new public management under the dictates or pressure of the donor agencies. IIPA is not above that. Now knowingly or unknowingly, deliberately or otherwise, it has become a tool of management. To the best of my knowledge, 9 universities have introduced it as part of their syllabus for public management. Now the Government of India is asking us to support their idea. The World Bank literature is entering into the IIPA library. If you look into the UNDP Report, it also speaks more or less on these lines.

PROF. NOORJAHAN BAVA: Public administration is an intellectual discipline as well as a profession, an instrument of the government. It (NPM) is an ideological model, which has to cater to the management needs, the top management policies. But somehow it is a theoretical problem for our people (the public administrationists), which need to be debated and discussed. We need not accept it, simply because it comes from a global agency like the World Bank. All of a sudden, a new model cannot be thrown up like that. Now we have one Super-Power. They want to have only one model of development with globalization and privatization everywhere. Have we in the developing societies reached that stage through which we can bring about those policy changes? What is good for the western industrialized and developed societies is not good for us. They are not to be tried in the developing countries, where our major basic problems are unemployment, inequality and poverty. Now who is the gainer in this game? The profit seekers in the developed rich countries. The rich people will have concentration of wealth while the poor will become poorer.

So, I do not think that privatization is the solution to the problems of the developing countries. That cannot remove poverty. Then corruption will further increase, unemployment will increase. Because, with the introduction of modernization and technology, with machines like computers, less people will be required to perform the same functions in factories and offices. So, there will be growing unemployment. It is an inhuman system. We are totally against adopting a system, which forgets its responsibilities towards the people. It is my own personal conviction. I do not know whether my colleagues here share my views or not. We have to tell our students, look, this paradigm has now come; do not think it is good or totally free from problems; you have to really subject that to scrutiny and make your own judgment.

MR. CHAIRMAN: I think you have stated a good point. I think as a teacher we must tell the students how this discipline was developed, what were the choices, how this has become public management, how many times they changed the names, from the school of political sciences to the school of public policies. I personally believe that as a teacher I should never impose my own political belief or ideology on the students. But as a teacher I must explain to them what is the ideology. I may be the worst enemy of Communism or Marxism. But I must study Marxism. Otherwise, how can I teach Marxism, if I have not studied it? I must tell the students what Marx said, what Engels said or what Churchill said. I need not agree with one word of what Churchill said, but it is my duty to inform the students what he stood for. I did my study in USA and even in the under-graduate class I knew what Marxism is because it was a compulsory subject. In India, the study of Marxism is prohibited. This is a wrong type of approach. It is my personal belief that the study of a subject is not confined to me; I must explain them to the students.

The other day one of the students was telling me, you are saying all the good things about the west, but what about India? I may tell you that in the West even the first year student can talk direct to the President of America and even question some of his actions. But the Indian students can see the President only on the television.

I think these are the various facets through which public administration has worked and will work. We should tell them what exactly is happening. Though all of us may have our beliefs, we have to explain to them the various schools of thoughts, including those with which we may not agree.

With these words, may I have the permission of Madam to declare the afternoon session of this Conference closed? Thank you very much for your kind cooperation.

PROF. NOORJAHAN BAVA: I thank Prof. Verma for the excellent conduct of the Session. We have, at least in the later part of the Session, been able to focus on the relevance and importance of the new approaches to the study of the discipline of public administration, apart from the practice of public administration. That is one of the purposes for which this Conference was organized. I am very happy that we are moving in that direction.

(*The Conference then adjourned for the day*)

BUSINESS SESSION-III

(13 December 2003 FN)

IT Revolution, E-Governance and Public Administration

PROF. NOORJAHAN BAVA: Let me call the House to order. This is the second day of the Conference and we are starting the proceedings. According to the programme, this is the Third Business Session, on "IT Revolution, E-Governance and Public Administration", to be chaired by Prof. Ramesh K. Arora, former Professor of Public Administration, Rajasthan University and now Senior Fellow in HCM Institute of Public Administration Jaipur,

I have received a phone call a little while ago, before I left home, that he is coming by taxi from Jaipur, there is a lot of fog en route, the taxi is coming at a snail's pace and he is afraid that he could not make it for this session. He also told me, "Madam, kindly do not wait for me. Please start the proceedings, as per the programme. I will try to come and join." I hope he has no problem en route and he reaches and joins us soon.

Prof. V. Bhaskara Rao is present here and he is the Chairman of the next session. But I would request him to swap the Chairmanship with Prof. Ramesh K. Arora. I now request Prof. Bhaskara Rao to come here and chair this session.

Now a word about Prof. Bhaskara Rao. He is one of the distinguished scholars, teachers and researchers in the field of public administration that India has produced. Formerly, he was Professor of Public Administration in Kakkatiya University, Warrangal. After a distinguished career, he retired from there a couple of years ago. He is a prolific writer on the subject. He has also written books in Telugu medium for the benefit of the students of the Universities in Andhra Pradesh.

He has been spreading the light of knowledge in the field of public administration through his writings, teaching and evaluation of examination papers in Telugu as well as in English. Apart from that, he is the Co-Founder of the New Public Administration Society of India. He is the Founder-Secretary of this Association for over 15 years. He is dedicated to the cause of the development of the discipline of public administration and has many more achievements to his credit.

I extend a very warm and cordial welcome to Prof. Bhaskara Rao and request him to preside over this session "IT Revolution, E-Governance and Public Administration".

REMARKS BY PROF. BHASKARA RAO, CHAIRMAN, III BUSINESS SESSION

Let me at the outset congratulate Prof. Bava for organizing this great Seminar on "Public Administration in the Twenty-First Century" and giving me this opportunity, not only to present a paper but also to preside over the session. I am very grateful to her.

I must tell you very honestly that I have gone through all the papers that have been written on the forecasts for the 21st century. It was a very pleasant experience to go through those papers. Apart from thanking her for giving me an opportunity to come over here, I am also thankful for her kind words about me.

I have served the cause of public administration all my life. I did it in my own way. Being in a rural area, being a rural University, there were many limitations, but I served the cause of pubic administration in a really sincere manner. It may not be a great contribution but I did whatever was possible. While I am satisfied with my work, I feel that there is a lot that needs to be done. I hope the younger generation, the young people who are present here, will take care of that job.

I must also confess here that I am not well versed in the IT revolution and e-governance in public administration. In a sense, I am a traditional public administrator, not knowing much about the happenings in the technology-dominated field. So, I would like to learn from our friends like Prof. Sachdeva and Dr. Pardhasaradhi. I would now request Prof. Sachdeva to present his paper.

In this session papers were presented by Prof. R.K. Sachdeva,

Dr. Y. Pardhasaradhi and Dr. Sujata Singh. They also responded to the questions raised by Dr. Asha Gupta.

PROF. NOORJAHAN BAVA: I want to thank Prof. V Bhaskara Rao for chairing this session and Prof. Ramesh K. Arora, Prof. R. K. Sachdeva, Dr Pardhasaradhi and other paper writers for their presentations. We will now move on to the next session.

INTERVENING SESSION

(13 December 2003 FN)

Key-Note Address by Gerard Lemos

PROF. NOORJAHAN BAVA: Dr. Sanjeev Reddy, Director, IIPA, Mr. Gerard Lemos, Vice-Chair, British Council and our Guest of Honour, ladies and gentlemen!

It is indeed a great pleasure to welcome Mr. Gerard Lemos, who is a distinguished scholar, administrator and also active social activist, the three rolled into one. He is going to give us his experiences – varied, diverse and exciting about the British administration and some issues of UK Government's policy. Since he has held very important positions as Civil Service Commissioner and Audit Commissioner in the Government and closely associated with NGOs run by social researchers like Lemos and Crane, who took up issues regarding the weaker sections and others, I think he has much to give us in terms of strategy, how to overcome the various problems, the racial problems, feminist problems and other problems. He has authored a few books. I think they are available in our Library. If not, I would request him to give us copies of his books for the use of our members.

As the Convener of this Conference on Public Administration in the Twenty-First Century, I request Mr. Gerard Lemos to address us. Actually, we were planning to request him to come here for the Valedictory Session at 4 p.m. today. But he has another appointment somewhere else at that time and we do not want him to miss that. I cannot call this as Valedictory Session, because we have two more sessions to go before we conclude. Therefore, I describe it as the Intervening Session. He is delivering the Keynote Address on "Issues of Public Policies of the British Government". I request Dr. Sanjeev Reddy, to chair this Session.

Aspects of British Policy: Mr. Gerard Lemos, Vice-Chair, British Council

May I just say what a pleasure it is to be here on behalf of the British Council? I am also supposed to be here for personal reasons. I think you all know of my Indian origin and I am not tired of mentioning that. It is a great pleasure to speak as an Indian and it is a large community in UK.

I am also coming from generations of civil servants on both sides of my family. All my forefathers have been civil servants. Since they have been civil servants in India, Lemos must have been amongst them. So, from that point of view also I am pleased to be here.

I am going to say a little bit, and I intend to say it very briefly, about the conduct of public administration in the United Kingdom at the moment, especially in the context of the regulation of public administration in the United Kingdom, which is burgeoning. I read in *The Financial Times* yesterday, that the Government of the United Kingdom now spends 12 billion pounds on the supervision of public service and on the regulations on them. It is an extraordinary amount of money to pay to people to watch other people work.

I want to say a little bit about how that is working and the lessons that I have learnt. I would also spend a little amount of my time on the regulation of the financial service industry in UK. It seems to me that it is an instructive comparison between how you regulate the private sector and how you regulate public service.

Before I go on to that, I should say a few words about the context we find ourselves in the UK. Despite being an enormously wealthy country, there are many elements in UK that do not work. Those in Government, and indeed the Opposition, have very high priority about the need to improve the services. There is particular concern about the National Health Service, shall I say the last impact or legacy of the great establishment, of Welfare State by the British Government.

It is widely felt that we have to provide good quality and cost effective treatment. Now people have to wait too long for that treatment and the physical conditions in which that treatment is delivered are often unappealing and uncomfortable. It has also an ideological background. The civil service has a profound distaste for performing patient chores associated with health and there is also the problem with education at all levels. Apparently, there is the inexcusable rise in certain types of crime and disorder. ***So, health, education and crime lead the indictment of public service.***

Problems of U.K. Minority Ethnic Community

In my personal point of view, ***by far the largest concern is the continued social and economic exclusion of a significant minority of the population, many of whom are what we call members of UK minority ethnic community.*** Within this broad notion of social exclusion are communities in which there is persistent high level of crime, unemployment, ill health—physical and mental, illegal drug use and poor housing. All these together, along with cultural exclusion, pose a sense of anger, a sense of alienation and a feeling of having been left behind. That feeling is felt perhaps by about 15 to 20 per cent of the UK population. So, ***our sense of community and our sense of national well-being is undermined.*** In short, we regarded all these problems for many years as beyond the reach of solution, as the wicked issue of racial and minority problems.

State's Regulatory Role

Against this backdrop, the role of regulation of both public and private sector is being redefined. The public is no longer content because the regulations go no further than providing the insurance of privacy, integrity and honesty. As I said, 12 billion pounds a year are spent in UK on regulation. That is a lot of money. They feel the regulator's job now has become the facilitation of change and improvement. The regulators must now make their contribution to ensure that the working of Government at all levels improves as fast as citizens' expectations, and faster than the emergence of new problems, such as Internet crime or money laundering.

Impact of Globalization, Information and Communication Technology

Without straying too far from my reasons, it is just worth saying that it is obvious to all of us that ***globalization and information and communication technology are adding enormously to the economic***

prosperity. But the social impact has been profound and destabilizing. We are struggling to ensure that the government's responsiveness to change is based on better policy to service delivery, and more efficient use of financial resources, particularly since the British public has lost their appetite for paying ever more taxes.

I am involved, I would say, with three independent regulatory regimes in the UK. So, I want to tell you a little about all the three of them. I do not make any special claim they are relevant to the Indian context, probably not, but they may nevertheless be of interest.

British Civil Service Commission

The first is the Civil Service Commission. I am one of the 14 Civil Service Commissioners. The first Civil Service Commissioner of Indian origin is Baron Prasad, one of our distinguished public servants. The Civil Service Commission was set up by William Gladstone in 1854, when he was the Prime Minister. The job of the Civil Service Commissioner is to regulate the recruitment and employment of the permanent civil service.

Audit Commission

I am also one of the 15 Audit Commissioners. The job of the Audit Commission is to audit and inspect most of the public services delivery by local authorities and urban local bodies, which includes housing, police, probation service, health care bodies and a number of others. There are separate inspectors for education and social services but they work rather closely with the Audit Commission. The cost of the Audit Commission on public service is more than 125 billion pounds.

Banking Codes and Standard Board

The third one is being the Deputy Chairman of the Banking Codes and Standard Board, which regulates the retail banking industry, such as cheque account, savings account, credit cards and so on. I should say these are not my real job. These are the things, which I do in my spare time.

These regulators are very different bodies with different

powers and different ways of working. Their differences are more revealing than their similarities. Now I want to turn to what I have to say.

The British Civil Service Commission was established in 1854, based on the North Cote-Trevelyon Report which wrote about the setting up of the Civil Service Commission. It commences in a language that could only come from England. It says: "The admission into the civil service is indeed eagerly sought after. But it is for the unambitious and the indolent or incapable. It is greatly desired by those unfit to be active physically. Those with indolence of temperament or physically infirm and unfit for physical exertion would look for civil service that may entail normal and honourable livelihood with little labour and no risk." It is not our intention to suggest that all public servents under the employment of Government have such dreams, but we have to apprehend among the seekers a large proportion of them. These motives more or less influence those who opted for this in the choice of the profession. Well, on the other hand, there are probably very few, who have changed this line of life and risen themselves to public eminence.

The suggested response to this strong indictment, which in a sense was the charge of nepotism, was that henceforth, from 1854, the permanent civil service should be recruited on merit, through open and fair competition and that these principles should be regulated by these independent commissioners. The principles of merit, openness and fair entry into the civil service still govern our work more than 150 years later, as the Civil Commissioners know. ***These principles of fair and open competition based on merit foster a wide commitment of permanent civil service to integrity and political impartiality.*** We, as commissioners, as stewards, feel that these values to recruit them are still relevant, and are likely to remain relevant for a long time to come.

The challenge to these principles comes from more modern sources. The challenge is coming under the headline I have already read out. The British civil service stands indicted for failing to deal effectively with some of the most intractable problems in the society, not responding to the rising expectations of the consumers and citizens, and failing to ensure that increase in public spending reach their target, improve service delivery, without being diversified into bureaucracy and other forms of apparently futile activities. I share the view that the bureaucracy is not at all totally free from blame. But, on the contrary, ***efficient administration is essential and bureaucracy can be self-serving and wasteful, a substantial obstacle to speed and efficiency.***

So, how is the civil service to be cured of these errors or these perceived errors? Well, some suggest more political appointments, senior people with explicit party loyalty, who believe in certain things, and they make things happen and make them happen quickly. I believe they are wrong. I regard this argument as trivial and shallow. I see no evidence of political loyalty leading to greater achievement or dynamism. For that matter, I see no convincing evidence that the civil service is dragging its feet to this or that wish of government out of ideological distance.

I am much more persuaded by the argument that the permanent civil service, entirely groomed in the hot house of White Hall, is unlikely to contain the range of skills to develop policies and deliver service outcome, which address the problems that I mentioned. According to the current head of the home civil service, what they are lacking are human resource management, financial management, IT management, project management and communication with 24-hour media.

My own experience as a Civil Service Commissioner involved in senior level recruitment very much tends to support this view about the skill deficit. Indeed, I will add to the list one more missing point. There is the absence of strategic marketing of public service, reflecting the era of the rational, not the era of consumer choice we live in. In terms of regulating civil service, one might argue that the regulatory regime should go beyond the principles and go more deeply into the contours.

The Audit Commission, because of the extensive audit activities that I have already described, finds itself in the opposite end of the spectrum. The Audit Commission collects massive data and use it to provide public assurance that it is honestly spent with the least expenditure to ensure value for money spent. Here at this juncture I would add one more test. Are we getting better worth for the money that is being spent? Whether the most vulnerable citizens are more or less effectively having their needs and aspirations met is being questioned. Despite all the data collection, we tend to get the answer that begins unhelpfully with the classic English equivocation "it all depends".

The challenge for audit based regulatory regime is, therefore, enunciation and communication of clear principles that can be readily understood, not only by public servants but also by ordinary citizens and users of public services and their advocacy. Once these principles are clearly established in the public mind, we should only be able to collect the data to test these principles. Then the inspectors can only be the tellers. When these high levels of framework are being complied with, the question is whether the citizen can conceive of receiving his entitlement and preferably much more.

I come last to the regulation of the financial services. Uniquely, in the European Union, UK has at least partly a voluntary regime for the regulation of retail financial services or some of the retail financial services. The banking and building societies voluntarily join the compliance club. They subscribe to the code of practice compliance, which is managed by independent organizations run by a board of four independent Directors, including myself. This regime combines voluntary compliance with an agreed code of practice that is permanent, largely undeclared thread than the more detailed and prescriptive statutory regulations. The outcome of threat of statutory regulation would be active voluntary regime. Transparent products and services replace the unresponsiveness to consumer pressure. Fair and open competition leads to sponsoring innovation and choice. That is the regime that I regard as a good one. It will create the requirement for the regulators to balance the creation of level playing competitive field with the consumer friendly environment, placing particular emphasis on the obligation of providing towards the worse off and the most vulnerable.

So, what general lessons might one draw from these observations about our regulations in the Twenty-first century? One would be that it is quite easier to regulate competitive markets than it is to regulate public service, where the consumers have little choice about the provider. Therefore, the provider is put to much less pressure to improve the quality or to reduce the prices.

My second inclination would be that regulation is not a substitute for choice and nor can regulation be a guarantor of quality in every circumstance. Competition and other mechanisms are needed to achieve choice of quality. High quality comparative information is critical about the services provided. There has to be a determined campaign of public education on the rights and responsibilities of the citizens, the consumers of services. This has to be vigorously debated in the independent media with vibrant advocacy through NGOs and civil society organizations.

My third conclusion would be that both principles and practice should be regulated. These are the things that obscure top performance measurement. Publication of performance measurement services is essential. Exhortation of principles, which nobody would dispute, is no regulation.

Can I return to my heritage, my own background in the non-government sector, in the non-profit sector? Ironically, given my extensive involvement in government regulation, which I have described, the NGOs and civil society organizations probably experience the least regulation. They are very independent with synergy and freedom, and continue to be regarded as fertile area for innovation and fountainhead of social change. So, ***government and business should learn from civil societies, which started in India. So, I think UK should start learning from India rather than the other way*.** **Thank you very much. (*Loud Cheers*)**

Observation by Dr. P L Sanjeev Reddy

Mr. Gerard Lemos, Mrs. Morna Nance and Mrs. Kamaljeet Singh: I would like to extend a very warm welcome to them. We have just heard one of the very illuminating speeches on comparative public administration systems, in UK and India. Some of the shared perceptions are equally applicable to the Indian context, because we have a sharedhistory with UK, a long association and we have learnt quite a lot from them and we also improved upon those.

I would like to assure them that since Independednce things are changing in India for the better. The permanent civil service is in place here, it is trained now, extremely professionally competent and fully geared to address the issues facing the country, both social, political and economic.

The performance of the civil service in the Indian context, I think, is improving from time to time, from Plan to Plan. So far as the quality of governance is concerned, of course, there is scope and there is a lot of space for improvement. That is where interaction and candid exchange of views, which we have been having for the last two days, is going to contribute to a great extent. I think a lot of interesting interactions are taking place here on the new public management system, which can be developed in the Indian context.

First and foremost is the impact of globalization. A lot of supra national bodies are coming in, whether it is the WTO, World Bank or the IMF, and they are affecting the sovereignty of the state. There is information dissemination, and a lot of protocols, treaties and covenants we are signing. A lot of their goals are affecting the macro economic policy of the various nation states in Asia and Latin America. The aid givers are setting up a lot of conditions, which are basically impinging on the sovereignty of the state.

Secondly, international terrorism is taking place and it is having its impact on the quality of governance. There is cyber crime through Internet. All these things have a global impact. So, it is no longer a national government insulated from the international processes. Therefore, we have to keep in mind the international developments and the various changes that are taking place all over the world.

Thirdly, the development of IT, communication and information technology is affecting our aspirations, response systems, knowledge dissemination and public welfare. Just before you came, there was a presentation on e-governance, how it can bring the citizens and the government together, how the government system can be on line and how there could be the least delay between demand and response and how everything can be made hunky dory.

Then, so far as the rural administration and urban governance is concerned, several State Governments have taken up initiatives, which will enable and equip the State Government authorities, even NGOs and citizens, to get their problems sorted out across the table. On line programmes like Bhoomi, Sauthalyam, e-Sewa, about which some presentations have been made have made problem solving simpler.

Take the introduction of the Citizen's Charter. You were the first to do that. We have adopted the British system. Now in most of the Ministries, Departments and organizations the citizen's charter is in place. This is one of the steps towards making the government responsive and accountable.

If you take the Tenth Plan, there is one chapter where governance through alternative models is being discussed. One is planned and anticipated changes. Then there are ad hoc changes in the institutions. What are the changes in the global economic and political order? What are the unanticipated changes? How the government system can be engineered to take up the responsibility of good governance? Now that Mr. Gerard is here, let me state that increased accent on people's participation is one of the crucial things here. In the new system of government, there is increased participation of the people.

After the adoption of the Seventy-third and Seventy-fourth Amendments to the Constitution, election to the local bodies should take place every five years. You cannot delay or postpone it. There can be no excuses. There is one-third reservation of seats for women and weaker sections. This has made the government system a little more democratic and egalitarian.

Decentralization has already been mentioned. Then the Right to Information Act has been passed in various States. So, the people have the right to know and they can have access to information. There is reform of the revenue administration. They are also taking up mobilization of other resources from the public and other organizations to carry on governmental activities. There is increased role for civil society. There is involvement of the voluntary sector in the task of planning and implementation.

Some of the other steps are: interface with the public, especially at the cutting edge level, developing core competencies in the voluntary sector, promoting symbiosis between voluntary organizations and PRI, monitoring and evaluation of the 11 monitorable projects of the Tenth Plan, internal shift towards increasing the financial contribution of the civil society to the various projects, enforcing the right to information, greater transparencies in policies and procedures, minimizing the discretion so that everything becomes rule-based and transparent.

Every authority must be made accountable. So, the accountability system is coming in place. Then, revamping the system of rewards and punishment, and review of the functioning of the government, weeding out the redundant ones. We were discussing right sizing and down sizing the bureaucracy, increasing professionalism, capacity building and training.

The next reform is towards procedural streamlining. As per the recommendations of various committees, set up for the purpose procedural streamlining is taking place. There is project based and reform linked support, synergy and coordination between different public and parastatal agencies, and rationalization of Centrally sponsored schemes and Central sector schemes. There is the use of zero-based budgeting. Fiscal Responsibility Act has been passed by the Lok Sabha. Regarding the empowerment of the marginalized and excluded, which is very dear to our heart, we are now considering how the marginalized sections, women, the disabled, the weaker sections, harijans and girijans, how they can be brought into the picture. The judicial reforms are also taking place.

There is use of information technology for good governance. These are steps already taken by the Government. E-Government is coming in a big way. Standardization of e government activities is taking place. Resources from both the public and private sector are brought within the ambit of e-governance.

The path ahead appears to be very rosy. Good governance is perhaps the single most important factor in ensuring that the objectives of the Tenth Plan are achieved. Steps will have to be taken to address the issues relating to improved people's participation. Effective decentralization of government, involvement of civil society, especially voluntary organizations, the crucial right to information, these are some of the steps. E-government and IT have already been mentioned. These are the things that are likely to give a big push to increased transparency and fair play and make the systems user friendly.

Yet another aspect we are discussing is the United Nations Millennium Goals, so that the governance systems in most of the member countries are being directed towards achieving those goals. Some of the objectives of the Millennium Goals are freedom from hunger, literacy, health, housing amenities, law and order and various monitorable targets. We are giving a new thrust and new orientation to the governmental activities in that direction.

So, what is to be done? Some of the steps are training, capacity building, institution building, attitudinal change, establishment of best practices, and development calendar, making it available to our people so that it can be replicated and up-scaled and tried out through appropriate training programmes. I am sure these steps will make good government a reality, though it looks distant now. There is constant scope for improvement. It is not as if good governance is the finishing line. It has to go on improving, go on evolving.

You have referred to corporate governance, including Board of Directors, and responsibility statement. The Government of India and the Company Law Board have already taken various initiatives. I was myself permanent Secretary dealing with Company Affairs, dealing with 5-1/2 lakh companies in the whole country. We brought in lot of changes for protection of rights of minority shareholders. Representation for women has been considered as compulsory. There would be specific audit committee recommendations. All financial transactions would be subject to scrutiny by an independent board. The AGM is very powerful. The management must make everything clear to all the shareholders so that they can debate and discuss all the issues concerning the company.

The shareholders living in remote areas have been given the opportunity to exercise their vote through postal ballot. I do not know how many countries have adopted this practice. India is one of the few countries that has adopted postal ballot. A person living in Assam cannot attend the Board Meeting in Delhi or Bombay but can send his vote through postal ballot. He can even send through e-mail or through a computer kiosk his preference on any investment or policy decision, which the AGM is supposed to discuss.

Corporate democracy, better corporate governance, and better government system, are building blocks towards real democracy, the essence of which is that there must be healthy interface between the government and the citizens. This interaction must be fulfilling and comfortable and as good as possible.

These are some of the comments that I would like to make. Now the floor is open. We have been greatly benefited by the inputs, which our Guest has given us. It has been a very great privilege for us to be having him with us. I was extremely delighted to listen to the speech of Mr. Gerard Lemos, Vice-Chair of the British Council, who has addressed us. All of us are lucky to have him with us. In fact, it is the icing of the cake, because we were already having a wide discussion since yesterday. You have really taken it to the pinnacle of fulfilling the object of the session. You were Audit Commissioner, Civil Service Commissioner, Government Adviser on Racism, Adviser in several government departments, including the Treasury and Cabinet Office. You have referred to social exclusion and the practical aspects of governance. So, it is our good luck to have you here and listen to your address.

We have many social researchers here in this Conference. You can ask him whatever question you would like to ask on social policy, racial equality or what both countries can jointly do. We have a common history. The civil service system, and its instruments, parliamentary democracy and institutions - all these got a common history, a common background. So, let us exchange our views and try to get the best out of it. The floor is now open.

We have got here a Legal Counsel, Ms. Mahajan. She is a widely travelled person. She can tell us about the legal system obtaining in the country. She has come specially to listen to you. She is a busy lawyer in the Supreme Court.

MS. MAHAJAN: I am honoured to have this opportunity to speak on the topic. I will just say a few words to explain the present legal system that is prevailing and what is really the reason for the great delay in delivering justice and the great backlog of cases pending in the various courts, right from the district level to the High Court and the Supreme Court. We are just trying to find that out.

To my mind, the main reason for this is that there is too much of patronage. If it is not really corruption in the monetary sense, then it is procedure. Everybody thinks, including the common man, that he can get away with anything by delaying things. So, one lawyer is brought in to apply brake and to delay the thing. The other lawyer tries to hurry up. The courts are caught between the two. So, they say, all right, we adjourn the matter. That is the main reason. Because people are not really serious about settling cases when they go to court in most cases. In my experience of almost 35 years at the bar, I have found that in most cases people do not go for justice and very few people expect justice from the court. In most cases, by pressurizing the opposite party, they want to arrive at some kind of settlement which is in their interest.

For instance, if a businessman owes government Rs.10 lakh and if he can hold up payment for another 10 to 15 years, the interest the court would award would not exceed 9 or 10 per cent, whereas he is going to make 20 to 25 per cent profit from that amount, which he is holding up. So, it is in his interest. Nobody really cares. When I say "nobody", I say generally nobody really bothers how much loss is being caused to the country and to the people. Do they think whose money is being used like this?

No matter what the Supreme Court says, no matter the number

of judges, which are added to the Supreme Court or the High Court, or even at the district level, unless there is an earnest endeavour to deliver justice, the position will not improve. It is not only a question of the quality of the judges, but also of the bar, the people who are manning the judicial system that has to be improved.

At a Seminar some time back, we discussed this question how things are going to be improved, if the quality of the members of the bar does not improve. I have a very recent experience of somebody coming to me from UP, holding a law degree. He does not know even the ABC of law. I do not know from where he got this degree and how he got enrolled with the Bar Council. This is one major problem we are facing in the judicial system.

Of course, we are following the Anglo Saxon system of jurisprudence, the same as the British. We have inherited the British sense of giving opportunity to the person to be heard. All these principles we have adopted. But, in actual practice, we are overwhelmed by our own weaknesses, the weaknesses which have crept into the system through 200 years of slavish mentality, which says, "I know somebody; so, I will get it done; do not worry". This is the attitude that generally prevails.

Yesterday I got a call. My client says, the opposite party is going to give money to the judge; so, I am going to lose. Therefore, the major problem we have to solve is corruption, no doubt. Otherwise also, the procedures are getting very cumbersome.

I would say that we have to think of some very far-reaching changes in our judicial system and adopt some of the better avenues that other countries have adopted. There is the procedure of settling the issues in the chamber and coming with only one or two issues before the court. This is one thing that we have been trying to persuade the Government to accept by amending the law. It cuts out or shuts out all the miscellaneous hearings, which take so much time and end all adjournments after adjournments.

I think we do appreciate the jurisprudence that we have inherited and its principles. Even now we look at those very wise judgments given by the British Courts. I am a great admirer of Lord Denning, though many people may not agree with me. I admire his simple and short judgments, very clear cut and insightful. I wish our judges also adopted that kind of a system.

I tried to express the problems, which we are facing, I am facing as a lawyer. I suppose it is for us to find a way out. I would say that we have to adopt very drastic changes in the system, in the civil and criminal administration, in the judicial administration. Most important of all, we have to clear all the muck—sorry for that word, which is a very harsh word. I hope I have not been too harsh in my opinion anyway. Thank you very much.

DR. P.L. SANJEEV REDDY: We will take a couple of questions collectively and then the Chief Guest will respond. Prof. Renuka Garg has done quite a lot of work on public private partnership in a place called Surat, which was one of the dirtiest cities, plague affected city. It is one of the centers of cut diamonds and major exporter of zari silk and various other products. Now it has been converted into one of the cleanest cities largely because of private public partnership. Prof. Garg may briefly explain it and then seek some advice from the UK model. You can briefly explain the position, what has happened here and then ask questions.

PROF. RENUKA GARG: Good afternoon everyone. Yesterday I tried to bring forward the Surat model for overcoming the various difficulties being faced by the city in the wake or the aftermath of the plague. If you look into it closely, there is partnership from three quarters in the whole operation. One is definitely the Surat Municipal Corporation. The second is private sector and the third is the people, NGOs played a leading role initially. Later on, it was more of private initiative. When we talk here of these four parties, now only three, we find that they have gone in for utilizing a major share of the management practices and management partnerships, which they tried to bring in.

One was with regard to the planning part of it. When we talk of the overall planning, we have to be very much conscious of the threshold expectations of the public. At this time we found that the threshold limit happened to be cleanliness. So, cleanliness was the first thing that we did. The second was building the infrastructure. These were the two areas, which required instant action, and this is what the Municipal Commissioner tried to solve.

One major problem that we face in the Indian conditions is the issue of corruption, the nexus between the executive, the political parties and the private parties. We tried to break it. The Municipal Commissioner took a very strong stand and, as he put it, the big heads have to roll. That created a kind of demonstration effect. There was a demolition drive going on. There was no major opposition and in some cases it was voluntarily being done. There was no barrier from the public side. In fact, the public was fed up with these things. So, when the Municipal Commissioner took strict steps, nobody came forward to appeal. In fact, the people were opposed to the then political set up and the role being played by the private sector.

The second instrument, which we used in bringing about change, was the use of the penalizing power, the legal part of it. The Commissioner used his official power, the legal power, on the economic field. I asked him, why not on social marketing? He said, punishment on the social marketing will not have any effect here; the first part will have to be the legal part. One is recovery of user charges. The second economic aspect is technology and the third is infrastructure building. These were the three major strategies, which were initially initiated by Shri Rao.

He said that social marketing was not going to work. We have spent a lot of money into it. The awareness has already been created. We want a clean city. Everybody wants it. There are more than 30,000 units near and around Surat. One is art silk industry. It is exporting Rs. 3,000 crore worth of diamonds. It is very much industrially developed. Plague affected the exports. So, the business people and traders were very keen that this image of the city should change and it should become a clean city. Wherever we found the people were making the city dirty, there was on the spot penalization, which gained support from the business people. In fact, the business people sponsored the drive for cleaning the city. Earlier, the city was marked by certain neat islands surrounded by dirty slums. Now the whole city has become beautiful and the private sector has helped us in this effort.

Coming to NGOs, Gujarat has been a model in terms of micro financing. You must have heard of SEWA. When we talk of micro financing, women entrepreneurs play a leading role. It is very much evident in Gujarat. The street vendors are more of women and they are doing extremely well. They are very much conscious of their rights. If you visit the city at any time, may be even at night, women are freely moving around. This is the environment that we have created in Surat. I am sorry to say that it is a sort of environment, which is very different from what is obtaining in the northern part. Here I am not very sure whether women can travel at night and whether it is safe for them. In Gujarat it is very much different.

This is all due to people's initiative with sufficient good governance from the Municipal Corporation, with the private sector chipping in. The NGOs were doing their part. So, all these four quarters have contributed in making this a clean city. It remains a clean city and a green city.

DR. INDERJEET KAUR: Thank you for giving me this opportunity to ask a question. In his thought provoking speech, Mr. Lemos, was talking about the impartiality and integrity of the bureaucrats and he was feeling that it is in tact and it will remain in tact. But we have been watching serials like "Yes Minister" and we have been reading textbooks that are being published nowadays after Mrs. Thatcher's period, which show there was deviation from this impartiality and integrity. How would you react to it? Please give us your firsthand experience.

Secondly, I would like to seek some information on the public grievance redressal system, which is working in India. You are calling it complaint-handling system in UK. I explored the Internet, but I was not getting the public grievance redressal system as such or the complaints handling system, the term you are using. How is it being managed in UK?

Thirdly, before you came here, we were talking about e governance and Prof. Sachdeva was talking about pseudo democracy for the way democracy is working these days. What is the nature of the democratic system in England?

DR. AASHA GUPTA: Thank you for the very illuminating lecture. My question is of a general nature. Could some sort of incentive work where regulation is not working?

MR. GERARD LEMOS: It is certainly a big question and a very strong question, but I would answer it. On the question of the justice system, as you probably know, we are going to review it in the United Kingdom. In the process, the place of the Lord Chancellor is being abolished. It is causing consternation, particularly in some quarters, where there is a feeling that it is time that we split Parliament from the judiciary in a cleaner way, keep them separate and have separation of powers, clear separation of powers. You have a Supreme Court, which we do not have. You may think it is a simple principle to enunciate and simple procedure to enact. In fact, it is proving extremely messy, the disentanglement of the constitutional arrangement. Like all constitutional arrangements in UK, it is going by the cliché in terms of its mark, as you have heard today. I think it is proving very difficult.

I think there are some very legitimate concerns being expressed by the judiciary, or some members of the judiciary, some very senior members, like the Chief Justice, for example, about whether the judicial independence would be compromised by not having any say to choose a judge as a member of the government. This is an ironical way to look at it, theoretically at least.

I think there is concern already, particularly about the appointment arrangement to the judiciary. It is very well known that it is proposed that instead of the British Chancellor there should be one judicial Appointments Committee, on very similar lines or on parallel lines to the British Civil Service Commission, so that you would have independent people who will run the system based on merits. There is the interesting and complex notion, which presents some challenges like writing the CV. It would be self-defeating. Let me not be frivolous about it.

So, there is the question of how you appoint judges and how you guard their independence, how you have real separation of powers. As I said, it is proving more complex and challenging than we first imagined. Overlaid are the great norms of judicial review, which many Cabinet Ministers at least in private mirror as more than adequate. So, there is a real problem—I would not go to the extent of calling it a struggle for power; that would be an exaggeration but there is real tension between Parliament on the one hand on judicial independence, or the right of the judiciary in courts to comment on laws, which in the judicial review cases, may not have been properly framed or probably incapable of conveying that intention. The executive, on the other hand, has the feeling that this is showing us down, get in the way of making things happen. Let me give one or two examples. One is the disposal of the Shalimar case. As you know, in UK there is tension on what is described as the slowness of the process, which is a highly controversial subject for those who live in UK. Here I would say that the British Council consists of lawyers while I am not a lawyer. So, the comments I make are as it were above my pay grade. But I would say this that we are undergoing a very complex process to change ourselves in that regard. One can still remember the jurist system went out of teaching first. The Lord Chancellor is the lone Speaker of the House of Lords. As you have the Supreme

Court, we have the highest court still interfaced with the House of Lords definitely. I think for judicial appointments it is not a very big enough base.

I was completely fascinated by the point made about how the public private partnership worked in Surat. While in some areas we have badly failed, in some fields we have succeeded. Financial exclusion is a serious problem in UK in a way, which is not the case in many middle income and developing countries. Women entrepreneurs is an area where you may feel you have a lot to do on that. The key that we have learnt is the public private partnership, very similar to the ones that you were describing. We would certainly learn about the importance of civil society, NGOs and so on, that being the kind of transition through proper representation and participation, if you like, to come and join.

If I may be slightly pragmatic about it, it is clear that the presence of the diamond industry created, (to go back to the point that was made about incentive) enormous incentive to solve the problem. Indeed, it produced enormous revenue flow. If we look at the history of private public partnership, and in UK also, it is very much the same case, if there is revenue flow to support the partnership, it will work. If there is no revenue flow, it would not work. For example, it would be much easier to get private public partnership work in areas such as transport, where there are clear revenue streams to be touched, but much harder in areas such as public health and education, which are universal services, which are largely free. So, certainly these are some of the lessons.

You have raised some challenging questions on impartiality and integrity. I think the key concern about the impartiality and integrity of the civil service crystallizes on the question of what is the role of the Minister's Special Advisers. Do the Minister's Special Advisers have the right to give orders to civil servants? Are the civil servants obliged to follow the instructions of political appointees?

Although this issues is a theoretical one, of course, it has crystallized into a major national controversy over the question of so-called ... Dossier in the case of Weapons of Mass Destruction in Iraq, which led to enquiries and it has produced its results. One way of interpreting all that is where the civil servant influences too much on political appointment and lends political consideration? You are right there that we are feeling challenged on that subject.

I have to say that my own view would be that it is a good story for the press all right. There are 72 political Special Advisers and 650,000 civil servants. So, you have got a sense of where the balance lies. I think a vast majority of the civil servants continue without undue political influence. But you would be surprised that the political influence, which was the most challenging, if you like, was the high public concern. What can be a higher public concern than whether or not to go to war? So, I would not say it is a crisis of integrity. But there are concerns.

I think it is also bi-partisan political point of view. I do not think Mrs. Thatcher's Government was worse or better. I think all political parties regard civil servants to a great or less extent as a constituent in the slow or hopeless task of bringing in the political point of view. I think it is a bi-partisan point.

On the question of public grievances system, I think quite a lot of ideas came from Scandinavia about the Ombudsman. I think it had a lot of impact, particularly in relation to the private sector, but also in the public sector. To me this is one of the interesting discourses that I have been listening to and I have learnt it only from India.

The Government has decided to introduce the Equality and Human Rights Commission. At the moment, we have the Equality Commission, but no Human Rights Commission, except in Northern Ireland. One of the discussions has been whether we are going to have Human Rights Ombudsman, Non-Discrimination Policy Ombudsman or Women's Policy Ombudsman. I think we have generalized it too much, the way we are going on dealing with complaints. Certainly, their decisions are not exactly precedents, but they influence the regulatory framework, even if they do not look into the legal consequences. I think it is going on now.

On the question of incentives, I am not quite sure what you have in mind. You can tell me what you have in mind.

DR. AASHA GUPTA: In a country like India, where directly and indirectly so much reference has been made to corruption, regulation is not really yielding the desired results. I was wondering, instead of regulations, if we start thinking of incentives, may be monetary, may be in terms of prestige, may be in terms of facilities, that might work.

MR. GERARD LEMOS: If you are thinking of incentives, I think we have a very complex historical system of incentives in UK. It is not financial by any means, but there are all kinds of other incentives. One of the dangers is that the incentives may create unintended consequences. I may be rather old-fashioned, but nevertheless I feel that you can inadvertently create perverse incentives. Take one Chinese example. The Government passed a law saying that women who have been abandoned can declare the identity of the father of their children so that he can be called upon to support them legally and financially. The only exemption to this rule was where women experience massive violence, where they did not have to declare the identity of their partner. You would be surprised to hear that massive violence against women increased four-fold. It is clearly a perverse incentive. Obviously, the measure did not undergo minute scrutiny before it was introduced. It created a perverse incentive.

Let me give another example. A lot of manufacturing industries closed down in Koman, Stewart and so on in 1980s. A number of people, a hell of a lot of people were rendered unemployed. Millions of people became unemployed. They started claiming disability benefit and their number started increasing enormously. It led to corruption. So, you could perhaps argue that it is a form of perverse incentive in a way, which make things happen. But it does not make any difference to the people at large.

Allow me to introduce my final observation. Before any step is taken, the State has to consider not only the beneficial consequences but also the unintended consequences.

DIRECTOR (Dr. P.L. Sanjeev Reddy): We have a few researchers, who have prepared their papers and they want to present them. Would it be all right if we give opportunity to some of them to present their papers before lunch? There are four speakers, who are scheduled to present their papers. We can continue that till 1.30 p.m. when we break for lunch.

PROF. NOORJAHAN BAVA: I want to take this opportunity first to propose a Vote of Thanks to Mr. Gerard Lemos for his scintillating talk. He has given a lot of insight on the practice of public administration. Theory is one thing but practice is yet another. With his rich experience as Commissioner of Public Service Commission of UK on the one hand and as a Member of the Audit Commission on the other, and as a very active social worker dealing with racial problems, he has given us a lot of food for thought. Thanks to his talk, we are really benefited and enriched.

I once again thank Mr. Gerard Lemos, Vice-Chair, British Council, Ms. Kamal Singh and Ms. Nancy for having taken time off and come over here so that Mr. Lemos could share his thoughts with us. Now I would invite all of you to join us for lunch at 1.30 p.m.

BUSINESS SESSION-IV

(13 December 2003 FN)

New Paradigms in Public Administration

PROF. NOORJAHAN BAVA: We have still 40 minutes left for lunch. We will straightaway proceed to the paper presentation. I would request Prof. Ramesh K. Arora to chair this Session. He is a distinguished former Professor of Public Administration from Rajasthan University. He has done monumental work in public administration. There is no student of public administration, who does not know Prof. Ramesh K. Arora. He has endeared himself not only to the student community in his own university, but also to the students of other universities through his books. He has authored large number of books on public administration. I remember at least one of them, which I used to understand what is comparative public administration 20 years ago. We know that it is the outcome of behavioural movement, but he was the first public administrationist to have authored a book on comparative public administration in India. Prof. Arora tells me that it used to be a Bible for comparative public administration in many universities and it continues to be so even today. That is the kind of work that he has authored.

Prof. R.K. Arora is a Visiting Fellow at the HCM Institute of Administration in Rajasthan, which is the state equivalent to the IIPA at the Centre. Another aspect of his profile is that he is the Chairman of the Management Development Academy. He is propagating in a big way the management approach posed in public administration, with which all of us do not agree anyhow. He is the Editor of *Administrative Change*, which has been very a useful journal to the student community and for researchers who want to publish their research papers.

He is also the Secretary of the Rajasthan Regional Branch of IIPA. The main purpose behind my invitation to him is that we have decided as a principle at the Executive Council of the IIPA to involve the Regional branches in the celebration of the Golden Jubilee of the IIPA. So, he represents the Regional Branch of Rajasthan on this occasion, besides being the Chairperson of this session, which he has earned in his own right as an eminent Professor of Public Administration in this country.

He has undergone a lot of problems in reaching Delhi by road this morning because there was a lot of fog. He was to have chaired the previous session. He rang me up and informed me that he is coming but he may be a little late. Now that he is in our midst, let us give him a big hand. (*Loud Cheers*)

He has a paper to present, besides chairing the session. So, if he has some thoughts to share, he can do it first and then request other speakers to present their papers. He has the discretion to do whatever he deems fit, because he is the Chairman. We have to break for lunch at 1.30 p.m. I now request him to chair the session.

Remarks of Prof. Ramesh K. Arora, Chairman IV Business Session

I am very happy to be here. Now we will have a very brief session of about 38 minutes. I would like to close the session at 1.30 pm. because lunch cannot wait. So, I would request the speakers and participants to conform to the time. First of all, I would request Prof. Noorjahan Bava to present her paper on "Post Modernism and Public Administration".

PROF. NOORJAHAN BAVA: How much time do I have?

MR. CHAIRMAN: 15 minutes.

PROF. NOORJAHAN BAVA: The Main theme of my paper is Post-modernism and Public Administration.

This Business Session is on "New Paradigms in Public Administration". Since the 1950s, a large number of paradigms have emerged in the discipline of public administration and more and more are still emerging. I am only going to talk about just one paradigm—Post Modernism which I felt is important, and not very well-known. It is a very new theme.

In the United Kingdom, United States and many other western capitalist industrialized economies people believe that whatever is happening in their system, be it polity, society or economy, is applicable to the rest of the world. But we in India, and other developing countries, cannot just blindly adopt any model, any paradigm per se. So, the purpose of this session is to have insight into the new paradigms, and ask a basic question, what are the new paradigms, be it post modernistic or new management, and are they relevant to the developing countries whose population constitute three-fourth of this world? Can we be on par with the developed capitalist industrialized societies and talk on equal terms and in the same manner on who benefits out of it? These are theoretical issues, which we, as theoreticians, students, scholars or teachers of public administration have to raise, as to the relevance of these models. This is my brief introduction about the new paradigms in general.

Coming to my own paper, it is already circulated and so I would not take much time. I will just focus on a few important points in my presentation. In the first place, in the 1990s, a new paradigm entered the intellectual field of public administration. What is the paradigm shift I am talking of? It is the paradigm shift from modernism to post-modernism. So, I am talking of post-modernistic public administration. Before going into that, what is post-modernism? There seem to be all kinds of thoughts, notions and ideas about it. I was trying to read, understand and figure out what it is.

According to my understanding, post-modernism is a paradigm or model. It is a theory, it is a method and it is a movement. It is a social theory and method, an intellectual model. It originated as a social theory long ago and today it has entered almost all social sciences. I have given a graphic picture of post-modernism in my paper. I have called it as POMO for the sake of brevity. It is now the in thing, not only in political science and public administration, but also in all other social sciences, as shown in the chart of my paper.

As theory and method, post-modernism debunked all the established analytical categories of thought, modern thought, in all the social sciences, including our own subject. Ideas and concepts like bureaucratic institutions and politics—administration dichotomy, or the scientific management, or the Weberian command and control model of bureaucracy, all these are under fire, devastating fire, and the call is that you give up all these "reified" institutions. They have become deified institutions. They do not have any purpose to serve today in the late 20th or the 21st century. We have to go in search of new concepts, because these concepts have changed, and they create unreality, not reality.

Similarly, in the intellectual field, post-modernism attacks all the modernistic theory of social sciences including law, all the theories and thoughts that exist in various disciplines, including science, hard sciences and the scientific method. So, scientism, monism, universalism, essentialism, foundationalism, structural functionalism and many more may turn erratic in the post-modern language. Meta-narratives, including capitalism, technicism, Marxism, all these have to be thrown out; they are attacked, they are challenged. (I am not going to give you all the arguments of that challenge). Do not accept all these things, you think of the shift to new theoretical framework for our analysis.' That is the clarion call of POMO, in short. POMO as a movement, as I said, has spread very wide. It has spread its tentacles through all social sciences and even literature.

What are the post-modern conditions? Can we picture the post-modern conditions? Yes. I will just give you 6 or 7 characteristics of post-modern societies. The post-modern society is characterized by the hyper reality of **epiphenomenalism**. It means that the areas of symbols, areas of signs do not have any meaning; they have lost their reality. They lead to virtual unreality. They have no stable or lasting meaning. This is the phenomenon of epiphenomenalism.

This leads to another characteristic called **self-referentiality,** which means the words refer to themselves. They have no meaning; they have lost their meaning. So, we are made to live in a make-belief world, not a real world. What is recurring social reality is not social reality, but it is what is called **hyper reality**. We are living in a world of post-modern society. We are having what is called hyper reality, that is, there is a gap between words and deeds.

All this leads to what is called **symbolic politics**. The politics that is played in post-modern society is not the politics that ought to take place, ought to play the game of politics that came down from Aristotle and others. That has no relevance. We have today in the post-modern set up or context, the post-modern politics, which is called symbolic politics.

In such a situation, what happens is a sequence of images bombardment on public consciousness, where we are introduced to simulation, what is called media spectacle. The public debate is lost with the result we find that our politicians take advantage of it. They indulge in malfeasance, mal-administration, corruption and failure in their public duties. The people are taken for granted, their rights and liberties, everything at stake are lost.

So, public politics is no good in the post-modern conditions. Even representative democracy is under attack by the post-modern scholars. In the United States, which is a citadel of Presidential form of democracy, as we all now, it is a form of representative democracy which in POMO perspective is neither "democratic" nor "representative." That is the conclusion drawn by post-modernistic scholars. What should we do? It is the citizens who are the losers. The politicians are gaining their selfish interests and the bureaucracy becomes the instrumental rationality in the hands of the politicians to self-serve their interests, or in collusion with the politicians to taint the system. That is what is happening.

Another characteristic of the post-modern society is that the society has become **consumerist**. The importance is on buying goods and services. Your development lies in increasing your consumption, going to the market, buying things, it is a pleasure to buy goods and services. Your progress and development is measured in terms of how many TV sets, cameras, this and that you have. So, production is put to the back burner and consumption is gaining the upper hand. There is consumerism plus symbolic politics together, they are aided by the modern media, with the bombardment of TV advertisements, which they think are the best, on line shopping, everything. We have become part of it and today it is all happening.

Under these circumstances, another thing has also happened. In the intellectual world or literary world, post-modernists have destroyed, or they want to attack and destroy all the **meta-narratives**, which emerged during the modern period, starting from democracy, socialism, Marxism, structuralism, the systems theory in political science, anthropology, sociology, economics etc.

So, where are we? What are we doing? I am thoroughly confused on how to proceed ahead. I have been teaching my students for more than three decades within the framework of these theories. One is certainly the democratic theory. Now post-modernism tells us, abandon all that, as far as public administration is concerned. Take our modern democracy. It is the British democracy of the Westminster model that India has adopted. We are running the government for the last 50 years under this model. Now the post-modernists say it is no good. So, what should we do?

Post-modernists say there is the "accountability loop model" in representative democracy. In this type of democracy, the citizens just cast their votes; the individual choices or preferences are aggregated into the political will during the electoral process. Once the verdict is clear within the electoral manifesto, they are translated into laws. Our law-makers give legal sanction to these policies.

The bureaucracy implements these policies. The modern rules are imposed on the bureaucracy and the bureaucracy is accountable to politicians, the politicians are accountable to the people. This is the loop model. In this, the citizen's voice is minimized, the voice of the voiceless is nil, the weaker sections is nil. The prominent/powerful sections of the society are the gainers. So, this is where their interest lies, with the weaker sections like women, the down trodden and the disabled having no voice. The distributive society has to play an important role in the formulation, implementation and evaluation of public policy. That is the post-modernist model of public policy and administration.

Now coming to the **theoretical underpinnings of post-modernism,** as academics, you cannot just accept any theory or every theory without supporting evidence. Are there any theoretical foundations behind post-modernism? Yes, not one but a number of them. All these theories are mind-boggling. I have spent quite a bit of time, trying to learn and understand them and then put down those thoughts in the paper.

POMO is rejection of **orthodoxy**. By orthodoxy what Waldo, one of the great intellectuals in the field of public administration, meant was the classical administrative thought in Wilson's politics and administration dichotomy, Taylor's scientific management, Max Weber's hierarchical control and command and control model of bureaucracy. These are regarded as orthodoxy and orthodoxy has been the paradigm of development in the study of public administration, even in practice from the day Wilson published his 'Study of Administration' in 1887, till 1950, when Behaviouralism came into the field. Still, orthodoxy continues to hover over the intellectual field, and also in the practice of public administration. There is no country in the world without a bureaucratic arrangement. So, it is still there, as part and parcel of the post-modernist society as well.

But the post-modernists say, you throw it out, we will have a new—not a new institution but a new idea. The new idea is **'public energy field'**. The concept of public energy field is complex and it will replace the concepts of bureaucracy, scientific management and constitutionalism. It is a better paradigm, it will work better for the satisfaction of the people. After all, the people are sovereign and the government has to serve them. Yesterday the UGC Chairman talked about the need for the 'government of peace'. So, it will work towards the government of peace in specified areas.

Secondly, post-modernism is grounded and rooted in three other theories. The first is **Phenomenology**, which you must have heard of. The second is **Social Constructivism**. The third is what is called the philosophy of **Structuration theory**. So, if you want to know anything about post-modernism, you must first go to the theory of phenomenology, existentialism, post-structuralism, communitarianism as well as constitutionalism. Constitutionalism and communitarianism are under attack. But these three other theories—phenomenology, social construction theory and structuration theory, constitute the base for post-modernism.

Now what is phenomenology? I have explained it in my paper. I am not going to explain it here. There are certain key concepts with which these three theories are interwoven. I have put them in a Glossary so that we can easily understand them. (This has been given in the second half of my paper). Phenomenology talks of **subjectivity, the body subject**. It talks of other rationality.

Similarly, you have under constructivitism the concept that all social realities are created by human beings and social reality is constructed in a social manner through interaction, action interaction flow, by human beings. But what has happened in modernism is that all human creations have been given immutability, reification that means they cannot be changed. They are immune to change; they (modernists) are opposed to the process of change, though they were created by human beings once upon a time. Why were they elevated to the status of god when they are used in our discussion, policy making etc?

The social construction theory opens up avenues for dialogue. So, post-modernism stands for dialogue or discursive matter. It is all about discursive theory, debate, discussion and dialogue.

Conversation must take place in as many groups as possible, not only amongst administrators but also amongst citizen groups. The citizens have to govern themselves.

So, post-modernists really believe and start conceptualizing and practicing these concepts. If we start to operationalize these concepts, we hope to land in the land of what is called paradigm of **participatory democracy**. In a participatory democracy the citizen is there everywhere. He will not allow corruption to take place—we will not allow anybody in the bunch of officials sitting in the government institutions to reap the profit for themselves, the advantages for themselves, forgetting public interest for which they were appointed and recruited by the Public Service Commission. We in India have the Union Public Service Commission and State Public Service Commission in each State. Therefore, we have to substitute modern concepts and theories of representative democracy by the public energy field.

In their book ***Post Modernism and Public Administration*** Hough and Miller are proposing a new model in the place of bureaucracy. They have used post-modernist concepts and theories to attack bureaucracy and orthodoxy. So, post-modernists do not want to have anything to do with bureaucracy. They start with the as public energy field.

I have deliberately not made a critique of the post-modern theory. I am not accepting all that they say is true and correct. Finally, even post-modernism is subject to criticism. We just cannot take it for granted. But that criticism, I will leave it to you to consider in the spirit of post-modernism, because everyone has the right to critique and find a way out.

MR. CHAIRMAN: Thank you very much for giving a very lucid presentation on a complex subject. You have taken 25 minutes. Believing that this watch is fast by 5 minutes, we have 15 minutes. All the three papers of this session will be indeed taken up in the next session, says Prof. Noorjahan Bava. So, what I am planning to do is that I will just present my paper in 10 minutes and leave some time for discussion, because both these issues are related. I am not going to take even 10 minutes, may be less.

My humble submission is regarding new public management that Prof. Noorjahan Bava talked about. We do believe in management as the major focus of public administration theory. L D White in the First Textbook on Public Administration in 1926 said that public administration has better grounding in management than in law.

In fact, the whole movement of public administration started, not with Woodrow Wilson, his article was totally forgotten after 1887. It was basically because of the movement in the United States of America in the beginning of this (20th) century, namely the scientific management movement became the credo of administrative systems. When President Taft appointed the Taft Committee, the basic agenda was how to employ and apply the principles of scientific management to government systems. Even we learnt and talked about scientific management in the Soviet Public Enterprises. I think in 1976 the Department of Personnel of the Government of India brought out the management in government. So, let us not try to quarrel with management. It is a sister discipline.

Look at their generosity. The most popular degree course of management is MBA. This is known as Masters in Business Administration, not Masters in Business Management. They have borrowed the word "Administration" from us and used it forever. They have not quarreled with the word "Management" and said "we want to be MBM, Master in Business Management". They have not said so. So, let us be more liberal and not have the capitalistic attitude towards management.

There are two aspects of public administration—external environment and internal environment. Law, politics, sociology and anthropology of course guide the external environment and the internal has to be guided by management. There is no harm, because public administration is not a discipline; it is multi-disciplinary, it is inter-disciplinary. It has the capacity to absorb, adopt and imbibe all these qualities in these disciplines and that is what makes it a vibrant discipline.

The 1970s saw a great debate on New Public Administration (NPA). After the Minnowbrook Conference in 1968, we had new public administration. What was new public administration? It was a younger discipline and so they used the word "new" public administration. There is no new sociology, no new political science, no new economics, no new anthropology, but only new public administration. Now it is New Public Management (NPM). Is "new" qualitative adjective or temporal adjective? I think it is a temporal adjective. Chronologically we have a movement.

What I want to emphasize is that the new public administration was a value-based movement, focussing on responsive citizen orientation, equity and justice. This was basically a value-laden approach. The crux of administrative activity and the process was not highlighted in the new public administration. But the impact of NPM had led to a new policy, **a public policy approach.**

When Dwight Waldo became the Editor of ***Public Administration Review*** of USA for about five years, all the issues were focussed on US public policy. The new public administration laid emphasis on the problems that are faced by the people. So, all the problems that the people in the United States were facing, were highlighted in the ***Public Administration Review.***

Then came the **policy science approach**, along with public policy approach. The **post-modernism, reinventing the government** movement of 1992, is the basis of the new public management. Although the word "new public management" was being used in USA and Britain at the end of 1970s and the beginning of 1980s, it got a big fillip in the intellectual field after the reinvention of government movement. So, remember, the codified title of the book Reinventing Government. It is about how the management of American companies, American systems are changing. It means that the change of government is already there. It is then codified and mentioned in detail and elaborated by others in 1992.

In 1992 the good governance movement started. The World Bank Report on Good Governance came in 1993. So, these nine years have been very crucial for the development of ideas and issues in public administration. The new public management, it is considered to be the paradigm today. It has all the features of public administration, as far as we are concerned, re-inventing government, public policy approach, but not post-modernism.

Post-modernism is primarily a negative approach in the sense it rejects a lot and accepts very little. We are still not post-modern in India. My basic assumption or submission is that most of these theories are developed in US, UK and Western nations for flavour of their own ambience, ecology and their own environment. They are not applicable to India in totality. Parts of that are relevant. For example, parts of the new public management are relevant in India, not the whole of it. This is going to be my thesis for the next 5 minutes or so.

My submission is that public administration in these countries is only equal partner with private sector, NGOs and civil societies. In India it is the dominant partner. So, most of the assumptions concerning public management that are very much inherent in this movement of new public management are not relevant to India, because here the dominant guiding spirit in national development and nation building is government.

So, here the government role cannot be marginalized in any way. It can be done in a small country like Denmark, Sweden or Switzerland or New Zealand, but not in India, not in China. So, the regulatory role of the government is not going to diminish in India. As long as there are inequalities in this country, the social welfare role is not going to diminish in this country. Therefore, only a very small portion of the government, which is the commercial role of the government, that is being affected by new public management. They apply to public sector undertakings. Yes, make administration more efficient, make it more responsive, and make it more citizen-oriented. We agree with all the basic premises of new public management, which are relevant to the Indian situation, but most of them are really not reflecting the Indian milieu and Indian traditions.

There are so many discontinuities in the United States and Great Britain. We are not in times of turbulence at all. When Dwight wrote that book Public Administration at the Time of Turbulence in 1971, it was the time of turbulence for USA, not for India. India is a perfectly continuous static but stable society. The type of capacity that India has in absorbing change is absolutely phenomenal. Therefore, we are not hard-pressed to change the modes and methods of administration in this country.

What happened in the last 20 years? You know the famous story of Rip Van Winkle. He slept fort 20 years and found everything had changed. Suppose Rip Van Winkle had slept in 1983 and woke up in 2003. Would he find a great change in Indian administration? No. In the collectorate, in the tehsil or taluk, the village panchayat, the zilla parishad, in the departments of the secretariat, everywhere the system is the same; the noting, drafting, filing, audit, accounting, accountability system is the same. We have not changed the administration, except for certain cosmetic changes like IT, a few changes here and there. Even the IT is only a part of the movement for efficiency, for responsiveness.

In 1951 we had A.D. Gorwalla Report. According to that report, the three basic purposes of Indian Administrative Reforms are efficiency, economy and integrity. They are still important. Economy is part of efficiency. So, economy, efficiency, effectiveness, integrity, responsiveness and democracy, these are very significant. We have to be citizen-oriented and democratic.

We have been fighting on two fronts—democracy without and democracy within. The administration should respond to democracy without, that is the environment. Within the administrative system, there should be more of delegation and more of decentralization. So, the basic problem in India is as to why we cannot really transplant the new public management model.

We are a country where individual leadership role is very important. Officers belonging to IAS, IPS, or state level officers, the chief executives, they can bring about changes. The systems do not change in India. People bring about change in the system for a short while. They are the people who have really done marvellous work in innovations and creativity.

The NPM is basically a system-oriented model. Unfortunately, we have not been able to change the system in a large country. The big problem is motivation in government. The problem of motivation in the private sector is totally different. They can say, okay, have incentive according to productivity. Can we have that in the governmental system? Can we pay an officer more if he has produced more in a district? We cannot.

Therefore, remember one thing. If you want result-oriented or output oriented incentives, it is impossible in a governmental system like ours. So, we have to devise new methods in the Indian ambience. Is it possible to measure performance of the government at the micro level or the administration at the micro level in a welfare state? It is really not possible. So, we cannot measure even the performance of our administrators or the administrative system, except in terms of qualitative indices of people's satisfaction, which is of course reflected in the elections.

Look at what happened in the recent elections. I come from Rajasthan. Our Chief Minister Ghelot has done a wonderful job. He was a very good administrator. He used to take care to see that the administration was done properly. Yet he got defeated at the hustings. Why? The people did not feel that they have got enough. Fair.

Prof. Noorjahan Bava talked about phenomenology. That comes into the picture. People did not perceive that the government was doing enough. So, there is a crisis of rising expectations, which is not there in the USA, not so much in Great Britain, because the people's dependence there on government is very limited. Here the dependence of the people on the government is a huge one. Therefore, we cannot really think in terms of following the model of NPM to measure the productivity of Indian situations. We have weak civil society movement. We cannot really downsize the government or right size the government. It is very difficult. Therefore, the emphasis should be more on better governance than on less government.

If you reduce the number of people in the government, there will be a great movement against it. In Rajasthan one of the reasons why Shri Ghelot lost was that he did not agree to create new jobs, or even fill up the existing vacancies, which were already there in the MOU with the Government of India. When the Fifth Pay Commission scales were given to the government employees in Rajasthan, the condition was that they would not increase the number of posts, rather decrease it. He did it and he lost. If we do that, we have to pay the political cost.

So, we have to think in terms of lateral entry from government into business, from business into government. Let us make our service rules flexible. Let us not have rigid rules. Let us have contractual jobs within the government. Let us have a compensation policy, which would be flexible. Let us reward risk-takers in government. The innovative administrators always suffer because they make mistakes. Let us have a system of whistle blowing. Outsiders cannot prevent bad things from happening. Only insiders, who know more, can do it.

Let us have technology expansion. This will help in strengthening ethics. Let us develop a knowledge society in government. Let us have individual accountability associated with the government system. The top-level leadership should be given responsibility and targets and they should be accountable and given rewards. If one IAS officer has done good work, you need not change his scale of pay, but give him Rs.50,000 as reward or some prize posting, when you can distinguish between man and man.

Reservation in the Indian civil service is 50 per cent. Max Weber talked about the levelling impact of bureaucracy that people really get equated. But look at this. The most representative bureaucracy is in India, say David Russell Bloom, Crislock and Subramaniam. As a result, there is an assumption that because of reservation there is lower efficiency. I would not believe so. I have no statistics to show that it is a true assumption. Therefore, you should not go into this. Yes, you cannot follow the Weberian model of bureaucracy and recruitment in a system where reservation is up to 50 per cent.

So, we have to think in terms of a better incentive system and more delegation within the government. There is so much of centralization in the Indian administration. All the files go to the Chief Secretary, all the files go to the Director, Head of Department or the Vice-Chancellor. In a federal or monarchical system, people have the tendency to concentrate power in their hands. That mindset has to change. Let us develop a team within the administrative system and delegate powers. If that is done, then the top-level administrator will have more time for vision and mission. That is very significant.

We have to think in terms of cost accounting in government. Look at the money that is being spent on government. If 60 per cent of our government revenue goes into payment of interest or repayment of loan, what is left for development in a poor country like India?

So, my submission is that we have to inculcate in our administrators a new ethics. I think we are not giving great importance to the change of attitudes. That is very important. If you look at the whole training, I am also doing training at present, the focus of training is on skills and knowledge and not on attitude. It was in 1976 that Indira Gandhi said that you couldn't change the Indian administration, unless you change the attitude of the bureaucracy. But, then, why bureaucracy only at the top level? What about the middle level leadership? What about the bottom level people, the clerks? As Gorwalla said, the real bureaucracy is Babu Bureaucracy. If a Babu writes on a file, nobody even at the top level has the courage or the gumption to go against the Babu's comments.

In the National Museum, Delhi, there is a file of the old British period, where the LDC made a note, the UDC approved and signed it, the Assistant signed it, the Section Officer signed it, the Deputy Secretary signed it, the Secretary signed it. Then it went to Lord

Curzon, after 9 people have signed, endorsing the view of the LDC. Lord Curzon wrote with a big big loop, "I agree with him"!

There is no need for any change in the Indian bureaucracy. In fact, I believe that there is no need for change in the system. The process is very good. How can NPM say that it should not be process-oriented, it should be resulted oriented? If you deviate from the process, you will be caught in India. There is so much of distrust against people who violate the process. There is nothing wrong with the system, nothing wrong with the people.

I end with one statement of Shri P L Tandon, who was the Chairman of Punjab National Bank and Chairman of the State Trading Corporation. He wrote an article in ***Seminar*** in 1973 with the title "Low Cost Reforms", wherein he said, we do not need any reforms in this country; if the senior officers supervise, control, guide and regulate the junior officers with care, there is no need for any reforms.

I think there is a lot of food for thought. There should be thought of food now. We all go for lunch now. The rest of the papers will be taken up in the next session. I thank the Director for giving me this opportunity.

DIRECTOR (DR. P.L. SANJEEV REDDY): I would like to take your permission to say a few words in two minutes. It was wonderful listening to Prof. Arora. I would like to make a couple of points, which I think should serve as appetizers for you when you go for lunch.

The common perception of the people in the Indian society is they would like to have a government which works better, a government which costs less. They do not want to be taxed too much, they want the government to be efficient, as lean as possible. This has led to a concept called SMART Government, which most of the State Governments have adopted. SMART is an acronym, which stands for Simple, Model, Accountable, Responsive and Transparent.

Actually, these things would imply demystifying the administration, making it simple, intelligible so that everybody would understand what we are doing. The state should not be like a monolith, highly impersonal, complex. The Chairman of the University Grants Commission told us yesterday that the government institutions have proliferated so much that even officers in the departments do not know how many governmental organizations exist. They come to know about it only from the budget papers in a country like America, because the whole thing is so complex and so impersonal. Hence, we need de-mystification, delayering, delegation, de-bureaucratization and decentralization. These are some of the initiatives that are being taken.

The next point is that people want the state to steer and not row. The state must only give directions that you achieve this. They should not get into the messy things of doing things. The state is not cut out for doing these things. The public functionaries, because of their attitude and incompetence, they will not be in a position to perform. If they perform, there will be lapses. So, let it be done by somebody else, who is well equipped to perform with the involvement of the civil society. Let them only steer and not row.

Then the State has to perform the supportive role, regulatory role, maintenance of law and order, communal amity, taking care of core sectors like health and education, where the returns are late and low, where no private entrepreneurs will ever go. They have to do it upfront with objectivity and cater to the poor and needy, socially and economically excluded. The State should also hive off activities to performers, who can deliver fast, rather than trying to perform those functions themselves.

Actually, this leads one to the conclusion that in the Indian context there is too much of government, but too little of governance. What they ought to do, they must do it perfectly. What they ought not to do, let them leave it to others. Now the government has a huge infrastructure, huge outfit, panoply of people, machinery office buildings, vehicles, all of them symbols of the status and power of the State, the sovereign government. This has become an anathema to the people. Their performance is spiked. So, they get dis-spirited and frustrated. This is what happened in Rajasthan, as was mentioned by the Chairperson. So, there must be some serious attempt or mission on the part of the government servants to be seen less but doing more. If a lot of government servants go to the villages just to distribute Rs.10 or 20 per family, it really causes frustration to the people. It is not worthwhile having such sort of schemes. This is the first point I would like to make.

Secondly, I would like to comment on what Prof. Noorjahan Bava was mentioning. There is a good book, which is highly relevant in today's context, by Farid Zacharia, the Editor of

Newsweek International and a regular columnist. I would like to quote one or two sentences from his book, or a couple of ideas from him, because they are really inspiring. He says that the American form of democracy is one of the least democratic in news today. The American Government today is more democratic than ever before and also most dysfunctional. In the world's greater democracies, such as India and Britain, and in many parts of the world, the approach to democracy is not production but expanding the growth in liberty. He also says that from Russia to Venezuela, the Palestinian Authority, instead of being a strategic preacher, is an elected autocrat. The societies, particularly in the Arab world, are trapped between repressive dictatorships and fanatical men.

Is there a way out? There is. In fact, he sums up which should really provoke us. Woodrow Wilson said, the challenge of the 20th century was to make the world safe for democracy. As we enter the 21st century, the challenge to the entire conventional thinking, he warns, is to make democracy safe for the world. So, democracy itself has to be made safe for the world. The type of democracies that we are seeing here, with all the aberrations would make us sit back and think whether this sort of democracy will lead us anywhere.

The modern democracy will find it difficult to meet the challenges of fighting terrorism, adjusting to globalization and the aging society, and they will have to make their system work much better than it currently does. That means making democratic decision-making effective, reintegrating constitutional liberalism into the practice of democracy, and rebuilding broken political institutions and civic associations. Perhaps, most difficult of all, it requires those with immense power in our society to embrace their responsibilities and leave a set of standards that are not only legal but also moral. Without this innate suffering, democracy will become an empty shell, not simply inadequate, but potentially dangerous, bringing with it the erosion of liberty, the manipulation of freedom and decay of common life. This would be a tragedy because democracy with all its flaws represents the last best hope for people around the world. But democracy itself needs to be secured and strengthened for our times. Eighty years ago, Woodrow Wilson took America into the 20th century with a challenge to make the world safe for democracy. As we enter the 21st century, the new millennium, our task is to make democracy safe for the world. So, this is the question we can think over. (*Loud Cheers*)

PROF. NOORJAHAN BAVA: We are now going to break for lunch. Time is 1.45 now. We will be back by 2.30 so that we can continue this session, when the left over papers would be taken up. We have to see how we can cope with time management. All of you are cordially invited for lunch at the hostel lounge.

(*The Conference then adjourned for Lunch*)

CHAIRPERSON (PROF. RAMESH K. ARORA): So, we were discussing about food for thought and thought for food. The transition from food for thought to thought for food was very easy. But for some the transformation from thought of food to food for thought is always difficult.

Well, in this session, which is in fact a continuation of the previous session, we have three eminent speakers, who would be making their presentations. Prof. V Bhaskara Rao would be speaking on "Public Administration in 21st Century". He will be followed by Dr. Harbans Pathak, who would be speaking on "Civil Service Reform for the 21st Century". The topic of the third paper by Dr. Radhanath Tripathi is "Police Administration and Custodial Death in Delhi in the Context of human Rights".

Prof. Bhaskara Rao, as you all know, is the doyen of public administration in this country. He is a person, who has been associated with IIPA, the Indian Public Administration Association and also the New Public Administration Society. He has written a large number of books and articles in the field of public administration. Presently, he is associating himself with a large number of NGOs. He has retired from the Kakatiya University. I would now request him to make his presentation. Since we are short of time, I would request him to try to confine himself within 21 minutes.

PROF. V. BHASKARA RAO: presented his paper on "Public Administration in 21st Century".

CHAIRPERSON: Prof. Harbans Pathak is Professor and Head of the Department of Public Administration, Punjab University, Patiala. He has been with teaching profession for three decades. He has written and spoken a lot about public administration. After his introduction Prof. Pathak presented his paper on 'Civil Service

Reform in the 21st Century'. After him Dr. Radhanath Tripathi, Lecturer in Political Science, ARSD College, Delhi University made his presentation on "Police Administration and Custodial Deaths in Delhi in the Context of Human Rights".

Prof. Pathak responded to a question raised by Dr. Inderjeet Kaur.

CHAIRPERSON: You have a very well prepared paper, which is very comprehensive with a lot of suggestions. The debate of having a humanist police has been going on for quite some time. All the human right activists will talk about changing the attitude and approach of the police in investigation and trying to prevent such events, which really defame and bring a bad name to the police. But the counter point is that if you really become soft, the crimes will go up. The criminals will really feel absolutely relieved of police pressure. So, there is no solution, which can be cited as to what should be the moderate way of reforming police. Is that the only way? Yes. There should not be custodial death. Every custodial death should lead to an enquiry and punishment to the persons responsible for the custodial death.

But we cannot talk of not having third degree methods at all. Then will 2-1/2 degrees be all right? But something has to happen. If you study the police, you cannot really do away with it. I have been a Member of a Committee for the training of police officers of Tamil Nadu, Rajasthan and Assam, one UNDP project. We have suggested a lot of ways of humanizing the police. But we have come to this conclusion that both have to go together. Good policemen have to really use sophisticated methods for getting a confession and punishment to the guilty. We do not know what is the method. But no point black, straight jacket method for reforming the police or punishing the criminals.

CHAIRPERSON: There is a paper "Politics Administration Dichotomy in the context of NPM" by Prof. Raghavalu of Nagarjuna University. I am very sorry to say that paper could not be downloaded. It will be included in the volume.

Friends, this is the end of this session. I am really grateful to the paperwriters and presenters for presenting their views in a most effective manner and Prof. Noorjahan Bava for giving me this opportunity. But I want to end the discussion with a little note. I was a student of public administration in the 1960s. There were a lot of articles on public administration in the '70s, challenge to the public administration in '80s, challenge to public administration in '90s. Then, 10 years later, at the end of the 20th century or the beginning of the 21st century, if you look at all the articles, the problems remain the same, as also the solutions! Thank you very much.

PROF. NOORJAHAN BAVA: It is my pleasant duty to thank Prof. Ramesh K Arora for patiently presiding over the session, which was in a truncated manner, before lunch and after lunch. It was a good performance on the part of him as well as the paper presenters.

(The Fourth Business Session then concluded)

BUSINESS SESSION-V

(13 December 2003 AN)

Decentralized Governance and Development

PROF. NOORJAHAN BAVA: We are now in the last Business Session of this Conference. This session on "Decentralized Governance and Development" should have started at 2.30 p.m. We have overshot the time. Now it is 3.45 p.m. But it can go on for one hour. There is no problem.

The Chairpersons for this session are Prof. R.K. Sachdeva and Prof. Renuka Garg. Seven people were slated to present their papers according to the Programme. Fortunately or unfortunately, only three paper presenters are physically present here. They are Prof. Shiv Raj Singh with his paper 'Women's Empowerment', Dr. B.V. Chalapathi with his paper "Urban Governance: An Appraisal" and Dr. Sangita Dhal with her paper "Women's Empowerment in the Panchayati Raj System: the Case of Orissa". The remaining papers have reached me. They are in the set of papers circulated to you. But the paper presenters are not present here. So, we will take those papers as read.

Now I entrust the responsibility of presiding over this session to Prof. R.K. Sachdeva, who has been waiting since this morning to perform this duty. He would preside over for the two papers "Women's Empowerment" and "Urban Governance: An Appraisal". I would request Prof. Renuka Garg to preside over the last paper "Women's Empowerment in the Panchayati Raj System: the Case of Orissa".

Here I may mention that Prof. R.K. Sachdeva was my teacher in 1977-78, when I did the Advanced Professional Programme in Public Administration (APPPA) at the IIPA. I was sponsored by the UGC and Delhi University and was the first academic to undergo this Programme as the UGC Fellow and DU Fellow. In the APPPA Programme, there is one course on management information system. At that time, computer had just come in. I am talking of the period before 25 years. He taught us management information system. So, he is my teacher, and with all due respect I welcome him to this Session. He has already presented his scholarly analysis on IT yesterday.

Prof. R.K. Sachdeva is an alumnus of the IIT Delhi. He has done his Ph.D. in this field. He has been a very dedicated teacher here at the Institute. He has run many training programmes, including the course on Masters in Public Administration and Computer Management in this Institute.

With this brief introduction, I now request him to preside over this session.

REMARKS BY PROF. R.K. SACHDEVA, CHAIRMAN, V BUSINESS SESSION

Thank you, Prof. Bava. It is very kind of you to have called me your teacher, because I have never studied public administration formally. I have never run any course in public administration. So, I cannot really be a teacher to a person, who is a Professor of Public Administration in Delhi University. Nevertheless, she was a participant in the Third APPPA Programme, in which I had taught one of the papers on Management Information System. So, my basic area is management information system, not public administration. My knowledge of public administration is what I learnt in my 31 years of stay in IIPA. It is quite a bit of time to have a good overview of what is public administration.

Coming to the topic of the session, "Decentralized Governance and Development", I remember, in the '70s we used to have a lot of seminars in this very room and there used to be a lot of talk about decentralization. Everybody used to recommend that we should have more and more of decentralized form of government and all that. But, at the same time, we used to see in the country that we were moving towards more and more centralization. So, we used to listen to all the experts in the seminar hall talk of decentralization and then we were experiencing the process of more and more of centralization in the country. So, you can say this dichotomy was there in those days.

We are now glad that the Seventy-third and Seventy-fourth

Amendments to the Constitution have been passed, wherein one-third of the seats in the Panchayati Raj system have been reserved for women. These are concrete steps towards the process of decentralization and women's empowerment. So, we are actually moving towards a more decentralized system not only in terms of seminars and conferences but also in practical life.

We have some eminent speakers here with me. Perhaps, they definitely know more than I do in terms of women's empowerment and urban governance, the topics on which they are going to speak. As Prof. Bava said, there are two chairpersons, three speakers and more audience! I would now invite the first speaker, Prof. Shiv Raj Singh, to speak on "Women's Empowerment".

PROF. SHIV RAJ SINGH: Co-Chairperson Prof. Renuka Garg and distinguished scholars! Before I present my paper, I would like to extend a hearty thanks to the Director of the Indian Institute of Public Administration and Prof. Bava for inviting me to this Conference. I am really enlightened by attending this Conference. I am really grateful to them.

CHAIRPERSON: Thank you very much, Prof. Singh. I remember, when we passed out of school, the analysis of the school result always showed the boys used to perform over the girls. In the last elections, out of the four states, three states have chosen women as Chief Ministers. I wonder who calls women as the weaker sex. I have always understood women as the stronger sex. Now whether there is reservation or not, whether there are incentives or not, women are going to come up. Nobody can stop it.

Now the next speaker according to the list is Dr. T. Satyanarayana. He is not present. I now request Dr. B.V. Chalapathi to make his presentation.

DR. B.V. CHALAPATHI: Here I am going to present a case of study from Kadapa district. It has two municipalities; one is Kadapa Municipality and another is Prodattur Municipality. My paper is a modest attempt to make a study of the Prodattur municipality, an important town in Kadapa district of Andhra Pradesh.

CHAIRPERSON (Prof. R.K. SACHDEVA): Thank you very much. I think we have been very unfair to Dr. Sangita Dhal, who has been waiting for so long, because she is the last speaker. But I think the last speaker is going to be the most interesting speaker.

PROF. NOORJAHAN BAVA: I thank Prof. Sachdeva for conducting the session so well. Now I call upon Prof. Renuka Garg to be the presiding officer for one paper presenter. Dr. Sangita Dhal is going to present her paper. Both are ladies. How nice? It is women's empowerment!

Prof. Renuka Garg is Professor of South Gujarat University. In fact, she is in the Department of Business Administration. But her sister, Dr. Preeti Garg, is Associate Professor in the Department of Public Administration of South Gujarat University. Both of them have jointly prepared their paper on Public-Private Partnership in Surat. Therefore, I have invited both of them and they are here. Prof. Renuka Garg impressed me as a very efficient teacher. She delivers her goods on time and she is very efficient because her field is business administration. She not only teaches but also practises it with efficiency. I met her in Jaipur last December. I was very much impressed, because they are working in the civil society field. I thought civil society and public administration interface would be covered by inviting them. So, both of them are here.

I now invite Prof. Renuka Garg to conduct the proceedings of this session.

CHAIRPERSON (PROF. RENUKA GARG): Thank you, Prof. Bava, not only for inviting us, but also for encouraging us.

The topic that Dr. Sangita Dhal is going to present is "Women's empowerment". Now different definitions have been given with regard to what is empowerment. The dictionary definition says it is enabling. That is fine. But if we look into the present condition of women, I have certain issues to raise.

Firstly, it came out yesterday, though not very explicitly, and it is this: Is there a class feeling for women?

Secondly, I find there are many welfare measures for women. But what about women's development? Are we just going to relegate it by giving some sops through welfare measures? Or is it development that we would be looking for?

Thirdly, what is the responsibility of the media? Evidently, we are talking in terms of very regressive kind of design systems, which we watch on the television. Even if we look at the print media or any other media, they are raising women issues, but they never take them to the end. The cause remains unaddressed. So, the third point is the role of the media in addressing the issues of women.

Fourthly, I am deeply pained by the role model for women that is depicted. If we take the 1994 Miss World and Miss Universe titles, we have this whole beauty business developed in the country. We do not just require beauty business. We require the role model. I have no hesitation in saying that Prof. Bava has been a role model that makes a story. I think we require many more like her. By saying this I am not flattering her. This is a business pattern. We require role model so that young ladies may pick up from there. So, what about their promotion by the media and other sources?

The other thing, which needs to be pointed out, is the attitudinal change. When I talk of this, I do not refer only to women but men also. How far this attitudinal change has come about? Prof. Shiv Raj Singh talked about so many laws for the protection of women, like the Dowry Prevention Act. They just remain dead letters and nothing gets implemented.

But we found something very refreshing in Gujarat, because of the role played by Pathak. Now a very small village of Jalore has become the hub of activity because of the Pathak brand and they are doing extremely well. She was felicitated by Economic Times last year. She got the award last year. One woman entrepreneur got the award this year again in Gujarat from SEWA. So, when you talk about grassroots, certain developments are happening and women are coming to the fore. But we require many more of such models.

With these words, I hand over the floor to Dr. Sangita Dhal for whatever she wants to say about women's empowerment.

DR. SANGITA DHAL: First of all, I would like to thank Prof. Noorjahan Bava for giving me an opportunity and an occasion to address a gathering on the Golden Jubilee National Conference of the IIPA.

Having said that, I would like to say that the paper I am going to present gives an empirical survey of two districts in Orissa, where I have tried to find out the nature and extent of women's participation in the political process at the grass roots level. Here I have selected one tribal district and one advanced district. I have tried to analyze how the women sarpanches played their roles after getting elected. My study shows that women sarpanches need personality, character, ability to withstand pressure, education, and accessibility for people.

PROF. NOORJAHAN BAVA: I want to thank the two

Chairpersons, Prof. R.K. Sachdeva and Prof. Renuka Garg and the three paper presenters of this session.

I want to make an announcement. We have now reached the final stage of our Conference. So, it is time now for the presentation of the reports by the Rapporteurs of the various sessions. Dr. Sangita Dhal, who has just now completed her presentation, is the Rapporteur for the First Business Session. Dr. Inderjeet Kaur is the Rapporteur for the Second Business Session. The Third and Fourth Business Sessions were covered by Dr. Durgesh Nandini. Dr. Radhanath Tripathi was the Rapporteur for the Fifth Business Session. I would request each of them to present their brief reports, before we go to the Valedictory Session.

Presentation of Reports by Rapporteurs

DR. SANGITA DHAL: In the First Business Session, presided over by Prof. S R Maheshwari, the first paper was presented by Dr. S.C. Arora on "Good Governance at the Grassroots Level". He emphasized the need to improve governance at the grassroots level, because of its close proximity to the people and because an organization should focus on the development of the society for which good governance is the medium.

In his perception the passing of the Seventy-third and Seventy-fourth Amendment was a positive step in the direction of good governance. He bemoaned that adequate powers have not been delegated under the Eleventh Schedule, to PRIs; the gram sabha meetings were not conducted, the emerging leadership was not qualitatively better; the ward committees have not been constituted in the urban areas; and suggested that financial empowerment should be available to the local bodies, in order to enable them to function very effectively.

Dr. Priti Garg and Prof. Renuka Garg in their ppaper "Delivering Social Services—A Case Study" on the Surat Municipal Corporation presented the success story of how public (government)—private partnership and NGOs transformed plague ravaged Surat into a clean, green and prosperous city.

In her paper "Public Grievance Redressal System in India" Dr. Inderjeet Kaur after touching upon the theoretical aspects of the public grievance redressal system, referred to the role of the Department of Administrative Reforms and Public Grievances, in improving the government structure and making the administration more citizen-friendly by simplification of procedures and citizen charters. Need for effective monitoring system, courtesy towards the citizens, commitment to work, and deaddiction of the lower class employees from alcohol and drugs were also emphasized by her.

DR. INDERJEET KAUR: Thank you, Prof. Bava, for giving me this opportunity to present a report on the Second Business Session of the Conference.

Chairing the Session Prof. S.P. Verma observed in his opening remarks that IIPA should not act as an adjunct department of the government, rather it should try to protect its dynamic character by focusing on the reinforcement of the links between IIPA and various Departments of Public Administration of the Universities, as visualized by its Founder. This will also develop public administration both as a discipline and a profession.

"HRD Initiatives for Organizational Growth" by Prof. Bharati Sharma. (In her absence, the abstract of her paper was read) emphasized that the growth of any organization is linked to the growth and development of the people in the organization and therefore, technology and equipment are no substitute for dedication and commitment. She suggested that a good strategy of orientation, training and development changes, and maintenance of employees be adopted as HRD Initiative.

In her paper on "Internationalization of Public Administration" Dr. Sujata Singh, examined the barriers that hinder public administration from becoming an international discipline; and pointed out that while business administration has conquered international frontiers, public administration has developed as two separate disciplines, one for the developed west and the other for developing countries.

She cautions that in the context of NPM the blurring of boundaries between public and business administration undermines the importance of public administration as a field of enquiry.

Dr. Lipi Mukhopadhyay's paper on "Gender Issues in Global Development" focuses on the socio-psychological issues in the context of the ongoing global economic restructuring processes and their legal impact on gender, employment and human resource development in future. On the basis of research evidence, she tries to prove that women are in a disadvantageous position, despite new opportunities and free trade system, and they bear a disproportionate burden of society, irrespective of the community, nationality or class. She has suggested strengthening of the social safety net for the people with the active participation of NGOs and local organizations to check this discriminatory trend.

The paper on "Globalization, Technological Innovations and Public Administration: Challenges and Constraints" by Dr. Aasha Gupta highlights the changes brought about in the discipline of public administration by globalization and technological innovations. The shift from public administration to public management, has substituted the assumption of sufficient direct control, uniformity of purpose by way of accountability; and standardized procedures of traditional administration by assumption of team work, networking and partnership among public and civil society in the modern administration; and the values promoted by new public management are paving the way for a culture that is bound to extol the role of managers as heroes, profit as success, more consumption the social status and an end in itself.

Some of the challenges arising form the paradigm shift include the retreat of public administration from its intellectual tradition roots and the public is left to the vulnerable general behaviour principles of management of business administration; E Government and networking involve huge cost besides the complete overhaul of the mindset; and it will lead to not only in shaping values but also in conflict of values.

The Coordinator of the Conference, Prof. Noorjahan Bava, observed that the shift to new public management is not healthy and it is not totally acceptable, as it undermines almost all values and ethos of public administration.

PROF. NOORJAHAN BAVA: I would now request Dr. Durgesh Nandini, the Rapporteur for the Third and Fourth Business Sessions, to present her report.

DR. DURGESH NANDINI: In The Third Business Session on "IT Revolution, E-Governance and Public Administration", chaired by Prof. Bhaskara Rao. Prof. R.K. Sachdeva presented his paper on "Social Value Creation through Information/Knowledge" in the 21st century.

Prof. Sachdeva described the role of information technology, social value creation, problems of organization of government for information management and indicated the various challenges ahead in a knowledge-based society.

In his paper on "Electronic Democracy: Concepts, Trends and Implications for India", Dr. Y. Pardhasaradhi explained e-democracy, ICT and the benefits and limitations of ICT on democracy. In addition to the future prospects of e-democracy in India, he analyzed the implications and has given some recommendations.

Dr. Pardhasaradhi presented another important paper on "Public Administration and ITC paradigm". This paper covers ITC governance, efficiency of e governance, ITC and decision making, paperless administration and its various scales. He has also presented some case studies. One of them is CARD or Computer Aided Registration Department in Andhra Pradesh. Lastly, he has highlighted some performance indicators of e-governance.

Then the Chairman requested Dr. Sujata Singh to present her paper "Internationalization of Public Administration: Overcoming Historical Barriers". Dr. Singh critically commented on the landmarks in the history of American public administration and Wilson's view of public administration in the developed world. In addition, she expressed her anxiety on the impact of NPM on the public administration movement. Mr. Gerard Lemos, Vice-Chair, British Council, delivered the Keynote Address of the Intervening Session.

Mr. Gerard Lemos is a partner of social researchers Lemos and Crane, which has research studies on social policies including homeless and racial equality. He is the author of several reports and books, including the newly Discriminated Homeless People. Since he serves as the Audit Commissioner, Civil Service Commissioner and Board Member of the British Council and Deputy Chairman of the Banking Board, and Standards Board Mr. Lemos shared his views on the problems of minority ethnic community in UK, the enduring principles of merit, openness and fair entry into the British Civil Service, and State's regulatory role in the context of globalization in the British system.

In the Fourth Session, on New Paradigms in Public Administration chaired by Prof. R.K. Arora. Prof. Noorjahan Bava presented her paper "Post-Modernism and Public Administration"—a new paradigm that has arisen in the field since the 1990s. She said that it is based on phenomenology, social constructivism and structuration theories and it questions the orthodoxy in public administration. Prof. Arora spoke on New Public Management and its relevance for India. Dr. Radhanath Tripathi expressed his views on Police Administration and Custodial Deaths in jails in Delhi in the context of Human Rights" and made many suggestions for improvement of Police administration.

Prof. Harbans Pathak presented his paper ("Civil Service Reform for the 21st Century") on the basis of his experience and study of the subject. He has proposed many reforms in Indian administration.

PROF. NOORJAHAN BAVA: I would now request Dr. Radhanath Tripathi to present the Report of the Fifth Business Session.

DR. RADHANATH TRIPATHI: The Fifth Session of this Conference devoted to "Decentralized Governance and Development" was chaired by two distinguished scholars, namely, Prof. R.K. Sachdeva and Prof. Renuka Garg. Three scholars presented their papers.

The first paper by Prof. Shiv Raj Singh was on "Women's Empowerment", where he rightly pointed out the role of women in nation building processes of the country. He has tried to highlight the various constitutional provisions and the different Acts, which have been enacted, for the development and protection of women from atrocities committed in the society. He was of the opinion that the government have failed to implement the various Acts, which is one reason for the backwardness of women. He feels that there is improvement in the condition of women after the passing of the Seventy-third and Seventy-fourth amendments, which gave reservation for the participation of women in the local government. He has made several suggestions for Women's empowerment.

In his paper "Urban Governance: An Appraisal", Dr. B.V. Chalapathi, gives the findings of the case study of Prodattur municipality that he conducted in this important town and commercial centre in Kadapa District of Andhra Pradesh. He has highlighted some of the important problems related to local government of this municipality. These include problems of the municipal committee, irregularities in the conduct of the meetings, ignorance of the councillors about the rules and regulations, insufficient powers of the Chairman, lack of administrative coordination, lack of training to the municipal officials, and lack of an efficient system of accountability as no disciplinary action is taken against erring officials.

He concluded that the successful working of any municipal corporation depends on various factors like political will, financial viability, social awareness, environmental conditions and committed and competent municipal staff, who can develop a good work culture.

The abstract of the paper on 'Glocalization in Mumbai' by Dr. Marino Pinto was read out by the Convenor Prof. Noorjahan Bava.

The last paper by Dr. Sangita Dhal is on "Women's Empowerment in the Panchayati Raj System: The Case of Orissa". She has done two case studies, one in Jajpur, a progressive district, and another in Keonjhar, a backward tribal district. The samples were drawn from two panchayats each in these two districts.

After the Seventy-third Amendment women have taken advantage of reservation and they have come forward and participated in the elections and different development activities of the panchayats. This participation has increased their political consciousness and awareness and encouraged them to participate more and more in the political process. She has highlighted three types of participation, namely, electoral participation, institutional participation and decision making participation and five basic qualities and characteristics of women panchayat members. This includes personality or character of the woman sarpanch, accessibility the woman sarpanch and reachout of the people, minimum educational qualification, sufficient training, and network system among all the organizations working at the grass-roots levels.

PROF. NOORJAHAN BAVA: Thank you, Dr. Radhanath Tripathi. I thank all the Rapporteurs, who have presented the reports of the various sessions. With this, we come to the end of this session.

(*The Fifth Business Session then concluded*)

VALEDICTORY SESSION-VI

(13 December 2003 AN)

PROF. NOORJAHAN BAVA: Dr. Sanjeev Reddy, Director, IIPA, Shri B. C. Mathur, Hon. Treasurer, IIPA, distinguished guests, ladies and gentlemen! We have reached the Valedictory Session of the two day Conference. At the outset, I would request Dr. Sanjeev Reddy to preside over this session. We welcome Shri B.C. Mathur to deliver the Valedictory Address. Before that, we offer him a floral welcome. (*Loud Cheers*)

REMARKS BY DR. P.L. SANJEEV REDDY, CHAIRMAN, VALEDICTORY SESSION

Hon. Shri B.C. Mathur, Treasurer, IIPA and the Chief Guest of the Valedictory Session, Prof. Noorjahan Bava, Convenor of the Conference, distinguished participants and friends!

We have come to the fag end of this two-day Conference and it looks as though all of you enjoyed the two-day discussion. All the inputs that have come about are extremely useful in building up new paradigms for public administration in the modern context.

The previous session was attended by the British Council people, who showed a remarkable amount of interest in pursuing this proposal. They also assured us that they would be in a position to help us, in bringing to us all the best practices which are prevalent, not only in UK but also in all the Commonwealth countries. That would be a good feast of ideas to all of us and it will be shared amongst all of you. You can see to what extent they can be replicated and even upscaled in your field areas.

I am also happy to tell you that Secretary, Department of Personnel, and Training showed enormous amount of interest in this Conference. He was to have come here yesterday and today. But as his mother has to be operated today, he has expressed his personal regret. He has also said that he would be missing the very inspirational and very edifying session today. He has sent his good wishes for the Conference.

Thirdly, Shri K.C. Pant was supposed to have come here today. He has sent a communication yesterday that "due to preoccupations, the Hon. Deputy Chairman of Planning Commission is not in a position to accept your kind invitation. However, he conveys his good wishes for the success of this endeavour."

We were very hopeful of Shri K.C. Pant's presence in this Session because the entire Tenth Five-Year Plan is dedicated to governance. There is an entire chapter on governance. If you ever happen to go through it, you will find that they have identified that this is a very key and sensitive area, which will determine the success or otherwise of various attainable targets set out in the Five-Year Plan.

We have also been discussing in various forums e governance, transparency, accountability, bringing administration closer to the people, empowering the socially and economically excluded categories like women, weaker sections, Scheduled Castes and Tribes. About 29 per cent of them are below the poverty line. Almost 47 or 48 per cent of them are women. If you take the children, their position has deteriorated, as per the UNICEF report, which was submitted only a few days back, according to which India is not in such a happy position.

All these things will indicate that there is plenty to catch up and we want to catch up. The new public administration system has really to gear itself up to take on the new challenges. We have also to take into account the UN Millennium Goals, where also India is far behind. In order to create a hunger free India, egalitarian India, a democratic India, and India as a knowledge society with all the people living above the poverty line, also having an acceptable level of quality living, a lot of resources have to go in. Well-targeted programmes have to be promulgated and implemented. There must be responsive government with a lot of options.

You are aware of the new concept of development as freedom, which Amartya Kumar Sen has been advocating of late. ***Development itself is freedom for him.*** In other words, development must unfold before the people various types of freedom, freedom to choose, freedom to work, freedom to get educated, freedom to have information. He says there are 7 unfreedoms and they can be unshackled only if development takes place.

Development, at the beginning, of the development process itself will empower people, will give them liberty, will give them not only material objects and material comforts, it should also give them other non-material things like good education, good quality of life, good quality of living, good habitation, good environment; and all of them will constitute a living environment or ambience in which a person lives. Any State worth its salt must ensure that such ideal, conducive and supportive environment is created, where people are free to achieve their goals, to find self-actualization and find the entire life a richer and more varied thing, with a lot of options. It is for him to do things in his own way and for that freedom is most essential.

As I was telling you in the morning, Zakaria came out with a book, which says that democracy itself is becoming unsafe in this world. The type of democracy that is taking place is dysfunctional, with a lot of powerful entrenched interest to hijack the whole thing, to satisfy their own agenda of mutual interest or powerful interest, to the great detriment of the interests of the larger sections of the people. That will make the entire democracy unsafe for the world. So, he says, first of all make democracy safer thus far.

The type of democracy that you want to build, the type of development you want to bring in will certainly depend upon the type of public administration you want to have. We need a public administration, which is very sensitive to the needs of the people, which can achieve the larger goals of the state, which can be non-invasive, non-obtrusive, trying to create facilities to all the people so that they will blossom and they will realize their potential in various ways. Give them these conditions, create the necessary milieu so that nobody is exploited, everybody is encouraged, facilities are given to everybody to come up in life.

Secondly, all the disenabling circumstances or handicaps, all the constraints, whether natural, inherited, artificial or statutory must be removed so that nobody is handicapped, and everybody is free. Create a level playing field for all where there is opportunity really to improve oneself.

I draw your attention to the circumstances in which the poorer sections have to live. Take, for instance, the remote areas, the tribal belts, non-connected areas, where the development process itself has not gone. They are outside the pale of market, outside the process of development. How will they really live there? Reach the unreached, hear the voiceless or unheard, hitherto unheard, bring them to the mainstream. Everybody must be brought into the mainstream, so that they are taken care of by the State, which has been created to see that all these sections of the community are properly looked after, their interests are protected, and their aspirations are fulfilled. We need that sort of government, which can really provide the best opportunities to the people, remove all the impediments, empower the weaker sections and enable these people to really perform.

The State function now is only to steer and not to row. We need a government, which works more and costs less. In the theory of reinventing government this has been the main principle. It has to take up a supportive, facilitative and creative role. The private individuals, the civic society and others, who are most efficient to deliver things, must do the entire operational work. The State should not get into fields, where its inefficiency will be compounded, where you will not get value for money. These are the areas from where the State must immediately withdraw. The state must vacate these sectors, leaving it to efficient people to perform.

The state must not vacate areas, which are exclusively the domains of the State. For instance, law and order, basic health, education, external policy, defence, currency, these are the various crucial sectors where the Sovereign State should not withdraw. The rest of the less productive services and other areas of services, like the production of goods, can certainly be delegated to the cooperative sector, public sector, private sector, joint sector; or pubic-private partnership can also come in.

The British Council Vice-Chair was telling me during the lunch time that in UK most of the services are now being privatized. The civil society will take up those functions, form a society or a registered body. He was saying that the company or corporation with which he was associated had a turnover of 12 million pounds. A number of other things like consumer retail shops, consumer protection, schools, hospitals, are being organized by private trusts, private groups or private associations. They charge what is called user charges and sustain themselves. That is the way you can have a decentralized setup, which will not take away state resources.

They will invest and they will recover the cost from the consumer. The consumers are also totally happy that the State does not come into the picture. The State will cover only those areas, which it could not vacate or really hive off.

A point was raised yesterday that we have too much of government and too little of governance. The less complex the government the better. Now in every field there is government. Wherever you go, there is regulation, there is a law, there is an office, everything in place, and lawyers make money out of the situation. Is it possible for us to scrap all the old laws? In fact, Shri Mathur was just now mentioning to me that when he was in the administration in 1947, there was a form which they had to fill up, which contained a column, how many villages were still with the Japanese. It was relevant in 1942. Though it was no longer relevant, it was there in the forms of 1947 and 1950. This sort of archaic forms and archaic laws have to be given the go by. Make them simple, make them relevant, and ask only for that information which is necessary, which is monitorable and implementable.

It is in this context that I was suggesting a zero-based budget or approach for all the forms and all the regulations. If the State wants to do a particular thing, let it be decided first why it has to do it, why others cannot do it. If others cannot do it, then the State should take over. If others can do it better, why get into this? You have much better things to do. That must be the approach. The State must do things only by exception and not by rule.

If anybody is willing to step in, if anybody else can do it better, you can regulate, you can be a whistle blower. That sort of approach has to come. The state has to vacate the unnecessary spheres and get into the most necessary, crucial and vital fields and do it well, instead of doing it inefficiently in all the sectors and all the activities. Choose critically the main core areas and perform exceedingly well. Let others perform in other areas, where they can perform better. You can empower them, regulate them and you can be a whistle blower. In that way, the resources of the state can be very optimally utilized. These are some of the points, which are coming up in these discussions.

The new areas of public management necessarily means a professional approach, managerial approach, e-technology for instance, e-marketing or even management of technology like CPM, areas of inventory control, network systems of budgeting, proactive planning, monitoring through qualitative and quantitative techniques, citizens' charter, getting reports from the people about the performance of the government and trying to improve. A review for review's sake is no good. A review for improving the quality of administration should be taken up.

In fact, in Bangalore there is an organization, which is taking up rating of all the civic services every three months. It appears in the papers. The people concerned have to reply about their performance and they have to improve their performance over a period of time, over time and over space. The people audit it.

This is where the accountability comes. In the recent elections performance audit was an issue. They have decided which government has done well and all that. It has come up in *India Today* report. They have really brought out what are the indicators, what are the factors which led to the swing, swingometer as it is called, why it has swung and what are people's perception. It may be correct or not correct, but people's perception has to be really assessed from time to time by public administrators, practising public administrators even for theoreticians.

You are now dealing with human beings and human beings react. Whether the customer is happy with the public administration or not is the real thing. You may think sitting at the top of the table that you are doing a wonderful job. That is one side of the picture. But how does the common man feel about it? Does he think that you are efficient, cost-effective, optimal and doing things with a smile? How does he feel about it? While dealing with people's interests, their reaction should also be taken into account and it has to be calibrated to meet the requirement. You have to see how you could give the maximum of citizen satisfaction, as that is the acid test for good governance. These are some of the ideas, which came mostly from you. I am only trying to recapitulate them.

Now I would request Shri B.C. Mathur to deliver the Valedictory Address. As all of you are aware, he is one of the senior-most civil servants, who has worked in various capacities. He has a lot of experience, and a lot of empathy for the common people. He is extremely patriotic and professional in his approach. We would like to request him to address us.

But, before that, I would like to compliment Prof. Bava for taking the lead in organizing this Conference and inviting all of you. We feel so much at home because all of you have come in with a lot of academic inputs. We badly needed these inputs, we needed a whiff of fresh air, fresh ideas. You have brought all of them with you. I would like that this sort of thing continues for a very long time. It may be a continuing affair, not just one short affair, but may be once in a quarter or once in six months, at your level or at our level. You can have a series of such scintillating seminars, which would be mutually beneficial.

With these few words, I would like to extend a very warm welcome to Shri B.C. Mathur. (*Loud Cheers*) Now I would request him on your behalf and on my own behalf to kindly deliver the Valedictory Address.

Valedictory Address by Shri B.C. Mathur (IAS Retired)

Thank you, Dr. Reddy. In the IIPA Golden Jubilee Celebration Year, I must congratulate the Director, Dr. Sanjeev Reddy and Prof. Noorjahan Bava for starting a programme on public administration.

Public administration has been changing a lot, and will continue to change, because of the aspirations of the people, what they want. Yesterday I was telling you how technology has changed and how at one time I used to get information through pigeons, which is not required now. But I can tell you how attitudes have changed over time at various levels.

Way back in 1955, one day I was sitting in my residential office. Somebody was talking outside to my peon. I asked him who is there. He said, one MLA has come to meet you. I said, send him to me. The MLA came to see me, took about one minute or two and went away. After that, my PA, Sham Babu, came to me and reprimanded me. I was the District Magistrate and he was my PA. He said, "what have you done?" I asked, "What had happened?" He said, "This MLA would come to me first. Then I would tell him that the Collector is very busy and will give him time after one week. Now you have straightaway called him. So, who will listen to me?" It shows that public administration has changed today and the Collector has to receive the MLA and see him off also. So, the attitudes also have to change. I am just giving my personal example to show how things were and how things are today.

When we went in for democracy, we really did support this. I hope that when these seminars pointedly report on various forms of actions like this, as to what has gone wrong with our democracy and how we can improve it, I am sure that things are bound to improve. Whether we like it or not, today some hooligans have taken over and we have to change it.

The Prime Minister has already said that people who change sides will not be taken in the Ministry. So, things are happening in a positive direction. Now CBI investigation is going on against people who occupy high positions, which was not there earlier. Scams were there even earlier, but now they are publicized, people listen to the news, the TV and the print media, and find out what happened in a particular case, because the people have the curiosity to know it. TV has now reached the villages. So, even the villagers know what is happening and they feel that something has to be done. Once people come to know about these things, you cannot keep them under the carpet, because they are there for people to see.

Somebody was talking about the empowerment of women. ***I am all in favour of 30 per cent reservation for women.*** But I can tell you from my own experience. When I joined the IAS, there was no woman IAS officer at that time. They started coming from the next batch in 1951. Today the way the girls are passing out from class 10 and class 12, and every year they beat the boys, very soon you will see that they will be occupying all the senior positions and then we would be asking for 30 per cent reservation for men! So, do not bother. One never knows.

Today we have five women Chief Ministers. If we include Mayawati, she is the sixth one. When she was the Chief Minister, she went about suspending Collectors and Commissioners and did anything she liked, which was something impossible earlier. So, these things are happening. Still, those things, which were prevailing for thousands of years, cannot be changed in one year or in 10 years. Yet they are changing very fast. Our methods also have changed.

Yesterday the Chairman of the UGC brought out a very important point that not only the administration has to be efficient, but also there has to be peace of mind. You have to provide peace of mind, not only to the persons involved in public administration, but also to others. For that you have to work hard, you have to be devoted. Then you do not have to be anti-somebody or having fear all the time that because of this over-competition in the world you will lose your job. You have always that feeling or fear. So, you do the work all the time and you have no time for your family. Now not only the senior people are not having enough time to devote to their families, even the junior people are not having enough time for family life.

My son works for Maruti, the Japanese company. There is a punch card and if he is late even by a minute, half the salary of that day is gone. But if you go one hour earlier, there is no advantage. In our days, we also used to work hard. But nobody said in the evening, I am so tired that I have to go to the pub to chill myself. In my working days, I went straight home to my family and chilled myself or refreshed myself, by talking to my wife and children, which was very satisfying. If your family life is happy, your work would also improve.

I can understand that occasionally when things are moving on a war footing, may be for one or two days you may have to sit late in office. But if you sit in office till 10 p.m. every day with no time for the family, your productivity will certainly go down. When you are tired, you will take 3 hours to do a thing, which normally you could do in one hour. Clarity will also be lacking when you are tired.

In our universities, the curriculum must take into account the changes that are taking place in the field of public administration. To that extent, you have to keep on reviewing public administration. At one time, nobody thought of public administration as a discipline. We thought learning about Locke and Rousseau will be enough. It is not so now. We have to know also of the impact of science and technology, how it affects administration. What are you going to do about it? We may have very bright people, but then if we compartmentalize everything then we need somebody to moderate it. It becomes very difficult.

We may pass resolutions, pious resolutions. I have seen in the Chief Ministers' Conference, presided over by the Prime Minister, resolutions are passed saying we will do this or that, especially in the field of public administration and personnel administration. One is that there should be a definite policy for transfers and posting. But even before they leave the Prime Minister's office, they forget it and start doing the same thing. If you take it at the lower level, 3,000 teachers are transferred at a time in UP.

The average tenure of a District Collector or a Superintendent of Police at the moment is less than six months in UP. It takes more time to understand a district, what are the problems of the district. By the time you have understood them, you are transferred. [Frequent transfers] ***Apart from demoralizing the bureaucracy, it is a very costly business.*** Because, when you transfer a fellow, you have to pay him TA, plus salary for one month and cost of transportation of luggage. If you add up the whole thing, it costs several crores of rupees every year, which could be used for development work. Therefore, this becomes a criminal act, especially in a poor state.

This knowledge should become available to the public. I have seen that the UP Regional Branch of IIPA have brought out several papers with statistics to show how much damage it (frequent transfers) has done to the finances of the state. If this is known to the people, they would revolt, they will insist that such reckless acts should stop. Now we have left all this, which should rightly be done by the executive, to the High Courts and the Supreme Court through PIL. Now the Supreme Court tells the executive, you clean this malaise, you do this and you do that, though it is not the job of the judiciary.

The judiciary also does not do their job properly. In the case of corruption or misappropriation of funds, the charge sheet can come within a week. There are still some honest people in the judiciary and in other fields. If they are kept for at least 3 years in a place, the judgment can be given within three months or six months. Of course, the lawyers would ask for adjournment. Then the High Court has to observe a certain discipline and say, "look, you pursue the case; when the decision has been given, you can always come to me for a review or for appeal. But let us do the job of disposing of the case." The judge at the lower court also knows the law. If he is functioning properly, do not interfere with his work and do not ask him to give a stay order. Once you get a stay order, the case goes on for years. This is what lawyers and litigants are doing now.

I knew one of the district officers of UP through a friend. I used to meet him at some social functions. My friend was narrating the incident. He said, he came to see me. His son was involved in a murder case. He said, "Sir, I do not want you to do anything; but please do not oppose the bail. If he gets the bail, the rest is okay."

Then the case would take 10 years for regular hearing. By that time, some witnesses will die, some will be won over; some will forget the details of the incident vividly, whether it is a black coat or white coat and the benefit of doubt will be given to the accused. Therefore, they are all interested in that. My point is that the judiciary has also to cooperate with the legislature and executive in these matters.

What all can be studied in public administration? The study of public administration will certainly take into account what goes on in the name of e governance. I am not here to discuss it, because this has already been done and our Rapporteurs have very rightly explained to you what has happened in the various sessions. So, let me not go into that.

But the point is that ***we have to see that there is delegation and decentralization of power.*** Let us see that it works. We have to decentralize. We have to see that we provide only the guidelines. We cannot run the State Government or the local government or panchayat system from Delhi.

Take tribal welfare. I have been in the Planning Commission. I am talking of what happened 30 years ago. We did not even know that a tribal from the northeast is very different from a tribal in Kholapur district or Bastar district of Madhya Pradesh or the Meenas of Rajasthan. Even within a district, say Kholapur, there is Gonda and Gonda Paraya, both very different in every respect. Gonda is a very gay person, whereas the Gonda Paraya is a very rude person. At the least provocation, that fellow will cut the head of somebody, just like that. So, we put the police there but nothing happened. This was in 1951.

One day the medical officer in charge showed me one police officer, who was suffering from gonorrhea. He said, look at this fellow; I actually thought that all probationers under training should be shown that fellow, so that they will never venture to go to that side. The doctor said, even if he gets well through penicillin injection, he would start it again. So, this is the job they are doing in the tribal areas! I hope things are better now.

Unless we have full facts and figures about the living conditions of the tribals in different areas and their differences, we will never be able to administer the tribal areas. The mere issue of rules and regulations will not do. What is applicable to the people in Nagaland will not apply to the tribals of Bastar. So, we must have intimate knowledge of their working conditions, which only the local people can supply. Therefore, we have to give them opportunity to rule themselves. They may make mistakes, I have no doubt about it. Everybody makes mistakes. But they will learn very soon. Leave it to the people. ***So, decentralization is very important in a democracy.***

How is this taught in the universities in our curriculum? It has to come out very clearly by various case studies, by various studies that have been made by the learned teachers, professors and research people that these are the impacts of the various policies. In the case of Orissa one presentation was made about the impact of decentralization and village panchayats in the last session. Then one of our own Professors has done a study of a panchayat in West Bengal.

As long as this knowledge is there and people know about it, if it is also taken up through the media, things will certainly improve. ***Public administration will certainly have to be people-friendly, because people want democracy.*** They know it is a useful tool. There is no doubt that people can play a part only in a democracy. But it should be democracy of a type that works. I hope this is certainly possible and we should really do it.

As the Chairman of UGC has brought out very clearly, computer technology has to be introduced. At the same time, we have to see how useful it could be in bringing peace, how comfortable it could make life, instead of using it for killing each other. Today public administration can be used by two parties to kill each other, I mean killing the other party. If it is used as a method for that purpose, we are in a very difficult situation.

Public administration has to ensure that it is a tool to bring about welfare for the people. While a robot can be used in warfare, it could also be used in the hospital for open-heart surgery. You can avoid the opening up of the chest. You have only to make two holes, put two robots, they will do the job, you can see on the screen and the patient can be discharged on the same day. If public administration methods were used, if computer is used, if Internet is used like that, it would be useful. Then people will understand and appreciate it. They do not appreciate it all the time.

The computerization of railway reservation has not eliminated corruption completely, but 80 per cent of the reservations are done through computers. There is very little that the unscrupulous people can do about it, because the reservation can be done from anywhere in the country. Now you do not have even to go to the reservation office. You sit at home, do it through the Internet, you get your ticket at home, without all the botheration, at a cost of Rs. 30, instead of the usual Rs. 20. No doubt, it can still be improved.

Now take a service like the STD, which is now provided by the private people. If you take any colony in a big city, there are 50 or 60 STD booths and they are providing efficient service to the people at the minimum cost. You do not have to travel far away to get this facility. People will appreciate such facilities.

If you want to come from NOIDA to Delhi via the Maharani Bagh side, there is a big fly-over and they charge you a toll of Rs. 15. In the beginning, I was very much annoyed that they are taking from me Rs. 15. Then somebody explained to me that if I do not avail of this facility, I would have to come by a longer route and the petrol charges for the extra mileage would be around Rs. 30. So, by using the toll bridge and paying Rs. 15, I am actually saving Rs. 15. Such things have to be explained to the public.

Public administration has to function for the wellbeing of all sections of the people. I will give you an example. When I was Secretary, Supplies Ministry, I found that it took about six months time for the supplier to receive the payment after the bill was submitted. We went through the whole procedure, what are the reasons for such inordinate delay and we brought out a booklet explaining how delays in payment could be avoided. I told the concerned people that the payment must be made within three days. If you do not make payment within three days, you must show it to your senior officers and explain why you are rejecting the bill, or delaying the payment. Otherwise, you will be held responsible for the delay and the consequences flowing out of it.

I found that our turnover was around Rs. 5,000 crore. If the payment of the bill takes six months, the supplier has to take into account that aspect while quoting his price. Since his working capital is blocked for six months, he has to take a loan from a bank and pay some interest. If it is assumed to be 10 per cent, then it will come to Rs. 500 crore for a total turnover of Rs. 5,000 crore. If he could really get the payment earlier, his quotation will be lower. Even if we cannot save Rs. 500 crore, but if we save Rs. 100 crore for the government and also increase the satisfaction of the suppliers dealing with the government, it benefits both parties.

I learnt this long long back when I went to the United States. I went to a bank there, which has computerization and ATM facilities, which we did not have in India at that time. I went there with my wife and showed her all the facilities. They gave me the cheque, the ball pen and everything. I signed it and gave it. At the end of the transaction, the girl at the counter gave me 10 dollars. I asked my wife how much we took for the entire transaction. My wife said that it took only 30 seconds but you must be knowing that girl and that is why she gave you that money! I said, do not get any wrong ideas, I do not know any girl here, it is their system.

Then I asked the manager, "don't you get cheated?" He said, yes, we do get cheated. I asked "how much in a year?" He said, "it may be around one million dollars a year". Then I asked, "why don't you check it?" He said, "look, if we check this, we will not be able to pay in one minute; it will take two minutes". Then he explained, we have gone through various alternative procedures and finally decided on this that up to 100 dollars we do not check at all. If we take two minutes, we will have to have extra staff, That extra staff and the more time taken to check each transaction will make me a bankrupt. The clients will shift to the neighbouring bank from me. This is not a government bank, but a private bank. If I do not give good services, say one minute or less, my bank would be closed. So, considering all aspects, even though they knew some clients will cheat them, they have adopted this procedure.

So, there are hundreds of methods by which you can save money. You have to see which method works. It requires a lot of devotion, not sycophancy. If you want to be a sycophant, be sycophant to the people. You meet them, listen to them, and find out their problems. They do not cheat you. Generally, poor people do not cheat. It is the richer fellows who find methods to cheat you.

In Delhi, as in other places, power is costly. The rate can be reduced. It is not very difficult. It can be done, provided you have the will. It is a very simple thing. Every sub-station or a transformer has a meter. You know how much power you have supplied to every place in this area and how much money you will get out of it. The department will immediately give you the names of areas where the theft is the maximum. Concentrate in that area, put some people there and see who is not paying. Be ruthless about it; cut their power connection. It is possible and it is such a simple thing.

We generally say that the politicians do not let you do it. But that is not the only reason. We are also a party to it. It consists of people like me also. Vice-President Shekhawat was telling me that the senior bureaucrats have also become facilitators by making money from both ends. If that is the Mafia, we cannot help it. But if such instances are brought out in seminars like this, if case study after case study is publicized, you cannot escape it. People will be forced to install power meters. People will see in which area you are getting the maximum load and not getting money out of it. Concentrate on it.

We say *Chaltha Hai*. But *Chaltha Hai* will not work after some time. People are conscious of these things. They will not allow this attitude of *Chaltha Hai*. You cannot get a seat in a cricket team by paying Rs. 10 lakh. Now that scam has come out. They will be afraid of doing it that way, until they find some other ingenious methods. They will find out some other methods, but you have also to find out methods all the time to prevent it.

So, in the study of public administration, you have to highlight these things. ***In the curriculum you bring out what is good administration.*** What should be the personnel policy? What is the role of the governmental machinery? What is the role of the state? All these would be coming in public administration.

I hope that some very nice papers have been presented in this Conference. I have seen some of them. I could not go through all of them. They are all of a very high order. They would be printed. ***I certainly feel that the UGC people will also look into these things and introduce the discipline of public administration in those Universities where it has not been done.***

I can tell you that the IIPA has done good work. When the Administrative Reforms Commission was looking into personnel administration, we from the IIPA presented a number of papers. We sat with the members of ARC, with its various sub-committee members and presented some papers. A lot of work has been done by IIPA and is still being done.

We have a good faculty. The only thing is that they need some sort of incentive to do this. How to address this problem? It is prevailing all over the country. Sometimes I feel very sorry for our country. In my days in the school and college, we used to revere our teachers. Even though I was Secretary to the Government of India, whenever I used to meet my high school teachers, most of them are dead now, but whenever I still see some of them, I always say, 'Namaskar. How are you, Sir?" He will say, "good, thank you". He deserved it. But what happens now? They think, "they are all thieves".

How do you get respect? This is a problem that we are facing in bureaucracy also. I can tell you that if you have done good work, if you have been honest, if you are cooperative, you will get the proper respect. Even when we follow the rules strictly, there should be some humility about it. Sometimes some person may have a real genuine problem. If he knows that you are helping him, you are a good fellow, he will help you.

I will give an example. My chaprasi in the Steel Ministry was the General Secretary of the Class IV Union. He asked me one day, "why are you eating cold food? You bring it from home at 9 o'clock in the morning and by 1 o'clock it is all very cold." I remarked, "What can I do?" He said, ""I will bring it from house." I said, "No, why should you bring it?" All the same, he used to go to my house, bring my food and I was eating it. Then he kept the tiffin carrier in my car. I never paid him anything. The only thing he knew was that I was his well wisher and it is true.

He was in class IV and I was in class I, but it is all a matter of luck. If I had appeared in an examination for LDC's post, I would have been rejected. It happens. I am not joking. The gentleman, who topped the IAS and I, we both appeared for an interview for the post of Senior Research Officer in the Historical Division of the Ministry of External Affairs. The minimum qualification was First Class in MA History and both of us had that qualification. After some days, he got the letter "we regret to inform you that you have not been selected". He did not feel the impact because on the same day the IAS result had been announced over the radio, stating that Ramachandran had topped the IAS list. But the same person, who topped in the IAS, was not selected for a lower post. It is all a matter of luck. It is a matter of chance that we get an opportunity to serve top personalities, you get a chance to talk to the Chief Minister, and it is a matter of chance that you are in positions where you can meet those who wield influence.

So, there is nothing special in your being in that position. Therefore, you have to have certain humility. People like Shri Tarlok

Singh, who built up the Planning Commission, if you see him, he sits on the ground. Even though he is 90 now, he writes with his hand. He remembers everybody. He met me one day and he said, "Mathur, do you remember that I met you at such and such place?" Though I did not remember it, I said "Yes, Sir". I have seen such fellows, working very hard and yet full of humility. Even though he retired about 30 years ago, people still like him because of his manners.

How do we teach humility to government staff is something that we have to consider. Then what do we do with all the money? There is no limit to greed and power. Try to be happy. Just because I can go and eat dinner at Maurya Sheraton does not make me feel very happy or good. I went there one day, but not at my cost. My brother in law from London had come here and he took me there. We had great difficulty in getting a seat. It was full. Then they said, we will give you seat on the pool side. But near the pool side, they have put some purdha. So, we could not see the pool, even though we were sitting there. It was too dark and you cannot see what you are eating. One prawn plate came. Though I did not pay for it, I found that it costs Rs. 800 per plate. This was about 10 years ago. What kind of nonsense is it? What could we do? People have money and they want to spend it. But I can tell you that it does not make them happy.

One of my nephews is touring all the time and taking food in five-star hotels. Day before yesterday he came to my house after a very long time. He said, today I have got good food, I am sick of the five-star food. For one or two days, or perhaps even 5 or 6 days, you can go to a five-star hotel and eat there. Then you get sick. It happens.

From outside everything looks very green. When I joined as a Collector, I was also like that. As a young fellow, you go there, everybody salutes you, you give orders. After 5 o'clock, I used to get down from the office, go to the treasury, I used to take the salute and come back and feel exhilarated. But after some time I no longer enjoyed it; in fact, I took a different route to avoid all this. It happens. So, do not get impressed by all these showy things.

The real thing [that it matters] is how much you have done for the people. When I went to the outskirts of Balasore district, I saw people were sitting and eating outside in the open. There was a pond near the sea, which had only 3 or 4 feet of water. People will go there, wash their mouth and spit it. They were easing and washing in the same water. They were also taking bath there. I thought what a dirty people they are. I wondered, why can't they take a bucket of water outside and do all these things.

Then one of them said, what happens in the month of May, when there will be no water? What do you do? Something must be done. You have to provide water in some way. We thought of installing tube-wells. But it will take some time for people to use the tube-wells, because they are used to that type of pond water. They have become immune to that. So, what is necessary is that you do not look down upon anybody.

I thought that having gone from Delhi I had unfortunately got into such a dirty place in Orissa. Later on I found that the people were good, the place was excellent. I learnt the local language and a little Bangla also. In Delhi I knew only Hindi. Here I learnt two more languages.

It was a very good place and I was very happy. I tell you, I spent the happiest of times in that State, which I thought, has the highest incidence of malaria, highest incidence of filaria and tuberculosis. Many of the officers used to say, we are posted here, one day we will die of malaria. But it has not happened to me. We have to see the actual realities and what we could do, because we have been given certain powers.

You are all academicians and you are teaching them. Teach your students properly. Get into the curriculum all that you need. Bring out all those case studies that you have done, bring out the various research projects, which have been done by your faculty colleagues. Teach them those things, which make them good administrators. Merely saying e governance is not enough. What does it mean? What are its implications? What are its drawbacks? What is worth doing? What are the world trends?

We have to compete. We have to accept the reality. Whether we like it or not, globalization is a reality. We cannot get out of it. Whether we like it or not, WTO is a reality. We have to face it. But we are not fools. Our people who go abroad are doing wonderfully well. The average income of the Indians working in America is twice that of the American citizens. Our own people can do that much abroad. And yet they are not the best people. The best people still remain in India. Only people with a lot of money can go abroad, not everyone.

But the point is what happens here? Can't we do the same thing here? Our culture is different. We are individualistic. We do not like to see our colleagues going up. If you are doing very well, perhaps somebody under you will try to pull you down saying you are either untrustworthy or incompetent, because he wants to come up. I have seen many such cases. When I was the Chairman of the Industrial Development Corporation of Orissa, I had two Managing Directors. One of them was travelling with me in the plane and during the entire journey he did nothing except saying all sorts of bad things about the other fellow. It took me six months to get the correct position. He was all wrong. The other person had done wonderful work.

We have to explain to the people[officials] what is to be done. There has to be teamwork. We have to tell them how to do team work when there are five or six people. However intelligent a person might he, he cannot do everything himself. He has to depend on other people in the organization. So, we have to place trust in them and train them. Unfortunately, when there is shortage of funds, the first casualty is training, though it is a very foolish thing to do.

Whenever we have any training programme here, they-Government Departments send the so-called sparables. I told somebody, "Every time I come to IIPA, I find you here". He said, "The Government is sending me alone. I asked even the Chief Secretary. He says, there is nobody else willing to go. So, I am sent every time".

You have to have a purpose. Public Administration is a very wide field. I am sure, this Seminar will be found very useful. Once again I express my gratitude, especially to Prof. Noorjahan Bava, who has done a wonderful job, and of course to Dr. Sanjeev Reddy and his colleagues. Thank you very much. (*Loud Cheers*)

PROF. NOORJAHAN BAVA: We have now come to the fag end. Before I perform the Vote of Thanks, I would request the Director to give the certificates to the participants through Shri B.C. Mathur.

DIRECTOR (DR. P.L. SANJEEV REDDY): All of you have spent two good days here. In token of your presence here and active participation in this Conference, we have great pleasure in distributing some certificates. I will read out the names of the participants. I would appreciate, if they could kindly come over here and receive the certificate from the Chief Guest, Shri B.C. Mathur.

(The certificates were distributed to Prof. V. Bhaskar Rao, Prof. Ramesh K. Arora, Prof. Noorjahan Bava, Dr. Y. Pardhasaradhi, Dr. Harbans Pathak, Prof. Shiv Raj Singh, Prof. Renuka Garg, Prof. R.K. Sachdeva, Dr. B.V. Chalapathi, Dr. Lipi Mukhopadhyay, Dr. Sujata Singh, Dr. Priti Garg, Dr. Aasha Gupta, Dr. Inderjeet Kaur, Dr. Radhanath Tripathi, Dr. Sangita Dhal and Dr. S.C. Arora.)

In token of our appreciation of the initiative taken in this regard, with your permission, we would like a bouquet to be presented to Prof. Noorjahan Bava. We would request the Chief Guest to kindly hand over the bouquet to her. (*Loud Cheers*)

I would like to thank all of you for having participated in this two-day Conference. We hope to see you very soon. We wish you a very happy journey back home. We wish you a Merry Christmas and a Happy New Year. (*Loud Cheers*)

PROF. NOORJAHAN BAVA: Prof. Pathak wants to say a few words on behalf of the delegates about their experience of this Conference.

PROF. HARBANS PATHAK; Hon. Chief Guest, Shri B.C. Mathur, Director Dr. P.L. Sanjeev Reddy and friends: On behalf of the delegates and participants of this National Seminar, it is my pleasant duty to propose a hearty Vote of Thanks to the Director of the Institute, who deserves special recognition, because it is under his Directorship that the Golden jubilee of the IIPA is being celebrated. (*Loud Cheers*)

I would like to express my gratitude and thanks to the Registrar and supporting staff for making excellent arrangements for the delegates.

The most important person, whom we would like to thank, is Prof. Noorjahan Bava, Professor of Political Science, University of Delhi, an established scholar of Public Administration. We had long interactions with her right from the days she was in the Delhi University. She has taken a lot of pains to see that this National Conference should be a grand success. I think if we see it in retrospect, and I hope all the participants agree with me and we are speaking with one voice, that she deserves a very special congratulatory message.

I would only make one request to the Director. In the celebrations connected with the Golden Jubilee of IIPA, the

Regional and Local Branches should be involved. I am very happy to report to you that the Patiala Branch of IIPA has already organized three functions so far. We had a talk by the Chief Secretary of the Punjab Government on the Reforms in Punjab. Secondly, we had a Panel Discussion on Development Administration, where Prof. Shiv Raj Singh from Himachal Pradesh University, Prof. R.K. Sapru from Punjab University and Prof. Usha Kaur from Guru Nanak University spoke. Shortly, we are going to have other functions also with the patronage of our Director. I think the Regional and Local Branches should be equally involved in the celebrations by IIPA at the centre. I thank you very much once again.

DIRECTOR (DR. P.L. SANJEEV REDDY): I mentioned in my concluding remarks that we will meet very soon. It was not a slip of the tongue. We will be meeting very soon, at 7 o'clock, for dinner. So, that would be an occasion when all of us can meet.

I would like to take this opportunity to thank all the officials. Registrar Naresh, Deputy Registrar Kaul, our training staff, including my PS Shri Arora, all of you who have made it our day.

VOTE OF THANKS

PROF. NOORJAHAN BAVA: This is my last act in this Conference, proposing a Vote of Thanks, and I should perform this with all the solemnity and happiness, that the occasion demands.

Shri Mathur, Dr. Sanjeev Reddy and distinguished guests! It was way back in September, 2002 that I dreamt of this Conference. Because I am in the area of Public Administration, I have worked in this area for over 40 years and I have studied at IIPA so, there is some affinity and some sacred relationship between me and the subject, and between IIPA and me. In this historical context, I just dreamt that, in the Golden Jubilee Year of IIPA, I must do something for the Institute and the Subject. It was a sheer coincidence that, I dreamt so and submitted a proposal to the Director and the Executive Council, IIPA that we should celebrate this occasion in a befitting manner. I made a few suggestions on how to go about planning, how to go about celebrating this great day.

One of the things I mentioned was the holding of this Conference and I came forward to organize this Conference, if I was given an opportunity. The Standing Committee recommended the proposal and the EC happily accepted this. Then a High-Powered Committee was constituted under Shri T.N. Chaturvedi, who is now the Governor of the State of Karnataka. It also approved my proposal.

This is how the preparation for this Conference began. We had no financial resources in the Institute to host a grand conference, but we had plenty of will power. I tell you that there is nothing to beat the will power. If you have that in plenty, you can overcome all the hurdles, difficulties and problems. You can find ways and means to overcome them. This is what had happened. Even to this day we have not received any funds from any funding agencies, from any sources.

I should thank Director Dr. Sanjeev Reddy for taking up this initiative with all the available funding agencies in Delhi. He wrote letters, he met people in person, talked to them and persuaded them. He asked me to go and meet people in ICSSR. Just a week before the Conference, the Deputy Registrar (Academic) and myself went to ICSSR, met people there and persuaded them to help us. So, somehow, because of this will, interest and enthusiasm, the Conference began.

Director and I sent an invitation letter to all of you 4 months ago. IIPA sent out 122 letters, because our decision was to invite the Readers and Professors of Public Administration/Political Science from the various Universities across the country. Out of 122, invitees 40 of them responded and about 30 of them have written papers. Out of the 30, who wrote papers and sent to me, 25 have come here to attend the Conference and the rest could not make it.

We had a problem. There was a catch in my letter. I could not openly commit the reimbursement of conveyance expenses. People were coming from different corners of the country to Delhi to attend this Conference. It is unfortunate that we could not tell you, "Look, please write your paper, we will reimburse your ticket money at least". That is what is done usually in all the conferences, it is nothing out of the way; but because of the financial crunch we could not make a open commitment.

To this day we do not know how much we are going to get from any of the finding agencies. But it sounds really bad if we do not meet at least partially your expenses. So, whatever payment we have made to you is just a token. We do not want to disappoint you, make you go back home empty-handed, high and dry. So, this is just a token payment.

Secondly, I thank all the delegates for having braved the weather of Delhi. I had warned you about it in my letter that the temperature can range from 25 °C to 5 °C, so please come fully protected. The Registrar and the Director have seen to it that every room in the IIPA Hostel was provided with a heater, so that it could be utilized if the temperature went down because we had bad weather here two weeks back, when the night temperature used to dip to 7 °C. Now, luckily and happily, there is very great improvement in the weather situation for the last two days.

So, whatever shortcomings are there on our part, whatever limitations were there, inconveniences were felt by you, please forgive me in the larger interest of our study of the discipline of Public Administration.

I feel so immensely happy that despite all the hurdles, we have succeeded and it is a grand success, I should say. Only very serious people will always work hard and never give up. So, the handful of people who participated did an excellent job and all the good ideas were presented in different forums. We hope that in the future we will bring out the Golden Jubilee Volume of all the papers, may be before the end of this financial year. I have planned that to be out by 31st March.

Having said all that, it is my duty to thank the Chief Guest of the Inaugural Session of this Conference, Dr. Arun Nigavekar, Chairman of University Grants Commission, for having come over here and delivered the Inaugural Address. There were other dignitaries present on that occasion yesterday. I thank all of them, including the Additional Secretary of the Department of Personnel and Training, Shri Suvaratan.

Our own Vice-President, Shri G.C.L. Joneja, presided over the Inaugural Session and Shri B.C. Mathur proposed a Vote of Thanks. Our thanks are due to them. I literally gave them very short notice because we were not sure till the last minute as to who were going to come. We were what you call on tenterhooks. We were so hopeful and at the same time not so hopeful too. So, we wanted to put their names, but we could not put their names. Then Shri B.C. Mathur and Shri G.C.L. Joneja came to my rescue. They were here for a meeting, I requested them and handed over the letter of invitation to preside over the Inaugural Session/deliver

Valedictory Address. So, I thank Shri Joneja and Shri B.C. Mathur profoundly for having come here at short notice and performed a wonderful task.

Now it is my duty to thank the Administration of the IIPA starting with the Director. We took work out of the Director and his office staff. They performed all the work I entrusted them with a smile on their face. They never hesitated to do whatever we wanted for this conference. My thanks are due to Shri Gulshan Arora, PS to Director, Shri Rana and Ms. Geeta and other staff.

Next my profound thanks go to Dr Naresh Kumar, Registrar of IIPA, and Shri T.K. Kaul, Deputy Registrar (Academics). So far as the Deputy Registrar is concerned, the responsibility was thrust on his shoulders. I said, "you are Registrar, Academics; therefore, it is your responsibility". He never said anything except "Madam, it will be done". He has done it from day one to this day. He was available all the time and he did all the work. If the Conference is a success, a large share of the credit goes to him and his staff.

The same with regard to finances. My profound thanks are also due to Dr. P. Bapiah, Deputy Registrar (Finances). He has discharged his duties and responsibilities in an excellent manner. Within the resource constraint, I think all the dues that have to be given, (the token money that has to be given to you), have been paid and hope there is no case of non-payment for paper writers. Similarly, I hope all the Rapporteurs have received their honorarium and nobody is left out. It was all done in a very satisfactory manner and in a subtle manner, because nobody knew who was getting how much. We have devised a formula and strictly followed it. We have not done full reimbursement of your TA but the formula evolved was uniformly followed.

I thank Dr. B.D. Singh and his staff, who have done their work in an excellent manner. So also Ms. Sarita and others at the Registration Desk. My thanks are also due to the two young photographers with their smiling face, who were on duty from 9 a.m. yesterday. They did an excellent job and our thanks are due to them.

Last but not the least, I thank the entire IIPA, the faculty and others who came for the Inaugural Session, in particular the five Faculty members, who presented papers.

I have one announcement. The Editor of the Indian Journal of Public Administration was not present here yesterday. There was some problem and he could not make it. He sent me a note stating that he would come today. But today also he did not come. The purpose of mentioning this is that we are going to bring out the Golden Jubilee Special Number of the Indian Journal of Public Administration, for which the theme chosen by IIPA is "Governance for Development". This will be the Special Issue for the period January-March 2004. So, you have at your disposal about four months or even less. The details about this will be printed in the Newsletter. It is a five-page letter. It will take a lot of time if I am going to read it out. So, I am not reading it. Dr. Sanjeev Reddy, who is the Editor of the Newsletter of IIPA, I am sure, will see to it that it is published in the next issue of the Newsletter. My humble request to all of you is to take interest in this because it is the Golden Jubilee Volume.

With these few words, I once again express my profound and heartfelt thanks to all of you who are here, and also who are not here, for having made a big success of this Conference and thus enabled me to realize my dream. I thank you all once again.

(The Conference then ended)

PART II

PAPERS PRESENTED IN THE CONFERENCE ON

Public Administration in the 21st Century

CHAPTER I:
Public Administration: Trends, Challenges and Reforms

1

Trends in Public Administration

Prof. S. Bhoopathi Rao and Mr. M. Lingaiah

Ever since Public Administration took its birth as an intellectual field of enquiry it encountered from time to time one crisis or other. 1970s saw Dwight Waldo's book entitled "Public Administration in a Time of Turbulence". He has suggested that New Public Administration would help us to encounter the crisis. Some scholars of contemporary time are perceiving similar crisis. It is felt that the developments taking place since 1990s have been shown as contributory factors. It does seem to a serious student of public administration "that public administration is always in a time of turbulence."[1] Public administration as a dynamic discipline was successful in the face of adverse currents emanating from various quarters.

Public Administration retained its robust and dynamic character as identity crisis perceived by its critics proved to be ineffective in shaking the basic foundations. Perceived threats, however, were transformed into strengths. Public Administration its made it possible by carefully chartering the progress of their academic aircraft. New avenues were discovered. Scope of the discipline got diversified. Non-public administration scholars have developed interest in the field of public administration. Their contributions caused emergence of a number of paradigms. Theoretical diversity became a prominent feature of public administration.

"Unlike many academic disciplines-even those in social sciences-ours is a porous field imbibing as much in"[2] as possible from the field of practice. This article makes no effort to sketch the course of development involved in the growth of the field as there is no dearth of literature in so far as the evolution is concerned.[3] Attempt of this article is to highlight a few select aspects which in our opinion, were crucial to the development of the field. The scope of the paper is confined to concerns and issues faced by the public administrationists of contemporary era. The intention is to share our understanding with the academics and practitioners of public administration.

CONTROVERSIES ABOUT PUBLIC ADMINISTRATION

Public administration as a discipline is characterized by a wide range of disagreements and debates on various themes. Herbert A. Simon,[4] Dwight Waldo,[5] Robert Dahl[6] are considered pioneers in bringing this trend into focus. The contemporary era is facing a multitude of thematic concerns. The following themes constitute some of the important ones.

Definition

Public administrations are not able to evolve consensus on the definition. Ever changing contexts have created formidable problems and complex situations. The difficulties involved in defining the field are increasing year after year. It is increasingly felt that public administration is broad ranging and amorphous combination of many things including concepts, theories and practices. As a result some scholars have taken a stand that it is better not to define the field. This situation has prompted some scholars to project public administration as discipline without a field. However, some scholars have attempted to define the field in a comprehensive manner. Eagerness of the scholars to cover as many variables as possible, has resulted in lengthy and non-cohesive definitions.[7] A careful examination of different views, reveals that the context is a crucial factor. Globalization, for instance projects more variables as compared to localization. Multiplicity of contexts, complexities involved in understanding the contexts and dynamic nature of variables have become major hurdles in the way of formulating an acceptable definition.

Status of the Discipline

Public administration picked up academic legitimacy in 1926. This was made possible by the then evolving situation characterized by the publication of Leonard D. White's "Introduction to the Study of Public Administration", the textbook totally devoted to the field. White's text reflected main thrust of the field, viz., public administration lends itself to scientific study. This position, from time to time, became an objective of questioning by the critics. Scholars like Nicholas Henry have tried to put an end to the discussion on the status of the discipline. His works have attempted to conclusively prove that since 1970 Public Administration has secured an identity of its own.[8] Scholars like Waldo preferred to call public administration as am applied field. They prefer to identify it as a profession. 1970's and 1980's witnessed some serious efforts to strengthen this view point. In America, for instance, founding in 1967 of National Academy of Public Administration, and emergence of the National Association of Schools of Public Affairs and Administration as a formal professional accrediting agency for master of Public Administration Programmes is seen as an important development.

There are certain doubts as to whether the time is ripe for identifying public administration as a profession. Absence of uniform curriculum in public administration graduate programmes, lack of institutional framework to regulate qualitative aspects of teaching and practice, non-insistence on public administration degree for the entry of civil servants are shown as reasons for their arguments. Some scholars are not willing to accord the status of the discipline to public administration. Arguments are advanced to the extent the public administration is an integral part of political science. Their problem appears to lie deep into their loyalties and difficulties involved in overcoming methodological hurdles. Bava's work makes a good attempt to identify as to why reservations are coming in the way of recognizing public administration as a discipline.[9]

Core-Periphery Debate

Policy-administration dichotomy remained during the early era as core of public administration. Despite formidable limitations, it has served several purposes. Public administration secured academic legitimacy. Merit principle was firmly implanted. Principles mooted in the era of "Orthodoxy" continue to influence the practice. Policy-administration dichotomy crumbled to dust on account of ravaging attacks from "administrative Platonists."[10]

Public policy, since 1970's bagged the central place in a most comfortable manner. In a short span of time, it became an unwieldy field due to prattle gathered by it. Protagonists of policy science, in pursuit of their ambitious plans made several extensions and encroachments. As a result, public administrationists began to think in terms of searching for an alternative. Some scholars like Nicholas Henry suggested that public bureaucracy should remain as a locus for the study of public administration. His works on public administration proved that his suggestion holds some firm ground. Bureaucracy, however, is facing formidable challenge from three directions: organizational humanists, left-wing theorists and new-right theorists. Value loaded judgments of these theorists condemn bureaucracy, for different reasons. Death of bureaucracy[11] according to them, holds the key to good public administration. Practice of public administration, during the last few decades, indicated that death of bureaucracy is an unattainable goal. Operational imperatives dictated that the bureaucracy cannot be dispensed with Post-1990's theorists, therefore, advocated down-sized bureaucracy as a mark of good governance.

Focus

The endeavour to evolve principles of public administration to promote efficiency and economy remained as a focus of the subject, during the early period. The 1950's saw suggestions to bring public interest into the central focus. But difficulties involved in identifying as to what is public interest[12] dislodged public interest as a focus of the discipline.[13] Administrative humanists have tried to project employee's self-actualisation as key to effective administration. This view faced a challenge from 'rationality' advocates.[14] They felt that agency's rationality should occupy the central part of the focus. Post-1970 theorists of public-choice disagreed with Simonian perspective and advocated freedom of choice for the individuals who reside in 'public' domain rather then people employed by the public organisations.[15]

Public administrationists failed to develop consensus on methodology. Adherents of classical school relied on the distilled experience of practicing administrators. Behavioralists rejected the method employed by the classists. They have advocated experimental method. Tools employed by the sociologists and social psychologists were found to be useful. Normative theorists found the approach of behaviouralists as untenable and advocated the methods employed by the political scientists irrelevant.[16] Evaluation studies or programme evaluation is held in high esteem. Tools employed by the management science including operations research, systems analysis, cost-effective analysis are found useful. Theorists holding allegiance to policy science approach have summarily rejected these tools and advocated policy analysis.[17]

Competing Models

Because of extraordinary interest in public administration in the last few decades, there appeared a number of models. Their variety and the large number of persons who espouse them have caused a great deal of confusion as to what public administration is? What public administration theory is? And how public administration should be approached for study and analysis. The principal reason for theoretical diversity is lack of consensus as to what the core concepts are and lack of agreement as to what meaning can be assigned to given concepts. Concept of 'organisation' for instance, is defined in a number of ways. Each explanation emphasizes certain select aspects of administrative phenomenon to the exclusion of others. Inclusions and exclusions are guided by the opinion, interests and academic background of academician(s) concerned. The following discussion covers a few models which we consider to be of significant variety.

(a) Procedure-bound Command and Control Model

The Classical era has contributed this model.[18] The public administrator, under this scheme, is a career civil servant, who is appointed on the basis of merit. Principal goal setting and value-setting activity falls outside the scope of the administrator. Policy makers-those who determine the will of the State/the political executive and the legislature provide them. The role of the administrator is to mobilize and utilize the resources, in pursuit of given goals and values, and achieve the results. Operational freedom of the administrator is governed by a set of procedures which are pre-set. The administrator gets a fixed salary as a return. The administrator is accountable to the Policy-makers for their actions, in-actions and procedural violations. Performance of the administrator is periodically evaluated and "level of compliance with the procedures" is used as yard stick for promotion. Career advancement may run into difficulties in case procedural violations are noticed.

(b) Rationality Model

1980's saw the emergence of this model.[19] It has cast a very wide ranging impact. The public administrator is seen as a man who has a recognized role to play and a set of duties to perform. The particular organizational context provides the roles and duties. Organisations are seen as solutions to the wicked problems faced by a segment of public. They emerge out of articulations attempted by interested elements. While the government gives the formal approval[20] for forming the organization, the civil servant, in order to enact his role and discharge his duties, makes a number of decisions. Decisions are seen as emanating from the value premises and factual premises. The focus of the decision of the administrator is to influence the man at the operational level in such a manner that the decision taken by the latter subserves objective rationality rather than the subjective rationality. Several incentive models including rewards and awards are employed by the administrator. The rationale behind such actions is to influence the actions of the men working at the operational level. The extent to which organizational goals are achieved with due emphasis on efficiency and economy, is taken as the benchmark to evaluate the administrative behaviour.

(c) Satisfaction and Redressal Model

This model emerged during 1960's and 1970's.[21] The Public

administrator is seen as one who assumes responsibility for achieving his agency's effectiveness. Organisational effectiveness is perceived as a human function of aggregating the amount of satisfaction experienced by the people associated with the organization. Human satisfaction, in turn, is seen as a function of redressal of human deprivations. These include a multitude of needs including related needs and growth needs. The key lies in understanding of the human behaviour. The administrator should focus his attention to identify the needs-hierarchy of individuals and provide for the satisfaction of employee's needs. Deliberately fashioned programmes and informal level endeavours are employed, to achieve the intended results.

The Public administrator's focus has to be/to create/provide the conditions conducive to ensure a "satisfied work force", the basic assumption here being that a satisfied man is a productive worker.

(d) Interests Articulation/Aggregation Model

This model became famous after 1970's.[22] The Public administrator, as a member of bureaucracy, actively pursues his intellectual activity to look for avenues of participation, in various interfaces of the policy process viz. Policy making, policy implementation and policy evaluation. Public policy is perceived as the process concerned with authoritative allocation of values. The Public administrator looks at himself as one among many individuals, groups and institutions who are actively involved in interest articulation and interest aggregation activity. His focus is centered around opportunities to gain as much advantage as possible. The gain earned is ought to be shared by all those who actively support the administrator from within and from without. The agency to which the public administrator belongs, makes some marginal gains. Ability to secure as much gain as possible is seen as the benchmark fo evaluating the performance of the public administrator.

(e) Equilibrium-Bound Scan-Adapt Model

It is the most popular model[23] and its roots are traced to Chester. I. Barnard. The Public administrator, as a member of managerial sub-system has a goal to maintain the dynamic equilibrium between the outer system and the administrative system. Environment holds the key to the survival of the system. Environment provides the inputs and accepts the output. While demands, resources, and supports constitute the inputs, public goals and services constitute the output. Environment comprise socio-economic and political systems operating at local, national and international levels. The Public administrator should actively involve himself in scanning environmental changes and initiate changes within the system so as to develop its capacity to absorb the disturbing changes emanating from the environment.

CHALLENGES OF 21ST CENTURY

The 21st Century has brought about a number of developments. These are potential enough to create a sense of "turbulence". The ground under the base of several disciplines became shaky. Public administration as a discipline is facing a unique situation with equal amounts of threats and opportunities. The following are some of the important developments which have impacted both public administration theory and practice.

(a) Emergence of the Concept of Global Village

Economic compulsions of the world community caused the emergence of "globalisation".[24] This phenomenon has made us realize that 'mutual dependency of the members of the world community is an inescapable reality. Each country has to seek the cooperation of others for solving its domestic problems of all kinds—economic, political, social and administrative. Economic integration of the world is an overt aim of globalisation. It is sought to be achieved through free trade *i.e.* free flow of goods, services and money. Experience has demonstrated that the flow of commodities is accompanied by a number of non-material currents including ideas, opinions, sentiments, aspirations and motives. The free flow of all these things created new problems and unique issues, calling for new public-policy initiatives and innovative administrative practices. Further, policy implementation is facing formidable challenges as the concerns of public policy are crossing the borders of one or more countries.

(b) Dawn of the Information Age

The Information and Communication Technology (ICT) has brought about sweeping changes in the contemporary society.[25] State of the art hardware, sophisticated software, networking systems and procedures, dedicated work-teams comprising highly talented and gifted individuals have contributed to the emergence of information age. I.T. industry, as a product of information age, has come to occupy an important place in the world economy. I.T. has also brought about remarkable changes in governance and administration. E-governance, E-enabled administration, E-enabled management have ushered in changes in the practice of public administration leading to speed, efficiency, transparency and easy delivery of public services. Public administrations of yester-years were very much concerned with the constraints imposed by the difficulties involved in information management. These constraints stand radically reduced. Decision-making and control have been made easier. Adequate ground is made available for organizational restructuring and business processes, and re-engineering exercises. However, the I.T. age has brought certain new problems. Cyber crime control, law and order administration, and prevention of financial frauds have become difficult tasks. I.T. has provided much leverage to criminal and anti-social elements. Law enforcing agencies are facing a number of I.T enabled-hurdles. At the social level, IT has created the 'digital divide' between the information rich and information poor.

(c) Rise of the Unipolar World

With the collapse of the Soviet Union and the rise of the unipolar world with America as its navigator, economic strength, military supremacy, and advancement in science and technology have made the West to establish its dominance. It is in a position to dictate terms to the East. Recent developments in Afghanistan and Iraq indicate that the dissent is severely dealt with. The West has its own overt and covert agenda and it appears that it has no hesitation in pursuing its agenda in an aggressive manner. The UNO is too weak to stall western adventurism. Because of the failure of movements to unite the Third World, the West has consolidated its position.

(d) Rise of the New Right Economic Philosophy

Failures experienced by the erstwhile Soviet Union and East European countries are seen as weaknesses of the Leftist philosophy. The New Right Philosophy is seen as the lone alternative. Academic community of the west is given ample back-up to work towards securing academic legitimacy to the concepts, constructs and arguments advocating New Right thinking. Alternative ideas, native wisdom, tradition based thinking have become objects of neglect. Public policies are coming under the influence of the New Right.[26]

(e) Radical Reform as Strategy for Change Management

Institutional failure is seen as a world-wide phenomenon. The developed world and developing societies have similar experience in so far as mounting problems are concerned. It is increasingly believed that slow pace reform process is incapable of solving societal problems. Radical and comprehensive reform carried out at a rapid pace is perceived to be the only solution. The world community, especially the developing world, is assured of adequate support from international funding agencies like IMF, and World Bank which have assumed responsibility for initiating, monitoring and evaluating reform processes. As a result, economic reforms, political reforms, administrative reforms etc. are vigorously pursued by several countries.

(f) Increasing Hurdles in Macro Economic Management

Ever-increasing financial deficit has become a common feature of many countries Resource crutch is a world-wide experience. Governments are compelled to seek help from international lending agencies like the World Bank and International Monetary Fund. These institutions, are not willing to lend money unless the borrower shows a positive interest in their agenda of reforms. This reform agenda includes wide ranging areas of public financial administration, micro-economic management, public personnel administration and public policy management. Most of the governments have a feeling that they have no other option.

EMERGING TRENDS

Public administration as a discipline has responded to the currents emanating from various directions. There is an increasing realization that it should shed its 'orthodoxy' and display dynamism. A perusal of contemporary literature reveals the following important trends.

(a) Wider Appreciation for Multi-disciplinary Thrust

Earlier thinking depreciated the multi-disciplinary nature of public administration. Complexities involved in understanding warrant that the public administrationist should consult concepts, ideas and theories of social and physical sciences. It is increasingly relised that the theories and tools of political science are inadequate to facilitate comprehensive comprehension.[27] Multi-disciplinary thrust is seen as a formidable strength rather than a weakness[28] of the discipline. There are several scholars who subscribe to the view that public administration is a meta-discipline rather than discrete discipline.[29]

(b) End to 'Dichotomic Thinking'

The earlier literature was characterized by politics-administration dichotomy, public administration-private administration dichotomy and the like. Arguments were advanced that the public administration is 'different'.[30] Some political scientists were seem showing eagerness to use public administration-private administration dichotomy in pursuit of their 'mission' to cast a firm hold over public administration. Public administrationists faced formidable problems in establishing a firm base for public administration as a discipline, Now, it is increasingly realised that 'dichotomic' argument holds no ground. It is felt that the 'interface' and 'inter-dependency' thinking should be strengthened. Politics, administration, management techniques, ethics, economic events, socio-cultural dynamics, geographical dimensions, ecological changes, technology and international developments should be taken into account to understand an administrative situation.

It is increasingly felt management of business and management of public business are not totally different from each other.

Therefore, it is believed that association business organizations, their ideas, ideals and theories will provide much support to the public administrator in solving problems faced by the management of public business. Theories like New Public Management which advocate this view point are receiving greater acceptance as compared to theories like New Public Administration which disown such thinking. Ideas like customer choice, clientele satisfaction, Total Quality Management (TQM), cost-effectiveness, rapid speed, greater flexibility etc., are finding greater accommodation as compared to political ideas and ideals like public interest, political direction and social justice.

(c) Abandoning the Search for Uni-disciplinary Theoretical Framework

People well acquainted with management literature are well aware of 'management theory jungle' arguments advanced by Koontz and others. Public administration is no exception to this phenomenon. Non-dogmatic thinkers have realised that no comprehensive theoretic framework can be developed as far as public administration is concerned. Models have serious limitations to address all the problems which an administrative situation entails. It is increasingly realised that the administrative phenomenon is a product of multi-causal dynamics. Further, all situations are not alike. Nature and scope undergo radical changes as and when contexts such as goals, cultures, and technologies vary. Under these compelling circumstances it is felt that multi-paradigmatic nature of public administration is most suitable to address problem solving. The practitioner of public administration can illuminate his understanding better and choose one model or other. His judgment plays a crucial role in producing outcomes from an administrative decision and action.

(d) Search for New Forms of Theory and Practice

Normative theories advocating market friendly policy regime[31] are receiving increasing legitimacy. Public choice theory, theory of good governance,[32] reinventing the government theories[33] and the like fall under this category. Privatization, dis-investment, co-option of third party, balancing of the budget are emerging as some of the important "value-goals". Descriptive theories explaining the virtues of flat-structures, decentralization and outcome based controls are enjoying high level of exposure and attention. Assumptive theories painting satanic models of public bureaucracy with magnified pathology of bureaucracy as its central part are getting illumination and appreciation. Instrumental theories like New Management, Electronic Governance, Entrepreneurial governance are being sold with aggressive marketing strategies.

(e) Increasing Demand for Public Administration Educational Programmes

Public administration education programmes are increasing day after day. More and more Universities are coming forward to offer Public Administration programmes. The number of the students who opt for these programmes is continuously rising. More and more journals devoted to public administration are launched to cater to the requirements of research students. The governments around the world are showing interest in securing public administration education for their officers and employees. Unlike in the past, almost all the teachers possess a basic degree in public administration. They are functioning under an organizational context provided by the independent department.

(f) New Agenda for Crisis Management

In modernizing societies like India, the operation of socio-economic and political processes has received limited success in arresting institutional decline as well as declining moral standards. Electoral process, for instance, is facing formidable challenges. These include criminalization of politics, free play of money and muscle power, and populism characterized by false promises. Parliaments have become every weak and are not in a position to protect public interest. Judiciary is overburdened with increasing litigations. And corruption has become a world-wide phenomenon. Against this depressing scenario it is increasingly felt that public administration should be entrusted with the responsibility to correct the distortions and pervasive trends found in various institutions including its own with the active participation of citizens and civil society organizations.

DEVELOPMENTS IN INDIA

The intellectual field of public administration began to acquire its academic legitimacy in India as early as 1926 when the University of Madras was the first in the country to offer diploma course in public administration in addition to providing for teaching the subject as an optional paper in the post-graduate course on Political Science. Since the 1930s Lucknow University got the credit of teaching Public administration as compulsory part of Political Science. Its position was strengthened in post-II World War Era. In 1949 Nagpur University constituted a separate department for public administration. A number of universities followed suit. Further several political science departments were reconstituted as departments of political science and public administration. Besides, political science departments began to offer post-graduate programmes in public administration. Some of the Universities like Osmania University have taken initiatives to develop the programmes on the lines suggested by H.A. Simon. Due emphasis was given to mould the discipline as administrative science. Indian Institute of Public Administration assumed responsibility to encourage study and research in public administration. Observations made by Pai Panandikar in the first survey of research in public administration, to the extent that "lurking doubts exists...whether public administration could develop as an useful discipline," [34] was taken as a challenge. The discipline began to show a sense of buoyancy. Several studies were undertaken to suggest measures to enhance administrative competency.

Administrative reforms covering substantive and procedural aspects were suggested. Dissenting voices highlighted the need for initiatives to develop normative areas. As a response, some of the Universities like Kakatiya University took steps to enrich the discipline with the value dimensions advocated by New Public Administration theory. The Centre of Policy Research, New Delhi assumed lead role in initiating policy studies. In response to call given by Kuldeep Mathur, in his concluding observations on the state of the discipline on the second survey of research,[35] the public administrationists began taking interest in establishing linkages with other disciplines. As a result, multi-disciplinary approach began its beginning in India. Post 1980's developments saw tilt towards professional aspect of public administration. Practitioners of public administration have shown keen interest in promoting professional aspects. Developments of post 1990's display interesting trends. The discipline began moving towards novel fields including Governance, Good Governance and Electronic Governance. Osmania University, for instance, has taken steps to develop one of the units of public administration as Centre for the Study of Governance. Electronic governance became an important component of post-graduate programme in public administration.

SUGGESTIONS FOR IMPROVEMENT

Despite impressive developments in the field public administration still provides some scope for improvement. We hope that implementation of the following suggestions would go a long way in strengthening the position of the discipline in India.

(*a*) Cooperative human action in pursuit of solving the problems faced by 'the publics' should be taken as defined field of public administration. Such a view embraces operational areas in which public bureaucracy, private corporations and voluntary groups participate in social action and administrative process.

(*b*) Managerial responsibility should be viewed as the central part of public administration. The public administrator, in pursuit of this responsibility, would have to make critical decisions.

(*c*) Decision making should be seen as an exercise of judgement in respect of various forces operating in the internal and external environment.

(*d*) Components of the context cast uneven impact, depending upon the values and facts involved in an administrative situation. Therefore, giving undue importance to one aspect to the neglect of others may cause irreparable damage. (Public Administrationists should resist from giving undue importance to political context).

(*e*) Policy-making is only one aspect of managerial responsibility. Its importance cannot be over-emphasized. The tendency towards treating public administration as concerned with policy making amounts to giving overemphasis to the policy-making function. Over emphasis may prove fatal to the identity of the discipline. The Public administration community should therefore, address themselves to this problem.

CONCLUSION

Public administration as a discipline has traveled its way for the last 100 years. Very often the question of its academic legitimacy is raised. This trend had its beginning in 1947. Simon, Waldo, Dahl who raised the problem of "crisis of identity" for public administration caused serious thinking amongst public administrationists and paved the way for gradual ascending of the subject to higher levels of academic achievements. Since the 1970s public administration was experiencing (self confidence) largely due to the contributions made by students, academics and practitioners of public administration. The discipline of public administration has received considerable amount of recognition among academic circles.

Despite this achievement there still remains a number of questions which are left unanswered and continue to engage the attention of academics. This article has highlighted a few important themes which are causing continuous debate among the public administrationists on one hand and between public administrationists and the critics of the subject on the other. These include definitions, core and periphery, status of the discipline and methodology and the like. The discourse reveals that no consensus is possible on these themes. Public administration has to operate under varying contexts, in pursuit of multifarious goals and values, using divergent techniques and technologies under variant cultures. Administrative process and nature undergo radical change as and when one of these variables change. Thus the problem is with the variations in contexts rather than concepts of the discipline. Further, none of the models developed by public administrationists is exclusively capable to cater to the needs of every situation. The challenges posed by the developments taking place in the 21st century have spawned a series of trends in public administration thinking and practice. The multi-disciplinary nature and multi-paradigmatic character of public administration and application of discretion in employing models in different situations have become some of the inescapable characteristics of the discipline. Various theories such as normative, descriptive and assumptive will have their relevance in so far as their utility in illuminating the understanding of the practitioners is concerned. However, much depends upon the discretion employed by the administrator in the discharge of his role in a context provided by the organisation in pursuit of his administrative responsibility.

REFERENCES

1. Astrid E. Merget, "Donald C. Stone Lecture", *Public Administration Review,* Vol. 63, No. 4., July-August, 2003, p. 390.
2. *Ibid.*
3. See E.N. Gladden, *A History of Public Administration* (Vol. I and II), London: Frank Cabs, 1972; Robert T. Golembeiwski, *Public Administration as a Developing Discipline, Part-I, Perspectives on Past an Present,* New York: Marcel Decker, 1977; Nicholas Henry, *Public Administration and Public Affairs,* Sixth Edition, New Delhi: Prentice Hall of India Private Limited, 1995.
4. See Herbert A. Simon, "A Comment on the Science of Public Administration", *Public Administration Review, No. 7* (Summer 1947), p. 202.
5. See Dwight Waldo, *The Administrative State,* New York: Ronald, 1948.
6. Robert A. Dahl, "The Science of Public Administration: Three Problems", *Public Administration Review* (Winter, 1947), pp. 1-11.
7. See John J. Corson and Joseph P. Harris, *Public Administration in Modern Society,* Mc Graw Hill, 1963, p. 24.
8. See Nicholas Henry, *Public Administration and Public Affairs, op. cit.* p. 44 (sixth Edition).
9. See Noorjahan Bava, *The Social Science Perspective and Method of Public Administration: Public Policy and Development Administration Approach,* New Delhi; Uppal Publishing House, 1992, pp. 130-38.
10. For an elaboration of this term see Glendon A. Schubert Jr., "The Public Interest in Administrative Decision Making", *American Political Science Review,* 51 (June 1957), pp. 346-68.
11. For inevitable demise of bureaucracy thesis see Warren G.Bennis, *Changing Organisations,* New York, Mc Graw Hill.
12. Glendon Schubert, after discussing public interest in an exhaustive manner concludes that there is no such thing. See Glendon Schubert, *The Public Interest,* Glencoe; The Free Press, 1960.

13. Michael M. Harmon, Richard T. Mayer, *Organisation Theory for Public Administration,* Glenview: Scott, Foresman and Company, p. 37.
14. See Herbert A. Simon, "Organisational Man is Rational or Self-Actualizing?" *Public Administration Review,* 33.4(1973):352.
15. See Vincent Ostrom, *The Intellectual Crisis in American Public Administration,* Rev. ed University, Ala; Uniersity of Albama, Press, 1974.
16. See Nicholas Henry, *Public Administration and Public Affairs, op. cit.* p. 22.
17. See Y. Dror, "From Management to Policy Science" in M.J. White *et al.,* (ed.) *Management and Policy Science in American Government,* Lexington Mass; D.C. Heath, 1975.
18. For a good treatment of this model see Mark Considine, Jenny M.Lewis, "Bureaucracy, Network, or Enterprise? Comparing Models of Governance in Australia, Britain, the Netherlands, and New Zealand", *Public Administration Review,* Vol. 63, No. 2., March-April, 2003, pp. 131-40.
19. See Simon, Dold W. Smithburg, and Victor A. Thompson, *Public Administration,* New York, Alfred A. Knopf, 1950.
20. *Ibid.,* pp. 30-31.
21. Frederick Herzberg's Satisfiers-Dissatisfiers hypothesis provides substantial ground to this model. For a critical appraisal of his hypothesis, see Chunoh Park, Nicholas P. Lobrich, and Dennise L. Soden, "Testing Herzberg's Motivation Theory in a Comparative Study of U.S and Korean Public Employees", *Review of Public Personnel Administration,* Vol. 8, Summer 1988.
22. "Interest group liberalism" thesis I sat the foundation of this model. For an evaluation of this thinking see Theodore Low, *The End of Liberalism,* New York, Norton, 1969.
23. The Concept of Organisational Rationality and Organic Metaphor thinking form the basis for this model. For a good outline of systems theory see James D. Thompson, *Organisation-in-Action,* New York: McGraw Hill, 1967.
24. C.P. Bhambri, "Globalisation, Liberalisation, and the Welfare State", *The Indian Journal of Public Administration,* Special Number on Liberalisation and Social concerns, Vol. XLII, No. 3, July-September, 1996, pp. 258-63.
25. See Dennis P. Curtin, Kim Foley, Kunal Sen, *Information Technology: The Breaking Wave,* New Delhi, Tata McGraw Hill Publishing Company Limited, 1999.
26. Grant Jordan and Nigel Ashford (eds), *Public Policy and the Impact of the Right,* London, Pinter Publishers, 1993.

27. See Noorjahan Bava, *The Social Science Perspective and Method of Public Administration: Public Policy and Development Administration Approach op. cit.*
28. Astrid E. Merget, "Donald C. Stone Lecture".
29. This type of thinking pervades the works of those scholars whose basic training is in public administration and whose commitment to the discipline is at an unquestionable level. See, for instance, Noorjahan Bava, Social Science Perspective and Method of Public Administration, Public Policy and Development Administration Approach, *op. cit.*
30. Appleby, "Government is different" in Jay M. Shafritz and Albert C. Hyde (eds.), *Classics of Public Administration*, Oak Park III, More Publishing Co., 1978, pp. 101-05, reprinted from Paul Appleby, *Big Democracy*, New York, Alfred Knopf, 1945.
31. For a critical appraisal of this trend see Mohit Bhattacharya, "Rolling back the State, Public Administration in the Age of Market Supremacy, *IJPA*, Vol. XLII, *op. cit.*, pp. 245-57.
32. See *IJPA*, Special number on Good Governance, Vol. XLIV, No. 3, July-September, 1998
33. For good coverage of reinventing theories see Sofi Ali and Anita Rao, "Reinventing Public Administration for 21st Century", *IJPA*, Vol. XLVI, No. 2, April-June 2000, pp. 169-88.
34. ICSSR, *A Survey of Research in Public Administration*, New Delhi, Allied Publishers, 1973.
35. See Kuldeep Mathur, (ed.), *A Survey of Research in Public Administration, 1970-1979*, New Delhi, Concept, 1986.

2

Internationalisation of Public Administration: Overcoming Historical Barriers

Dr. Sujata Singh

The Paper examines the barriers that hinder Public Administration from becoming an International discipline. Whereas Business Administration has conquered international frontiers Public Administration has developed as two separate disciplines—one for the developed West and the other for developing countries. The paper traces the problem to the legacy of the post World War II initiatives taken by the West.

Public Administration of the 21st century has its roots in the 20th century discipline of public administration, which had a distinct American flavour. However, the trajectory of Public administration in the developing countries was vastly different from that of the West. The paper examines the legacy of public administration in the developing countries to assess its impact on the internationalisation of the discipline.

A combination of factors gave America an advantage over the other super power as far as global leadership was concerned. Britain, had entered a state of decline in the 1940s and 1950s with the stigma of colonialism attached to it. The then Soviet Union, the only other contender to super power status came to be associated with the evils of communism. Another important factor, which worked to America's advantage, was the spread of English language, which the British had helped internationalise. This facilitated the dissemination of American innovations throughout the globe, especially in the newly emerging independent countries of Asia and Africa, which were earlier British colonies.

A challenging opportunity was provided to American public administration wherein as leader of the free world it was called upon to design the vehicle for administering development. However, this opportunity created serious implications for the internationalisation of Public Administration. American Public Administration not only looked to other disciplines for assembling this vehicle but also in the process created a separate sub-field for the developing countries. What emerged were two separate theoretical and conceptual approaches with common tools and techniques of Administration.

A parallel move necessitated by the globalization of commerce saw the internationalisation of business administration. The reason why America plays a leading role in business education is obvious. It was in America that the business school curriculum was first developed which was later adopted by business schools around the globe. This is not to suggest that business administration was not aware of differences in culture and the general environment prevailing in different countries, especially in the developing countries. The emphasis was on the universality of business tools and techniques. In sharp contrast, American Public Administration highlighted the cultural differences to such an extent that it made the universal application of tools and techniques impossible. In fact, two separate fields were created one for the developed and the other for developing countries.

By the end of the development decades (the 1950s and 1960s), public administration theorists were still optimistic about the future of the enterprise called comparative and development administration. The general consensus was that there would be a convergence of the parent field American Public Administration and its sub field comparative and development administration. Whereas scholars such as Riggs (1976) and Henderson (1971), believed the main field would become a part of the sub-field, Jong S. Jun among others felt the sub-field should merge with the main field.

The global nature of problems places comparative and development administration in a prominent position, Riggs argued convincingly. He added: "The American dimension of these problems will surely come to be seen as a 'sub-field' or a parochial aspect of the broader subject. As our consciousness expands, we shall no longer need to speak of 'comparative administration', but only of the study of 'public administration', and of its sub-field, the study of 'American public administration" [1]

Waldo appeared equally convinced that there would be a convergence in "development". This would be brought about through reciprocal learning and mutual adjustment.[2] In their enthusiasm these scholars seem to have paid insufficient attention to the differences between the parent field and the sub-field which could hinder such a convergence. The incompatibility of the two fields was largely ignored.

Landmarks in the History of American Public Administration

American public administration had already overcome its major problems by the turn of the 19th century. These hurdles were the direct outcome of the spoils system. American public administration during a large part of the 19th century was far from the Weberian legal rational authority system.[3] Infact, the most rapid phase of development had been accompanied by large-scale corruption in public life. The development of the merit system had been a slow process, which however was expedited with the assassination of President Garfield by a disgruntled spoilsman.

Woodraw Wilson's 1887 essay "The study of Public Administration," acknowledged as the starting point in the study of public administration in the United States provides clues regarding the status of the discipline or at least what it ought to be. He advanced the thesis that there is but one best rule of public administration, irrespective of the form of government. Wilson wrote at a time when spoils politics dominated United States.

Wilson attempted to lay the foundation of the discipline of public administration by demarcating its boundaries through the separation of politics from administration. He spelled out issues that had to be addressed by public administration as a distinct discipline. He saw civil service reform as a prelude to a more thorough administrative reform for achieving greater efficiency in government. The purpose was to devise more efficient methods for administration and cleanse the moral atmosphere for it to function in a nonpartisan business like manner.

Wilson's views can thus be summarized

"The field of administration is a field of business. It is removed from the hurry and strife of politics...Administrative questions are not political questions. Although politics sets the tasks for administration, it should not be suffered to manipulate its offices...This discrimination between administration and politics is now, happily, too obvious to need further discussion."[4]

In the United States the operationalisation of the concept of civil service neutrality was sought through two important acts: the Pendleton Act of 1883 and the Hatch Act of 1939. The Pendleton Act has been hailed as the first pronouncement on the neutrality of public service in the United States. The most important development under this legislation was the establishment of the semi-independent civil service commission, which was to serve on the question of the merit system. In 1939 the Hatch Act came as an answer to the incomplete civil service reform inaugurated with the Pendleton Act. The Hatch Act prohibited federal employees from taking part in any political activity. It prohibited employees from soliciting funds for political purposes, participating in campaign activities and seeking political candidacy.

Waldo wrote about a "reform" movement starting with the civil war and which continued until the period he was writing...the 1940s. The reform literature that came out of this movement stressed merit or training in place of party allegiance as the basis of selection for administrative positions. Superimposed upon this reform movement was the personnel movement which was a combination of what constituted the original reformist sentiment, personnel management ideas and techniques drawn from business administration and ideas such as professionalism and equalitarianism. As Waldo points out, "professionalism was becoming a prominent characteristic of American life, and specialization a key to prestige."[5]

Essential to the personnel movement was the training movement devoted to the development of training programmes for government employees. Stimulation for training of administrators came from industrialization, urbanization and the demand for professionalization of public administration. The scientific or "positivist" mood of the times also provided impetus to the concept of training. Established in 1906 the Bureau of

Municipal Research marked the beginning of the research movement that would have a tremendous impact on the history of public administration in the United States as personnel trained by the Bureau moved into positions throughout the country.[6] The natural outcome of all these movements was the "Administrative Reorganization Movement" which produced its own distinct literature.

Waldo highlighted the similarities between the scientific management movement and the public administration movement. They were driven by the same positivistic spirit with scientific management contributing many techniques to public administration. The administrative science movement provides ample testimony for the wide-ranging impact of Taylorism on the students of public administration. Thus, Public Administration came to share many common ancestors with business administration. Waldo also documented the influence of business on the development of public administration. Woodrow Wilson as early as in 1887 had envisioned a business like role for public administration. He provided a clue for later writers, observed Waldo.[7]

The 1930s produced works on the "principles" of public administration by scholars such as Luther Gulick and Lyndall Urwick which were published as papers on the science of administration in 1937. These principles of public administration spelled out the hierarchical functioning of the organization; the distinction and relationship between line and staff agencies; the functions of an executive and mechanisms for achieving coordination. The term POSTCORB was coined to describe the work of the Chief Executive. It stood for planning, organizing, staffing, directing, co-ordination, reporting and budgeting.

Economy and efficiency were the two predominant values inspiring administrative theory. "For 'economy and efficiency' have inspired reformer and researcher, teacher and student. They have often been held to be the ultimate administrative values, serving to unify and direct all inquiry".[8]

Another important development that had an impact on public administration was the behavioural movement. However, behaviouralism affected the main field and sub-field in different ways. Behaviouralism helped conceptualise rational behaviour for the main field whereas it explained irrational behaviour for the sub-field. Simon's administrative Behaviour described decision-making in America, again, in the context of rational choice, whereas Riggs wrote about prismatic behaviour in the developing bureaucracies. The main field and sub-field dealt with different levels of development and with behaviour in two entirely different contexts.

Public Administration in Developing Countries: Relationship between the Main field and Sub-field

American public administration as a field of inquiry had already passed through several stages of development when it was called upon to design its sub-field comparative and development administration. Historical developments on the world scene as mentioned earlier, called upon American public administration to contribute an important component of the development paradigm—the administrative vehicle for ushering in development. The important questions American public administration theorists asked themselves were: what are the characteristics of transitional societies? How do they impact on public administration systems in such societies? They argued that the conceptual framework had to be developed first in order to assess the requirements of development administration. Also the conceptual framework had to be relevant to the transitional situation. This basically led them to look for models that dealt with traditional societies. It was generally argued that the multi-dimensional nature of these societies defied a clear-cut demarcation between the social, political and economic spheres of activity. This perhaps explains why comparative and development administration had more in common with development theories...social, political and economic...than with its parent field American public administration. Schaffer highlights the difference between the "public administration movement" and the "development administration movement." The "public administration movement' as inaugurated by Woodraw Wilson defined public administration as a practical science. The "development administration movement" on the other hand ignored research, which actually was very relevant to its interests.

Whereas the "public administration movement" derived its ideas from scientific management and army reorganization, "development administration movement" got its ideas and motivation from non-administration and anti-administration sources.[9] He found the development administration movement uncritical of the prevailing condition of Western administration and over-critical of traditional administration.

Modernization/development theory conceptualized transitional societies in terms of interrelated social, economic, and political spheres. Hence, what affected the social, political, and economic arenas had a direct bearing on comparative and development administration. In fact, these disciplines were inseparable given the fused environment that characterized transitional societies.

Using sociological concepts, Fred Riggs (1964) developed the theory of the prismatic society to describe the situation in transitional societies where the old and new intermix to produce a complex cultural and administrative system. He argued that, in a transitional society, it is not possible to separate the administrative from the social, political, and economic aspects of society. Only with differentiation would the prismatic society become diffracted like the Western societies.

Perhaps the single most influential factor that dominated development theories was Max Weber's ideal type constructs. Weber's comparative and historical approaches came to have tremendous influence on American social scientists. The translation of Weber's works by American social scientists made his works available to social scientists in the United States as well as other English-speaking countries.

The three authority systems that Weber had outlined—traditional, charismatic, and legal-rational—helped describe and compare conditions in different countries. As Pye (1966) pointed out, Weber's charismatic form of authority added a third category to the otherwise "dichotomous scheme approach" which placed societies in two categories—traditional and modern. Weber's charismatic authority system dealt with a transitional pattern which could be routinized in an anti-authoritarian direction. The transitional society was thus unraveled when Weber identified the charismatic form of authority.[10]

The Prismatic Society

Industria and Agraria described two extreme situations. What happens when the two intermingle became the focus of Riggs's prismatic model. Riggs argued that the "prismatic" society has not only the qualities of the traditional and modern societies, but also when the two intermingle, the result is a complex society. This is visible in its social, political, administrative, and economic aspects.

With the prismatic model Riggs set a new trend of research, a different way of looking at the transitional societies. These transitional societies were the focus of development and modernization research and almost all the developing countries were considered transitional.

Drawing terminology from physics and the analysis of light, Riggs constructed two polar models to represent traditional and modern societies. At one end of the spectrum is the "fused" model, which is structurally as well as functionally highly diffused. The "diffracted" model on the other hand is structurally and functionally specific. The prismatic model represents societies placed between the two poles.[11]

According to Riggs, the prismatic stage of development represented a unique intermix of administrative, political and social elements. The bureaucracy could be analyzed only as part of its socio-economic environment. While the diffraction process has commenced, it remains uncompleted. Riggs asserted: "Ecdnomic behaviour in a prismatic society is also unintelligible without noting its interaction with politics and administration".[12]

The key to understanding the administrative system of the prismatic society lies not in merely examining the mixture of modern and traditional institutions. What is more important is the product of the mixture, the shape of new administrative structures that are different from both modern and traditional structures.

Riggs labeled the administrative sub-model of the prismatic society as "sala". The essential components of the prismatic society are heterogeneity, formalism, overlapping structures, nepotism, and poly-communalism. All these factors have a direct impact on the sala.

Social, political and economic theories of development shared a common goal—development. This was conceptualized in terms of stages based on what the Western nations had experienced in order to modernize. The role of administration varied with each stage of development, and the social, political and economic theories had their own set of expectations from the bureaucracy.

The development package was full of contradictions. On the one hand, the conceptual framework belonged to a different period whereas the tools that were to be transferred came from the business civilization which was part of the American culture specific public administration. The general consensus of Comparative Administration Group (CAG) scholars such as Riggs (1964), Weidner (1964), Gant (1979), and Siffin (1976) among others, were that the developing countries had not reached the stage where they could use the techniques developed in the West. As a result the development administration package reflected the skepticism of CAG scholars. The idea of transferring advanced technology driven by a philosophy and culture of efficiency and rationality appeared ill suited for the developing societies. What worked in a developed country could not be applied in an emerging situation, most CAG scholars argued. What would be more useful was to reflect on their own past so that the stages through which the Western societies had passed in their quest toward development could be anticipated and planned for the newly emerging independent countries of Asia and Africa.

Opinion converged on the view that development is a long, drawn out, gradual process and that the key to understanding this process did not rest with one discipline alone. The result was a multi-disciplinary development paradigm, a worldview shared across disciplines.

Perhaps it was for this reason that when development programmes aimed at poverty alleviation were launched in the United States in the mid 1960s, the model designed for the developing countries was not explored for application in the United States. The new public administration theorists were quick to point this out.

The New Public Administration Movement

The question of how comparative and development administration could be re-energized was the concern of yet another intellectual enterprise which went by the name "New Public Administration'. In the late 1960s and 1970s when comparative and development administration was being scrutinized, its parent field American Public administration was facing rougher weather. Serious doubts were being aired regarding its relevance. The New Public Administration grew out of this concern. Central to the New Public Administration and the "counter culture" it came to represent were the issues of equity, a client centered approach and humanizing public administration.

The "New Public Administration" scholars such as Henderson (1971) and Jowitt (1971) were firmly convinced that comparative and development administration was in a position to invigorate its parent field American Public administration. American public administration, Henderson argued, could gain by tapping the vast reservoir of talent available with the CAG for solving the problems of cities and developing areas within the United States. According to Jowitt the works of scholars such as Riggs have relevance to the conditions prevailing in America.

Henderson among others utilised the intellectual rigor as well as the theoretical and methodological sophistication of comparative and development administration. Whereas American public administration was non-comparative and culture-bound, comparative administration engaged in comparative and cross-cultural insights. American public administration was highly practitioner-oriented and avoided theory whereas comparative administration was theory driven. More than any other sub-field comparative administration could invigorate public administration was Henderson's firm belief. He predicted that, "comparative public administration would assume intellectual leadership of the field, extending its concerns into 'United States Culture' public administration".[13] Similar views had earlier been voiced by Riggs (1976) and Waldo (1976).

Jowitt observed that the body of theoretical statements that came out from the works of scholars such as Riggs has great practical significance to the political-administrative conditions prevailing in America. He notes that American administratiOn theorists as well as practitioners lack conceptualization skills which are all the more important given the crisis in the United States.[14]

The pertinent question to be asked is whether comparisons

are possible between situations that were treated as basically different. Issues associated with the politics-administration dichotomy, the concept of rationality and the problems of poverty in developing countries were believed to have their origin in fused structures, undifferentiated norms, values and orientations. These very questions distinguished the developed from the underdeveloped. Under these circumstances, how could the conceptual framework developed for the underdeveloped be relevant to American Public administration?

Riggs pointed out that American public administration remained parochial by failing to take note of developments in other parts of the world.[15] His later writings provide an explanation for this attitude. He wrote: "now it so happened that in the 1950's and 1960's in the Western world there was a complacent sense of self-satisfaction, a belief that we had arrived in the US and England and France and other Western countries at some kind of developmental plateau".[16] We need to interpret the aloofness of American public administration in the light of the above statement of Riggs. The answer to why a common framework for dealing with the global problems of development has eluded public administration could be found here. The convergence of the parent field and the sub-field on development remains elusive.

Public administration for the transitional societies and its export package from the very outset was plagued with contradictions. First, rational tools and techniques for enhancing and promoting rationality had been developed by the master discipline to meet the efficiency standards of American society. They were then transferred to the developing nations. Second, development theories—social, political and economic pointed to the undifferentiated nature of transitional societies and implied that these societies were not ready for rational tools and techniques. The inevitable failure of rational tools and techniques in an undifferentiated society served as a convenient explanation for the failure of development programmes.

The major items in the technical assistance programme in public administration created for export to the developing nations were concentrated in the areas of Budgeting, Organization and Methods (O&M), Personnel Administration and Executive Development. Much of the technical assistance programme in public administration came to be placed under the title of development administration.

The 1950s and 1960s saw the establishment, with the help of Ford Foundation grants, of institutes of public administration in the developing countries. These institutes were set up to train civil servants for the ever expanding bureaucracies. They were designed to play a central role in the dissemination of information. This was to be done through training programmes, conferences, seminars and publication of journals such as the Indian Journal of Public Administration and the Philippine Journal of Public Administration.

Implications of Two Separate Paradigms

The two separate paradigms—one for the Advanced West and the other for developing countries has had serious implications on the teaching of public administration in the developing countries. Successive generation of teachers have struggled to teach a discipline whose tools and techniques were at variance with its conceptual framework.

The question whether Western innovations can be transferred to the developing countries continues to be raised. The New Public Management movement is the latest to raise the issue of transferability of Western innovations, this time from the United Kingdom.[17] It may perhaps be argued that these apprehensions arise mainly on account of the insecurity of the Main field American public administration which has failed to overcome its own intellectual crises on account of a porous boundary.

In Search of a Core?

Bureaucracy has over the years vied for the core place in the discipline. Public administration literature grew around the role of bureaucracy in both policy formulation and implementation. Decision-making theories revolved around the bureaucracy and the myriad characteristics that were associated with them. However, with liberalisation and globalisation, the role of bureaucracy as the central actor is diminishing. The growing emphasis on downsizing of bureaucracy further reduces its role. The core issues may include the role of public administration as regulator, design and management of contracts, social welfare administration, implementation and evaluation theory and practice.

Public administrationists, the world over need to wake up to some hard realities. The inroads that business administration is making in what was traditionally considered the domain of public administration is sufficient cause for this wake up call. Business administration continues to march ahead co-opting the different regions of the world whereas public administration continues to look inwards. In fact, public administration faces the danger of getting engulfed by business administration. The rise in the public service MBA programmes bears ample testimony to the dangers that lie ahead. Public administration has always looked to Business administration for rational tools and techniques to be applied in public administration. However, its earlier fascination was with techniques of business administration, which now extends to business philosophy as well. This is not to suggest that public administration lived up to its ideals but at the same time it cannot be denied that its mission and vision were different from and more broader than that of business administration. Thus, the blurring of boundaries between public and business administration undermines the importance of public administration as a field of inquiry.

REFERENCES

1. Fred W. Riggs, "The Group and the Movement: Notes on Comparative and Development Administration," *Public Administration Review,* Washington, DC: American Society for Public Administration, 1976, p. 652.
2. Dwight Waldo, *The Enterprise of Public Administration: A summary View,* Novato, CA: Chandler & Sharp Publishers, Inc., 1981, p. 134.
3. Joseph LaPalombara (ed), *Bureaucracy and Political Development,* Princetton, NJ: Princeton University, Press, 1963, pp. 3-33.
4. Woodraw Wilson, "The Study of Administration", *Political Science Quarterly,* New York: Academy of Political Science,1887, pp. 197-222.
5. Dwight Waldo, *The Administrative State: A Study of the Political Theory of American Public Administration,* New York: The Ronald Press Company, 1948, p. 29.
6. *Ibid.*, pp. 31-32.

7. *Ibid.*
8. *Ibid.*, p. 192.
9. Bernard B. Schaffer, "The Deadlock in Development Administration," In Colin Leys (ed), *Politics and Change in Developing Countries, Cambridge*: Cambridge University Press, 1969, pp. 177-211.
10. Lucian Pye, *Politics, Personality, and Nation Building: Burma's Search for Identity*, New Haven, CT: Yale University Press, 1962, p. 35.
11. Fred, W. Riggs, *Administration in Developing Countries: The Theory of Prismatic Society, Boston*: Houghton Mifflin Co. 1964.
12. *Ibid.*, p. 28.
13. Keith, M. Henderson, *"A New Comparative Public Administration?" In Frank Marini (ed) Toward a New Public Administration: The Minnowbrook Perspective*, New York: Chandler Publishing Company, 1971, p. 245.
14. Kenneth Jowitt, "Comment: The Relevance of Comparative Public Administration", In Frank Marini *(ed), Toward a New Public Administration: The Minnowbrook Perspective*, New York: Chandler Publishing Company, 1971, pp. 250-260.
15. Fred W. Riggs, "The Ecology of Development", In Fred W. Riggs and Daya Krishna, *Development Debate*, Jaipur: Printwell Publishers, 1987, pp. 1-29.
16. *Ibid.*, p. 36.
17. See, Nick Manning, "The Legacy of the New Public Management in Developing Countries", *International Review of Administrative Sciences*, London: Sage Publications, 2001, pp. 297-312.

3

Public Administration in 21st Century

Dr. V. Bhaskara Rao

In the context of Independence, the constitution, and democracy public administration in India as an instrument of action, as a profession is only half-a-century old. Prior to independence, there might have been good/ efficient administration under kings and the colonial rule. But that cannot be considered public administration because it was never 'of' the 'public' nor 'by' the 'public'. 'Public' administration cam into existence in India only with the establishment of the democratic polity under the constitutional directives. Hence, public administration in India owes its allegiance to the constitution. Its first and the last duty is to translate the objectives of the constitutions *i.e.*, the public law. The constitution of India in its preamble resolved to secure to all Indian citizens 'equality of status and opportunity'. It also aims at achieving 'socio-economic transformation within the framework of a free society'. The constitution prevents discrimination on the grounds of religion, race, caste, sex and place of birth. It created provisions for the protection of SCs, STs and other weaker sections of society to ensure social, economic and political justice. Therefore, socio-economic transformation is considered the most important task to ensure social, and economic justice to the masses. This will continue to be the duty and the responsibility of public administration in India even in 21st century.

"Public" Administration in India, in a way is the product of the constitutions framed under the influence and impact of post-second world war ideals of democracy, welfare state, and socialist planning under the leadership of freedom fighters. That world scene has now almost vanished as the ideals of welfare state, and social planning are being given up. The leadership of those freedom fighters who attempted to build a nation of socialist pattern of society, and secular state are now denigrated by the present leaders under the influence of New World Order and the impact of Liberalization, Privatisation and Globalization (LPG). Infact, both before and after independence, external factors have shaped much of the destiny of Public Administration in India. Therefore, in the last decade of 20th Century, the State in India, 40 years after its emergence nearly took a 'U' turn to fall inline with the global capitalism, a world-wide trend. Therefore, it is necessary to reassess the role and functions of Public Administration in India in the contemporary setting. In the new context, the state intervention in economic activity is not justified as the will of politics. All the changes through Structural Adjustment Programme have been introduced without making amendments to the constitution and enacting new legislation. Thus, public administration today in India is pushed out of economic activity of commanding heights by a political decision on New Economic Policy, 1991. The rainbow coalition government at the Centre, and the rudderless regional political party governments in different states are pursuing their 'own' brand of public administration.

During the last fifty years, in general, public administration in India, responded only when it was pressurized through organized agitations, movements and revolts. For, democratization, decentralization, participation, joint consultation, collective bargaining, and egalitarianism are not much palatable to the Indian Public Administrative System (Bhaskara Rao, 1989). The fact of exploitations, economic inequalities, social oppression, and political servitude of people explain the nature of public administration and political system in India (Moin Sakir, 1986).

The Present Scene

In the light of the past events and the current trends, it is intended here to make some exercise in projections rather than predicting the future of public administration in India in 1st Century. Under the present perspective, the meaning, nature, functions, role, and scope of the State is called upon to change. It is imperative for public administration as an instrument of action of the state to change as per the directions of the changing state and its politics. In a federal state like India the sovereignty of the state is vested in the constitution. The protection of the constitution is the duty of the legislature and judiciary, but the executive governments at the centre and the states have been tampering with the provisions of the constitution without consulting the legislature and not considering the judicial pronouncements. Public Administration as an executive agency has to follow the policies, programmes and activities of the governments at its level.

The present trends fully confirm the declining role of the State and the aggressive assertion of the Market. This leads to the 'decay' of public administration. During 80s and 90s a strong public opinion was mobilized that public administration can no longer be the agent of economic growth and development. It may be true, that public administration failed to play a welfare and transformative role envisaged by constitution. But, the fact is, it became ineffective only at the behest of the private interests played against the public interest. Public administration succumbed to the political game. Politics and bureaucracy and their nexus could successfully fail the public policy and its implementation. Corruption has been rampant in every walk of life. People, their representatives (elected), the bureaucracy and everyone was made to believe that public administration in India can not deliver the goods and services, and the objectives of the constitution like welfare state, secularism, etc. cannot be achieved under the direction of democratic socialism and planning.

The constitution also created certain institutions to protect and safeguard some of its essential features, like the independent judiciary, Comptroller and Auditor General, Election Commission, Union/State Public Service Commissions, Finance Commission. SC/ST Commission. The Government established other institutions like Vigilance Commission, Central Bureau of Investigation, Lok Ayuktas, autonomous universities, public sector enterprises, nationalized banks, cooperative sector, and panchayati raj. Many such institutions had to crumble under the misdirection of the ruling class and the bureaucracy for their self interests. Problems like poverty, unemployment, ill-health, illiteracy, over-population, lack of essential infrastructure facilities, etc. could not be solved, as the public funds went into the pockets of private persons with whom the politicians, and the public administrators shared the loot. Under these precarious conditions, instead of mooting reforms in politics and public administration, economic reforms are introduced under the threat of the external/ world bodies like World Bank/IMF/WTO. Market will perform the developmental tasks. Now that the state has changed its role, the scope of public administration, and the size of the bureaucracy is also reduced to a large extent.

The Future of Public Administration

Peter Self avers social scientists have a poor record over forecasting of the future. This is because of their endemic tendency towards 'trend planning' for simply extra-polating present trends into future. He continues: "At present, social scientists, and economists in particular, foresee little beyond inexorable progress of the capitalist economy, mounting statistics of economic growth and an unbelievable degree of affluence and mobility for the economically successful. The darker side of these forecasts is the fear of the growth of large proletariat of idle, casual or part-time workers suffering impoverishment among plenty, or even the emergence of 0-80 society, the 20 per cent very affluent and the 80 per cent struggling or poor" (Peter Self, 2000).

The status of public administration in 21st century can be better understood, after realizing the present trends in the world. The ruling ideas in the world have become those of 'free markets' and 'political democracy' representing 'individualism' and 'self-interest'. Powerful business and political interests, are currently in ascendency in the modern world. Formal democratic institutions and their actions are made to serve the interest of capitalism rather than democracy. The domination of negative liberalism and the individualist tradition are directed towards the corrupt state. The word 'public' in public administration has become almost a dirty word for many under the ruling market system. The state has almost lost its democratic trust.

The present and future political system can be mended only by collective democratic action, provided defects are clearly exposed. For this, in the foreseeable future the Indian nation state needs to play a key role in political life, devising a more balanced framework for the market and public services. The state has to rehabilitate/reassert its role as provider of public services against the current attack upon public administration. The State, in general has to reclaim its lost role for protecting social and community values.

The future of the State in India would be decided in the initial decades of the 21st century by two options: If it desires to be a positive state, it has to read the pulse of the people carefully and imaginatively adopt the people-oriented policies of development to maintain the social stability and order, and contain the social unrest and discontent. This needs not only keeping its own house *i.e.*, public administration clean and neat, but also regulate effectively the market-centred capitalism permitted by it (the state). The second option is: If the State is forced by its friends and desires to be a negative one, it has to strengthen its coercive apparatus and unleash rein of terror and treat the elementary problems of the people as law and order problems. The symptoms appear to be that the Indian state has already opted the second option/alternative/choice. Hence, the Indian politics/administrative order may well move towards authoritarian and semi-fascist model (Haragoapal, 96).

It is natural for a such a model of state which depends on its coercive apparatus to change its role, image and style of administration. It will strengthen military, para-military and police organs, both at the boarders and in the society. While giving up industry, agriculture, and welfare, it may still talk about relief measures, poverty alleviation, peoples participation, democracy, decentralization, and allocations for the welfare. But in reality as it is not the development agency, it must protect the interests of the market and profit.

India, though became part of "capitalist world system" or "global village", yet it has to understand its own problems, may be in a global perspective, but not knowing itself and its local problems. It is necessary to realize that in the 21st century also, the bureaucracy dominates the polity, because it has been although "semi-powered". Hence, heavy reliance on professionalism cannot be avoided. However, the so called myth of dichotomy between politics and administration and the political neutrality of administration must be erased from its administrative values. For, politics and public administration cannot be separated.

What Should be the Future: Decentralization

The survival of 'public' administration in 21st century depends on the nature and scope of the political system *i.e.*, the sate in India. The state, must be positive and resist the onslaught of the market. For the success of its institutions it must leek the cooperation and support of the 'community', and the civil society. The state must delegate much of its functions like schools, public housing, health etc. to partly autonomous local elected agencies. The functions and responsibilities on 29 plus 18 items stipulated by the 73rd and 74th Amendments to the Constitution respectively must be handed to the local governments along with financial resources and personnel. Thus, democratic decentralization will not only respond to the growing volume of protest but will also satisfy a large extent the local people who are struggling for political power and participation in governance and development. This empowerment of local people will spur the growth of local leadership and enable planning their own areas.

There should be a common interest between the state, governments and the community/civil society organizations for deepening, and strengthening democracy, and promoting the public services, securing peaceful social life, reducing unemployment and preventing violence and crime. The values of democratic decentralization and an active civic spirit can facilitate the achievement of regional economic and social development.

Democratic Reforms

Public administration in India in the 21st Century can be made more effective only by a more active, equal and responsible democracy. This is possible through electoral and democratic reforms. The job of public administration must "begin at the ballot box".

Reforms on the following lines are necessary:

1. The working of democracy should be widespread throughout society.
2. serious and sincere electoral reforms for smooth, fair and fearless conduct of elections.
3. Strong curbs upon political donations, electoral

expenditure, criminalization of politics and use of muscle power.
4. Regulation of the activities of the recognized political parties by a specific law.
5. Small cabinets and more legislative deliberations and controls.
6. Citizens must be able to exercise their democratic rights with clear political support.

If people are to be empowered, the machinery of government must be made subordinate only to properly chosen peoples' leaders, who will then exercise their power, rights and duties in public interest.

Public administration's future must be change-oriented. Politics and administration must gain control over changes in science and technology. Public administration must be forward looking and focus on civic purposes. As civic society is changing, the goals will be dynamic and changing. Public administration has to change to meet the challenges of changing civil society and in turn, public administration also has to provide a direction for changing the society.

No body can set goals for the entire century—it is not possible to visualize, dream, predict, forecast beyond a period of 20 to 30 years. If public administration adopts the LPG model for 21st century, it may not continue after a period of time. On the other hand, if it adopts a people-centred vision, where people flourish based on justice, environmental sustainability and political inclusiveness, it will continue and change according to the needs of the people.

State as organized political community, market as organized economic community, and civil society as organized social community must be interdependent. As the market and civil society in India have not yet been organized effectively, the state has a special responsibility through its governance to maintain proper relations and manage the organized communities (political, economic and social). Public administration in India has to recognize in this context, that it has to involve the state, l market and civil society in a 'collaborative action and maintain balance' between them. The key challenge that has to be met is that the state, the rule of law and governance system actually protect and fulfil the civil and social rights of individuals and all communities alike (Thynne 2000).

It should be recognized that economic prosperity, social welfare and effective governance are interdependent. The importance of good governance will be magnified when the future ushers in greater change in global economies, technology and global threats to national security. Therefore, there is a need for an active and 'stronger' State to manage the interdependencies and interrelationships (strategic alliances and significant partnerships). The state has to achieve collaboration and coordination both horizontally and vertically within and among organizations and associated institutions.

Challenges

Today the market model of government in the form of New Public Management (NPM) is threatening to eliminate democracy as a guiding principle in public administration.

The vexing problems of the 20th century like poverty, poor quality education, and health, inequalities of gender and wealth, crime and violence, destruction of forest, and other natural resources, and pollution of air and water will continue in 21st century for many decades. The problems persist because people lack information, knowledge and political influence, to direct public administrative agencies to solve them (Richard, C. Box *et al.*, 2001). Information Technology, right to information, and transparency efforts may help to some extent.

The people in India have started loosing faith in the government. They are regarding politicians as corrupt and bureaucrats as self-serving and inefficient. For the government is "a matter of invisible negotiations conducted in public offices by public officials, experts and private interests" (King and Silvers, 1988).

Today, it is difficult to predict how the globalization of economies and how the expansion of the market concepts into the public administration will affect democracy and public service. India needs to adopt "strong" democracy *i.e.*, modern form of participatory democracy by self governing community of citizens. Public Administration must be a key actor in any effort to rediscover "substantive democracy" because of the complexity of providing public services in the present society. "Substantive democracy involves rekindling a public discourse about the purposes of collective action, accepting the role of citizens and public administration in shaping the future (Richard, C. Box *et al.*, 2001).

The present "phenomenon of economic imperialism" wherein the citizens are treated as customers, and separating public administrators from the public policy process, convinces that government is nothing more than a business. This poses threat to democratic governance.

The attempts at introducing NPM hinders "substantive democracy" and limits citizen participation in policy and administration. The NPM reforms fail to understand the basic foundation of public administration in a democratic society *i.e.*, what people want from government. The ideas of welfare society, citizenship, public interest, social responsibility and dialogue are treated a anachronistic. Whatever may be, there must be connection between public administration, governance and social life (Richard, C. Box *et al.*, 2001). Public administration is crucial and unavoidable for the social construction of society, for, the State, under the NPM avoids to address the issues that affect the society such as communalism, poverty etc. through substantive democracy.

Today the citizens are distanced from their public-service institutions. Therefore, public administrators and academics should play a part in the recovery of a 'substantive democratic' ideal. Democracy cannot be equated with consumer choice. Public administration does play a role in social order. People in public services not only deliver services but also serve as facilitators, interpreters and mediators of public action.

Public administration must not ignore its normative ground in public law. Customer satisfaction, and services would not serve as an effective proxy for public interest. There is lot of political pressure on public administrators to adopt the NPM's approach. But the NPM displaces the democratic foundation which is essential to public administrative leadership (Terry, 1998).

In the place of old Public Administration and the New Public Management, Robert and Janet Denhardt in their book suggested, the "new public service", for the future to:

— Serve citizens-Not customers,
— Seek the public interest,
— Value citizenship over entrepreneurship,
— Act democratically,
— Recognize that accountability is not simple, and
— Value people-not just productivity,

Now, the normative democratic context of public administration must be reasserted. This context includes achieving a democratic polity (Kirlin 1996). The central element should be a collaborative relationship between citizen and public administration. The citizens have the ability to self-govern. All citizens must be given an opportunity to participate. The emphasis on the collaborative mode is to give citizens the knowledge and techniques they need to deal with public policy issues and provide an open and non-threatening forum for deliberation and decision-making. This model is only one way to enhance substantive democracy. It is a well developed alternative that could be especially useful and powerful (Robert, C. Box, *et al.*, 2001).

"Substantive democracy" emphasizes on social equity and demands changes in the purpose and practice of public administration. It is against the old politics-administration dichotomy. Public officials and the elected representatives who interact with citizens can improve the quality of democracy by actively helping people govern themselves. This requires the courage and goodwill to share rather than control knowledge and administrative processes with the people.

In the twenty-first century, there is much for public administration in democracy to do beyond the mandate of perfecting mechanisms for service delivery. Public administration must have to contribute "for achieving a democratic polity, rising to the societal level; confronting the complexity of instruments of collective action and encouraging more effective societal learning" (Kirlin, 1996).

The British Government in March 1999 published "The Moderninsing Government White Paper". It set out a long-term programme of change for all UK public services. It had three aims: to ensure that policy is more strategic and joined up; to make sure that public services are focused on the needs of users, and to ensure to deliver public services of high quality and efficiency. The reform is based around six key themes: Strong Leadership, Improving business Processes, Performance Management, Improvement in diversity, Open to people and ideas, Better deal for staff (Dawson, 2001 p. 264).

Public Administration in India also should have this kind of long-term programme in 21st Century. This is not possible until a decision has been taken on the role of the state and 'desirable state'. It may be necessary to rebuild the state to create a 'smart government', which will focus on the field of social development in response to the large scale problems of India. The smart government focuses on its strategic roles in society with an institutional design and development of management capacities. It promotes the integration of economic and social development together with substantial improvement in equity. To achieve this, the state will have to take on the task of forging strategic alliances among these forces (Kliksberg, 2000, pp. 247-56).

CONCLUSION

Public Administration in the 21st century may have less scope and importance and its meaning may be changing from time to time but its nature must be oriented towards change, development, policy and welfare. Mobilization and allocation of human and material resources for human welfare must be its ultimate goal. Otherwise the very existence and survival of the democratic state in India will be in peril.

The future is uncertain. But the need for change is certain. The goal of strengthening democracy and democratic public administration can be pursued by political mobilization. The future of India can be helped or hindered by the future politics of India. While the LPG politics are dominating the present scene, it should be possible for piecemeal reforms and see that 'democracy is on the march' and the 'common good' is protected through public administration, in the 21st Century.

REFERENCES

Bhaskara Rao V., 'Colonial Structure, Capitalist Policy, Socialist Slogan, Hindu State: Indian Administration in the Nineteen Eighties', in Bhaskara Rao, V., *Public Administration in India,* Ajanta Publications, New Delhi, 1989.

Bhaskara Rao V., 'Administrative Personnel in India 1979-89', in Pai Panandikar (Ed), *Third Survey of Research in Public Administration,* (ICSSR), Konark Publishers, New Delhi, 1997.

Bhaskara Rao V., 'Liberalization Policy: Need for People Oriented Approach', *Indian Journal of Public Administration,* Vol.XLII, No.3, July-Sept, 1996.

Bhaskara Rao V., 'Paradox of Public Administration in India: Emerging Issues', *Indian Journal of Public Administration,* Vol. XL, No. 3, July-Sept., 1994.

Bhaskara Rao V., 'Re-engineering For Good Governance' in Sahni Pardeep and Uma Medury, *Governance for Development, Issues and Strategies,* Prentice-Hall of India, New Delhi, 2003.

Bhaskara Rao V., 'The New Policies: Some Emerging Challenges in Public Administration in India', in Sahni, Pardeep *et al.* (Eds), *Public Administration: Emerging Perspectives,* Gyan Publishing House, New Delhi, 1999.

Bhaskara Rao V., *'Public Administration'*, Ajanta Publications, New Delhi, 1989.

Box C. Richard *et al.*, 'New Public Management and Substantive Democracy', *Public Administration Review,* Vol. 61, No. 5, Sept./October 2001.

Box, Richard C and Deborah A. Sagan, 'Working with Citizens: Breaking Down Barriers to Citizen Self-governance', in Cheryl S. King and Camilla Stivers (Eds), *Government in US: Public Administration in Anti-Government Era,* Thousand Oaks, Sage, 1998.

Colonel Joseph R. Cerami, Review Essay: Rohr, Frederickson and Wolin on the 'Big Question: And the Future of Public Administration.

Dawson Malcolm, (2001), 'Leadership for 21st Century in the UK Civil Service', *International Review of Administrative Sciences,* Vol. 67.

Election Watch, Lok Satta Times, Vol. IV, No. 1, August, 2003, *Journal of Foundation for Democratic Reforms,* Hyderabad.

Elsenhans, Hertmut, *State, Class and Development,* Radiant Publishers, New Delhi, 1996.

Haragopal, G., 'Governance Through Participative Development: The Role of People's Movement', in Sahni Pardeep and Uma Medury, *Governance For Development: Issues and Strategies,* Prentice-Hall of India, New Delhi, 2003.

Haragopal, G., 'Public Administration in India: Does it Have a Future, in Bharakara Rao V. and A.K. Sharma (Eds), *Public Administration: Quest for Identity,* Vikas Publishing House, New Delhi, 1996.

Jean-Claude Garcia-Zamor and Renu Khator (Eds), *Public Administration in the Global Village,* Praeger, London, 1995.

Kettl, Donald F., 'The Global Revolution in Public Management: Driving Themes, Missing Links', *Journal of Policy Analysis and Management*, Vol. 16, No. 3, 1997.

King, Charyl S, and Camilla Stivers, *Government in US: Public Administration in an Anti Government Era*, Thousand Oaks, Sage Publications, 1998.

Kirlin J. John, 'The Big Questions of Public Administration in a Democracy', *Public Administration Review*, Vol. 56, No. 5, Sept./ October 1996.

Kliksberg, Bernando, 'Rebuilding the State for Social Development: Towards 'Smart Government', *International Review of Administrative Sciences*, Vol. 66, 2000.

Kothari, Rajni, *State Against Democracy: In Search of Humane Governance*, Ajanta Publications, Delhi 1988.

Kumar, Vijay, 'Re-engineering Indian Bureaucracy to meet the 21st Century Challenges', in Sahni Pardeep and Uma Medury, *Governance for Development: Issues and Strategies*, Prentice-Hall of India, New Delhi, 2003.

Maheshwari, B.L., 'Restructuring of Public Administration in South Asia: An Organization Development Approach', *South Asian Journal of Management*, January-March, 1995.

Moe, Ronald C, and Robert S. Gilmour, 'Rediscovering Principles of Public Administration: The Neglected Foundation of Public Law', *Public Administration Review*, Vol. 55, No. 2, 1995.

Pandey G., 'Future Public Administration in India: Some Projections and Suggestions', in Bhaskara Rao V, and A.K. Sharma (Eds), *Public Administration: Quest for Identity*, Vikas, New Delhi, 1996.

Prasad, R.N., *Governance of India: Issues and Perspectives*, Concept Publishing Company, New Delhi, 2002.

Sahni, Pardeep and Uma Medury, *Governance for Development: Issues and Strategies*, Prentice Hall of India, New Delhi, 2003.

Sakir, Moin, *State and Politics in Contemporary India*, Ajanta Publications, New Delhi, 1986.

Self, Peter, *Rolling Back the Market: Economic Dogma and Political Choice:* Mac Millan Press, London, 2000.

Terry, Larry D., 'Administrative Leadership, Neo-Managerialism and the Public Management Movement', *Public Administration Review*, Vol. 58, No. 3, 1998.

Thynne, Ian, 'The State and Governance: Issue and Challenges in Perspective', *International Review of Administrative Sciences*, Vol. 66, 2000.

4

Civil Service Reforms: An Agenda for 21st Century

Prof. Harbans Pathak

India, along with the rest of the world has entered into twenty-first century. But a moot question that should be asked in this context is: Has a proper preparation to face the incoming mighty challenges of Twenty-first Century taken place?

In my perception a totally new perspective, new thinking and new action programme are the essentials for this entry if it is to mean more than a mere count of dates in the calendar. Old hackneyed ideas of men and matters have to yield to new dynamism that should inform the new century and if one does not adjust to this, he will be left behind in the garbage bin of history. Therefore, the 21st century spells new challenges in the wake of globalization and liberalization-the terms which have acquired such currency within a short period.[1]

Process of Globalization

The economic LPG-Liberalization, Privatization and Globalization has been prescribed by the triumvirate international institutions-IMF, World Bank and the WTO, to all developing countries as a panacea for their speedy development. India cannot isolate itself from the world economy and, whether we like it or not, globalization will overtake us.

The forces of LPG and the revolution of information technology have shattered many a myth hitherto held sacrosanct about the government and more specifically concerning its primary institution of government and more specifically concerning its primary Institution of government and more specifically concerning its primary institution of governance-the public administration. No longer can governments afford to support rigid, bureaucratic, reactive, rules-driven administrative organizations. Rather today's administrative system must be flexible, consultative, result-oriented and pro-active-encouraging and supporting creativity and innovation from the bottom to the top in order to govern and provide services to the citizens at large.

Civil Services Reforms: Some Concerns

Civil Service constitutes the backbone of Public administrative system and its sub-systems. Since it provides consistency and continuity in administration, it is as important today as it was in the last century. Its importance should not diminish in the 21st century. The nation has a vital interest in preserving the image of its civil servants. The importance of the values of independence, efficiency, integrity, impartiality, objectivity and accountability is rooted in the characteristics of the tasks which the civil service is called upon to perform.[2] These values are as important to good government in the future as they have been in the past. It is, therefore, not only desirable but most essential that the general confidence of the citizenry in the civil service should not get impaired. In recent years, the political milieu in countries has tended to erode the qualities of independent thinking and expression of free, frank and fair views by civil servants. In addition, it is often asserted that the civil servants are rule-bound and obstructive. Such criticism and condemnation may be turned into potential points of strength in a system of the government under the law. By virtue of being rule-bound, it may function impartially, even-handedly and can resist political pressure. Unfortunately, the weakness has been exploited and the strength has been eroded.[3]

Civil service reforms are all the more important in the context of the adoption of policy of free market economy in the 1980's in UK and other Western countries and in the 90's in India. It is also known by different names viz. New Economic Policy, Structural Adjustment Programme, Privatization, Liberalization, deregulation and contracting out. The impact of free-market economy on the concept of government, structure of government and also, the way of governance are on the agenda of discussion world over. It is based on the perception that private is good and public is bad. The consequences of free market reforms on government and governmental business are generally described as the new way of governance,[4] government by the market,[5] reinventing government,[6] new public management,[7] sharing power,[8] slimming of State,[9] hollowing out of State,[10] really reinventing government,[11] and so on.

The Supreme Court judgment (2000) upholding the right of the government to deny two years extension of service to a civil judge in Orissa was in line with the earlier rulings of the apex court on the subject, which permitted the government to compulsorily retire employees after a review of their service records at the age ranging between 50 and 55 years. However, such powers were rarely exercised. The court also questioned the sense of security of service, which government servants cherish, and assume it to be a sacrosanct right, ignoring the fact that the founding fathers of our Constitution introduced Articles 309 to 312 to ensure that civil servants perform their duties without fear or favour.

On June 27, 2000 there was a very interesting discussion on a TV channel about the impact of the Supreme Court judgment on the security of service of civil servants. It was a pleasant surprise to hear the views of Mr. Munni Lal, Minister of State for Labour, who stated that 40 to 45 per cent Central employees were non-performers due to the sense of job security, and that he was in favour of the hire and fire policy as practiced in the private sector which ensured performance and the meeting of targets. Mr. Kutty, who represented the Confederation of Central Government Employees in the TV discussion, naturally, opposed such a view and said that within the framework of the existing Civil Services Conduct Rules errant civil servants could be booked for misconduct under the existing rules.

The issue being discussed was not misconduct, but non-performance and the work culture among government employees. They enjoy 104 holidays on Saturdays and Sundays, 16 gazetted holidays, 30 days' earned leave, 10 days' casual leave and another 10 days' sick leave, thus making a total of 170 days' holidays in a year. Their productivity and output on the days they are supposed to work is well known to the public.

The suggestion given by the apex court is about making the regulations under which only those civil servants whose skills and demonstrated performances match the needs of a modern civil service are retained in service. Is the government obliged to spend a major portion of public funds to keep millions of public servants on the rolls up to the age of superannuation when the nation cannot afford this colossal waste of the tax-payers' money? The civil servants have assumed the divine role of ruling the masses in a manner which even the British colonialists would not have dared. At least during the pre-Independence era even senior-most ICS officers, while replying to a letter or representation of even an ordinary citizen, would end the letter with the salutation, "I beg to remain, sir, your most obedient servant."

A large number of government jobs were wrongly created as a means to combat the problem of unemployment. The proliferation of government agencies and the creation of a large number of public enterprises, particularly in the states, were used as tools for extending patronage and for accommodating senior bureaucrats in ex-cadre posts which rightly should have been manned by professionals. Besides locking thousands of crores of rupees in unprofitable ventures, the government work culture was extended to public enterprises where the security of service is the only consideration. Even when state enterprises are being privatized the new owners have been asked to retain the existing work force as a precondition for the sale.

The British tradition of civil service neutrality had been adhered to for many years in India even after Independence. However, during the 1975 Emergency civil servants crawled and even the judiciary cowed down at the dictates of politicians and extra-constitutional authorities. After that there has been a continuous erosion of ethical standards. So there is a need to depoliticise Civil Services.[12] The politicians who have become the favourite targets of blame for this state of affairs are at least accountable and rejected by the voters and thrown into political wilderness for a few years. Has a single civil servant been made accountable and removed from service for inefficiency on for gross errors of judgements?

It is a sad fact that a vast majority of senior government

servants have failed to maintain a high degree of integrity and dedication to service expected of them. Even those who are honest have become subservient and lack the moral fibre and courage to resist when their superiors or even juniors act against public interest. At the other end of the spectrum are multitudes of junior governments employees who are given low-end responsibilities but are in a position to harass ordinary citizen as they are the ones who come into contact with them. Many government officials admit this state of affairs but declare that they are a part of a system which they can not change. They blame the politicians, staff unions and everybody else, totally ignoring the fact that as senior and responsible officers they have been ignoring the fact that as senior and responsible officers they have been vested with adequate powers but have abdicated their authority to enforce discipline in the offices which they headed.

The fact that a significant number of civil servants are recruited and subsequently promoted not on the basis of merit but on consideration of caste has certainly diluted the standards of the civil services. The nation had by and large accepted such a consideration for the scheduled castes whose forefather had suffered for centuries, but to extend such benefits (reservations) to other castes is nothing but a political ploy to create vote banks. The constitutional safeguard that such reservation should not be detrimental to administrative efficiency has been ignored.

A high level of ethical and oral standards practiced by our leaders who were in the forefront of the freedom struggle ceased to motivate the emerging political leadership which used political power for personal ends. In the initial years the civil services resisted them, but gradually they too succumbed to temptation and corruption crept into the government both at the level of petty officials and the senior civil servants to form a strong nexus. In such a system can senior officers afford to take action against anyone? So the principle of "live and let live" is the one which is being followed.

The system of selection followed for the recruitment in civil services gives weightage only to academic excellence. The other essential attributes like effective and practical intelligence, leadership qualities like decisiveness, ability to influence groups, integrity, moral and physical courage, dynamic qualities like determination, ability to withstand stress and strains both physical and mental and, above all, a deep sense of patriotism beyond narrow considerations of caste, religion and place of birth are ignored. It is a fact that the Union or State Public Service Commissions or Staff Selection Commissions neither have the capability of determining such attributes not the present system demands such assessments. After passing through the prescribed written tests, professionally trained selectors should be given the task of testing the candidates for such qualities before the final viva voce is conducted as the final selection point. As was the past practice, equal weightage should be given to the marks obtained in the written tests and personality evaluation for final selection. This system will entail additional costs, which can be offset by rightsizing the numbers of civil servants.

The duration of practical training attachment of All-India and Central services probationers must be increased considerably. At present the subordinate staff are put straight on the job and subsequently deputed to attend ill-designed training programmes in the training institutions which neither have adequate infrastructure nor the faculty to conduct proper training. In many cases, training institutes are used as dumping grounds for officials to cool their heels. Civil servants must be required to pass promotion tests for the first two promotions to ensure that they keep themselves updated professionally. For selection to higher posts, training programmes should be designed for preparing them for bigger responsibilities.

The inter-service rivalry within the civil services is also responsible for many of the ills. The other service have not yet accepted the supremacy of the IAS which controls every aspect of governance. While there is no doubt that those who join the IAS are higher in the order of merit compared to the other candidates allocated to other services. Whether such a halo effect should continue throughout their career is debatable. Heads of departments from the other services have been subordinated to IAS officers. There has to be a clear distinction between the staff function that an Ias officer is supposed to perform in the Central Secretariat and the line function, which is in the domain of the Heads of departments to other services.

In many cases, comparatively inexperienced officers have been given authority and responsibility beyond their capabilities. Senior and more experienced officers from the state services usually find themselves relegated to insignificant slots, and they are highly resentful of the all-India services officers. The position of the District Collector, which is the most crucial post, must be manned by senior IAS officers by upgrading the post and downgrading numerous posts in the Secretariat which are staff appointments. Before being posted District Collectors they should do at least two tenures as Sub-Divisional Officers.

Officers must be given at least a three-year tenure in a post instead of the present practice of frequent transfer. All senior officers must be away from their headquarters on tour for at least 15 days in a month. They must visit remote areas and meet the public to attend to their problems on the spot. Management by walking is the best method to assess the ground realities. Technocrats, as Heads of departments must be given the necessary authority to run their departments without interference and thereafter held accountable.

The question of downsizing the civil services must come into the open. It is an inevitable national need. Then, why not take the bull by the horn and devise a time-bound plan of action instead of beating about the bush. In the meanwhile, an example must be shown at the top by reducing the size of the Council of Ministers, both at the Centre and in the states, by 33 per cent. Similarly, 33 per cent posts at the level of Secretary and equivalent at the Centre and in the states must be abolished. All new designations like Director-General of Police, Chief Accountant-General, Chief Controller-General and Engineer-in-Chief created during the last decade must be abolished. The law and order situation was much better when there was only one Inspector-General of Police, a few DIGs and district SPs. There used to be only one Chief Secretary, a few Divisional Commissioners and District Collectors. The civil servants commanded more respect from the public as well as from politicians.

The salaries of senior civil servants could be increased to bring them on a par with that of the corporate sector but all the hidden perks must be abolished. Ministers, MPs and MLAs also should be given better salaries which should be transparent. But all perks which cannot be quantified must be abolished. The blatant misuse of government resources like housing, cars and telephones by ministers and civil servants must be stopped. The correct example at the top will give a loud and clear message down the line.

The masses are fed up with the attitude and the work culture of the government. Insurgency throughout the world has its origin in mismanagement by organs of the State. There is simmering discontent among the public. Many are more concerned with good governance rather than the forms of government. If things don't improve the public may take the law into its own hands, or, there can be a mass movement of civil disobedience on the lines advocated by Gandhiji against a colonial power. Now such agitations will not be controlled by Gandhians but by criminals and anti-social elements posing as Robinhoods to create chaos and anarchy which the civil administration may find difficult to handle. The other frightful alternative is the possibility of the emergence of a benevolent dictatorship which may assume legality under a new phrase, "doctrine of necessity". We have not reached the point of no return. If we cherish democracy, ethical governance and human rights, then as responsible citizens let us all ponder over the gravity of the situation and do our little bit to preserve our freedom and democratic values.

New Outlook

Marked changes in India with a new outlook in the direction of market friendly economy demand the administration including economic planning "to respond and adjust to the changes quickly and creatively to the market economy" "without tearing out socio-cultural fabric".[13] Till the beginning of 1990s essentially Indian socio-economic policy had been anti-market and greater emphasis used to be laid on justice and development. Following the Nehru-Mahalanobis strategy of development which equated development with industrilisation and modernization of the Western variety, desired results did not take place. As a result of rapid industrialization, it was expected that traditional forces and barriers of society would be gradually weakened; this would redistribute power leading to wider participation of the people ushering in political democratization under a 'developmentalist State'.[14] Unfortunately, this gradually resulted in a system of controls which C. Raja Gopalachari described as the 'Licence-Quota-Permit Raj' manifesting thereby the Leviathan hypothesis that when there is scope for government intervention it tends to grow. The growth of civil service in India can be traced to this phenomenon.

The capacity of the governments to discharge their burgeoning responsibilities has significantly declined which is now amply demonstrated by the tardy progress or failure of government programmes. Let us do no more than spending the next few years in honestly and assiduously restoring the essentials of governance.[15] Towards this end, it would be necessary to launch all necessary initiatives to start tackling the ailments of our polity which have already infected our society and denigrated governance and to introduce civil service reforms in order to check the decline of civil service.[16] The rising demands made on governments, vast role of the government in the economy and the society and increasing complexity of the tasks involved create 'overload' of demands on the decision-making bodies. In brief, as the modern State is loaded with more decision-making authority the more helpless it becomes. This has consequential effect on the imbalance between government commitment and government resources. The 'government overload' thesis strongly advocates shedding of government responsibility and welcomes a fresh look at the role of the State. The functions of the State, to quote Pandey, (1992)[17] are SEEDS *i.e.* 'Security, Equity, Ecology, Development and Safety'. Excepting 'Development' others are interwoven with the provision of stability. The State has to balance among these functions so as to combine stability with growth. In short, the State's role is precisely holistic and integrative. Rolling back of the State on the economic front underscores the need for its new role and re-examination of structures and procedures built up during the last few decades. Further, the State has to remain concerned with 'Development Dynamics' as catalytic agent of change. "The administrative machinery, men, work methods and processes have to be adjusted and conditioned so as to encourage privatisation, proper participation and incrementalism with flexible goals and ability to shift directions."[18]

The new approach appears to provide an alternative model to the panoply of problems arising out of administered development through 'de-administered' development. The model provides: (*a*) the bloated parastatals once deemed as administrative innovations are to be privatized because "over the years they have proven to be a bastion of patronage",[19] (*b*) varying sizes of government departments require down sizing and reorganization. In the 21st century civil servants at all levels hopefully should be fewer compared to the situation in 1980s. They should be better trained, more professionally-oriented, more aware of the world at large, more ethical, more productive and perhaps more humble.

REFERENCES

1. E.H. Valson, "Ringing out Rigidities," Special Onam Supplement. Indian Express, Kochi, September 1997, p. 2.
2. U.K., *The Civil Service: Taking Forward, Continuity and Change London*, Cm 2748 HMSO, 1995.
3. M.N. Buch, "Bondage of Bureaucracy", *The Hindustan Times*, February 10, 1996.
4. Australia, *The Changing Role of Government: Administrative Structure and Reforms-Proceedings of Commonwealth Roundtable*, Sydney, Australia, 24-28 February, 1992.
5. Peter Self, *Government by the Market?*, London (U.S.), West View Press, 1993.
6. David Osborne and Ted Gabler, *Reinventing Government*, Addison-Wesley, *1992;* Norman Lewis, "How to Reinvent British Government", London, European Policy Forum, May 1993; also Ronald C. Moe, "The Reinventing Government Exercise: Misinterpreting the Problem, Misjudging the Consequences", *Public Administration Review*, Vol. 43, No.2 (March-April, 1994), pp. 111-22.
7. Norman Lewis, "Reviewing Change in Government, New Public Management and Next Steps", *Public Law*, Spring, 1994.
8. Donad F. Ketle, *Sharing Power-Public Governance and Private Market*, Washington DC, Brookings Institute, 1993.
9. Peter Self, *op. cit.*
10. R.A.W. Rhodes, "The Hollowing Out of the State: The Changing Nature of Public Service in Britain", *The Political Quarterly*, Vol. 65, (April-June), pp. 38-54.
11. Peter F. Drucker, "Really Reinventing Government", *Span*, December, 1995, p. 11.
12. Harbans Pathak and Parul Pathak, "Depoliticise Civil Services: An Agenda for New Millennium", *National Seminar on Public Administration in the new Millennium: Challenges & Prospects*, Department of Public Administration, H.P. University, Shimla, April, 2001.
13. V.M. Dandekar, "Role of Economic Planning in India in 1990s and Beyond," *Economic and Political Weekly*, New Delhi, 11 June, 1994; pp. 1457-64.

14. Sudha Pai, "State, Class and Industrialization in Latin America: The Case of Brazil 1930-1980," *Teaching Politics*, Vol. XVI, (1990) pp. 1-120.
15. O.P. Minocha, Good Governance : Concept and Operational Issues, *Management in Government*, October-December, 1997.
16. Harbans Pathak, The Decline of Civil Service in R.B. Jain (ed.) *"Public Services in a Democratic Context"*, Indian Institute of Public Administration, New Delhi, 1983, pp. 286-291.
17. G. Pandey, "The Future Public Administration in India: Some Projections and Suggestions," paper presented in the National Seminar organized by IIPA, New Delhi, March 27-28, 1992.
18. Marina Pinto, "Challenge of Liberalization to Indian Bureaucracy" in R.B. Jain and Heniz Bongartz (eds.) Structural Adjustment, *Public Policy and Bureaucracy in Developing Societies*, (New Delhi: Har Anand, 1994), p. 321.
19. O.P. Dwivedi, "Structural Adjustment Programmes and Administrative Reforms in the Third World", in *Ibid.*, 358.

CHAPTER II:
New Paradigms in Public Administration

5

Public Administration and Postmodernism

Prof. Noorjahan Bava

What is Postmodernism?

The discipline of Public Administration (PA) has witnessed a paradigm shift in the 1990s from *modernism* to *Postmodernism* (POMO). The new paradigm is at once a model, a method and a movement in that region of the academic world known as social sciences. As a social theory and method POMO seeks to debunk well established categories in the literature on public administration such as bureaucracy, institutions, politics-administration dichotomy, scientific management, hierarchical control and so on. POMO also challenges the intellectual traditions and metanarratives in modern thought such as scientism, monism accompanied by reductionism, logical positivism in philosophy of science, the canons of analytical logic in philosophy, instrumental rationalism, universalism, foundationalism, constitutionalism (liberal, representative democracy within the framework of capitalist, industrial economy based on the fundamental law of the land), communitarianism, materialist dialectic in Marxism, structural-functionalism and systems theory in political science, anthropology, and sociology. In short it stands opposed to modernism and its theories in the social sciences.

Postmodern thinkers date back to Nietzche, American pragmatists John Dewey and Richard Rorty, and poststructuralist French philosophers Derrida, Lyotard, Foucault, Baudrillard and others. They were all skeptical of the typically modern claims towards universalism or essentialism- concepts that are now subsumed under *foundationalism or metanarrative.* Recent POMO theorists in public administration include David John Farmer, McSwite, Steven Seidman, McBeth and Clemons, James Scott, Charles J. Fox and Hugh T. Miller and Frank De Zwart.

Postmodern Movement

Postmodernism, like its rival intellectual cousin, Behaviouralism which, raged in the post World War II era, soon developed into a movement spreading its tentacles to the social sciences in the post-behavioural period. As is evident from the Chart-1.1, POMO has invaded architecture, economics, organization, political science, (Aryeh Botwinick), public administration, sociology, philosophy of science, philosophy, psychology, ethics and communication/ media sciences. In their thought provoking work—*Postmodern Public Administration: Toward Discourse,* Fox and Miller (1996, p. 45) graphically show the general traits of Modern vs. Postmodern cultures as follows:

Chart: 1.1 Pomo Movement in Social Sciences

Problematic	*Modern*	*Postmodern*
• Architecture	Functional, bauhaus	Eclectic, referential
• Mode of production	Mass assembly, factory	Postindustrial, information
• Organization/Pol. Sc./ Public administration	Weberian hierarchy Orthodoxy, Constitutionalism	Adhocracy, devolution Communitarianism, Neoinstutionlism, civil society
• Sociology	Nuclear family	Fragmented households

(*Contd.*)

(*Contd.*)

Problematic	*Modern*	*Postmodern*
• Philosophy of science	Logical positivism	Method. anarchy, interpretivism, Ideography
• Philosophy	Search for universals	Antifoundationalism
• Psychology	Integrated authentic self	Decentered self
• Ethics	Utilitarian, deontological, syllogistic	Situational
• Media	Print linearity	Video, montage, MTV, surfing

Note: Political Science and Public Administration in the chart are added by the author.

Differences between modern and postmodern trends/ tendencies may also be variously expressed as follows: (Fox and Miller, p. 45)

- Integration versus disintegration
- Centralization versus decentralization
- Centripetal versus centrifugal
- Totalization versus fragmentation
- Metanarratives versus disparate texts
- Melting pot versus salad
- Commensurable versus incommensurable
- The impulse to unify versus hyperpluralism
- Universalism versus relativism.

Postmodern Conditions

It is important to note that the distinction modern/postmodern highlights aspects of advanced capitalist societies such as the US, UK, France, Germany, Japan etc. These societies exhibit the following postmodern conditions: Postmodern societies are characterised by many features such as ***epiphenominalism, hyperreality, consumerism, self-referentiality, symbolic politics,***

incommensurability, and decentering self. In postmodern or post industrial societies people experience what is called epiphenomenalism, a situation in which words, signs and symbols have become increasingly divorced from "reality". They are increasingly unlikely to mean anything solid or lasting. Postmodern theory gives interpretive depth to these asocial aspects of language. People become "speechless" by media-induced consumerism, negative political advertisements, and sound-bite. In other words, signs through which the public conversation is communicated, have become self-referential and epiphenomenal (that is derivative or second order). The accompanying danger is that diverse subcultures talk past one another (*i.e.* language games are incommensurable) (Fox and Miller, p. 43).

The growing gap between words and deeds in postmodern societies leads to another strange feature namely ***hyperreality***—the "thinning" of reality into "virtual" reality. POMO societies soon tend to become ***consumerist societies*** because in these advanced industrial societies the emphasis shifts from production to consumption and information. As the viscosity of "reality" thins, it is exacerbated by the bombardment of TV advertisements that inundate consumers and informs and induces them to believe that consumption of goods and services is now vastly more important than production. Side by side another development takes place in these societies- just as Rome was battered and finally destroyed by successive waves of barbarians, so has the foundationalist/modern metanarrative canon been battered by Nietzsche, pragmatists, existentialists, phenomenologists, semioticians, poststructuralists, deconstructivists, hermeneuticists, and more (Fox and Miller, p. 50). These two developments/changes provide the historical conditions for this postmodern hyperreality. Under such conditions epiphenomenal signs rely more on each other, that is they become ***self-referential resulting in symbolic politics.***

The political implications of symbolic politics and hyperreality are many. One, rapid sequence of images and symbols with unknown and uncertain referents racing through the public consciousness results in "simulation and media spectacle displacing political debate". Second, the continuous struggle for meaning capture implies that symbolic politics is, largely divorced from material distribution of wealth and resources, which is an important function of the government. Ensuring distributive justice through such distribution which, is one of the essential tasks of governance thus gets neglected or relegated by the ruling political party in the POMO societies. Third, another implication of simulated and symbolic politics is the emergence of ***monologic communication in the place of communal or dialogical communication*** with loss of ***agonistic tension,*** which is inherent in dialogical communication. Thus inter-subjective social communication (dialogical) that creates "reality" is disrupted in conditions of postmodernity. Fourth, the roots of this disruption may be traced to modernist practices. Hummel (1994) links a monologic communication to a ***bureaucratized language*** in which the world of robust social action is displaced by the world of rationally organized bureaucratic action. The need to carry out hierarchically commanded duties pre-empts empathic relationships with clients. And in bureaucracy, because language is separated from the intentions of the speaker, the individual functionary need not be personally committed to his or her words. To treat the official statements of the bureaucrat with citizen/client for robust social conversations is fallacious. In other words, one does not have authentic conversations with bureaucratised functionaries: no problem solving or social sense making will occur because the problem has been pre-identified and its solution already put in its place (Hummel, 1994). There is no dialogue, no opportunity to express what Hannah Arendt calls the ***agonistic tension,*** no chance to engage in a verbal struggle to define a problem and to decide what should be done about it. This arrest of agonistic tension characterises postmodern language games (Fox and Miller, p. 51). Following the postmodern attack on modern foundationalism and its decimation of metanarratives, POMO, as a mode of thought is a celebration of ***"otherness" and "difference"***.

Modern Political Philosophical Theories

What is Postmodernism? It is the confluence and meeting ground of different philosophical schools of thought-Phenomenology, Social Constructivism, Structuration theory, Hermeneutics and Critical theory—all rolled into one. POMO aims (1) "to demarginalise...groups such as women, minorities, the economically disadvantaged...the colonized and others" (Farmer, 1999, p. 313) and give voice to the "voiceless" in the processes of governmental policy formulation, implementation and evaluation and thus ensure more genuine democratic governance-*more of participatory democracy*—than "the representative democratic accountability loop model of modernism (Fox and Miller, pp. 15-25); (2) "to demarginalise science, with its respect for facts and its attempts to find truth" (Zwart, 2002, pp. 482-83) because POMO denies "objective reality"; (3) to establish that "The reality we experience as "real" is actually a kind of virtual reality" (McSwite, 1997, p. 248); and (4) postmodernists "celebrate multiplicity- of culture, discourse, and knowledge...The latter, multiplicity of knowledge (some others indeed prefer "knowledges") introduces cognitive relativism, and cognitive relativism deprivileges science" (Zwart, p. 483). Last, but not the least, postmodernists celebrate the demise and burial of Orthodoxy/classical administrative thought; they argue that both Constitutionalism/Neo-institutionalism and Communitarianism are "not as satisfying" as the *Discourse* theory of policy and administration that they offer (Fox and Miller, p. 4) as the third alternative to Orthodoxy. Although all the three alternative models may be considered as "discretionist" (Fox and Cochran, 1990) - that is to say they affirm *a proactive public administration on behalf of the public interest* and all discretionist views imply a disdain for contemporary political authority, the first and second models are flawed as compared with the third according to these thinkers.

Orthodoxy, Constitutionalism/Institutionalism and Communitarianism: A Critique

Orthodoxy in public administration - the name given by Waldo (1948) to the enduring prescription of neutral public administration ascribed to Wilson (separation of politics and administration), Taylor's (scientific management), and Weber (hierarchical control) was the manifestation of the period of *high modernism*-the decades surrounding World War II - that 25 year period when the industrial economy matured and the ideology of technocracy and procedural democracy prevailed.

Since then orthodoxy has died a thousand deaths The increasing discretionary power enjoyed by administrators both in policy formulation and implementation, with the advent of the ***administrative state*** in western mature democracies and the nascent developing countries turned the Wilsonian dichotomy upside down. Taylorism was pilloried for three generations by human relationists and social psychologists. Weber's command-control model of bureaucracy was challenged by the behaviouralists and by contemporary developments. The latter include Japanese management thought- the Total Quality Management (TQM) movement, "reinventing government" approach, resurgence of liberalisation, privatisation, and economic choice theories, new public management, and the paradigm shift towards decentralised governance and development through workers' /citizens' participation in decision making in the fields of industrial management, applied political science and public administration.

Despite its death, orthodoxy continues to hover over the study of public administration, in all theories of governance, in every public agency, in civil service reforms and in academic curricula, legitimising a myth. However, two alternative models to the bureaucratic/neutral public administration contend "to displace" the orthodoxy. They are: (1) Constitutionalism/ Neoinstitutionalism and (2) Communitarianism/Civism. Fox and Miller seek to bring forth a third, the ***discourse theory*** (p. 14). They argue that all the three alternative models may be considered *discretionist* (Fox and Cochran)-that is "they affirm a proactive public administration on behalf of the public interest". Administrative discretion, in turn, is based explicitly or implicitly on the "incredulity of representative democracy". All discretionist views imply disdain for contemporary political authority, a strong tendency to dismiss the politics-administration dichotomy and leave behind partisan politics.

Prior to their enunciation of the discourse theory, postmodernists critique the modern representative democracy. Illustrating from American representative democracy, they correctly admit that it is founded on the doctrines of popular sovereignty, limited government and separation of powers- the foundational principles of the Constitution of the United States. Fox and Miller argue that it is "the representative democratic accountability feedback loop model of democracy" *i.e.* it is a "procedural" democracy in which the citizens' individual preferences are aggregated into the popular will through the process of election. The popular will, in turn, is codified into public law (legal public policy) by the legislature, which is implemented by the bureaucracy and evaluated by attentive voters. This loop model, they argue, not only lacks "credibility" as a whole process but also none of its stages functions as the orthodox theory supposes due to the fact that the political-administration dichotomy on which it is based, "does not work systematically in service to democracy". The corollary attempt to realise the popular sovereignty by precisely enunciating rules to bind the behaviour of governmental functionaries is "misguided" because of the dysfunctions of the loop. It is also "undemocratic" at the work site level. More and more rules are promulgated and enforced on the bureaucrats with the result they choose a particular concatenation of them (that suits them, or serves their purpose). Thus, the POMO thinkers conclude that American representative democracy is neither "representative" nor "democratic".

Although many of the maladies of the orthodoxy originate in the loop, people's representatives pass more reform laws assuming the "validity" of the loop. These reform efforts make the bureaucracy a scapegoat. Malfeasance and neglect of duty by elected politicians such as the President of the U.S. and Congressmen in the Water-Gate scandal resulted in the symbolic corrective of ethics reform and civil service reform. A whole new layer of regulatory rules was imposed by the government on the career bureaucracy, which turned out to be ineffective in preventing subsequent Iran-Contra scandal. For instance, both the U.S. Office of Government Ethics Act and The Civil Service Act of 1978 were passed by the Congress at a time when the decline in governmental legitimacy became an established fact, following the Water-Gate scandal. In short, the American federal bureaucracy was blamed for the malfeasance and failures of their political bosses and brought under their increasing control

Constitutionalism/Foundationalism/Neo-Institutionalism

A strong reaction to these conditions brought forth and evoked the academic defense of "proactive administration", like that found in ***Refounding Public Administration: The Blacksburg Manifesto*** by Wamsley and others (1990) who are staunch constitutionalists from the public administration community. These thinkers put forward a strong constitutional argument for treating American administrative branch/the permanent executive as the "fourth" branch of the Government. This represents an attempt to show that non-elected public servants owe allegiance *first* to the Constitution and only secondarily to the current incumbents of elected political offices. According to John Rohr (1986, p. 7), the leading proponent of constitutionalism and foundationalism "The Constitution is the symbol of the founding of the Republic and in politics, "foundings" are normative". He also asserts that "The source of authority of regimes is the founding act itself" (p. 179). On the issue of linkage between the founding of the Constitution and Public Administration, Rohr makes three modest claims: "The administrative state is consistent with the Constitution, fulfils its design, and heals a longstanding major defect' (p. 13). First, although public administration exercises executive, legislative, and judicial powers, it does not violate the relaxed standard of separation of powers, which standard can be traced to the founding argument. Second, the Public Administration provides a constitutional "balance wheel" originally assigned to the non-elected Senate. Third, the Public Administration provides a measure of (demographic) representation insufficiently fulfilled by the strictly constitutional branches. It is an innovative alternative to the loop model of orthodoxy.

Despite this virtue, Fox and Miller say, "the Blacksburg Manifesto fell short of meeting the need for an alternative model of public administration. They consider it as a weak attempt "to legitimize the administrative state... and too conservative to serve as the template for governance in the postmodern period" (p. 6). They further point out that defense of the status quo robs public administration theorists of the independence required to imagine more emancipating conditions of work and governance (p. 28).

Communitarianism

Communitarianism, is another contender to orthodoxy in public administration. It is a full-blown philosophical school strongly rooted in ancient (Aristotle), medieval (St. Thomas Acquinas) and contemporary thought (Johnson and Toulman, 1988, MacIntyre, 1984; Noorjahan Bava, 1984; C. Taylor, 1985; Bellah, Madsen, Sullivan, Swidler, and Tipton's (1985) ***Habits of the Heart*** and Bellah *et al.*'s ***The Good Society***). It is that philosophy which gives the pride of place to ***"the community"*** as opposed the ***"self"***. Traces of the philosophy can be found in the Aristotelian dictum that a person is a social/political animal, the full development of which only takes place in a well-ordered community (polis). This view is contrary to the modern *liberal* understanding of the *"Self"* which, supposes an atomistic (bourgeois) individual rationally maximising valuables unto its lonely self. According to the communitarians the atomistic self is not a recognisable self at all-being a cipher self having no concrete situatedness, no culture, no history. It is an abstract self and not embodied.

Another tenet of ***communitarianism is the primacy of the community***. Its analysis begins with the *context* not with the abstract atomistic sovereign individual. Individuals do exist in society as its members and are situated in a concrete socio -political, historical context. They, therefore, do not act in a vacuum. Orthodox-liberal-modernists view causality as emanating from autonomous individual consciousness and then proceeds to judgement or decision, from there to action. On the contrary, for communitarians, causality is the outcome of a dialectical, reciprocal process between individuals and the communal historical context through dialogue/mutual conversation with others in the society. The context is already well populated with significant others. Indeed, without the context, the human individual is unimaginable (Fox and Miller, p. 34). An important implication of this shift in locus is to elevate the community to coequal, if not, absolute primacy. For modern liberal thinkers, self-interest is the primordial force in life, coordinated by the "invisible" hand of the market and tempered by moral obligations dictated by reason. In contrast, communitarians assume that the community itself and other humans are a precondition for human life and happiness. Accordingly, human values, norms, and traits such as altruism, empathy and consciousness and concern for the common good, the public interest, and other group-based sentiments are "not eccentric deviations" from the norm of self- centred rationality, but are an integral part of being in a human society/community. This Communitarian view thus, militates against rational choice theory and dominant branches of economics. It has far reaching public policy implications.

Teleology of virtue and character is another essential principle of communitarianism. The cultivation of internal traits of character and virtue, then, are the goals of a well -ordered polis. Accordingly, citizenship of a polis, far from being a matter of convenient administration of affairs, is "a crucial part of the process of character cultivation". The telos of human life, namely, a fully developed virtue and character require the active participation of all people in communal governance. In other words, the process of discourse/ discussion/dialogue with other members of the society/community/state is essential for the full development of human potential. Communitarians privilege ***strong democracy that leads to justice.*** People should be involved in the decisions that affect their lives, not only for the sake of justice, but also because the full development of their human potential requires it.

If the constitutional model reminds the citizens of their sacred duty to govern themselves and live up to the noble values and cherished goals of the Founding Fathers of their Constitution, the Communitarian model of governance and public administration is a clarion call to strong citizen-administration relationship, and *direct democracy* as in ancient Athens, or the present Swiss Cantons or the new England town or towards ***Participative democracy*** in the contemporary society.

Communitarianism is not altogether free from flaws. The problem with this model is its assumption that communities are wholly or largely benign. Another problem is that it has totalitarian tendencies in that all aspects of life are brought under the teleological thrust towards well -ordered society. For instance, the right to privacy and freedom given to sovereign individuals by liberalism can be taken away in a communitarian system in the name of community integrity, solidarity, unity, or morality. Totalitarian regimes in fascist Italy and Germany and Communist Soviet Union are cases in point. Critics also point out that communitarianism is too idealistic to be practicable in the mass societies created by advanced and post-industrial capitalism. The greatest stumbling block to this model arises from citizens' apathy, indifference and lack of interest to participate in the process of governance and matters of pubic life in general. Government can only educate, persuade and motivate the citizens to vote, it cannot coerce them to do so. And if people do not actively involve themselves in governance or development, democracy will gradually cease to exist and tyranny of a person, or party or a ruling junta will soon emerge in such a society.

Postmodern public administrationists offer the ***discourse*** model to bury orthodoxy and to overcome the limitations of constitutionalism, institutionalism and the pitfalls of postmodern milieu entailing symbolic politics leading to malgovernance, corruption in public life and loss of governmental legitimacy. To assert itself, such a model needs to be placed on the strong foundation of the latest and most sophisticated underpinnings that social theory can furnish.

Theoretical Underpinnings of Postmodernism

POMO theorists like Fox and Miller attempt to provide such a sophisticated theory called the ***discourse alternative***. They write:

> *"Phenomenology as base to constructivism, and the two combined as base to structuration theory, and the three combined as base to energy fields has been our attempt to provide it"* (p. 109).

Defending such a heady mixture of four theories in the discourse alternative, they assert that "A phenomenological base avoids the pitfalls of foundationalism. We have appealed to no universal or essential first principle. We start with the proposition that body-subjects find themselves in situations in which their intentionalities find fruition. These situations include alter egos with whom we conspire to give, as well as to appropriate, meanings (but no fixed prior meanings). The use of structuration theory and pubic energy fields in the discourse theory does not imply any canon. Moreover, a public energy field can be positively or negatively charged in many ways - by many types of participants and ways of participating" (Fox and Miller, p. 109). Public policy is not the result of a purely rational discovery of objective Truth to which governments respond with solutions infallibly deduced from that Truth. Policy, on the other hand, "is the struggle for meaning capture".

The discourse theory is woven with certain key concepts borrowed from phenomenology, constructivism, structuration theory, critical theory, postmodern political theory, and energy field theory from physics. With a view to enable the readers of POMO public administration to easily grasp the meanings of these notions and ideas, the author of this paper has culled them out and put them in a glossary given at the end of the references. Familiarity with the denotations and connotations of these intellectual tools is a precondition for a clear understanding of POMO.

Phenomenological Insights

Phenomenology provides four conceptual tools necessary for a discourse theory. These are: (1) The body-subject, (2) Intentionality, (3) Sedimented habitual comportments, and (4) situations.

1. ***The Body-Subject*** literally means the concrete body of a person who is treated/spoken of as the subject. In the phenomenological perspective, the body subject is simultaneously both physical and mental. Our bodies literally incorporate objectivity and subjectivity. Because all consciousness occurs in bodies, discourse is possible. Ponty spreads subjectivity throughout the body, giving corporeality to subjectivity. Hence, it must be the body as a whole with consciousness, reflexes, and sedimental habitual comportments, with all its senses and powers pulling together, which must be the appropriate unit to consider. Our bodies participate in linking us to the environment, enabling us to have knowledge of the world. According to Merleau Ponty (1962), we must attempt to go beyond, behind, and below the "refied" abstractions of thought to our shared and indubitable experience of life. He observes:
   "The first philosophical act would appear to be a return to the world of actual experience, which is prior to the objective world, because it is in it that we shall be able to grasp the theoretical basis no less than the limits of that objective world **(p. 54).**
2. ***Intentionality in Situations***: "Intentionality" is often said to be the chief theme of phenomenology. Intentionality is the name given to consciousness which, can not be considered apart from its contents. Consciousness is not an empty container; it is predicated; it has always something, an imminent object to which it points (Husserl, 1962). Action is a physical expression of intentionality, conditioned by the sense one makes of the situation. Action is not separate from sense-making; indeed, sense-making is for action.

3. ***Sedimental Habitual Comportments***: Intentionality sparks out from body-subjects in the world, not for idle contemplation or interested observation, but for the motility, for the action, of those body-subjects. This phenomenon is common to all body-subjects. When intentionality sparks out from body-subjects, it bears the marks of their time, class, gender, and place. Body-subjects acquire "sedimental habitual comportments"—favoured styles of living in the world, which taken in aggregate make up infinitely varied but uniquely authentic selves.
4. ***Situation:*** Body-subjects are always "situated". In other words, the Cartesian imagination may wander where it will, but in the case of competent human actors, human consciousness always comes home to the situated body-subject in the world.

Constructivism

In their very influential work—*The Social Construction of Reality* Berger and Luckmann (1966) observe that a constructivist view combines, telescopes, ontology and epistemology. They define constructivism thus: Humans who seek to know social reality are themselves the carries of it. Observers of social reality can not be external to it, nor can their observations be utterly isolated from that being observed. Conceptions of social reality then are, in a sense negotiated. This is called the social construction of reality.

Accordingly, a constructivist epistemology/ontology is radically *nominalist*—that is, the names we human groups give things are ultimately arbitrary. Names and symbols are not so much denotive of something as they are socially agreed upon gestures, various shorthand significations, for commonly accepted aspects of the lifeworld of that group for which significance has been mutually developed.

The human ability and tendency to *reify* (make real) can, over time, create thought patterns so grandiose that they obscure the daily practices of life from which these categories were primordially derived. The term "bureaucracy" is one such reification and gets in the way of explication of lifeworld practices. Such reifications then tend to ignore, even deny the most obvious evidence from the lifeworld. A "lifeworld" perspective is one that is eternally vigilant against such reifications. It will always question the relevance of theoretical constructs to the intersecting intentionalities of body-subjects in groups in their day to day life.

Structuration Theory

As developed by Anthony Giddens (1984), stucturation theory seeks to avoid giving reifications or immutability to human constructions, but without demeaning the subject-active-voluntarist side required for constructivism. Giddens observes:

> "One of my principal ambitions in the formulation of stucturation theory is to put an end to each of these empire-building endeavours (*e.g.* both one-sided voluntarism of hermeneutics, and one-sided reification systems). The basic domain of study of the social sciences, according to the theory of structuration, is neither the experience of the individual actor, nor the existence of any form of societal totality, but social practices ordered across space and time"(p. 2).

1. ***Recursive Practices***: Crucial to structuration theory is an understanding of *recursive practices*- literally meaning recurrence of practices time and again or "embodied cultural sediments" to use Merleau-ponty's words. Giddens argues that recursive activities are not brought into being by social actors but continually recreated by them via the very means whereby they express as actors (Giddens, p. 2). Humans are born into a world already rich in meanings, which they take up and in doing so re-create or reproduce them, although never exactly identically, for the present and the future.

   Although recursive practices channel and limit human creativity, it is important to emphasise that they are the occasions for its exercise. For example, language, rules etc. Recursivity is important because it neither denies nor demeans human agency. Indeed it only rarely wanders from well-known paths.
2. ***Reflexivity***: Humans exhibit *reflexivity*-consciousness of actions, intentionalities, recursive habitual practices but

that reflexivity takes place not in a vacuum but within the flow of action and interaction within determinable limits. These limits are formed by the expectations of others and co-created by competent selves grasping, accepting, and performing within the limits of those expectations. Such competent performances reinforce and validate those limits, which become structures of varying strength and duration.

3. ***Structures***: Giddens observes: "Social systems, as reproduced social practices, do not have "structures" but rather exhibit "structural properties" and that structure exists, as time-space presence, only in its instantiations (manifestations) in such practices and as memory traces orienting the conduct of knowledgeable people (Giddens, 1984, p. 7). In short, systems, institutions and the like owe their existence not to some objective realm outside the social practices of individuals in groups, but within them. Social reality is socially constructed or constantly socially renewed by human behaviour patterns regulated by recursive practice. Giddens calls "the most deeply embedded structural properties, implicated in the reproduction of societal totalities as "structural principles". Further, those practices, which have the greatest time-space extension within such totalities, can be referred to as "institutions".
4. ***Institutions:*** Understanding "institutions" is the most important aspect of structuration theory for the purpose of POMO. Institutions are habits. For Giddens, "institutions" are recursive practices sustained by resource appropriation and rules. Rules may be of different kinds, but certainly not limited to written rules, laws, or standard operating procedures. Rules may be classified as intensive-shallow, tacit-discursive, informal-formal, weakly sanctioned- strongly sanctioned (Giddens, p. 22). It is important to remember that recursive practices do undergo evolutionary transformation in everyday life and institutions of structuration theory are not like Weber's ideal type-unalterable slots impervious to the human beings inhabiting them. In other words, if reality is socially

constructed, that reality can, and will inevitably be reconstructed. This may happen due to unintended consequences or due to changes initiated elsewhere. But they may also be adjusted by discursive will formation, as Organization Development movement has shown in countless empirical instances (Fox and Miller, p. 90). In other words, institutions being habits not things, they keep changing; and they might look the same from outside but their practices must surely vary according to the intentionalities of those inside and outside.

Public Energy Field

The discourse theory of policy and administration is a paradigm shift from "bureaucracy" to "public energy field" similar to the shift from particle to wave in quantum mechanics has been in physics. This model seeks to substitute bureaucracy by the new concept of ***public energy field*** (PEF) by bringing under it all those activities and recursive practices currently conceived as agencies and institutions in organisational charts in the bureaucracy along with the closely related sectors of civil society like the social service sector, the fourth estate, and citizen groups of all kinds. In other words, the public energy field will comprise all civil society organizations, media agencies and all citizen groups engaged in activities with "public" implications and concerned with the question: what should we do next (Fox and Miller, p. 101).

To reconceptualise public policy and its administrative implementation as a public energy field is to remix several currents of thought. The *public* part in PEF is the borrowing and mixing of Hannah Arendt's (1963) conceptions of the ***"public sphere" and "agonistic tension"*** and *Jurgen* Habermas's (1989) concepts of *public sphere* and ***"communicative competence"***. But "energy" is a more robust and viscous term than "sphere". Fox and Miller (p. 105) are of the view that PEF is less abstract and entails situation, context, and historicity.

1. The concept of ***public sphere***: Both Arendt and Habermas theorised about "a public sphere" in their different ways. According to them a public sphere is one "where an autonomous political will formation might occur

independent of either the *state* or the *economy*" (Habermas, 1992, pp. 421-61). Writing from the Frankfurt School Critical Theory tradition which vehemently opposed the ideologies of ***domination/hegemony***, that is, capitalism, scientism, technicism, and bureaucracy that constrain fundamental human *equality* from asserting itself, Habermas and his colleagues worked to reveal the overt and subtle manifestations of fundamentally irrational enslavements of mankind. His theory of "communication competence" is one such attempt for "human emancipation" from unnecessary domination based on the fundamental structures of communication itself. Habermas interprets "rationality" as any action or statement that can be adequately defended (or criticised) by those performing the action or making the statement. His rationality is also emancipatory in that it requires that participants in the dialogue be essentially equal. If people are to talk genuinely to one another domination must be transcended. That is why "social equality" be pursued as a matter of public policy. Free communication is essential for our being social animals. Situated as we are in complex webs of community relationships, emancipation from dominating social structures is thus the ***telos of life***—the ultimate end, movement towards which defines human progress.

Thus, communication requires equal participants. Talk between unequals is either command or acquiescence. Habermas's argument focuses on political expression but it goes beyond free speech. Free speech is not sufficient; equal opportunity to engage in dialogue is also necessary. Authentic communication is the end towards which human progress is marching. To Habermas authentic communication leads to rationality. He lays down four different types of validity claims for a smooth functioning of a language game. These are: in the exchange of speech act, claims that utterance is understandable, that its propositional content is true, that the speaker is sincere in uttering it and that it is right or appropriate for the speaker to be performing the speech act (McCarthy, 1975). These four validity claims are what make communication *authentic*. Incorporating Arendt's "agonistic tension" in the discourse theory allows for pluralism of standpoints.

2. *Energy Field*: The dictionary meaning of "energy" is inherent power—the power of operating, whether exerted or not. For Aristotle, energy was the progressive actualisation of that which previously existed only in potentiality (Jammer, 1967, pp. 511-17). Adding to energy the notion of "field" connotes a space-time extension within which energy is potentially or kinetically manifest. In our use, "'energy field" describes phenomenological *present or now* charged with human intentionality. An energy field is composed of bundles of human intentions, enthusiasms, purposes, and motivations arising from varying "nows". "The energy field concept directs attention to context, that is, to substantive events, and also to social interactions that constitute the sense-making process". Ideas are brought into "good currency" through interaction in particular setting with others. The ideas that circulate among participants, along with those generated in earlier processes, attract participation (Fox and Miller, p. 107). Thus, one can study human social behaviour in terms of the energy concept (Lewin, 1951). The concept of energy fields captures a more free-flowing interaction among organisational actors and environmental actors, their intentions, and the energy they bring to the world. The concept of energy fields invite "interpretations" and interpretations are themselves part of an energy field. Further, energy fields open up interpretations unavailable to top-down, bureaucratic command-control policy implementation. The energy field concept insists on radically" more interdependence and more permeable borders" than classical bureaucracy

3. ***Policy Analysis:*** Policy analysis or discourse is inherently ***political*** (Stone, 1988). Thoroughly dissatisfied with the highly rationalistic, objectivist, economic analysis of public policy Deborah Stone first distinguishes between political reason and rationalistic analysis based on the utility maximising, atomistic individuals. Then she asserts that policy dialogue occurs within a political

> community that does not resemble the economic market place, but the polis. Stone proceeds to argue that the objectivist policy analysts would have us believe that there is a single truth that can be found out about policies. She asserts that "policies are paradoxes wherein several contradictory truths may simultaneously exist, depending on one's point of view. This is so because policy disputes are instances of political reasoning, not some abstract logical calculus with discrete, fixed-meaning, invariant units. Political reasoning proceeds by metaphor and analysis and discourse participants try to persuade each other that some problem or solution is like one thing rather than like another thing".

Use of Constructivism to Deconstruct Bureaucracy

Bureaucracy, as a term, does not capture the totality of the public sector activities according to postmodernists. They regarded the term as a "reified conflated aggregation" -meaning a symbol that gathers up diverse and often contradictory lifeworld experiences and peremptorily subsumes them under that symbol. Hence the term need to be unpacked, deaggregated or "deconstructed" in POMO language. Under the constructivist approach, bureaucracy will stand deconstructed and become "neither a concrete entity nor a self-surviving organism" (Pfeffer, 1981). Accordingly, bureaucracy is no longer a term that appropriately subsumes sufficiently *fixed practices* as to have "rational critical utility". On the other hand bureaucracy, is more of rhetorical gambit in the game of meaning capture. This conclusion emerges when one traverses the evolution of the social science methods from determinism to probablism and finds how such a shift undermines the definition of bureaucracy as a determinate command - and control structure of Weber or Taylor's deterministic scientific management. The term has undergone substantial transformation. Further, the deterministic method assumes a commitment to cause-and effect knowledge, a belief in the presence of an "objective reality", and confidence that the researcher will conduct value-free inquiry leading to generalisations or statement of laws (Fox and Miller, p. 96). In the determinist conception bureaucracy is "a closed model of control".

The shift from determinism to probablism demolished and de-legitimised the Weberian claim of cause and effect knowledge and the scalar command model. It also became clear that Weberian ideal type is antithetical to probabilistic insights and methodologies. Weber's is a "quixotic" attempt to ensure "certainty" by way of initiating causal chains with "predetermined effects" (Fox and Miller, pp. 97-98). All these show that formal institutions exist in the context of legitimating value orientations like efficiency that are both culture bound and historically contingent and not at all "objective". In other words, Bureaucracy quite plainly has no objective existence outside of human social interactions. Neither separately nor combinedly determinism and probablism capture the evolution of recursive practices. Because both are based on "decisions" (to either command or to manipulate variables which elicit appropriate (to the manipulators) behaviour, they can not comprehensively grasp the implementation of public policy by public administration and all of its many co-constructors of realities (Harmon, 1981). Both determinism and probablism presuppose the efficacy of policy design from some centralised, top-down hierarchical, point of view. On the contrary, energy fields assume a public sphere with multiple sources, like sunspots potentially flaming up from any and all points. The energy from a flame-up then, pulsates out in waves of currency, affecting the field as a whole, as well as other nodes of potential flame-ups. ***In both philosophical and democratic theoretical meanings of the term, public energy field is a radically pluralist vision*** (Fox and Miller, p. 101). As Stone puts it, shared meanings motivate people to action and weld individual strivings into collective action. Ideas are at the centre of all political conflict. Policy-making, in turn is a constant struggle over the criteria for classification, boundaries of categories and the definition of ideals that guide the way people behave" (Stone, 1988, p. 7). As per constructivism, a successful policy will change recursive practices, those reiterative patterns of conduct that constitute our cultural habits and assumptions. Recursive practices can at bottom be changed only by changing human intentionalities and interpretations. Policy legitimacy is important, but it requires the participation of all. If legitimacy can not come from truncated participation of the loop model, alternatives available in discursive ways need to be explored.

Glossary

Hyperreality:	The use of words, symbols and signs which are unlikely to mean anything solid or lasting, leading to virtual reality.
Loop Model of Democracy:	Refers to procedural democracy wherein individual preferences are aggregated to popular will, codified by laws and implemented by the rule-oriented bureaucracy. Popular sovereignty is sought to be realised through enforcement of more and more rules to control the behaviour of governmental functionaries.
Modernism:	Signifies rationalism, scientism, universalism, positivism, reaching objective truth, secularism in politics and culture, industrialism and metanarrativism.
Phenomenology:	A philosophical tradition involving human situations, perceptions, consciousness, action and intentions.
Postmodernism:	Meeting ground of three philosophical traditions namely, phenomenology, constructivism and Structuration theory.
Postmodern Society:	Postindustrial society; a society characterised by symbolic politics, hyperreality, public policies based on facts and claims of truth of science, marginalisation/ exclusion of weaker sections from decision making process.
Postmodern Public Administration:	Rejection of Weber's bureaucracy and adoption of the Public Energy Field instead. It is a discourse theory ensuring truly democratic model of legitimate government based on discourse structures for formation of the sovereign will of the people.
Reified:	Human practices, though created by human beings, are objectified as immutable forces of nature.
Self-referential Words:	In conditions of hyperreality words lose their capacity to signify and instead become self-referrential, *i.e.* meaningful only in a narrow

context, that is either not shared by every one or fleeting in the sense that there is nothing beyond the moment to digest.

Subjectivity: According to the Cartesian view Consciousness is the centre of subjectivity and concentrated in the mind. But Merleau-Ponty spreads subjectivity throughout the body thereby giving corpo-realtiy to subjectivity. It implies that the human body as a whole with consciousness, reflexes, all its senses and powers links us to the environment and enables us to have knowledge of the world.

REFERENCES

Arendt, H. (1967), *On Revolution*, New York: Penguin.

Bava, N. (1984), *People's Participation in Development Administration: An Empirical Study of Tamil Nadu*, New Delhi: Uppal.

Berger, P.L. and Luckmann, T. (1966), *The Social Construction of Reality*, Garden City, New York: Doubleday.

Botwinick, A. (1993), *Postmodernism and Democratic Theory*, Philadelphia: Temple University Press.

Farmer, D.J. (1999), Public Administration Discourse: A Matter of Style? *Administration and Society*, 31 (3) 299-320.

Fox, C.J. (1990), Implementation research: Why and how to transcend positivist methodologies. In Palumbo, D.J. and Calista D.J. (Eds.), *Implementation and the Policy Process: Opening up the black box* (pp. 199-212).

Fox, C.J. and Miller, H.T. (1996), *Postmodern Public Administration: Toward Discourse*, London: Sage.

Giddens, A. (1984), *The Construction of Society: Outline of the Theory of Structuration*, Berkley: University of California Press.

Habermas, J. (1989), *The Structural Transformation of Public Sphere*, T. Burger and F. Lawrence, Trans. Cambridge: MIT Press.

Habermas, J. (1992), In Calhoun, C. (Ed.), *Habermas and the Public Sphere*, Cambridge, MIT Press.

Harmon, M.M. (1981), *Power in Organizations*, Boston: Pittman.

Husserl, E. (1962), *Ideas: General Introduction to Pure Phenomenology*, London: Collier.

Jammer, M. (1967), Energy. In Edwards, P. (Ed.), *The Encyclopaedia of Philosophy*, (Vol. 2, pp. 511-17), New York: Macmillan.

Kockelmans, J.J. (1967), *Phenomenology: The Philosophy of Edmund Husserl and its Interpretation*, Garden City, New York: Doubleday.

Lewin, K. (1951), Field Theory. In D. Cartwright, (Ed.), *Field Theory in Social Sciences*, New York: Harper.

Lyotard, J.F. (1984), *The Postmodern Condition: Report on Knowledge*, Minneapolis: University of Minnesota Press.

McBeth, M.K. and Clemens, R.S. (19), Postmodern Policy Analysis with Postmodern West: Problem definition in the Yellowstone Bison case, *Administrative Theory and Praxis*, 21 (2), 161-75.

McCarthy, T. (1975), Translators' Preface. In J. Habermas, *Legitimation Crisis*, Boston: Beacon Press, (pp. i-xxiv).

McSwite, O.C. (1997), *Legitimation in Public Administration: A Discourse Analysis*, Thousand Oaks, CA: Sage.

Pfeffer, J. (1981), *Power in Organizations*, Boston: Pittman.

Ponty, M.M. (1963), *The Structure of Behaviour*, A.L. Fisher (translated). Boston: Beacon Press.

Rohr, J. (1989), *Ethics for Bureaucrats* (2nd ed.), New York: Marcel Dekker.

Scott, J.C. (1998), *Seeing Like a State: How Certain Schemes to Improve the Human Condition Have Failed*, New Haven, CT: Yale.

Stone, D. (1988), *Policy Paradox and Political Reason*, Glenview, IL: Little Brown.

Waldo, D. (1948), *The Administrative State: A Study of the Political Theory of American Public Administration*, New York: Ronald Press.

Wamsley, G.L., Bacher, R.N. *et al.* (1990), *Refounding Public Administration*, Newbury Park, CA: Sage.

Zwart, de. (2002), Administrative Practice and Rational Inquiry in Postmodern Public Administration Theory. In *Administration and Society*, 37 (5), pp. 482-98.

6

New Public Management: Emerging Concerns

Prof. Ramesh K. Arora

Ever since the discipline of Public Administration was given an identity more than a hundred years ago, there has been a constant confluence of Management Science and Public Administration. The impact of F.W. Taylor was evident in the writings of L.D. White and W.F. Willoughby; French scholar Henry Fayol built bridges between Management and Public Administration; Chester Barnard was the prime motivator of Herbert Simon; the contemporary Management super-guru, Peter Drucker has perspicaciously analyzed government bureaucracies from a management angle; the fusion theory of Chris Argyris has been tested in the context of American federal government; and today the burgeoning world of Management Science has its penetrating effect on the intellectual development of Public Administration. This convergence appears as a natural consequence of the integrated development of the discipline since the core of Public Administration has always been its external political context as well as its internal organizational (read managerial) dynamics. What is internal to a public administrative system is its process of management and what is external to it is its political (hinging also on socio-economic) environment in which it functions. It is universally accepted that most maxims, principles, guidelines and dictums of efficiency, economy and effectiveness have emanated from the writings of Management thinkers and that they have been adopted and adapted by the scholars of Public Administration in their distinctive intellectual ambience. Both Management and Public

Administration are applied science. Hence leaving aside their individual contexts of control and accountability, there is no drastic differentiation between the two as far as their cardinal goals and roles are concerned.

Currently, if there is one 'paradigm' in the discipline of Public Administration, it is perhaps 'New Public Management' (NPM).[1] This paradigm of NPM emerged on the heels of the movements of re-inventing government (1992) and good governance (1992). The sub-title of the book ***Re-inventing Government is How the Entrepreneurial Spirit is Transforming the Public Sector.*** If we closely examine this sub-title of book by David Osborne and Ted Gaebler, it would be evident that both these scholars were 'describing' what was already evident on the administrative scene. Hence, they were not essentially prescriptive but primarily descriptive while highlighting the presence of entrepreneurial governments. Truly, the movement of managerializing the government had started even before this monumental volume was published. Writings of these and other scholars had already appeared in 1980s (and even earlier) which highlighted the need for adopting in an effective manner sound management practices in government systems. One is reminded of what was happening about nine decades ago when Taft Committee was appointed to transplant Taylorism into the government system. Little wonder, certain scholars have branded NPM as neo-Taylorism. Even if we avoid a debate on a neologism like 'neo-Taylorism', it must be contended that public administrative organizations have liberally borrowed, models and modes from its more vibrant sister discipline, Management.

A historical perspective would reveal that bureaucracies throughout the world have rarely responded effectively to environmental challenges on their own. They have generally lagged behind the times. In 1968 itself, when Dwight Waldo was organizing the first Minnowbrook Conference, Peter Drucker had come out with his perceptive volume, ***The Age of Discontinuity*** which made a prescient analysis of the incompetence of bureaucratic government. One can even see this exasperation with straitjacketed bureaucratic system in the writings of Harold Laski, Warren Bennis, Robert Reich, Tom Peters and Alvin Toffeer and others.

And it is ironical that remedies to bureaucratic ailments have been offered more by scholars of Management than by the wise men of Public Administration. But what goes to the credit of Public Administration scholars is their alacrity and competence to imbibe and incorporate the pertinent and the precious from any other discipline and mould it as per their own intrinsic agenda and ambience. New Public Management is only one such manifestation of this resilience of Public Administration.

The OECD believes that through NPM, public sector is being made more managerial-the introduction of a more contractual, participative and discretionary style of relationship between levels of hierarchy, between control agency and operating units, and between producing unit, be they public or private. Further, the OECD avers that most countries are following two broad avenues to improve production and delivery of goods in services in public organizations. These two avenues are:

1. Raise the production performance of public organizations (to) improve the management of human resources including staff, development, recruitment of qualified talent and pay-for-performance; involve staff more in decision-making and management; relax administrative controls while imposing strict performance targets; use information technology; improve feedback from clients and stress service quality; bring supply and demand decisions together (*e.g.* through charging users).[2]
2. Make greater use of the private sector (to) promote a dependable, efficient, competitive and open public procurement system for contracting out production of publicity provided goods and services and contracting in intermediate goods and services and, end monopoly or other protection for suppliers.[3]

In sum, the OECD view on NPM involves the following aspects of administrative management:

- Improving human resource including performance pay.
- Participation to staff in the various stages of decision making, relaxing control and regulations, yet prescribing and ensuring the achievement of performance targets.
- Using information technology to an optimum level in

order to make MIS more effective and enrich policy and decisional systems.
- Providing efficient services to clients and treating them as customers and even as members of the organization.
- Prescribing user charges for services in order to make the customers as more integral part of the public sector management.
- Contracting out services as a part of the privatization plan.
- De-regulation of monopolicies and deconcentration of economic power among various organizations.

There has been a plethora of literature of New Public Management and one finds in the myriad writings certain common concerns and foci. Briefly, the most common attributes of NPM are:

- Focus on outputs, with greater stress on results rather than procedures.
- Strengthening professional management.
- Ensuring high standards and measures of performance.
- Greater emphasis on output controls.
- Increasing de-centralization of business decisional power.
- Greater accept in the public Sector on adoption of private. sector style of management practices, discipline and parsimony.
- Ensuring accountability, progressive leadership and greater understanding between political leadership and the public.
- Added responsibility of managers for results.
- Gradual decrease in the size of government.

Over the years, there has been one important shift in the thinking of NPM. In the early stage of entrepreneurial government, there was stress on de-governmentalization and privatization which was sometimes called downsizing of rightsizing. The government was expected to be lean and mean but now once again, it has been recognized that the imperatives and inevitability of government's role and responsibility as a crucial facet of national life cannot be undermined. For developing countries particularly, the role of government in engineering socio-economic change and bringing about goal-directed progressive multi-dimensional development is likely to remain supreme. Therefore the contemporary emphasis is not on less government but on better government. This is where the value of sound managerial practices has permeated the field of public administration.

A question arises as to why the scholars of Public Administration have not resisted the 'onslaught' of a New Public Management on their discipline. Perhaps it is primarily because of the fact that howsoever new-fangled New Public Management might appear to be, it has its organic linkages with 'old' Public Administration. Accordingly, one can surmise that traditional administrative and managerial theories which emphasized efficiency, effectiveness and economy have assumed a new form as integral components of New Public Management. The difference, of course, lies in the goals of the administrative systems in two divergent settings, but then NPM is not so much concerned with the goals of public administration, as with the strategies to achieve them. In this context, it ought to be appreciated that while the foremost concerns of New Public Administration has been with the goals, values and the spirit of public administration, New Public Management, on the other hand, is principally interested in the structure and style of public administration. There are certain elements of new Public Management that are perceivable in New Public Administration and vice-versa. Essentially, both are complementary to each other.

As we move towards the future we are likely to witness two parallel administrative realities. The first, anchored in New Public Management, would be more germane to the milieu in developed nations where the government is emerging as a facilitator and moderator of goal-directed change. The other reality will be more reflective of the enterprise of change in developing nations where the government's responsibility and role in tackling poverty and backwardness will remain prominent and legitimate for many more years to come. In a country like India, the traditional public administration focusing on organizational re-structuring and managerial efficiency will continue to be ensconced on a pedestal of time-tested authenticity. And besides, the principal values and concerns of New Public Administration as well as New Public

Management would also continue to perennially re-energize the discipline as well as the profession of Public Administration. Thus, in the foreseeable future, Public Administration is destined to flourish in a poly-paradigmatic environment facilitating its multi-faceted growth.[4]

REFERENCES

1. See for a perceptive analysis of the theme, Hughes, *Public Management and Administration;* and Halachami and Bouckaert, eds.; *The Enduring Challenges in Public Management.* For a comparative perspective, see Christopher Pollitt and Geert Bouckaert, *Public Management Reform: A Comparative Analysis* (New York: Oxford, 2000). Also see, L.K. Kaboolian, "The New Public Management Challenging the Boundaries of Management vs. Administration Debate, "*Public Administrative Review,* Vol. 58, No. 3 (1998), pp 189-193; and D.G. Mathiasen, The New Public Management and its Critics," *International Public Management Journal,* Vol. 2, No. 1 (1999), pp. 90-111.
2. Hughes, *Public Management and Administration,* p. 67.
3. *Ibid.,* p. 68.
4. For a glimpse of the multi-faceted character of Public Administration, see Bidyut Chakrabarty and Mohit Bhattacharya, eds., *Public Administration: A Reader* (New Delhi: Oxford, 2003).

7

Politics: Administration Dichotomy Revisited in the NPM Context

Prof. C. V. Raghavulu

Very few themes have endured in the discourse on public administration as that of politics—administration dichotomy. In the early period two different strands of thought, quite unrelated to each other, provided the basis for the doctrine. Woodrow Wilson was the father of the conventional view of separation between politics and administration. The formula is simple: politics is concerned with policy, the higher order things, and administration deals with implementation of policy. The second strand of thought comes from Max Weber. According to him a division between administration and politics is a central organising principle in all modern political systems. The division is again based on the simultaneous application of two principles: subordination to a hierarchy and separation of the careers of administrators from partisan politics. It should, however, be pointed out that in the Weberian framework, the neutrality of the civil service/ bureaucracy is related to professionalisation.

Politics-Administration Dichotomy: Specification of Variables

On issues such as the neutrality of the civil service and its politicization, normative approaches often get mixed up with analytic concerns. A normative framework tends to be based on a heuristic distinction between absolutes or ideal-typical characteristics. In reality, a multitude of variables appear to interact in influencing the outcomes *i.e.*, the degree of politicization or the limits to neutrality of the civil service. Moreover, further specification of the details in operationalising the concepts would contribute to greater clarity to a discussion on the theme. Both Wilson and Weber advanced their respective formulae in the context of an open, democratic polity. Any exploration of these themes should, therefore, reckon with the nature of the polity, and the strength of the administrative tradition, as measured by the degree of professional independence. Conversely, the degree of politicization of the bureaucracy seems to vary from one political system to the other, and among countries wedded to the same political system, and within the same country from time to time. For instance, the nature of the relationship between the political executive and the civil servants differs among Commonwealth parliamentary democracies such as United Kingdom, Canada, Australia and India. The involvement of bureaucracy in the political process and the extent of power wielded by it in developing countries, according to Fred Riggs, depends on the relative strength of other organizations in the society. Turning to the next point, we note that there is considerable evidence in support of the view that the degree of politicization of civil servants varied from time to time within a given country.

Politicization of the higher civil service is a phenomenon that finds wide variation across countries. Direct involvement of civil servants in political life, as measured by their capacity for collective political mobilization, is far higher in France, Germany, Sweden, Spain, Austria, Belgium, Netherlands and Japan than in U.S.A., U.K. or India. In Japan, the bureaucracy controlled economic policy until the mid-1990s when strenuous efforts were made to reduce its power. Governments based on coalitions also offer greater scope for politicization of civil servants.

Within bureaucracies of the developing countries, discrete networks of influence exist. Besides providing channels of access and informal communication, they allow influence to be exerted in all critical matters of importance to the civil servant, such as career advancement, placements, etc.

Critique of Civil Service Neutrality

Owen Hughes observes that it is always a flaw to think that bureaucrats would be impersonal, neutral arbiters and not involved in politics. Vincent Ostram, a votary of public choice theory, observes that bureaucracies wield considerable power and it is reflected in various forms of self-enrichment. Referring to the situation in the developing countries, Ahmed Huque notes that bureaucrats exercise a substantial amount of power and that there are possibilities for acquisition of improper benefits by interpreting or bending the rules in favour of certain groups or individuals.

Paul Appleby was one of first analysts to explode the myth behind the classical formulation of politics-administration dichotomy. He argued that bureaucrats do participate in policy making in a number of ways. This theoretical stand is now widely accepted. Equally important is the recognition that it is difficult to localise each decision, let alone identifying the role of each player—bureaucrat or politician—in the outcome of each decision on a policy matter. The involvement of bureaucrats in the definition and implementation of public policy is also a bye-product of the complexity of the policy requiring the inputs of experts as also the latitude available to the official applying it. In this sense, the bureaucrats accomplish work of a political nature. In the process of carrying out political decisions, the bureaucrat has to adapt them, articulate the explanation and use discretion wherever necessary. And in some instances, decisions made by bureaucrats may replace decisions made by elected functionaries. In sum, much of the administrative activity affects 'who gets what' from government; it should, therefore, be considered 'political'.

There is a large grey area between politics and administration. In this zone of what Peter Self calls 'administrative politics' politicians and bureaucrats mingle. A simplified distinction between politics and administration at the higher levels is, therefore, not very realistic. The dividing line between the two is always an artificial one, drawn between the more general and the detailed aspects of governmental administration. It may be worthwhile, as R.G.S. Brown suggests, to make a distinction in terms of a spectrum of contributions ranging from a specific–technical–factual end to a general–political–value end.

Politics and Administration: Context of New Public Management

Reforms based on the paradigm of New Public Management (NPM) were widely adopted in the developed countries and find high receptivity in many developing countries. NPM has a few implications for the relationship between political executives and senior civil servants and the balance of power between them. Adherents to neo-classical economic theory and public choice theory had a profound impact on NPM; they argued in favour of roll back of the state, that the latter should confine itself to 'steering instead of rowing' the economy, and the state's role is mainly that of a catalyst and facilitator. NPM holds that markets are superior in every respect to the public bureaucracy in improving aggregate welfare and economic efficiency. One unintended consequence of privatization and outsourcing is in terms of ensuring the recovery of political control of the economy, subjecting the bureaucracy to the rules of competition.

A second consequence of NPM and reform consciousness is centralization of decision-making authority. Multilateral agencies have suggested time and again that reforms would find widespread adoption if they are backed by political will. The accent is on political leadership and assertiveness. Margaret Thatcher is a role model in this regard. The main thrust of NPM also is to place the onus of responsibility for adoption on the political leadership *i.e.*, the chief executive. To ensure the effective implementation of NPM, the rise of prime-ministerial/chief-ministerial power, therefore, becomes inevitable. It is a structural change rather than one based on personality. The need to control public expenditure, through techniques such as zero-based budgeting and performance appraisal, has brought the political chief executive to centre stage. With the rise of the career politician, it is felt that the capacity for self-regulation on the part of the Finance Minister or other individual Ministers has been on the decline. As economic management and budget control become the prime concern in the new governance strategy, the Prime Minister/ Chief Minister appropriated from Finance and the spending departments the authority for decision-making, direct monitoring and overall direction.

A third development from the application of NPM is the loss of standing of senior civil servants with regard to monopoly over policy advice. Their monopoly in this sphere has been broken with the lateral entry of a wide range of policy entrepreneurs and analysts from international agencies, think tanks, consulting firms, the private sector, etc. Though the formal structure is undisturbed and bureaucrats continue to play an important part in policy making and advising, some significant changes in norms and practices are noticeable. There is lot of grumbling and evasive behaviour on the part of a sizeable proportion of senior civil servants to being lectured and sermonized on the best practices. They consider themselves as repositories of conventional wisdom on administration, distilled from their long experience. However, dissent is not open, but resistance is very much there.

8

Globalization, Technological Innovations and Public Administration: Challenges and Constraints

Dr. Asha Gupta

Poised at the turn of the 21st Century, the world today is experiencing both quantitative and qualitative change-quantitative in terms of economic growth and technological innovations and qualitative in terms of a new paradigm of a new society governed by an altogether different values and ethos. Public administration is no exception to this silent revolution creeping the developed and the developing world alike. During the past quarter century, the focus has shifted from 'public administration' to 'public management'. The not so gradual retreat of public administration from its intellectual tradition rooted in public law has left it vulnerable to the generic behavioral principles of management taught in business schools.

Whereas the traditional public administration was based upon the assumptions of self-sufficiency, direct control, uniformity of purpose, upward accountability and standardized procedure, the modern administration is based on the assumptions of teamwork, networking and partnership among public, private sectors and civic society. Such a partnership has become inevitable to be able to meet the challenges thrown by globalization at all levels of government—local, regional, national and transnational. The networked government is a challenge in itself requiring a greater amount of information, transparency, efficiency and public accountability.

The modern administration requires an altogether new modus-operendi. The pace of reform is driven by rapid technological and communication innovations. The integration of financial markets round the clock severely constraints the time frame available to the public policymakers and administrators to be able to take informed decisions. Hierarchical and bureaucratic structures do not permit them as much adaptability and flexibility as desired or required. Moreover, e-governance, made possible due to technological innovations, has put the citizen at the center, keeping the government and public servants at their toes. Though e-governance is supposed to be cost-effective in the long term, it requires huge investments into information technology at the initial stages. Besides huge costs and efforts involved, it requires a complete overhaul of the mindset.

This paper seeks to focus on some of the challenges and constraints faced by public administration in the era of rapid globalization, technological innovations and proactive civil society and media. The values promoted by public management are likely to promote the culture that is bound to extol the role of managers as heroes, profits as success and conspicuous consumption and social status as an end in itself. It is likely to result not only in 'shift in values' but also 'conflicts in values'. The methodology adopted is analytical, comparative and empirical.

Why Globalization?

Globalization requires us to think afresh how we mange our joint activities and fulfil our obligations as public administrators. There are many challenges and constraints that are being faced by those in public administration in the wake of globalization process. Earlier the states created the nations of citizens by conscripting, disciplining, monitoring and regulating their activities through public administration. Today they are required to adjust their domestic policies to serve the global economic and political hegemony (Gupta, 2004).

Though the global transformations in economic and political spheres are well noticed and studied, it is not easy to visualize the impact of these transformations on public administration. We find a decline in the sovereignty enjoyed by the states all the world over and the rise in extra-territorial hegemony. Just as we find links between the rise of industrialism and democracy, similarly we find links between post-industrial, rather deindustrial world and the spread of globalization and market economy to the first world, the 'so called' second world and the majority or 'so called' third world.

Earlier the idea of democracy was vigorously promoted not primarily in the interest of the masses but in the interest of the capitalist class that sought freedom of movement to cut down costs of the finished goods due to toll tax at various provinces or countries. Now the advanced capitalist economy seeks further movement from advanced countries to developing ones not only to promote their goods but also trade in services. Even higher education falls in the category of services as reflected by the latest trends in GATTS and WTO agreements. This time they have sought recourse in deterritorialization and extra-territorial jurisdiction in the name of globalization. The breathtaking speed and technological innovations have given vent to their dreams and designs.

The process of globalization didn't start one fine day. Nor was it started at one particular place by one set of people or group. Nor it can be stopped by another set of people or group at a particular time or place. It is the inevitable outcome of the late capitalism and deindustialism. All the states are trying hard to cope up with it. What we can do is to reflect deeply and find out what can be achieved out of it and how best can we cushion the worst. The realistic and upto date knowledge can help us in taking the right steps and it can also help us in overcoming some of the apprehensions.

There is a Chinese proverb: ***when winds of change blow, some build walls other build windmills.*** Darwin stated "***it is not the strongest species that survive, nor the most intelligent but the ones most responsive to change.***" Today's motto seems to be "***reform or perish***". But we should ask ourselves: reforms for what? It is true that only thing that is constant is change but changes do not occur in a vacuum. Nor are changes sought without certain motives. At the realm of public administration, we must govern better at the national level and learn to govern together at the international level. Effective public administration is a must at both the levels.

Public administration must adapt to the realities of the new era. We need to form coalitions for change with partners beyond the precincts of officialdom. Mobilizing skills and the necessary resources has made it imperative for the state governments to form loose and temporary alliances cutting the institutional, regional, national and disciplinary lines (Annan, 2000: 64). The new problems, such as, protection of environment, controlling AIDS, combating corruption, fighting terrorism, require new solutions with the help of new alliances with the private and non-state actors both at the national and international levels.

In an interdependent and complex world, collective action is possible through modern communication and outsourcing. The connected nature of the problems implies that the innovations and changes at the global level are bound to affect the national politics and public administration and vice-versa. Therefore, current governance challenges and new forms of cooperation I the networked world have to be tackled across different sectors and across different levels—local, regional, national and global (Benner, Rienicke and Write, 2002: 7).

The transnational and multi-sectoral initiatives have brought together the public, private and the non-state sectors into loose issue-based networks. The hierarchical and bureaucratic structure are ill suited to respond to globalization as a process of acceleration, driven by rapid technological changes and integrated by 24 hour operation of global financial markets and the media. It requires adequate knowledge, flexibility, adaptability, quickness and readiness to take the risks.

Often the policymakers and the administrators find themselves form between the issues of legitimacy and accountability. Now Public policymaking at the national level has to keep in mind the economic interests at the international level and act at the dictates of political and economic hegemons at the national and international level. In today's rapidly changing world scenario, geo-economics dominates geo-politics. We no longer find the fights over the control of territories and administration but we do find stiff fights over the markets. Under these circumstances, the hierarchical approaches are no longer relevant. Rather, too much reliance on public bureaucracies can prove counter-productive.

No wonder, we find a shift in paradigm from 'public administration' to 'public management' instead of administrative expertise the focus is on managerial skills. A shift in paradigm occurs when we discover 'a dramatically new way of conceptualizing and thinking about some areas of concern' (Sheafor and Horejs, 1997: 101). A shift in paradigm takes place when commonly held value consensus is replaced with a new set of values and assumptions (Kuhn, 1970). Though it is difficult to say whether the shift from 'public administration' to 'public management' amounts to a 'shift in paradigm' (Moe, 1994:119) or not, one thing is clear that there is a major shift in the very focus.

While the traditional public administration was based on the assumptions of self-sufficiency, direct control, uniformity of purpose, upward accountability and standardized procedures, the modern administration, on the lines of public management, is based on the assumption of teamwork. Instead of quantity, the stress is now laid on quality, instead of equality, the stress is now laid on liberty and instead of uniformity, the stress is now laid on wider choice (Stewart and Waish, 1992: 499-518).

Instead of following policies and directions of hierarchical superiors, the public administrations cum managers are now required to play a positive role in policy making. It ha led to conflicting roles. While entrepreneurship requires autonomy, personal vision of the future, secrecy and risk-taking behaviour on the part of administrative managers, the democratic administration, on the other hand, calls for accountability, citizen participation, openness, and transparency in policy-making and public dealing. The governments are now required not to just spend money but also earn it as well by entering into joint ventures, public-private partnerships, user charges and entrepreneurial loans. The public administrators are also required to select alternatives, such as, contracting out, franchise, lease, vouchers and *quid proquos* to reduce fiscal constraints.

Traditionally, the public administration was seen as an 'adjunct of politics and its practice'. The Weberian model of administrative structure—hierarchical, rule bound and neutral was seen as adequate. With the advent of globalization, the cardinal values of traditional public administration have come into conflict with market oriented public management. Now the emphasis is more on performance monitoring and management rather than on administration of government made programs and policies (Woodward, 1991). With the shift towards public management, we find a shift in accountability towards the citizens as customers.

As such, the insistence on standardized procedures has to be replaced with the motivation, new pay scales and flexibility. While under the traditional public administration, the personnel are either recruited on the grounds of merit or seniority, under globalization, the stress is on contractual arrangements. While under the traditional administration, a bureaucrat tries to maintain good relations with his or her immediate administrative and political bosses, in the marketized form of public management, he or she is also required to deal with the NGOs, voluntary organizations and third parties, requiring altogether different skills.

From Public Administration to Public Management

The smooth transition from 'public administration' to 'public management' depends upon the shift in the core values. The underlying model needs some stimulation as well as some form of ecological adaptation in response to external stimuli, greater to private capital, discipline exercised by the stock market and the threat of competition, etc. These external stimuli are supposed to generate a response in terms of prices, financial viability, operative efficiency and customer satisfaction. The public administrators are now required to be adept economic and political entrepreneurs simultaneously. It can be explained in the form of the following table (Lan and Rosenbloom, 1992: 536-37):

Criteria selected	*Public administration*	*Public management*
Constitutional function	Execution, legislation, adjudication	(*a*) Executives as analysis, Contract negotiators and Program evaluators (*b*) as conducts for citizen's demands (*c*) judges as adjudicators
Political referent	Developmental	Populist
Core values	Efficiency, economy and effectiveness	Cost-effectiveness, entrepreneurship, competition and quality
Views of the individual	Impersonal case citizen	Consumer of public goods and services participant
Preferred way of knowing	Observation (quantitative and qualitative)	Public opinion Market outcomes

(*Contd.*)

(*Contd.*)

Criteria selected	*Public administration*	*Public management*
Constitutional function	Execution, legislation, adjudication	(*a*) Executives as analysis, Contract negotiators and Program evaluators (*b*) as conducts for citizen's demands (*c*) judges as adjudicators
Political referent	Developmental	Populist
Core values	Efficiency, economy and effectiveness	Cost-effectiveness, entrepreneurship, competition and quality
Views of the individual	Impersonal case citizen	Consumer of public goods and services participant
Preferred way of knowing	Observation (quantitative and qualitative)	Public opinion Market outcomes
Proposed structure	Hierarchical Principals and agents flats	Team work multi-layered citizen participation
Decision making	Rational Comprehensive	Utility Optimization
Rule-making	Centralized agenda	Negotiation
Budgeting	Benefit/cost Incremental	User pays decremental
Implementation	Forward mapping Principal agent	Backward mapping third party
Personnel	Merit, seniority	Contractual

The questions arise: how can we synthesize managerial efficiency with public accountability? How can we synthesize efficiency with equity? How can we synthesize the values of individualism, professionalism and competition with those of social justice, egalitarianism and community life? How can the pursuit of power and material gains be synthesized with the ethos of public service? How can we stop the 'commercial culture' from pervading the 'managerial culture' required to provide a boost to the public administration? How can we reap the benefits of managerial culture without changing the administrative structure of public organizations and efficiency managers and entrepreneurs' overnight? How can the public administrators reconcile their new role of public managers with democratic values, etc. All these questions await honest answers.

The move from 'public administration' to 'public management' may not only result in 'shift in values' but also 'conflict in values'. In the coming decades, the able 'entrepreneur' and not the efficiency 'administrator' is likely to be the hero of the society. Public administrators as 'entrepreneurs and agents of entrepreneurial states' are required to seek new sources of revenue besides the traditional tax support. But it may lead to a conflict between the two roles. While the entrepreneur role may enhance the autonomy and discretion of public managers cum administrators, it may make public accountability more difficult to be achieved—once the focus is shifted from the inputs to the outputs. There are also many difficulties in measuring the performance of public managers cum administrators in terms of outputs alone. There are many ethical questions involved too.

A Reassessment of the Shift in Paradigm

It is feared that the dynamics of management careerism may out weigh the dynamics of administration in public interest. Management advocates those values which have proved to be the most damaging ones to an organization, namely, the pursuit of career advancement and personal acquisitiveness, rather than working for the common good, common purposes and common benefits of the entire organization, if not the society as whole (Woodward, 1990). Public management is bound to bring commercial culture that extols the role of entrepreneur as a hero, of profits as success and conspicuous consumption and social status as the 'end' of one's life. What seems lacking in this culture is the moral dimension that produces genuine heroes with a sense of community purpose (Woodward, 1991: 27).

Usually this political dimension of the debate on public management is often overlooked. The whole debate needs to be studied in the context of shift in political ideology and economic theory in the form of neo-conservatism and neo-liberalism. The government is now seen as 'steerer' rather than 'rower'. From this perspective, 'public management' is offered as a 'neutral' or 'transferable technology' to save the 'public administration' from demise. But, in fact, the thrust of the reform agenda may prove to be hostile to the traditional values of public administration. Under 'public management', there is too much focus on the cost, price, market and customer to the neglect of equity, service, need and social justice. The very location of public management studies in shifting from he traditional university departments of political science and public administration to business schools.

Whereas traditional public administration was based on certain values and assumptions with regard to bureaucratic model of state structure and operations, we find no such consensus on 'public management'. This concept is being used in gague and imprecise manner. Although public management of goods and services is supposed to be more efficient and flexible, there is not much empirical evidence to justify such claim. On the other hand, we may find 'public management' trapped in the spiral of 'competitive deregulation' and 'limitations in terms of capacity'. It might result in a gap between the rising expectations of public management and its potential output. Even if we have administrative flexibility and autonomy, we may lack the same at the political level (Hambelton, 1992: 9-20).

As such, the public management theory is neither coherent nor neutral. It is based on an altogether different political perspective not only on the structure and functioning of public organizations but also on the political basis of the public sector itself. The objective of public management appears to be 'to de-politicize the operations of governmental process and to redefine accountability relationships' (Gray and Jenkins, 1995:92). We find sharp differences between the values and assumptions underlying traditional public administration and modern public management edifices. In the new world, it is possible not only to separate politics and administration but also separate them from public accountability. The move from 'public administration' to 'public management', as such, cannot and should not be simply seen as a step forward in a linear way. Instead, it has to be seen as 'a discontinuity rather than a continuity in value systems' (Kuhn, 1970).

While public administration was still the preserve of political science and constitutional law, public management comes under the purview of business schools and economics. Prior to 1980s, finance and expenditures were not considered as subjects warranting detailed consideration by a select group of specialists. The 1980s and 1990s became the age of financial manager. Accounting, budgeting and auditing have dominated the discourse about the resource allocation to education, health and social welfare, on the one hand, and delivery and distribution of public goods and services, on the other (Gray, Jenkins and Segsworth, 1993). It is more result-oriented than service-oriented. As such, 'public management' cannot really replace or be the substitute for 'public administration'.

Myths of 'unfettered enterprise' and 'individual reward' have proved problematic even in developed market economies. They are likely to be out of place in developing nations having altogether different cultural traditions. The rising consumerism and market economy is bound to lead to a decline in moral values (Featherstone, 1990:115). People are already rebelling against a world that turns them into 'mere consumers'. Too much stress on excessive acquisitiveness leads to dehumanization in terms of noble values.

Economic Growth, Environmental Conservation and Human Development

If communism failed for lagging behind in terms of economic growth, neo-conservatism may fail too for breeding excessive consumerism, to the neglect of humane aspects of development. In the absence of social justice we may only have economic growth without any development, depending upon how we interpret the term development. It is usual practice to define development not in terms of what people are or what they would like to be, but in terms of what they do have and what others think they should become. But the traditional one dimensional approach of measuring development in terms of GDP needs to be replaced with a more complex but multi-dimensional measure of human development, based on quality rather than quantity.

Excessive materialism and conspicuous consumption have to be checked if we really want to avoid the environmental disaster threatening the survival of 'spaceship earth' (Simonis, 1990: 118). In pursuit of economic growth to the neglect of humane development, modern technology has failed to realize the inner limits of human society and outer limits of spaceship earth. As such, it has disturbed the ecological equilibrium, jeopardized the ecosystems stability and the quality of human life both in physiobiotic and sociocultural terms (Mohan, 1993: 39-41).

Growth is important, but contentment is far more important. Instead of pursuing a path of abundance, we must learn to delimit our needs and desires. Already on the threshold of the twenty first century, when we are moving into a highly uncertain and ambivalent future, we need to rely on a new perspective that goes beyond the state and the market, in general, and public administration and private management, in particular. The pursuit of inner growth and humane development is far more important than the mere pursuit of external goods and comforts. In fact, the well being of an individual depends upon his or her happiness, and the happiest person on earth remains the one who is most content.

Happiness does not always lie in attaining power, position or materialistic goods. It is a personal experience, varying from individual to individual, depending upon his or her temperament, biological inheritance, aspirations, abilities, upbringing and circumstances around. In fact, it is an inner experience that comes in the form of mental serenity and emotional equilibrium. It is the mind alone that is the abode of human health, happiness and harmony. Encouragement of self interest in the tradition of economic growth cannot lead to humane development. Instead, this linear approach towards market economy worldwide, marked by increasing cultural, psychological, social and ideological homogeneity and politico-economic centralization, can pose a serious threat to the very notion of individualism (Gupta, 2000: 211).

Paradoxically, economic progress may impede inner growth and holistic development of individuals, and the market economy may lead to the corporatization of society and the diminution of self (Whiston, 1991: 163-78). Market-based efficiency may bring surplus wealth and wider choice, but at the cost mental health and freedom of mind. The market economy makes us think in a single predetermined direction, sacrificing many creative talents, on the way. Therefore, corporation should be questioned in all forms—economic, political, sociocultural or ecological. The feminist theory also aims at deconstructing the very public-private dichotomy to expose the psychic opposition between male and female. In fact, the true emancipation lies in attaining power over the self.

A creative society need not be sacrificed at the altar of mass society, nor should individuals be treated as conforming ends rather than potential gods. Nor should any nation be subsidized at the economic growth can be a worthwhile exercise only if it leads to a positive contribution to human development. Though economic growth can be seen both as the cause and consequence of human development, myths of unfettered economic growth need to be shed by all means (Srinivasan, 1992:8).

Infinite growth in a world of finite resources is neither possible nor desirable. Nor can the problems of citizens pertaining to rising expectations, consumerism, political violence, economic and regional disparities, Mafia, private accumulation by public officials, nexus between the politicians, businessmen and bureaucrats, restlessness among the youth and loneliness among the elderly in the wake of high-tech and post modern societies cannot be solved either by public administration or by public management. These can be solved only by laying stress on the 'being model of development' in lieu of 'having model of development', emphasizing on 'what you are' rather than 'what you have'.

Let us hope that in the twenty first century, stress will be laid on human development and quality of life. The pursuit of economic gains can be a worthwhile exercise only if it makes positive contribution towards human development. A passive non-interventionist government can neither cope with the unfolding crisis in terms of widening economic disparities, economic recession, unemployment and rising social costs, nor can it provide the much needed guidance and support for human development. Public management as much needs the stimulus from the theory of public administration as far as the human values are concerned, as the latter needs from the practice of public management as far as the *modus operendi* is concerned.

Impact of Technology

Rapid changes in information and communication technology during the past few decades can be considered both the cause and consequence of globalization, having tremendous effect on the functioning of the states, in general, and public administration, in particular. These innovations have provided both the opportunities and constraints in the ways and means of bridging the gap between the developed and the developing countries (Singh, 2000).

These innovations have paved the way for electronic governance, which has already become a subject of political and economic discourse all the world over. It has provided the citizens a choice and a possibility of easy access to government information and services. By putting the citizens at the center means more focus on the supply side of economics. It also implies empowerment of the ordinary citizen if we believe in the dictum that knowledge means power.

Whereas e-governance helps the state in saving scarce resources, it also helps the citizens in getting fast and quality service. The twenty-first century requires real "SMART" governance implying Simple, Moral, Accountable, Responsible and Transparent government. Even the Government of India has made huge investments in information and communication technology, both in terms of human resource and infrastructure. Various governments at the state level have also framed their own ICT policies and have started implementing them. Andhra Pradesh is the leading example of e-governance.

The emergence of e-governance has kept the public administrators on toes, as the citizens are becoming more demanding and quality conscious even at the local level. It requires tackling the issues at three levels, (1) technical, (2) managerial and (3) funding. The Centre and state governments need to identify the appropriate software and hardware packages for cost effective delivery of public services, making this knowledge widely available through demo-mechanisms and customizing it as per local and work specific requirements. Duplication should be avoided to save costs. While e-governance can be cost effective in the long run, it requires huge investments initially (Budhiraja, Ranu, 2002. www.mit.gov.in/eg/article2.asp).

What is difficult to change is the mindset of the people, particularly at the top echelon of bureaucracy and policymaking. It is very difficult to foster trust among the various stakeholders. Lack of trust and misperception among the various actors in the networked and interdependent world can cause tremendous obstacles. It is equally difficult to overcome the strained relations among various actors coming from various sectors. Usually they nourish stereotyped perceptions and prejudices towards one another (Nelson, 2001: 35). Regular orientations and training programs can be of little help.

The developing countries are made to feel that unless and until they adopt modern technologies, they are likely to be left out from the bandwagon of globalization. But the governments in these countries face several constraints, such as, the commitment on the part of top leaders is found missing or lacking, infrastructure for e-governance and technology-based administration is invariably inadequate, the resources required for initial investment are not available, the political and administrative set up is not fit to be able to absorb the new technology successfully, heavy bias towards English as a medium of communication, lack of adequate awareness and technological skills among the masses and absence of desirable rules and regulations over the use of cyberspace, etc. (Singh, 2000).

The G-8 summit has taken a proactive stance to bridge the digital divide and promote good governance. It has recommended that the general awareness should be promoted about the role of good governance in socio-economic development. Private and non-governmental sectors should be encouraged to provide assistance and funding towards improving connectivity and accessibility by integrating the information and communication technology with socio-economic development. Steps should be taken to harness intra-regional competencies and promote pro-competitive, flexible and socially inclusive policy.

But the developing countries, comprising the majority world, need to come forward. They should not shy away from shedding not only the feudal structures but also colonial mentality. Instead of being at the receiving end and suffering at the hands of political and economic hegemons both at the national and international level, they should take the advantage of technological innovations by forging strong and meaningful alliances among themselves and turning the table against the hegemons.

The emerging economies and not so technologically advanced countries must insist upon humane and communitarian development instead of economic growth of few individuals at the cost of the vast majorities. The technological revolution contains both opportunities and challenges. The days of dependency are gone and he developing countries must realize that the developed world needs them as much as they need the former in an interdependent world. They must also realize that cyberspace is neither emancipatory nor oppressive, but a politically and philosophically contested space. The Internet is neither good nor bad, but certainly, it is not neutral. It is used by the economic and political hegemonic powers to fulfill their neo-colonialist designs.

The only way to fight an adversarial network and encroachment upon cyberspace is to fight with a network. The governance of cyberspace imp[lies shift in power relationship based upon identity and territory. While the concept of governance is still based upon the capitalist world system and ceaseless accumulation of wealth, the concepts of state, government and public administration have withered away or replaced with service industries. We are caught unaware in the fight between the capitalist world economy (in terms of controls, regulations and exploitation for profit) *versus* the sub-politics and anti-systemic movements (in terms of free and open access to information regardless of content) on a global scale.

REFERENCES

Annan, Kofi A, 2000, *We the Peoples: The Role of the United Nations in the Twenty-First Century.* New York: United Nations.

Benner, Thorsten, Reinicke, Wolfgang H. and Witte, Jan Martin, 2002. 'Shaping Globalization: The Role of Global Public Policy Networks', *Cooperation-Responsibility-Transparency,* Gutersloh: Bertelsmann Foundation.

Featherstone, Mike, 1990, *Consumer Culture and Post Modernism,* London: Sage Publications.

Gray, Andreas and Bill Jenkins, 1995, 'From Public Administration to Public Management: Reassessing A Revolution', *Public Administration,* 73 (Spring).

Gray, A.G., W.T. Jenkins and R.V. Segsworth eds, 1993, *Budgeting, Auditing and Evaluation,* New Brunswick: Transaction Publishers.

Gupta, Asha, 2004, 'In Search of New Identitites:Universities in the Era of Political and Economic Hegemony'. A Paper prepared for presentation at the ISA convention at Montreal, March 17-20.

—— 2000, *Beyond Privatization,* UK: Macmillan-IPSA Series.

——1994a, *Changing Perspectives of the Welfare State: The Issue of Privatization,* New Delhi: Pragati Publications.

—— 1994b, 'Privatization: A Political Strategy or An Economic Device?' in Rudra Dutt ed., *Privatization,* New Delhi: Pragati Publications.

Hambleton, R., 1992., 'Decentralization and Democracy in UK Local Government', *Public Money and Management,* July-September.

Kuhn, T. 1970. *The Structure of Scientific Revolutions,* Chicago: University of Chicago Press.

Lan, Zhiyong Lan and David H. Rosenbloom, 'Public Administration in Transition?', *Public Administration Review,* November-December, 52(6).

Moe, R.C., 1994, 'The Reinventing Government Exercise: Misinterpreting the Problem, Misjudging the Consequences', *Public Administration Review,* 54(2).

Mohan, Madan, 1993, 'Ecology and Development', *Third Concept,* January, New Delhi.

Nelson, Jane, 2001, 'Cooperation Between the United Nations and All Relevant Partners, in Particular the Private Sector', UNO A56/323, New York.

Rhodes, R.A.W., 1994, 'The Hallowing Out of the State: The Changing Nature of Public Service in Britain', *Political Quarterly,* 65(2).

Sheafor, Bradford W., Charles R. Horejs and Gloria A. Horejs eds., 1997, *Techniques and Guidelines for Social Work Practice,* Boston: Allyn and Bacon.

Simonis, U.D.O.E., 990, 'A Development Strategy for the 1990s', *Inter Economics,* May-June.

Singh, Subir Hari, 2000, 'Ways and Means of Bridging the Gap between Developed and Developing Countries', A paper presented at High-Level Panel on Information Technology and Public Administration at United Nations, New York, September 26.

Srinivasan, T.N., 1992, 'Human Development: UNDP's Flawed Index', *The Economic Times,* January 1, New Delhi.

Stewart, John and Kieno Waish eds., 1992, 'Change in Management of Public Services', *Public Administration,* 70(4).

Whiston, T.G., 1991, 'Forecasting the World's Problems: The Corporatization of Society and Diminution of Self', *Futures,* March, London: Butterworth-Heineman.

Woodward, Nick, 1990, 'Public Enterprise, Privatization and Cultural Adoption' in John Heath ed., *Public Enterprises at the Cross Roads,* London: Routledge.

—— 1991, 'Ownership and Management—The Concepts' in V.V. Ramandham ed., *Privatization, Ownership and Management,* London: Routledge.

CHAPTER III:
Human Resource Development/Human Rights

9

HRD Initiatives for Organisational Growth

Dr. Bharati Sharma

Introduction

The commitment and dedication of the people have an overwhelming impact on the success of an organization. If commitment and dedication is total the achievements is only a matter of time. Inspite of poor capital equipment and not too advanced technology, a determined group of people have done wonders. Whereas the latest in technologies and the best of equipment have yielded poor results because of lack of peoples' involvement and motivation. Although it is possible to buy technology best suited for business and design good management system, dedication and commitment of people is not readily available. This has to be carefully nurtured and developed.

Since the time it was realized that human beings are resources of an organization, Human Resource Management (HRD) became an essential component of any organization. HRD system is perhaps the most important element in organization's effectiveness which not only ensures present performance but also long term survival and growth of the organization. HRD acts as a catalyst in keeping the organization profitable and alive.

There is a growing awareness in Indian industry of the importance of Human Resource Development. HRD focuses on development not control. Development however needs an integrated approach. It must strive at developing the peoplé in such a way that they are motivated and dedicated so as to contribute whole-heartedly to the growth of the organization.

If HRD is to aim at playing a pivotal role in improving productivity and competitiveness of the organization, it should have a meaningful human resources management system as its base. It should cover the different aspects of the role of HRD—its roles in strategic planning, performing, developing, processing, change and enabling (Krisna, 1990).

There is a realization in one and all that organizations that focus attention on human resources are the ones that are able to grow in this competitive world of business. Growth of any organization thus is linked to the growth and development of the people working in the organization. But the issue of dealing with people is not an easy task. It is often said that in business we have more of "people" problem than any other problem. If people problems are solved our business problems will be substantially resolved. The only way we can solve these problems is through some HRD initiatives. A good strategy on orientation, training and development, change strategy, action for learning, proper integration and maintenance of employees will change the work organization into a family and the employee to a member of a family.

Orientation

The modern society preoccupied with wages, salaries and dividends often forgets that job has some more important purposes to serve in the form of satisfaction of needs, fellowship and development of human personality. Considering these purposes, the need of the hour is proper orientation programme which will enable the new employees to adjust to the culture of the new organisation. This will be truly in tune with the HRD philosophy which is based on the premise that "Every human being has immense inherent potential and is basically willing to contribute his best and he gets best satisfaction in doing so" (McGregor, 1960).

New employees are vulnerable to influence. They are in Kurt Lewin's term 'unfrozen and ripe' and can be influenced and made to move in the desired direction. They will be refrozen in the new settings and the orientation process adopted will have a major role to play in this refreezing process (Lewin, 1951).

Orientation is essential for the will being of both the employees and the organization. All organizations engage in orientation in some form or the other. Some do it formally with some programme and others put the employees directly into their jobs with little special attention. But orientation goes on formally or informally. Some organizations have fixed period of transition from a trainee to an executive, or from probationer to permanent. On the other hand, the transition could be so varied that the adaptability of the employee alone will decide when he is ready to be called permanent. Responsibility of socializing new employees is usually given to a person or a group or persons. But often the new employee is left on his or her own to figure out things. At the time of selection itself certain qualities are looked for in the employees and the organization makes investment on these qualities. But sometimes orientation tries to strip away certain characteristics of the recruit and reshape them so as to fit them into the organization culture.

Any socialization process has to keep the following objectives in mind:

— Help employees to adjust
— Make employees satisfied
— Bring about commitment
— Reduce anxiety
— Remove reality-shock

It must be kept in mind that the effectiveness of the transition process from gathering information to mastering the relevant job components affects the outcomes of socialization. Ineffective socialization is related to increased turnover, lower performance, dissatisfactory negative work attitudes and stress (Ostroff and Kozlowski, 1992).

Career Development

Immediately following induction is the function of developing the employee's ability to do the job. Development would include both training to increase skill in performing a specific job and education to increase general knowledge and understanding of one's own total environment. Planned development programmes will return values to the organisation in terms of increased productivity, heightened morale, reduced costs, and greater organizational stability and flexibility to adapt to changing external requirements. However, along with developing employees to achieve the organizational goal both employee and employer should be concerned with the long-term career objectives. Career planning is one such system which will keep the motivational level and help the employees take this career as a challenge and make it more satisfying. "It is ironic that what is most precious to the individual in so far as work is concerned, that is, the career, is given the least attention by the organization" (Leach, 1977).

While adopting various methods to help in the growth and development of an employee importance should be given to developing career paths. The purpose of career planning is to lay out a future programme of work activities and development experiences in order to prepare a person for fulfilling work, to show logical progression of people between jobs. The concept of career paths can be made useful only when they are formally defined and documented. The task of developing realistic career path may involve some steps. First, through job analysis the skills, knowledge and other quality required to perform various jobs may be determined. In subsequent step, it is desirable to identify similarity among jobs based on their content and skills/knowledge requirements, and to group similar jobs into job families. Thereafter it is required to identify logical possible progression among these job families, which will represent career paths. The possibilities for multiple career paths to which workers and employees can adapt their personal plans for movement may also be explored. The most crucial and delicate issue concerning career development plan is communication of the career development paths to the employees.

Change Strategy

Organisations that enjoy enduring success have shown that the business strategy and practice must keep adapting to the changing world. Today's organisations are operating mostly under uncertain and changing environment and therefore, need to be more flexible in order to cope with the environmental demands.

This characteristic of adapting to the environment makes

organizations similar to living systems as only those who are able to adapt and can survive. This link between the organization and environment is not only confined to the type of input provided or the output elicited, but determine the very act of strategy formulation. Organisations whose prime aim is to achieve their goals and objectives must develop strategies depending on the demands of the environment and change these accordingly.

Change is moving from present state to a desired state in response to dynamic internal and external factors. Growth takes place only through the forces of change. Technology, economic conditions, global competition, world politics, social and demographic changes, and internal problems are some of these forces.

As changes in organizations are stimulated by multiple external and internal forces, organizations, in order to survive and prosper, must respond and adapt to these forces. They must innovate continuously and improve their products and services to meet changing customer demands and competition. Technologies must be updated and new and better ways to organize and manage must be found. Complacency and the status quo are dangerous for any organization. The individual managers and organizations that recognize the inevitability of change and learn to adapt to manage the organizational personnel will be most successful (Cook, Hunsaker and Coffey, 1997). It is true that although change is inevitable and perhaps it is the only constant thing in the world, there is always resistance to change. Resistance can take place either at the individual level or at the organizational level. At the individual level resistance is caused due to selective perceptions, lack of communication, fear of the unknown and resentment towards the initiator. Organisations too resist change for most of the same reasons as individuals do.

Often during changes in decision-making, authority and control of resource allocation threaten the balance of power in organizations. Units benefiting from the change endorse it, but those losing power resist it. Organisations resist change when there is a structural instability due to change, since basically organisaitonal structures, rules and regulations are designed to develop consistent, predictable behaviour An organization is a system of interrelated structures or subsystems. A change in any area will have effects on others, which may not be acceptable.

Organisational culture, which is so carefully created and maintained, may also cause resistance to change. Organisational members will resist changes that force them to abandon established and approved ways of doing things.

However, resistance can be overcome by education and communication. Knowledge of the reasons for change and the likely consequences make people accept change gracefully. Participation and involvement in the change process too minimize resistance as it is difficult for people to resist changes that they themselves have helped to bring about. Helping those affected by the change to new requirements through support, training, consulting may reduce resistance. Negotiation and agreement are often important tools for dealing with powerful resistors. Although not a positive approach, application of threat measures such as decreased salaries, lay off and the like may also have to be taken into consideration to overcome resistance to change.

Action for Learning

Organisations learn everyday while planning their activities quietly, interacting with people, reading internal documents, performing tasks and watching work being done. Organisations are what they are because of learning and adapting to change. The moment they stop learning they will cease to be organizations. They will either be killed by other successful organizations or die a national death. Organisations that are learning constantly attempt to figure out what works and works better through learning. Organisations acquire and apply knowledge, skills and values, beliefs and attitudes that enhance and maintain growth and development of the organization. Statistics say that out of the list of 500 companies in America in 1956 only 29 from the top 100 on the original list remain today. Although no such data are available in our country we often hear of companies either going sick, winding up or acquired by other successful companies.

Strategic Planning today is more about organizational earning than about programming; a series of activities to attain an objective. A planning head of a reputed company once noted that the real purpose of effective planning is not to make plans but to change the mental models that decision-makers carry in their heads. Today's strategic planning and strategic thinking involve envisioning and planning a workable fit between organizational competencies and limitations on the one hand and opportunities and threats on the other, with the aim of serving customers better. Thinking strategically means anticipating what actions are most likely to help the organization prosper in a changing environment. The strategic side of management is the craft of balancing stability and consistency over time with change when needed (Mintzberg, 1987).

Sense of Belonging

The willingness of people to work is based largely on management's ability to integrate the interests and needs of its employees with the objectives of the organisaiton. There must be a reasonable merger of the persons and the organization if effective action is to result. It should be attempted that organizations are managed in such a way that what is good for the employee is also good for the organization. When there is proper identification with the organization, the employees feed proud of being the part of that organization and work for the growth of the organization as they do it in a family.

It is the sense of belongingness that knit together all employees through strong/shared values. This results in concern for their own well-being and also for thė organization. Effective HRD approach should help employees develop a sense of belonging and deal with any identify crisis. HRD system must creak on atmosphere where there is scope for development of concern for excellence and self-actualization.

Commitment to team which is rare in Indian organizations will also come from the sense of belonging and the team members will work as members of family. When individuals collaborate and jointly search solutions to problems, team performance should be higher than that of the most competent individual. In most cases, it is seen that there is negative synergy where team performance is poorer than the individual performance. A major concern of HRD should be to develop synergy and encourage improved group performance. This sense of belonging in the employees will bring in the concept of family-hood and team members will work as members of the family.

Conclusion

Success of HRD in an organisation depends on how these initiatives are carried forward. Whatever strategy an organisation adopts results can only be achieved through people and therefore, organizational growth is possible only through HRD initiatives. Initiative must be taken to develop a corporate citizenship among the people where rights and duties both play a very important role. Members of organisation enjoy many rights being its part and thus, they must never forget their duties. They are also stable holders in the organizations rise and fall, success and failure, survive or die. Organisations in which members remember both rights and duties and maintain a balance between the two are bound to survive.

REFERENCES

1. Cook, C.W., Hunsaker P.L., Coffey, R.E. (1997), *Management and Organisational Behaviour,* McGraw Hill, USA.
2. Krishna Suresh (1990), "HRD Issues/Opportunities—Top Management Views" in *Excellence through Human Resource Development, Tata McGraw Hill Publishing Company Ltd., New Delhi*
3. Leach John (1977), "The Notion and Nature of Careers", *The Personnel Administrator,* Vol. 22, No. 7, September 1977, p. 50.
4. Lewin, Kurt (1951), *Field Theory in Social Science,* Harper & Row, New York.
5. McGregor, Douglas (1960), *The Human side of Enterprises,* McGraw Hill, New York.
6. Mintzberg, H (1981), "Crafting Strategy", *Harvard Business Review,* Vol. 65, July-August.
7. Ostroff, Cherri and Kozlowski, Steve W. (1992), "Organizational Socialization as a Learning Process: The Role of Internal Acquisition", *Personnel Psychology,* Vol. 45.

10

The Government as Learning Organization: A Globalized HRD Model for Leadership, Creativity and Destress

Dr. Prem Saran, IAS

Introduction

As we move into the 21st century, things Indian will increasingly begin to come into their own. The distinctive Indic episteme would draw greater scholarly interest in a globalising world, given its potential relevance in many contemporary fields of application. Such traditional Indian knowledge systems can provide a powerful ecological model for land resource management and rural upliftment, human resource management and public administration.

It has been successfully used by a number of State Governments to train their senior IAS, IPS, and other officers. It has also been similarly tested successfully on senior officials working in major public sector enterprises. It is now being digitized for use as a Distance Learning tool by the Government of Assam.

In the following pages (Section I) an attempt has being made by the author to explain the global, cross-cultural character and outreach of this Model of Human Research Development; it operationalises Peter Senge's well known concept of the "Learning Organisation"; and believes that it can be fruitfully used in **Public Administration,** by treating government organizations as Learning Organisations and in Management by contemporary mangers for what has been called **rightbrain management** (Alder:1998b).

This paper draws partly from the author's personal (practical) knowledge and theoretical expertise from his training in ancient Indian meditational and mystic techniques as a student of Indology, Religious Authropology and Management and partly from the inspiring works of Peter Senge and Debashis Chaterjee. Based on both primary and secondary sources of data, the author has formulated an innovative eponymous model of human resource development (Christened as Saran's Model) for brevity and convenience.

Professor Peter Senge of the Sloan School of Management, MIT in his much acclaimed book, "The Fifth Discipline: The Art and Practice of the Learning Organization" (1994) identifies **systemic thinking**, as the fifth discipline' crucial to create a learning organization. It means that when one looks at an organization one sees the connection between its parts, and a process of change rather than stasis.

"Learning Organization" is one that recognizes the importance of the people within it, supports their full development and creates a context in which they learn" (O, Connor and Seymour, 1994). Indeed, *Fortune* magazine, recognizing the competitive edge that learning organizations would have, has identified them as likely to be the most successful corporations of the future. With the "knowledge society" in place, there can be no two opinions about the ever-increasing salience of effective learning processes, and of the kinds of organization that actively foster them.

A basic flaw in Senge's model is, that it does not indicate, the praxis that is needed for his fifth discipline to be inculcated. He admits, that a "sixth discipline", "a wholly new discipline that we cannot even grasp today" may be needed. He hints at the shape of that new discipline, in his Foreworld to Debashis Chatterjee's innovative book, "Leading Consciously: A Pilgrimage Toward Self-Mastery" (Chatterjee: 1999). Senge believes that Eastern cultures like India and China constitute a "unique storehouse of practical knowledge about consciousness" [emphasis added] and commends the author for "his vision of offering ancient insights in a way that makes them understandable to contemporary mangers".

Chatterjee's work offers a simplified version of ancient Indian meditative practices, (Indic meditative praxis) the fundamental goal of which is the attainment of the "mystical experience". Its holistic nature makes it cognate with the "systemic thinking" that constitutes Senge's "fifth discipline". These techniques have the potential to enable one to systematically internalize that organizationally desirable kind of thinking. In other words, these can very form the core of the required "sixth discipline".

In Section II, the author argues that since his model is based on the holistic modes of functioning of the rightbrain, it can potentially be **the sixth** discipline that is needed to effectively operationalize Senge's crucial (fifth) discipline of systemic thinking for the learning organization. He reaches the conclusion that it can even be considered **"the ultimate"** discipline for that purpose. For it is the distillation of over two *millennia* of yogic experimentation in the Indic civilization, which indeed is a culture specialized precisely in the kinds of praxis required for achieving that sort of learning-oriented mindset!

I. Saran's HR Model of Rightbrain Management: Features

After Roger Sperry's Nobel Prize-winning discovery of the special modes of functioning of the human rightbrain, there has been much research interest in finding ways of systematically tapping its vast potential. This interest has spilled over into the field of Management theory and practice especially in the area of Human Resource Management. The present model has also been influenced by Roger Sperry's discovery. The Model has four characteristic features:

1. It is **cross-cultural** in the sense that it makes use of both the Indian and Western philosophical thoughts and ideas, backed by the author's expertise as a practitioner and teacher of Hindu-cum Buddhist techniques of mediation.
2. The Model is very progmatic in that it is useful for the purposes of **Stress Control, Creativity, and Rightbrain Management.**
3. It involves techniques for doing meditation, which is performed in three stages, viz. **relaxing the body, relaxing the mind, and autoprogramming.** Finally, the model can be situated within the context of current mainstream research in the Behavioral Sciences.

The Indic Cultural Background: The Model rests on the foundation of four core themes in the Indic civilization. First, unlike the atomistic personality structure of the modern West, South Asian personhood is "porous". For it is "holonic", to use Arthur Koestler's term: everything in nature is a "holon", *i.e.* a whole, that is in trun, a part of other wholes. This holistic psycho-culture understanding of selfhood is seen crossculturally to be much more accurate than the Western, as anthropologists like Melford Spiro and Malcolm Crick have shown. That, in fact, partly explains why well-known transpersonally-oriented psychologists like Robert Assagioli and Abrahm Maslow have significantly enriched their work by the use of perspectives from Indic and related meditative traditions.

Second, as opposed to the Judeo-Christian Worldview of the Western civilization, with its distinctive and almost pathological Protestant work-ethic, the South Asian cultural ethos is more playful. This is indicated by the salience of the Indic (Hindu) cosmogony of "lila", which views the cosmos as the outcome of the (erotic) sport of the "devine". This cultural syndrome clearly has positive and humanistic effects, because it makes for a more relaxed and healthier attitude towards life.

Third, a corollary of the second theme, is the Indic cultural salience of the **pleasure-principle.** This is quite patently evinced by the pan-South Asian persistence of the Tantric cult, with its foregrounding of a balanced hedonism in order to attain the altered state of 'samadhi', which is the pan-Indic term for the mystical experience of union with the ground of being. This sophisticated appreciation of the role of Eros in human life also happens to resonate with Freud's realization, towards the very end of his long life, that the libido is naught but the life-force!

Finally, as against the androcentric, Judeo-Christian metaphysical and hence socio-cultural biases of Western culture, Indic philosophy and culture are pervasively imbued with the ancient bipolar ideology of Samkhya, with its characteristic and basic attitude of **gender-mutuality/complementarity**. This can perhaps be related with the Jungian speculations about the anima and animus, which allude to the psycho-spiritual basis of the relationship between the sexes. At any rate, it is this equi-gendered view of reality the underlies the centuries-old yogic technique of Kundalini-visualization, to which we now turn.

Kundalini-Visualization as HR Technique: Briefly put, the core of the Saran HRD model is a radically simplified version of the traditional Kundalini technique of bipolar yogic visualization. It basically consists of the following three stages. First, the body is relaxed by using a process of autogenic visualization. Then, the mind is put into an "altered state" by the visualization of an "inner body", within which is a fine tube running down its center, from its anal region to the crown of the head; thereafter, by visually directing the attention up the tube, from its bottom end to its top, a deep hypnogogic state is achieved. Finally, in this state of deep relaxation, one methodically programs oneself to achieve desired foals, personal and/or organizational.

The effectiveness of any tool or technique depends on how simple it is, as Edward de Bono has pointed out. The technique above is both simple and extremely effective, as experienced by the author whenever he used it in training courses for hardboiled professionals, such as senior Indian civil servants. For, within minutes, worldly-wise subjects such as these are enabled to enter a profound meditative state, within which they can then very easily learn to become better managers and leaders. That is to say, this technique can be profitably used for bottomline organizational objectives, through the synergic achievement of optimal Stress Control, enhanced Creativity, and a balanced Rightbrain-Management style, as indicated below.

Stress Control. There are about 2 dozen schools of yoga in the Hindu and Buddhist traditions. According to the eminent French Indologist Louis Renou, these Indic techniques of meditation are a veritable "discipline of the unconscious". Or, to use contemporary terminology, such techniques are effective ways to get out of one's normal leftbrain mode of consciousness, which constitutes merely the iceberg's tip of one's actual mental capacities. Thus, one can easily learn to systematically access the vast submerged and untapped potentials of the rightbrain. In other words, by regular practice of such rightbrain-manifesting states of meditative absorption, and thus of deep relaxation, one can effectively release the bulk of one's accumulated stresses. One can, thereby, increasingly operate at optimal stress levels, and as a result, significantly boost one's own performance.

Creativity. According to many experts, individuals, creativity depends essentially on the ability to make novel conceptual associations, whereby one is, then able to generate innovative ideas.

This is a process that is eminently facilitated by such techniques of rightbrain-tapping, which enable one to bypass the routine style of functioning of the leftbrain, in order to enter the visual mode of the rightbrain. This latter holistic mode permits one to make the imaginative leaps that constitute what de Bono (1990) calls "lateral thinking". The creative ideas that are thus generated can be critically evaluated later for their practicality and feasibility, by resorting subsequently to the logical activity of the leftbrain. The net result is that one begins to learn to operate in the whole-brain manner of the most effective CEOs and other top organizational leaders, as Harry Alder has shown.

Rightbrain Management. According to management writers like Edwad de Bono and Harry Mintzberg, even the well-known management schools are unable to produce the kind of a mangers that modern societies need. In Alder's (1998b) diagnosis, the main reason for this is that management-training programs are almost entirely leftbrain-oriented. For, they focus mainly on the over-valued skills of critical analysis, sadly neglecting the much more powerful rightbrian modes. Alder found that most of the top British CEO's he studied had actually learned to access their rightbrain capacities, and also to confidently trust the resultant outputs. There is thus a definite trend towards the "right brain manager" (Alder: 1998b), who quite clearly values this style of "creative management", as Gareth Morgan so aptly characterizes it.

Modern Perspectives and Saran's Model. To sum up this section, it will be an useful exercise to critically look at this Indic Model, vis-à-vis some cognate and interesting contemporary perspectives. We may start with Abraham Maslow's (1964, 2000) studies of "peak experience", which are complemented by Cziksentmihalyi's (1991) research on those mental states of "optimal experience" which he terms "flow". In such rightbrain states, one finds oneself functioning optimally precisely because one is so absorbed in what one is experiencing or doing, and is thus unselfconscious and oblivious of oneself. Both these researchers have also made explicit comparisons of these states with **yogic** experiences of meditative absorption.

Moreover, by putting one increasingly in touch with one's own internal resources, such "psychedelic" or "mind-manifesting' procedures help to cumulatively generate the positive mindset that Martin Seligman calls "learned optimism". This reinforces those positive feedback loops that synergize learning and growth, both in individuals and organizations. And that, in turn generates the high need-achievement described by McClelland, thereby reinforcing the motivation required to fuel the Maslowian drive towards self actualization and creativity. It is therefore not surprising that Alder's top business leaders are so dependent for their success on their constant recourse to the pleasurable, freewheeling modes of rightbrain thinking.

Again, in this global age of resurgent interest in non-Western modes of knowledge and praxis, it is only apt that Indians, Chinese and Japanese ideas should increasingly begin to cross-fertilize the field of management. We thus have the Japanese philosophy of *kaizen* (or "continuous improvement"),, and the Chinese "Tao of Leadership". And from Indian management theorists, we have S.K. Chakravorty's (1993) "Management by Values", Debasis Chatterjee's (1999) concept of "Leading Consciously", and the author's Indic Model of Rightbrain Management (Saran: 2000).

As already noted Senge has highly appreciated Chatterjee's work, and the latter was condescendingly cited by Harvard Business School for his salient contribution to management theory and practice. For, his model takes the "rightbrain manager" to the next turn of the spiral, where she/he comes face to face with the ultimate human need, as theorized by Maslow. This is the need for "transcendence", which holistically subsumes all the other needs in Maslow's hierarchy. At that stage, business management and public administration begin to get transmuted from a vocation into an **avocation,** with the concomitant optimazation of the pragmatic benefits that can accrue to both individual and society.

Thus, since it takes the above process of inter-cultural and cross-disciplinary fertilization even further, in terms of both theoretical rigour and practical efficacy, Saran's Model provides a basic tool for just such a radical and humanistic transformation. For we have seen that it is based on the highly sophisticated and time-tested Indic technique of *Kundalini-visualization.* And that in turn has been shown above to actually constitute a cross-culturally valid and powerful model of "rightbrain management", and therefore of optimal Human Resource Development. In other words, it can bring out more fully the human side of organizational enterprises. That brings us to Section II, where we can now examine how The Saran Model can be the sixth discipline anticipated by Senge himself.

II. Saran's Model: The Sixth and Ultimate Discipline for the Learning Organization

In this Section, the author first indicates why Senge's description of his "fifth discipline", viz. that of systemic thinking, is merely theoretical and exhortative, and therefore inadequate for its actual internalization and use. Subsequently, it is shown how Saran's Model can provide just the simple and empirical means needed to operationalize that "fifth discipline". In other words, it can be the required **sixth discipline** foreseen by Senge. Finally, he argues that this Model also constitutes the **ultimate** discipline for the learning **organizaion,** precisely because it addresses the crosscultural "meta-need" for the experiential knowledge of "transcendence" (Maslow, 2000), as well as because it has been finetuned through over two millennia of experimentation in the Indic civilization.

Now, as the subtitle title of his book would make one expect, Senge's description of his fifth discipline is probably intended to be a *practical* way of inculcating "systemic thinking" in the learning organization. Unfortunately, it remains only at the leftbrain, iceber's-tip level of cerebration, whereas effective learning has necessarily to engage the rightbrain, which constitutes about 90 percent of one's brain capacity! An apt comparison here would be the process of learning to drive a car, where a mere *verbal* description of gears and brakes and suchlike is in itself quite patently insufficient. One will have learnt to drive properly *only* when he has acquired the practical knowledge of driving- it has become his second nature, when one has reached the level of what is known as 'unconscious competence' in Neuro-Linguistic Programming, the wellknown contemporary technique of "learning to learn" (Andreas and Faulkner: 220-221).

However, it would be petty to fault Senge on this, given the overweening dominance of the leftbrain mode of cognition in the history of the Western civilization (Edwards: 1979, 1995). From the Greeks onward, through the medieval hegemony of the Christian Church, and right into modern times, the West has been a **talking** culture (de Bono: 1990). It has set its greatest store by the knowledge acquired through the verbal or leftbrain mode of ratiocination. It can therefore, aptly be termed a **leftbrain culture** (Alder, 1998b: 15-16), though it had increasingly begun to realize the limitations of its ovewhelming dependence on this mode of thinking alone. And that recognition has largely come through the increasing scientific interest in precisely those rightbrain modes of cognition that are systematically inculcated by the practice of the ancient *Eastern* techniques of meditation, such as the Hindu, Buddhist ang Taoist (Maslow:1964).

The Indic civilization, in remarkable contrast, has modally had an *inward*, yogic orientation, with resultant insights and learning being valorised as the summum bonum of all knowledge. So much so that the wellknown Indologist and Anthropologist Prof. Agehananda Bharati has rightly considered the yogic traditions of meditation to be the greatest contribution of India to the world (Bharati: 1976)! Moreover, this is a civilization that has specialized so highly in such techniques of rightbrain-tapping that it has developed over two dozen schools of meditation, both Hindu and Buddhist, in the course of over two millenia of highly individual experimentation and praxis.

In other words, since Indian culture places so much emphasis on the visual and holistic mode of cognition, such as that exemplarily developed by yogic discipline, it can very well be called a **rightbrain culture.** Further, the basic paradigm for much of yogic meditation is the ancient technique of *kundalini-visualization.* That is to say, the Indic methodology of *kundalini-visualization,* including its contemporary and user-friendly avatar of **Saran's Model,** has plainly stood the test of time as a proven technique of rightbrain-tapping. That being so, it will now be interesting to examine how exactly it achieves its aim of effective rightbrain management, in order also to see whether it can be the anticipated *sixth discipline* for the learning organization.

Saran's Model as the Sixth Learning Discipline. According to the reputed mangement trainers Joseph O'Connor and John Seymour, (1994) who use Neuro-Lingustic Programming (NLP) in their work, Senge's fifth discipline of systemic thinking is most undoubtedly an essential skill for mangement. However, as they go on to admit, (Western) mangers are still in the dark about how this kind of holistic (*i.e.* rightbrain) thinking is to be systematically and effectively achieved. And the reason for this is simply that the art oand science of systemic thinking is so antipodally different from the routine, linear (*i.e.* leftbrain) thinking that is so overvalued in the West, even though it actaully represents only 10 per cent—the *iceberg's tip*—of our mental capacities!

On the other hand, we have seen that Saran's Model can provide the required sixth discipline that today's global manger is looking for. And that is because it is based on the time-tested Indic paradigm of kundalini-visualization. To appreciate why this is so, we may now take a closer look at the effectiveness of yogic visualization, and thus of my eponymous Model. We may do this fruitfully by using the perspectives generated by the discipline of NLP, since it is explicitly about *íincreasing* people's effectiveness and *maximising* their potential" (Bradbury: 2002, 39).

According to NLP, which was developed in the 1970's at the University of California, the human brain receives inputs through the five outer senses, does its blackbox processing, and then the person acts as per the resultant mental outputs. Again, when a person thinks, he or she uses the corresponding five *inner* sensory modalities (Alder and Heather, 1999: 6-9). Of these, the three most commonly used are the visual, autditory, and kinesthetic (or feeling) senses. In a leftbrain civilization like the Western, with its historically anathematic attitudes towards inward experience, these inner or rightbrain modalities are of course grossly undervalued as Foucault points out.

Conversely, in a rightbrain civilization like the Indic, these same inner experiential modalities are given a very high and *positive* valorization. As a result, there is a rich cultural capital available on tap, insofar as the ability to access and use the imagination is concerned. The denizen of such a culture is also thus able, with a little bit of practice, to cathect the Indic knack for *systematic* visualization. For this ability to generate clear *mental images,* as cathected for instance in the typically Indic prax9is of kundalini-visualization, represents an innate (if *inchoate,* as in the Western civilization) potential of the human rightbrain in all cultures. Such disciplined visualization therefore only requires a little training, such as may be imparted with the Model described here, for it to be *crossculturally* replicated and utilized (Alder, 1998b: 33).

Accordingly, with approprite training in visualization, as with **Saran's Model** of kundalini-visualization, the nature of the human brain as a cybernetic (*i.e.* goal-seeking) mechnism (Alder, 1998b:

123-125) can be brough into increasingly fuller play. The basic principle underlying the operation of this "psycho-cybernetics" (Maltz: 1997) is the biological tendency to seek pleasure and aoid pain. Thus, to the extent that one can exercise greater control over this mechnism, say by the disciplined use of Indic visualization techniques (Alder, 1998b: 158), one cn begin to channelise one's inner resources optimally. This is simply and easily achieved by generating clear mental images of one's aims as aleady and pleasurably achieved such as one's career and organizational goals.

One can thus program oneself to achieve the vocational and avocational goals that one consiously sets for oneself, by the systematic and synergized use of the three sensory modalities of NLP practitioners term "generative learning", or "learning to learn" (O'Connor and Seymour, 1994: 20-22). In short, Saran's Model of Indic rightbrain-tapping quite patently constitutes the *sixth* discipline we are looking for, whereby we can **internalize** and thus operationalize Senge's fifth discipline of systemic or **holistic** thinking, in a simple and practical manner. So it remains now only to conclude this disquisition by briefly examining whether that Model can also be considered the *ultimate* desideratum for the learning organization.

Saran's Model as the Ultimate Learning Discipline. According to John Naisbitt (Buzan: 289-292), the metatrend underlying the ten global megatrends of the new milleninium is "learning to learn". And this is precisely the "generative learning" that is "needed to create a learning organization" (O'Connor and Seymour, 1994:24). For it is learning that is generated by oneself from *within*, by tapping one's own unconscious or *rightbrain* resources.

There is already a slew of such techniques that are becoming increasingly popular in the West. An interesting example of such larning is Georgi Lozanov's **superlearning** (Maslow, 2000:256). This however is much too passive since it is external to the learner, being based on certain kinds of music tha are played in the background in order to help the learner access her reighbrain. On the other hand, the Indic type of rightbrain-tapping that is epitomised by Saran's Model of kundalini-visualization is eminently *pro-active*, and therefore quite clearly constitutes the *ultimate* learning discipline, based as it is on over two millenia of intesive and specialized experimentation in the Indic civilization.

In short, theoretical system-builiding such as Senge's, in the timworn Western-philosophical mode of *leftbrain*-thinking, is no longer sufficient for organizations that hope to successfully operate in today's globalizing world. It is definitely inadequate if one is to **effectively** inculcate the fifth discipline of the *learning* organization, namely that of systemic or **holistic** thinking. For, ongoing by Sternberg's cruicial three criteria of successful intelligence (Sternberg:2000), Senge's model fails to satisfy the cruicial test of **practicality,** even though it does meet the other two conditions of *analytical* soundness and *creativity.*

Conversely, Saran's Model of *systemic thinking* meets all three of the above criteria. For it is eminently **practical** too, since it is both simple and effective, being based on more than two thousand years of orthodox and orthopractical finetuning within those timeworn Indic traditions of ípsycho-experimentation" (Bharati) that are subsumed under the rubric of yoga. It is indeed the Promethean tool sought by the new *learning culture* that is emerging globally, in order to *"learn to learn"*.

Finally, we may recall that yoga is nothing but a *"discipline of the unconscious"*, according to the French scholar Louris Renour. Or, to use a contemporary idiom, it is a systematic technique for *tapping the righbrain,* with its vast resources of *systemic* or *holistic* thinking. Therefore it can quite aptly be termed the **sixth and ultimate discipline** for the contemporary **learning organization,** for it provides the wherewithal to complement and thus *operationalize* Senge's overly cerebral and *leftbrain*-oriented "fifth discipline".

Conclusion: Saran's Model and the Government as Learning Organization

It remains now only to show how this Model can be applied to the functioning of Government organizations. This can be done quite easily since Government is also a type of managerial organization, which is after all why there has been so much contemprary interest in the very concept of "management in Government". In other world, **Governent** can also be fruitfully treated as a type of **Learning Organization.**

In fact, it is high time that we in Government look beyational development techniques. For instance, as McDermott and Shircore argue in their book on the "NewManager" (p. 1), athe stereotypical change management intervention that is usually essayed is one that goes by theoptimistic name of "sharing best practices"; unfortunately, however, that effort is at best a "hit-and-miss process".

In short, such methods have willynilly to be complemented by innovative HR practices, such as my own eponymous, cross-cultural Model. And indeed with the widespread use of Information Technology in governance, the practicality of the Model can also be strategically enhanced, by digitalising and then propagating it electonically. Thereby the said Model can be put to widespread use as a Distance Learning Tool, to provide"Training for All" as per the National Training Policy of 1996....

REFERENCES

The author acquired this knowledge during his field research conducted in Nepal, for a Ph.D in Cultural Anthropology at the University of California. The subject of the research was South Asian Tantrism, in which the author happens to be a traditional initiate and an international expert.

Alder, Harry (1998a), *Think like a Leader*, Bombay: Magna Publishing.

Alder, H. (1998b), *The Right Brain Manager*, London:Judy Piatkus.

Alder, Harry and Heather, Beryl.

Andreas, Steve and Faulkner, Charles.

Bharati, Agehananada (1976), *The Light at the Center: Context and Pretext of Modern Mysticism*, Santa Barbara: Ross-Erikson.

Bradbury, Andrew (2002), *Develop Your NLP Skills*, New Delhi: Kogan Page.

Buzan, Toy (1980), *Use Both Sides of Your Brain*, New York: E.P. Dutton.

Buzan, Tony and Buzan, Barry (1994), *The Mind Map Book*, New York: Penguin.

Chakraborty, S.K. (1993), *Management by Values*, New Delhi: Oxford University Press.

Chatterjee, Debashis (1999), *Leading Consciously*, New Delhi: Viva Books.

Crick, Malcolm R. (1982), "Anthropology of Knowledge". *In Annual Review of Anthropology*, 11:287-313.

Czikszentmihalyi, Mihalyi (1991), *Flow: The Psychology of Optimal Experience*, New York: Harper Collins.

De Bono, Edwrd (1990), *Lateral Thinking for Managers*, London: Penguin Books.

Dreher, Diane (1997), *The Tao of Personal Leadership: The Ancient Way to Success*, New York: Harper Collins.

Edwards, Betty (1979), *Drawing on the Right Side of the Brain*, Los Angeles.

J.P. Tarcher (1995), *Drawing on the Artist Within: How to Release Your Hidden Creativity*, London: Harper Collins.

Goleman, Daniel (1995), *Emotional Intelligence*, New York: Bantam Books.

Koestler, Arthur (1978), *Janus: A Summing Up*, New York: Random House.

Malta, Maxwell (1997), *Psyco-cybernetics*, New York: Prentice Hall.

Mc Dermott, Ian and O'Connor, Joseph (2001), *NLP and Health*, London: Harper Collins.

Mc Dermott, I an and Shircore, Ian (1998), *NLP and the New Manager*, L:ondon: Orion Publishing Group.

Maslow, Abraham (1964), *Religion, Values and Peak Experiences*, Columbus: Ohio University Press.

Maslow, A. (2000), *Motivation and Personality*, 3rd ed., New York: Longman.

Morgan, Gareth (1993), *Imaginazation: The Art of Creative Management*, London: Sage.

O'Connor, Joseph and Seymour, John (1994), *Training with NLP: Skills for Managers, Trainers and Communicators*, London: Harper Collins.

Saran, Prem (1996), *Yoga, Bhoga and Ardhanariswara: Individuality, Eucaemonism, and Gender in South Asian Tantrism*, Ph.D. Dissertation, University of California, Ann. Arbor: University Microfilms.

Saran, P., *Tantra: Hedonism in Indian Culture:* 2nd ed., New Delhi: D.K. Printworld.

Saran, P., 'Right Brain Management: The Need of the Hour', *In Management in Government*, 32(2),

Saran, P., "Ethical Issues in Governance: A Cross-Cultural HRD Model", *In ASTI Journal of Training and Development* II(1).

Senge, Peter M. (1994), *The Fifth Discipline: The Art and Practice of the Learning Organization*, New York: Doubleday.

Spiro, Melford E. (1993), "Is the Western Conception of the Self peculiar within the Context of the World Cultures?" *In Ethos*, 21(2): 107-53.

Sternberg, Robert J. (2000), *Successful Intelligence: How Practical and Creative Intelligence Determine Success in Life*, Mumbai: Magna Publishing.

11

Police Administration and Custodial Crimes in Delhi in the Context of Human Rights

Dr. Radhanath Tripathy

Public Administration in the 21st century, as it is commonly agreed, must be an effective, efficient, legitimate, accountable, transparent and sensitive machinery of the state. Beside all these qualities, its existence must be justified on the extent to which it promotes and protects the human rights of the people. The end of good governance remains unfulfilled in the absence of a sensitive public safety administration or police administration because it is that part of public administration which deals with the basic human rights of the people. Besides promoting its efficiency and effectiveness, the need of the hour is that police administration has to be accountable and sensitive to the rights of the people in general and the rights of those who come into its contact or into its custody in particular.

With individuals as their point of reference human rights seek to guarantee to individuals the minimum necessary conditions for pursuing a distinctively human life. The idea of human rights emerged against violence and atrocities against women and weaker sections of the society, xenophobia, war crimes and religious and racial persecutions perpetrated by some twentieth century political regimes (state authorities). The major objective of human rights is to protect the individual against abuse of power by the authorities, *i.e.* against the abuse of state power.[1] The Universal Declaration of Human Rights, 1948, made these rights "positive" and initiated a process not only to recognize but also to protect rights, even against the State which violates them. In the worlds of M. Freeden, "a human right is a conceptual device, expressed in linguistic form that assigns priority to certain human or social attributes regarded as essential to the adequate functioning of a human being; that is intended to serve as a protective capsule for those attributes; and that appeals for a deliberate action to ensure such a protection."[2] Thus, it becomes a duty of the state or administration to protect these rights. The enjoyment of these rights, thus, depends on the extent to which they are being protected by the state authorities, particularly by criminal justice administration and police.

Human Rights and Police

Human Rights vest in the individuals (communities) and are protected by the State and in this process the police administration or force which is the most visible symbol of state authority plays an important role. J.H. Skolnick rightly observed that, "in modern society police is the principal agency for the enforcement of law. The policemen symbolize state authority and also they are the custodians of the interest of the society as well as individual citizens as far as their basic rights are concerned."[3] Police acts as the watchdog and protector of human rights. At every step police plays an important role. Firstly, it prevents the occurrence of crime, so that our rights are not in jeopardy. Secondly, whenever our life and rights are in danger, police comes to our rescue. Thirdly, when our rights are violated, it is the police which helps in the prosecution and restoration of our rights. As an important agent of the executive, it plays an active role in democratic government. Even in most of the democratic societies there are situations requiring the attention of someone with a legitimate right to use coercive force that is police.[4]

The paradox is that, there are various occasions, situations and instances when police acts contrary to its chartered duties. Police who are the law enforcers themselves violate law and consider force not morality as the basis of law enforcement.[5] The possibility of the rise of a violent and repressive police force always exists even under a democratic regime, as has been argued by David H. Bayley.[6] The irony is that police which enforcing law, maintaining law and order and fighting with crime, deviate from their legally assigned responsibility and become unlawful, irrational and inhuman rights violation by the police. The reality is that the greatest challenge to the rights of the individual neither comes from the other individuals nor from the society but from the law enforcement agency of the state, more particularly from the police.

Custodial Crime

Violation of human rights as a result of police behaviour and brutality is universal and takes various forms. The most important form of violation of human rights which draws our immediate attention is that which takes place in the custody of the police. Custodial crimes otherwise known as "custodial violence" or "custodial atrocity" manifest themselves in three categories—torture, rape and death. The right to life and personal liberty of human beings remain under constant threat when a person is in the custody of the police. During investigation and interrogation, police adopt many inhuman and extra-legal methods (popularly known as Third Degree Methods) and in this process people (particularly accused or suspects) are deprived of their right to life and personal liberty in a grossly unconstitutional and immoral manner.

In *Kishore Singh vs. State of Rajasthan,* the Supreme Court of India observed, "nothing is more cowardly and unconscionable than a person in police custody being beaten up and nothing inflicts a deeper wound on our constitutional culture than a state official running berserk regardless of human rights".[7] The person in police custody is helpless and lonely; he is away from his family members, friends and society. What happens in police custody is not open to public scrutiny. Therefore, injuries sustained in custody are qualitatively different from, even graver injuries sustained during other circumstances. The custodial deaths are no less abominable than the brutality shown by terrorists or fundamentalists. Brutality shown to helpless people in police lock-ups has a tendency to perpetuate itself.[8] Ironically, it is committed by a person who is legally required to protect the life and liberty of the people. As Justice Louis D. Brandeis of American Supreme Court (in *Olmstead vs. USA case*) succinctly put it, "the police reflect the state and the state the society. If the government becomes a law breaker, it breeds contempt for the law; it invites every man to become a law unto himself; it invites anarchy."[9]

Under no circumstances custodial crime (custodial torture, rape and death) should be allowed by the state machinery (police) in a civil and democratic society. The very idea of custodial crime sounds barbaric and is a remnant of the pre-civilizational age of tyranny and cruelty. This inhuman behaviour of police not only violates human rights and the rule of law but it also undermines democracy and dignity of the individual. This barbaric act of police erodes the faith of the people in the efficacy or legitimacy of the democratic institutions and administrative machinery. As Bayley puts it, "the significance of police brutality transcends the quality of hurt that is done to particular individuals. It is a problem of political legitimacy. It affects the status of law and standing of governments. It tests the boundaries of trust and consent between government and people."[10]

Indian Experience

Violation of human rights by police in India, is a colonial legacy which continues in practice even after independence. It is a blot on Indian democracy. Five decades after establishment of democratic governance based on the rule of law in the country police brutality/custodial crime continues to be a routine affair in police administration. In spite of constitutional and legal provisions, debates, discussions and interpellations in parliament/state legislatures, public criticisms and sincere efforts on the part of judiciary, National Human Rights Commission (NHRC) and other civil rights organizations such as People's Union for Democratic Rights, People's Union for Civil Liberties (PUDR, PUCI) and Asia Watch, etc. to check and prevent the practice of custodial violence, this agonizing and brutal event is still reported everyday. A large number of suspects are tortured and die and women are being raped in police custody.[11]

Custodial crimes that the general public come across represent only a fraction of the total reality. Torture frequently goes unreported unless there is some form of public pressure or protest on a political level.[12] Reports of Amnesty International, NHRC, PUDR, PUCL and Asia Watch and the comments of the judiciary in some cases of custodial crime clearly establish that torture is a regular feature in police administration all over the country.

Legal Framework

Respect for human rights and human dignity and protection of life and liberty of the individual are the cardinal principles of Indian Constitution and legal system. There exists sufficient legal provisions to safeguard the human rights of the accused against the police in Indian Constitution, Law and Criminal Justice System.

Aticle 21 of the Indian Constitution provides that "no person shall be deprived of his life or personal liberty except according to the procedure established by law." The procedural safeguards against arbitrary arrest and detention are provided for in Clause (1) and (2) of Aticle 22. Clause (3) of Aticle 20 says: "no person accused of any offence shall be compelled to be a witness against himself."

The Criminal Justice System in India is based on accusatorial model as opposed to inquisitional system.[13] Accordingly, under Section 101-104 of Indian Evidence Act, the accused has a number of rights and he is presumed to be innocent until his guild is proved beyond reasonable doubt. Section 25 of this Act makes confession made before police inadmissible as evidence during trial.

Section 41, 49, 55, 56, 57, 58 of CrPC provide protection against arbitrary and unlawful arrest, and detention in custody and unnecessary restraint. Right to be produced before a magistrate within 24 hours of his arrest is provided under Section 57 and 76 of CrPC. Under Section 163, CrPC, offering of threats, promises or inducement to extract information is prohibited. The Indian Police Act (Sections 20, 23 and 29) prohibits unwarranted personal violence by police officers to any person in custody and it also prescribes punishment for erring policemen. Art. 5 of the code of conduct for Law Enforcement Officers in India clearly retrains the police to resort to any method of torture or inhuman treatment. In case of deaths in custody, an inquiry by a magistrate is mandatory under Section 176 of the CrPC.

The Indian judiciary, in a series of cases,[14] has grappled with lawlessness in law enforcement. The Supreme Court, in *Kishore Singh vs. State of Rajasthan* case, has held that the use of third degree methods by police is violative of Art. 21. The Supreme Court has taken a serious note of custodial deaths and torture in the cases of *Gouri Shankar and Arbinder Singh Bagga* respectively. In another landmark case *Joginder Kumar vs. State of U.P.*, the apex court dealt with the rights of the arrestee. In the judgment on *D.K. Basu* case, the scope of Art. 21 has been very much expanded and the court has laid down a long list of guidelines of arrest. Through its judgments, the Supreme Court has held that the rule of law imposes a duty upon the state to take special measures to prevent and punish brutality by police methodology.[15]

The efforts of the courts have further been strengthened by the National Human Rights Commission which is not only critical of custodial crime and police brutality, but it also investigates cases of custodial crime and orders for compensation to the victims. Besides, it lays down guidelines to government and police regarding protection and prevention of human rights violation by police.

Custodial Deaths and Delhi Police: Empirical Findings

Each custodial crime--Death, Torture and Rape—is different in terms of its nature, significance and causative factors. Because of the limitations of this paper, I have confined this study only to "custodial death", the widely debated and the most inhuman police brutality. All deaths that took place in the custody of Delhi Police during the period 1985-93 have been analysed to understand this issue to its core. The story in Delhi is not different from the rest of the country as it is a part of the larger police culture that prevails in India.

Custodial Deaths

I adopt a broader and comprehensive approach to the term "Custodial Deaths". I assume that all custodial deaths are not necessarily "custodial killings" as in most of the cases the police do not intend to kill the victim except in cases of purposeful encounter deaths. The term "torture death" excludes from its purview death due to reasons other than torture like heart attack, illness, suicide, etc. which take place mainly due to negligence of the police. "Lock-up death" is confined only to deaths in the police lock-up after a formal arrest, whereas the scope of custodial death is much wider which includes all deaths that take place under the control of the police irrespective of the place of death and nature of arrest (formal arrest or informal detention).

Nature and Causes of Custodial Deaths

Deaths in Police Custody in Delhi (1985-1993)

Year	*Number of Custodial Deaths*
1985	8
1986	5
1987	5
1988	7
1989	4
1990	4
1991	13
1992	7
1993	6
Total	59

Source: Delhi Police Headquarter, District Magistrate Office and Reports of PUDR.

A total of 59 custodial deaths (in police custody) have been reported in Delhi during the nine-year period—1985-1993 (both years included). From this figure it can be concluded that every year Delhi witnesses deaths in police custody and the minimum number of deaths has been as low as 4 and maximum as high as 13. Custodial death cases are not only found every year but in every police district though they are mainly concentrated in three districts[16]—West, North-West and North-East Delhi which account for 50% (30 cases) of the total cases.

In every case of custodial death, the police give their version of the relevant events and circumstances leading to the death, and cause of death. According to the records of Delhi Police, there are many causes of deaths in custody.

Causes of Deaths in Police Custody (1985-1993) in Delhi Police Record

S. No.	*Reasons*	*Number of Cases (N=59)*	*in %*
1.	Police torture	2	3.4
2.	Suicide	15	25.5
3.	Ill-heath	14	23.8
4.	Previous injuries	7	11.9
5.	Heart attack	4	6.8

(Contd.)

(*Contd.*)

S. No.	*Reasons*	*Number of Cases (N=59)*	*in %*
6.	Overdose of drug and alcohol	2	3.4
7.	Accident	3	5
8.	Not in custody	3	5
9.	Other reasons	4	6.8
10.	Not available	5	8.5

Source: Delhi Police Headquarters, District Magistrate Office and Reports of PUDR.

Police version of the causes of custodial deaths cannot be accepted on their face value without scrutiny because police, very often try to make fabricated stories of deaths. Therefore, on many occasions, one comes across inconsistencies between police version and reports of SDM inquiry in such cases.

Among the causes of death given by the police, "suicide" is the most common one occurring in as many as many as 15 (25.5%) cases. The methods of suicide as narrated by the police are: jumping from the top floor, hanging using a floor mat or shirt sleeves, consuming chemicals, etc. Police stories cannot be totally accepted as there is no witness either to confirm or to counter them. Medical evidence often contradicts these reasons of suicide. In many cases the methods of suicide seem to be practically not possible.

The second most important reason of custodial deaths, as per police record, is 'ill health'. Fourteen (23.8%) accused are alleged to have dies either of chronic diseases like tuberculosis, viral hepatitis, fits, etc. or sudden illnesses like high fever, chest pain, stomach pain, etc. This explanation of police seems to be unrealistic because of two reasons. Firstly, the victims in general, were in the prime of their youth (80% were below the age of 40). Therefore, it is very difficult to believe that those young people could have suffered from such chronic ailments. Secondly, it is very difficult to believe that all these ailments erupt suddenly and miraculously once the person is in custody, to cause death within few hours.

According to official explanation, even (11.9%) suspects died due to "previous injuries" which they received from public or private party. Prior injuries may not be fatal, but can lead to death in the absence of timely medical attention. In most of the cases police do not bother to perform the legally assigned duty (under

Section 53 CrPC) of getting the injured suspect medically examined at the time of arrest and providing him medical aid if required.

'Heart attack' is another official of death which might happen due to social pressure and shock that the accused experiences after arrest. But it cannot be ruled out that the condition of the accused gets further aggravated by the physical pain due to the application of their degree methods or mental torture inflicted by police.

There are other causes like overdose of drug and alcohol including the causes mentioned above for which police hold the suspect responsible or consider these deaths being caused due to natural reasons.

In some cases police do not accept that the death has taken place in their custody. This happens when a person is not formally arrested but has been called and detained in police station for inquiries or questioning, but dies in police station. It is alleged that police place the dead body somewhere outside the police station and deny the death in custody even if police admit that the person was detained. This practice of "informal detention" do not keeping a record of detention and release is useful for police in covering up cases in this manner.

Police approach of limiting "custodial deaths" to "deaths w .hin the Thanapremises" has to be rejected. In few cases the accused die due to police torture but police refuse to acknowledge those as custodial deaths if they take place outside the police station or lock-up on the ground that the victim had never been in their custody.

However, custodial death is defined as, "death occurring during the period when some limitation is placed upon the liberty of the deceased, and that limitation must be imposed, either directly or indirectly by the police."[17] This means that it is immaterial whether or not the death occurs within the premises of a police station or chowki. A person, who once comes to the control of police, looses his freedom of movement and is considered to be under the custody of police. Supreme Court in an important cases[18] observed that the issue in defining custody is not so much place or death, as the power of the police over the victim which was the cause of death. All deaths which take place under the control of police (due to police torture) are clearly 'custodial deaths' no matter where they occur or whether the victim was detained in police station formally or informally.

Out of 59 cases, police admitted torture as the cause of death only in two cases which is contradictory to SDM inquiry report. In

13 cases, out of the 38 for which SDM inquiry reports are available, torture was established as the cause of death. The magisterial inquiry reports along with our empirical study establish a reasonably acceptable proposition that the number of custodial deaths due to torture is much more than what the police version says.

Custodial deaths on the basis of its causes, may be classified into two broad categories: (*a*) deaths due to police torture (torture deaths), and (*b*) deaths due to reasons other than torture. In the former category, responsibility is directly established on the police personnel. But in other cases police refuse to take responsibility and make the victims or nature responsible for such deaths.

The causes of deaths in the second category seem to be natural or accidental but our study reveals that for all such deaths police is directly or indirectly responsible. Once in custody, a person is deprived of the freedom to look after himself. It is therefore, becomes the responsibility of the police (custodial authority) to monitor his physical condition and provide timely medical aid besides other basic necessities of life. Failure to do so makes the police responsible for the death of the person. The Supreme Court of India also upheld this position in *Parmanand Katara* case.[19]

Suicide takes place because of the failure of police to take proper preventive measures to check the accused from committing this act. Therefore, custodial authority (police) is held responsible for the custodial suicide in the same manner as he is responsible for the escapade of an accused from his custody. It cannot be ruled out that the aggravated mental and physical torture by police is sufficient to force the accused to commit suicide. Deaths due to previous injuries and heart attach might be caused due to the physical and mental torture inflicted by police. In case of ill health and previous injuries, police do not take the accused to hospitals until his condition becomes critical. Deprivation of timely medical help because of the negligence and indifferent attitude of the police aggravates the illness and leads to the death of the person. Therefore, the police is directly liable for criminal negligence.

Death due to police torture or "torture death" is a product of the larger system of the violent police culture. Torture by third degree methods, is mainly inflicted on the accused or suspects during interrogation with a purpose to extract confession and information about the crime and sometimes to recover stolen property and in few cases it is used as a form of punishment. Sixty nine per cent

(69%) of the respondents confessed that third degree is used in few cases when it is absolutely necessary but sometimes it is also used irrespective of its necessity as stated by 31per cent of the respondents. Torture in police custody, our study reveals, is systemic and systematic. Firstly there is always a specific purpose behind the torture or use of third degree method. Secondly, third degree method is often practiced by motivated, committed and responsible police officers, not always by corrupt, aggressive and inefficient ones. A large majority of cases of police brutality takes place not because of individual aberration but because of systemic compulsions.

Custodial deaths (deaths due to torture or any other reason) are not "custodial killings", because policemen do not intentionally want to kill anybody in their custody. Whatever may be the situation, any death taking place in the police custody, it is the police which is directly or indirectly responsible for this. Deaths in custody take place either due to police torture or negligent, indifferent, apathetic and insensitive attitude of police towards the life and liberty of the people in their custody.

Victims of Custodial Deaths

People from different communities, age groups and socio-economic backgrounds are found to be the victims of custodial deaths in Delhi. But people from the most vulnerable sections of the society form the majority of the victims of torture and custodial deaths.

Occupational Status of Victims of Custodial Deaths

S. No.	*Occupation*	*Number of Victims*	*in %*
1.	Low paid employees in shops and factories	8	13.6
2.	Labourers, daily wagers, casual labourers and migrant labourers	6	10.2
3.	Petty shop-keepers/traders and vendors	12	20.3
4.	Domestic servants	3	5
5.	Taxi/auto drivers	5	8.5
6.	Rickshaw/Tonga drivers etc.	5	8.5
7.	Lower class government employees	5	8.5
8.	Others	8	13.6
9.	Not available	7	11.9
10.	Total	59	100

The poor and illiterate people constitute 75 per cent of the death victims. Police use third degree methods against these people without much fear and botheration because they are helpless in protecting their rights through courts of law and more particularly, there is no social and financial backing behind them.

Nature of Crime and Custodial Deaths

Custodial Death Victims' Alleged Offences

S. No.	*Nature of Alleged offences*	*Number of Victims*	*in %*
1.	Serious offences (murder, robbery, kidnapping, burglary, arson, etc.)	9	15.2
2.	Theft	18	30.5
3.	Quarrel	11	18.6
4.	Terrorist activities	4	6.8
5.	Petty offences (pick-pocketing, public nuisance, missing court date, carrying knife, etc.)	5	8.5
6.	Trivial reasons (moving suspiciously or loitering)	3	5
7.	Others	2	3.4
8.	Not available	7	11.9
	Total	59	100

The understanding of the nature of crime and criminals is a key to the diagnosis and possible solution of this problem. This table reveals that the accused suspected of serious crimes like murder, kidnapping, burglary etc. and those suspected of petty offences like theft, quarrel, pick-pocketing, missing count date, carrying knife, etc., both are tortured to death. Even some innocent people who were not charged with any offence became victims. Majority of the victims of death are not habitual, professional and hardened criminals, but petty offenders, casual criminals or those who crime as a matter of chance and even innocent people.

What is the track record of Delhi Police—the largest metropolitan police in the world—regarding protection of human rights? The professionalism that it has displayed in the field of maintenance of law and order, crime-fighting and traffic regulation may be commendable but its role vis-à-vis human rights of the people (suspects) is still in doubt. The story in Delhi Police is not different from the rest of the country as it is a part of the larger police culture that prevails in India.

Suggestions (Recommendations) for Control of Custodial Deaths

The phenomenon of "custodial death" can be controlled by making the police accountable and taking some preventive measures. Since lack of effective system of accountable and follow-up actions create a feeling of immunity among policemen, the immediate need is to make the police accountable through stringent follow-up-actions for which the following recommendations have to be strictly implemented:

- (*i*) In each and every case of death in police custody, a criminal case should be registered immediately and investigation and prosecution have to be undertaken efficiently and impartially by an independent agency such as C.B.I.
- (*ii*) All police personnel connected with the death should be suspended till completion of inquiry/investigation. A time-bound judicial and not magisterial inquiry under Section 176 CrPC, should be made mandatory in each custodial death.
- (*iii*) Post-mortem examination in all such cases has to be conducted by a board of at least 2 doctors in order to check any kind of malpractices.
- (*iv*) Inquests to be made open and transparent.
- (*v*) Prompt communication of the inquest findings to the kith and kin of the deceased and the media.

Preventive Measures

The occurrence of custodial deaths due to reasons other than police torture can be checked and reduced, if not altogether eradicated by taking some preventive measures:

- (*i*) Medical examination should be made mandatory, of all persons taken into police custody immediately after their arrest.
- (*ii*) In case of pre-custodial injuries of a person under

influence of alcohol or drugs, the person should be taken directly to a hospital after arrest and not to police station.

(*iii*) Investigation officers and duty officers should take prompt action in case of an accused complaining of physical pain or other such problems. They should immediately inform the relatives/friends of the accused to accompany the injured to the hospital.

(*iv*) A particular hospital handling the medico-legal cases should be specified in each police district and arrangements for medico-legal work must be streamlined, so that deaths due to the medical negligence can be checked and reduced.

(*v*) Basic medical and first-aid training should be given to Duty Officers for better appreciation and response to medical emergencies relating to persons in custody.

(*vi*) An extra guard should be posted in the lock-up to have a constant watch over the physical condition and other activities of the accused so that no accused can commit suicide.

Reform of Police Administration

Custodial death, in a substantial number of cases, is a product of police torture. Therefore factors responsible for custodial torture also contribute a lot towards custodial deaths. Prevention and gradual eradication of torture and use of third degree methods from police culture need a comprehensive reforms in police administration. The following measures need to be taken on a priority basis, which will make the police accountable, humane and human rights friendly. This will go a long way to check custodial torture.

Excess pressure of work forces policemen (investigating officers) to adopt short-cuts to find quick result. Thus they adopt third degree methods to inflict torture. Therefore measures to reduce work pressure has to be taken on the line of the recommendation given by National Police Commission, Law Commission and Bureau of Police Research and Development (BPRD).

Departmental pressure from higher officers to detect crime quickly compels the already over-burdened police personnel to resort to third degree methods. The faulty yardstick of evaluation of the performance of the policemen, adopted by the department also creates a mental pressure on police. Therefore, it is suggested that the higher officers should not put unnecessary pressure to detect crime quickly. There should be change in the system of evaluation of police performance from purely 'statistical' to a more 'valued-based' review, as recommended by National Police Commission.

Tremendous degree of frustration, particularly at the lower ranks of the police personnel, due to bad working conditions, long hours of duty, less salary, lack of housing facilities, lack of promotional facilities, separation from family, etc., cause sadist behaviour among policemen which is the major cause of the police atrocities on the suspects in custody. To reduce the frustration, adequate steps need to be taken to provide good working conditions in terms of rest period, housing facilities, salary, etc.

Scientific methods of investigation and interrogation should replace third degree methods. Investigation Officers (IOs) should be properly trained in modern scientific methods and adequate facilities for such investigation should be made available.

There are many grey areas in the legal procedures which create the scope for police to misuse the law for their convenience. It is imperative to make a few modifications in the existing laws and procedures to curb the practice of custodial torture/crime. Law should be made to make the breach of Supreme Court/NHRC guidelines a punishable offence.

Besides strengthening internal supervision, **'Public Grievance Cell'** has to be instituted at least at the sub-divisional level. A special independent investigating organisation should be assigned the task of supervising public grievances against erring policemen.

It is suggested that a special institutional arrangement known as **'Accused Welfare Cell'** should be made in each police station. It should be manned by experts appointed from the field of social work (holders of social work degree) to look after the rights, interest and welfare of the accused. Those social workers will be very useful for the poor, illiterate and ignorant accused and will play a great role in reducing custodial crime.

Conclusion

To sum up, policing in a human rights conscious democratic society of the 21st century is a challenging task. Police Administration with right leadership needs to recruit, train, motivate and encourage its members to cultivate and practise such orientations, qualities, characteristics, professional skills and standards that would enable them to play their legitimate role and serve the members of the society in harmony with the needs and demands of human rights. There is a need of paradigm shift from the perceptions of police being "an executive arm" or "agent of the state" or a "brutal law-enforcing machinery into a people-friendly (Citizen-in-uniform police) or human-rights-friendly police.

REFERENCES

1. Peter R. Baehr, *Human Rights Universal in Practice*, London, Macmilian, 1999, p. 42.
2. Michael Freeden, *Rights*, Great Britain, J.W. Arrowsmith, 1991, p. 7.
3. J.H. Skolnick, *Justice Without Trial—Law Enforcement in Democratic Society*, New York, John Wiley and sons, 1966, p. 6.
4. Carl. B. Klockar, *The Idea of Police*, Vol. 3, Law and Criminal Justice Series, London, Sage Publications, 1985, p. 15.
5. K.V. Thomas, *Human Rights, Terrorism and Policing in India*, Delhi, Indian Social Institute, 1999, p. 3.
6. David H. Bayley, *Police and Political Development in India*, New Jersey, Princeton University Press, 1969, pp. 10-11.
7. *Kishore Singh vs. State of Rajasthan*, AIR 1981 SC 625.
8. James Vadackumchery, *Human Rights Friendly Police: A Myth or Reality*, Delhi, A.P.H., 2000, p. 156.
9. As quoted in Prashant Kumar Thakur, "*Custodial Torture by Police: Search for Alternatives and Accountability*", Paper presented in the VIIIa International Symposium on Torture, 22-25 September, 1999, Delhi, p. 3.
10. David H. Bayley, Quoted in Prashant Kumar Thakur, *op. cit.*, p.17.
11. For details, see-India, Torture, Rape and Deaths in Custody, 1992, (Report), Amnesty International; Annual Report of National Human Rights Commission (NHRC); Reports of PUDR, PULC and Asia Watch.
12. India-Torture, Rape and Deaths in Custody, *op. cit.*, p. 9.

13. V.P. Srivastav, "Criminal Administration and Justice in India" in V.P. Srivastav (ed.), *Indian Police: Law and Reality*, Delhi, Manas, 1999, p. 193.
14. *Kishore Singh vs. State of Rajasthan*, AIR 1981 SC 625; *Gouri Shankar v. State of U.P.*, AIR SC 656; *Arbinder Singh Bagga vs. State of U.P.*, Judgement Today, 1994 (6) SC 478; *Joginder Kumar vs. State of U.P.*, AIR 1994 SC 1349; *D.K. Basu vs. State of West Bengal*, AIR 1997 SC 610; *Khatni vs. State of Bihar*, AIR 1981 SC 928; *Hussainara Khatoon vs. State of Bihar*, AIR 1979 SC 1369; *Nandini Satpathy vs. P.L. Dani*, AIR 1978 SC 1025; *Maneka Gandhi vs. Union of India*, AIR 1978 SC 597; *Ravikant Patel vs. State of Maharashtra*, AIR 1991 SC 373 and *Neelabati Behra vs. State of Orissa*, AIR 1993 SC 1819.
15. K.V. Thomas, "Police and Human Rights Issues", *Indian Police Journal*, Vol. 40, No. 1, 1993, p. 56.
16. Delhi has 10 police districts including Railway District and one Airport District which has no territorial jurisdiction.
17. Capital Crimes, Delhi, PUDR, 1998, p. 18.
18. On 26 November 1987, Naresh, a nine-year old school boy died after he was beaten with bricks and rods in his own house, by the police, when he tried to protect his mother from rough treatment of policemen during a police search of his house, in a landlord-tenant disputes. The Supreme Court, in this case, held that the issue of defining custody in this instance was not so much place of death, as the power of the police over the victim which was the cause of death. AIR 1990, SC 513.
19. *Parmanand Katara vs. Union of India*, AIR 1989 SC 2039.

CHAPTER IV:
IT Revolution, E-Governance and Public Administration

12

Social Value Creation Through Information and Knowledge: Vision of the 21st Century

Prof. R.K. Sachdeva

Social Value Creation

It is commonly believed that organizations exist to produce goods and services, or to earn profit. This is at best a myopic view of the organization. Neither the production of goods and services nor the generation of profit is sustainable if the organization does not create social value. Traditionally, we have classified persons into a *yogi* or a *bhogi*. Literally, *yog* means to add and *bhog* means to consume. When a person gives more to the society than what he takes away from it, he or she is making a net addition to "social value", and hence can be called a *yogi*. On the other hand, the person who takes away more from the society than what he gives back is a net consumer of social value, and hence can be called a *bhogi*. Similarly, an organization that gives more to the society than what it takes away, is a value creating organization. The organization that takes away more from the society than what it delivers in return, is a value destroying organization. No society can sustain the survival of value destroying organizations whether they are producing goods and services or not, or whether they are generating profit or not.

Organization for Governance

For an organization, the customer is always right. This is not merely a well-accepted principle of marketing. Even the quality is determined on this principle. The goods and services that conform to the requirements or needs of the customer are of quality. An employee of the organization would treat his customer with care. But, if the customer also happens to be the owner or a shareholder of the organization, he would be treated with extra care. Imagine an employee deciding on the needs of his shareholder customers. The polity that provides for the right of the citizens to choose their masters who would rule over them once every five years, cannot be claimed as democracy. Democracy has to provide the individual freedom to realize one's full potential individually and collectively. The pseudo-representative system of governance in the twentieth century has failed to satisfy the aspirations of the citizens. They have realized that the business of governance is too important to be left to the government. They want to participate in the process of governance and control their own destiny. Would the current information and knowledge revolution facilitate the achievement of this goal?

Information Revolution

Information system is the nervous system of any organization and *sine qua non* for its survival. Information systems in organizations are as old as organizations themselves. With the growing complexities of modern organizations, not to speak of the systems of public administration, information systems are playing greater role in providing integration and enhanced customer service in organizational and public functioning. Developments in Information Technology (IT) during the last few decades have had profound effect on the style and quality of life in general, and operation and management of organizations in particular. The term IT has come into common use since the mid-80s with the integration of computer technology and communications technology and the emergence of the Internet. IT provides integrated solutions to different aspects of information systems in society and organizations. Information systems have become integral, on-line, interactive tools deeply involved in the minute-to-minute operations, decision making, and policy analysis in public and private organizations. The main components and sub-systems of information systems are: (*i*) Information storage, selection and retrieval (database) systems; (*ii*) Information consolidation (data and text processing) system; (*iii*) Information communication (networking) system; and (*iv*) Information analysis (decision support) system.

Role of Information Technology

Information Technology, especially the use of networks, can help organizations to reduce transaction cost of market participation, making it worthwhile for them to outsource processes instead of using internal resources. Reducing transaction costs and consequent outsourcing is likely to make the organizations shrink in size (the number of employees) without reducing their revenue. Information Technology can also reduce agency costs or internal management costs of organizations. By reducing the costs of acquiring and analyzing management information, it becomes easier for managers to oversee a larger number of employees, and for the organization to become leaner and flatter [Drucker, 1988].

Virtual Organization

Virtual organizations use networks to link people, assets, and ideas. Work is no longer tied to geographic location. Information Technology may encourage adhocracies and 'task force' networked organizations in which groups of professionals come together, face-to-face or electronically, for short periods of time to accomplish a specific task; once the task is accomplished, the individuals may join other task forces. In information partnerships, two or more organizations can link their information systems, without actually merging and achieve unique synergies by sharing information [Konsynski and McFarlan, 1990]. Firms can cooperate to develop industry standards in a number of areas; they can cooperate by working together to build customer awareness, and to work collectively with suppliers to lower costs [Shapiro and Varian, 1999].

Information Management

Information systems are too important to be left entirely to a small technical group in the organization. Executive managers must take the initiative to identify the types of systems that would provide a strategic advantage to the organization [Ross and Weill, 2002]. The doubling of computing power every 18 months has made it possible for most organizations to use information systems for their core production and delivery processes. As a result, dependence on systems and vulnerability to system errors and poor data quality has increased. Public rules and laws have not yet adjusted to this dependence. Standards for ensuring the accuracy and reliability of information systems are not universally accepted or enforced. Computers that are constantly connected to the Internet via cable modem or DSL line are more open to penetration by outsiders, because they use a fixed internet address where they can be more easily identified. The architecture of a web-based application typically includes a web client, a server, and corporate information systems linked to databases. Each of these components presents security challenges and vulnerabilities [Joshi, Aref, Ghafoor, and Spafford, 2001]. Wireless devices can form ad hoc networks that can be exploited by malicious entities to disrupt service, collect confidential information, and disseminate false information. Because wireless devices roam in and out of wireless zones, such attacks can be difficult to trace [Ghosh and Swaminatha, 2001]. Advances in datamining techniques for large databases enable companies to find out much detailed personal information about individuals. Put together and mined properly, this information could reveal not only credit information but also driving habits, tastes, associations, and political interests of people [Whiting, 2000]. Information from multiple sources can be combined to create electronic dossiers and detailed individual profiles. The impact of IT on employment and class divide is not yet fully understood.

Knowledge Management

Organizations possess tangible as well as intangible assets. While tangible or physical assets of the organization are well reported and get accounted in the financial statements of the organization, the intangible assets are not easily measured. The growing discrepancy between the book value and market value of listed companies is an indication of the growing proportion of intangible assets in the companies. These include assets such as brands, customer relationships, patents, trademarks and, of course, knowledge. The intangible assets of the organization can be broadly classified into four categories viz. Human Capital, Structural Capital, Customer Capital, and Intellectual Capital. Human capital constitutes knowledge, competence, experience, know-how etc. of the persons associated with the organization. Structural capital is that which is left after employees go home for the night viz. processes, information systems, databases etc. Customer capital includes customer relationships, loyalty, brands etc. Intellectual property includes trademarks, patents, designs, copyrights and licenses. These intangible assets constitute the vital resources of any organization.

Knowledge management deals with the explicit and systematic management of vital knowledge and its associated processes of creating, gathering, organizing, diffusion, use and exploitation in pursuit of organizational mission. It involves the management of both the 'explicit' knowledge, which is codified in documents and databases; and the 'tacit' knowledge such as knowing how to swim that resides in people's heads. Tacit knowledge is experiential in nature and is not easy to express in an explicit form. While the explicit knowledge can be managed just like other information objects by conducting information audits, populating intranets, creating best practice databases, classifying content and creating knowledge maps. But, since tacit knowledge is in people's heads, the emphasis here is on managing knowledge workers and the environment in which they work by nurturing knowledge networking. Creating 'communities of practice' [Wenger, 1999], designing sharing workspaces, encouraging learning and innovation, practicing skillful dialog and storytelling etc. Knowledge can be embedded in software systems and context specific knowledge can be provided in real-time during decision support [Davenport and Glaser, 2002]. A good knowledge management program supported by IT and software tools ensures creating valuable knowledge, efficient utilization of existing knowledge, and retaining organizational knowledge even when employees leave the organization. It is estimated that *Fortune 500* companies alone are expected to lose 31.5 billion dollars in revenues through poor knowledge management systems [Poynder 2000].

Interface with Government

The Government of India, while recognizing IT as a thrust area for growth, has taken a number of initiatives to promote it. A major effort to promote the sector is proposed in the Tenth Five-Year Plan. The main objectives are: ensuring the sustained growth of software and IT-enabled services and increase India's share in the global IT market as well as expanding the domestic market: putting in place a policy framework to make India a major force in the hardware manufacturing sector; greater use of IT in governance; bridging the digital divide; promoting the development of software in Indian languages; and improving the quality of manpower, skills and research and development in the sector. Electronic-governance (E-governance) is fast emerging as an important tool for achieving good governance especially with regard to improving efficiency, transparency and making interface with government user friendly. E-governance denotes the application of IT to the processes of government functioning in order to bring about better governance, which has been termed as SMART (simple, moral, accountable, responsive and transparent). Similar thrust in the introduction of IT has existed in the public and private sector organizations for improving the operation and management of those organizations. The Tenth Plan recognizes IT as an area where the country has a competitive edge and can establish global dominance.

Issues of Concern

The momentum of the IT movement has pulled many willing and unwilling, knowledgeable and pretending to be knowledgeable actors into the wave. Organizations are rapidly moving towards increasing use of IT to maintain their social prestige and economic value under competitive pressures. However, the failure rate of new applications has been rather high. Many initiatives fail because managements lack vision and do not fully understand how to use information technology to create value [Reimus, 1997]. Accepting failure in public is not in their organizational interest. Effective utilization of IT in the organization requires a clear understanding of the management and policy issues relating to the development, operation and use of IT. Haphazard growth of IT applications without proper understanding of management and policy issues can have serious implications for the nation for decades to come.

According to analysts from Gartner Inc., more than 60 per cent of e-government iniatives around the world fail or fall short of their objectives. The success rate of e-government projects in developing countries is only 15 per cent. Some of the reasons cited for these failures in India include lack of familiarity, digital divide, low expectations, lack of incentives, not ease of use, lack of trust, silo effect, budgetary constraints, human resources constraint, paucity of reliable suppliers etc. [Shetty 2003]. One of the states in India has already implemented the computerized land records system three times over.

Challenges Ahead

Managers and policy makers have challenges to deal with the following issues relating to the development, operation, and utilization of information and knowledge management systems / IT based applications.

Development

— Information System Planning
— Estimation and Scheduling
— Risk Analysis and Control
— In-house Development Vs Outsourcing
— Contract Management
— Quality Assurance
— Configuration Management
— Monitoring and Tracking.

Operation

— In-house Operation Vs Outsourcing
— Security and Control
— Ethical and Social Impact
— Privacy
— Re-engineering of legacy systems
— Personnel Redeployment and Training.

Utilization

- — Redesign / Re-engineering of Processes
- — Estimation of Cost and Value Creation
- — Logistics and Delivery Systems
- — Decision Support Systems
- — Policy Analysis
- — Intellectual Property Rights
- — Impact on World Trade and Balance of Payments
- — Impact on Employment
- — Impact on Class Divide
- — Research and Development.

Conclusion

Information and knowledge constitutes the vital resource of any society. Information Technology offers new opportunities for revolutionary improvements in social value creation. At the same time, it presents new challenges before managers and policy makers in order to make the best use of this opportunity.

REFERENCES

Drucker, Peter, "The Coming of the New Organization", *Harvard Business Review* (January-February 1988).

Konsynski, Benn R., and F. Warren Mcfarlan, "Information Partnerships-Shared Data, Shared Scale", *Harvard Business Review* (September-October 1990).

Shapiro, Carl, and Hal R. Varian, *Information Rules,* Boston, MA: Harvard Business School Press (1999).

Ross, Jeanne W., and Peter Weill, "Six IT Decisions Your IT People Shouldn't Make", *Harvard Business Review* (November 2002).

Joshi, James B.D., Walid G. Aref, Arif Gafoor, and Eugene H. Spafford, "Security Models for Web-Based Applications", *Communications of the ACM 44, No.* 2 (February 2001).

Ghosh, Anup K., and Tara M. Swaminatha, "Software Security and Privacy Risks in Mobile E-Commerce", *Communications of the ACM 44, No.* 2 (February 2001).

Whiting, Rich, "Mind Your Business", *Information Week* (March 6, 2000).

Wenger, Etinne, *Communities of Practice,* Cambridge University Press, 1999.

Davenport, Thomas H. and Glaser, John, "Just-in-Time Delivery Comes to Knowledge Management", *Harvard Business Review,* July 2002.

Poynder, Richard, *Knowledge Management,* Learned Information, Dec. 1999/Jan. 2000.

Governance and Implementation, *Tenth Five Year Plan, Vol. 1, Chapter 6.*

Information Technology, *Tenth Five Year Plan, Vol. 1, Chapter 7.4.*

Reimus, Byron, "The IT System That Couldn't Deliver", *Harvard Business Review,* May-June 1997.

Shetty, K. Ashok Vardhan, "Why Most E-government Projects Fail", *Bussiness Line,* November 15, 2003.

13

Electronic Democracy: Concepts, Trends and Implications for India

Dr. Y. Pardhasaradhi and Dr. J. Musalaiah

Introduction

E-Democracy is one of the hot issues in the present day discussions all over the world as governments are moving towards experiments with online administration and consultations. E-democracy is at that stage now that it needs to be explored as a subset to the greater, and more important, philosophical topic of democracy itself. There are some fundamental questions that arise from e-democracy practices: Can online consultations/debates enhance the present system and increase efficiency in government operations? Can people receive better solutions and speedy delivery of services? These pressing issues confront modern governments since new technologies are contributing to the creation of faster communications, sharing of information and knowledge, and emergence of new forms of cultures. Major changes are being witnessed in the society to-day. For instance, Networked Communities are quickly evolving through the Internet and, increasingly, citizens are using the new technologies to organize themselves so that their voices can be heard, as well as to develop tools to attempt to influence government policies and programs at the political and public administration level. This process has started in the developed world vigorously as compared with the developing world. Writers and researchers analyzing and assessing the emergence of e-democracy, often leave out, on the whole, the broader philosophical nature of democracy itself. For purposes of understanding the evolution of e-democracy it is important to raise the whole question of how Information Communication Technologies (ICTs) will be used for to benefit the citizenry and efficiency in administration. The working of public services, processes of administration, knowledge on public policy making are the important areas in governance which are kept under secrecy in the traditional model of governance, whereas e-democracy and e-governance can change these areas into transparent and open areas, by facilitating citizen participation and learning. Against this background the present paper seeks to study the concept of E-Democracy and analyse its implications to our country.

Democracy and People's Participation as a Requisite for E-Governance

According to standard Western literature on political science, Democracy is "a way of organizing government and citizens' participation in it" (Martinussen 1999, 171). The democratic way of organizing government involves; (*a*) Competition for government positions; (*b*) Citizen participation in the selection political leaders; (*c*) A number of civil and political liberties (Martinussen 1999, 172). The idea of democracy pre-supposes citizens' capacity to form a well-founded opinion coupled with their competency and effective participation to ensure that legitimate decisions are made. The term "democratic potential' has been widely employed to address citizens' capacity to participate (in an effective and knowledgeable manner) in socially constitutive processes to exercise power (Mouffe 1992). The model/level of citizen's political participation is ranked form the basic activities to the most complex and devoted ones in the following order: (*a*) Voting; (*b*) Campaign activity; (*c*) Particularized contacts (individual contacts with state for resolving problem on his/her own behalf or for public benefits); and (*d*) Cooperative activity (political community/virtual non-virtual).

Kees Schalken has identified four main characteristics of Information ad Communication Technology (especially, the Internet in general). These are (1) Decentralization, (2) Fragmentation, (3) Virtualization, and (4) Globalization and Massification (Schalken, 1998: 161). According to Schalken, the dynamics and complexity of ICT lies in its decentralized structure where power over information and communication is shifted from central institutions to individuals, where time and territory are relative, and where an overwhelming fragmentation of subjects, goals and interests are combined with a strong tendency towards globalization.

The above-mentioned Schalken' view on ICT is, in many aspects, quite relevant to the classical theory of political participation. That significant differences exist between the Shalken's profile of ICT and the composite definition of political participation can be illustrated. Although the mainstream idea of democracy does not necessarily require everyone to participate in public decision-making process, it requires minimal, requisite number of active citizens capable of expressing their views rationally. Apart from active citizens, the other requisites to democratic society involve an enabling environment entailing effective checks and balances system, norms of tolerance, legal-historical mechanism of limited state power, conflict solution mechanism, etc. (Laudon, 1977:64). These attributes and characteristics are necessary if democracy is to proper in a particular society. It is in these aspects of political requisite that ICT can serve well or supposed to serve well as the means or tools of democratization process. As in other areas of governance, ICT, due to its widespread and inexpensive nature should be utilized to revolutionize the way of enhancing and enlarging the prospect of peoples' active roles in democracy.

E-Democracy: A General Definition and Typological Frame of Reference

The term "Electronic Democracy" or E-Democracy has become one of the most used "buzword's for any one to address the interaction between ICT and political process. According to Martin Hagen, "Electronic Democracy" refers to ***"theories, which regard computer and/or computer networks as central tools in the working of a democratic political system"***. (?Hagen, 1997), Andrew Kakabadse (2003) defines it as ***"the capacity of the new communications environment to enhance the degree and quality of public participation in government"***. To put it in another way, E-Democracy represents any democratic political system in which ICT is used to carry out crucial functions of the democratic government such as supply of information, communication, interest articulation and aggregation, decision making, deliberation and voting, etc. The technological innovations that make these activities electronically possible include the use of increasingly sophisticated computer chips, lasers, fiber-optics, LCD, databases, public and commercial satellites, etc.

Occasionally, we may come across the substitution of electronic democracy by other related terms such as, "cyber democracy", "virtual democracy", "technopolitics", "virtual polis", or "Information age democracy" (Milward and Snyder 1996). Although they are hardly synonym to each other, some are more precise and relevant than others in addressing the application of interactive technology on politics. To overcome the confusing nature of categorizing these terms, Hagen proposes a typology of E-democracy by separating it into three different concepts: (1) Teledemocracy, (2) Cyber Democracy and (3) Electronic democracy. Direct or representative forms of democratic government and differ in terms of the expectation and activities held by advocates of each concept.

To be concise, teledemocracy strives to establish more forms of direct democracy within a particular political system and aims to employ ICT for this end. The underlining assumption of advocates of this concept (or "the teledemocrats") is that a representative government is no longer effectively and appropriately able to meet the ever-increasing plurality of political inputs in an information society (Becker 1995). Alvin Toffler, a well-known futurologist, claimed that representative institutions are not fit to deal with 21st century problems and proposes ICT for its crucial role in transforming representative democracy into direct (or, at least, semi-direct) democracy (Toffler 1980, 430).

Although the cyberdemocrats share the same aspiration with the telecdemocrats for a more direct form of government, they stress a different aspect of political participation. For the cyberdemocrat, their prime concern is to recreate (virtual or non-virtual) communities as a counter-base to centralized forms. As the cyberdemocracy concept was developed on an anti-statist assumption, it views the state as a potential threat both to individual freedom and the maximization of wealth. Generally, the advocates of this concept comprise a somewhat peculiar mixture between: (1) those who demand self-empowerment and (2) those who demand freedom of wealth accumulation.

In contrast to the teledomocracy and cyberdemocracy-concept, the Electronic Democratization concept does not want to establish direct forms of democracy, but wants to improve representative democracy. Electronic democratization is defined as the "enhancement of a democracy, already assumed to be initiated, with new communication technologies in ways that increase the political power of those whose role in key political processes is usually minimized" (Hacker/Todino 1996:72). Not surprisingly, the main champions of the electronic democratization concept are members of the public institutions and non-government sectors rather than private sectors and individual citizen.

The differences in the three concepts of E-Democracy can be summed up in a typology as presented in Table 1.

Table 1: A Typological Frame of Reference on E-Democracy

Concept	*Teledemocracy*	*Cyberdemocracy*	*Electronic Democratization*
Underlining Assumption	Government is not coping well with changes	The best government governs least	Enhancement of communication equals enhancement of democracy
Main purpose	To empower people and increasing public leverage	To establish (virtual and/or non-virtual communities)	To enlarge communication channel to the public
Forms of political participation	Information Discussion, voting	Discussion, political Activity	Information, Discussion
Preferred forms of democracy	Direct	Direct	Representative
Degree of political participation	Voting and particularized contacts	Cooperative activity and destructive political Behaviour	Campaigning activity

Source: Adapted from Martin Hagen (1997).

Benefits and Limitations of ICT on Democracy

Models of E-Democracy

The debates about benefits and threats generated by "electronic democracy" have been explored by European and American Scientists and Practitioners since the early sixties. In their overview on the literature published on the subject of technology and democracy, van de Donk and Tops (1994) aptly conclude that the attention has mainly been focused on two big scenarios for the future: "Orwell and Athens".

In the first scenario "Orwell", technology will place citizens under a continuous surveillance by government, commercial institutions, and perhaps even fellow citizens, while the second scenario, "Athens", represents the old Greek dream of an agora where all citizens can gather and have a direct influence on their government which will be realized by technology. Although now a days we may not be able to evaluate the pros and cons of E-democracy by simply relying on these two scenarios, they do provide us some idea on how ICT is supposed to serve humans in term of politics and governance. This pat of the essay explores the underlining potential of ICT—its positive and negative ramifications on democracy under five models of E-democracy.

Advantages

The literature on democratic significance of ICT has mostly focused on its ability to enhance mostly direct participation of the public in the political process. For instance, statements such as modern technology is of great value in registering the political attitudes and inclinations of the public; interactive media can accommodate dialogue that flows among citizens; and communication technology brings issues into public limelight and allows them to be justified illustrate the point (London, 1994). In order to avoid the problem of redundancy likely to occur between ICT advantages and limitations, the discussion below is organized on the basis of five E-democracy models that are commonly found in most literatures in this field. They are (1) electronic bureaucracy model, (2) information management model, (3) populist model, (4) civil society model, and (5) political campaigning model.

(1) *The electronic bureaucracy model:* It is another name for the electronic delivery of government services. This model already enjoys increasing success at the federal and state levels in the U.S., Australia and Singapore where "government online" and "one stop service" are actively operational. The benefit of E-democracy under this model is it success in allowing for easier, quicker, and cheaper transactions with government on behalf of citizens and to reduce the size of the public sector.

(2) *The information management model:* The electronic communication serves as a bridge connecting individual citizens to decision makers under this model. By using multimedia in public places or personal computers from home, citizens can obtain government information or send messages to their representatives or government agencies. This model should fall into the typology of "electronic democratization" commonly practiced in Presidential administration in the U.S. (Kakabadse, 2003).

(3) *The populist model:* It enables citizens to register their views on current issues. This model is often equated with the revival of "direct democracy" and received visibility as the term "electronic town hall" during the presidential campaign in the US in the 90s. ICT benefits, according to this model, lay in its ability to provide unmediated communication between citizens and officials. According to populist model, E-democracy facilitates that civic discourse that is quick, direct, interactive and inclusive and will finally help educate people to act and decide on policies (London, 1994).

(4) *The civil society model:* The transformation of political culture and its goals that takes place under this model is designed to strengthen connections between citizens and promote a robust autonomous site for public debate (such as those virtual communities on the net). These kinds of networks, now a days have been well-established among the citizens of industrialized countries especially the U.S., Sweden, Germany, Canada, France and Japan (Kakabadse, 2003).

Limitations and Disadvantages

Although much of the technology needed for electronic democracy already exists in a number of societies, no one can really tell whether these technologies will enhance participative democracy or lead to further political fragmentation. Apart from its various benefits on citizen's governance, E-democracy also possesses numerous limitations and may lead to several problems on citizen's governance.

1. *The electronic bureaucracy model:* The limitations and problems of e-democracy of this model are primarily related to the confidentiality of personal data (Dertouzos, 1997:121-2). Government may as well see ICT as a complex and potentially dangerous force that will need to be regulated (much as air travel, stock market or armaments are regulated today). The overarching question is ultimately non-technical, it is a matter of trade-off. People will have to decide whether they want to have the right of controlling the privacy of their information and communication or whether they are willing to share this right with their governments in order to be protected from those various types of computer crime or cyber-crime.
2. *The information management model:* The limitations of e-democracy under this model are concerned with government underutilizing the technology at its maximum potential, but rather in an instrumental fashion. Generally speaking, democratic activity on ICT network still follows an add-on strategy to existing institutions. Most governments lack the attitude to fully exploit the full capacity of ICT for enhancing democracy; they are more willing to follow the principle of "incrementalism" (Poupa, 1999:152).
3. *The populist model:* Democracy through information technology may not always replace face to face meetings, particularly in discussion and negotiation phases. For instance, the Internet is probably difficult to use in the process of negotiation. Nevertheless ICT still cannot handle very large meetings as do the traditional large

assemblies and town hall meetings. Just as we cannot understand anyone when numerous people are screaming simultaneously, likewise we cannot possibly read millions of e-mail without resorting to delay (Dertouzos, 1997:216).

4. *The civil society model:* Heavy reliance on ICT to carry on the process of democracy may reduce the ability of the government to layout, debate, analyze and implement its plans. For instance, turning to the use of instant polls too often may bring the issue/matter/subject closer to groupthink idea or it is tantamount to "ritual mob rule" or government paralysis (Dertouzo). In times of national crisis, the inability to reach a decision could be as dangerous as the captain leaving every shipboard decision to the passengers.
5. *The political campaigning model:* Problem of e-democracy may arise from the misuse technology to commit fraud or to modify the voting pattern. This problem of e-democracy is not a mere technical issue but it raises the broader question of political morality and integrity.

Future Prospect of E-Democracy in India: Implications and Recommendations

The pioneering work of Kenneth C. Laudon on the penetration of Information and Communication Technology into the political domain emphasizes that ***"implicit in the development of certain information technologies are very definite models of democracy which considerably differ from one another"*** (Laudon 1977: 14). Even in the present day as globalization reaches its zenith, Ludon's remark has proved to be prophetic. Indeed, a country's accomplishment on E-democracy depends on the democratic potential its society possesses as much as on the level of IT literacy among its constituents.

Given the current situation in India, we have to admit that the prospect of employing E-democracy is in a very infant stage as compared with the U.S. and European Nations where the trends of E-politics have long been operating almost at its full potential. Nevertheless, the future holds the prospect for E-democracy for India.

Present Status of IT literacy in India

In general, people's habit of utilizing ICT is more likely to be exposed on the receiving end than at the initiating stage (Boonsiripaunth, 1998). According to a survey conducted by different agencies in 2003, in India 1,65,80,000 persons are accessing the Internet, accounting for 1.65 per cent of total population in the country and it impacts 60 million people. This penetration rate is relatively low as compared with countries in the Asian region (no need for the benchmarking with Western countries). In comparison with India's negligent 1.65 per cent of total Internet users, the ratio of other Asian countries is much higher. This illustrates a huge intra-regional digital divide in the region. For instance the ratio in Hong Kong is 56.5 per cent, South Korea 54.3, Taiwan 51.3, Singapore 51.2 and Japan 36.8. Nor the Indian position vis-à-vis the East Asian countries is very impressive.

Number of Internet Users in Top 15 Countries in the World++

Countries	*Internet Users in Millions*
USA	160
Japan	64
China	54
Germany	30
United Kingdom	27
South Korea	26
Italy	20
Canada	17
France	16
India	16
Brazil	15
Russia	13
Australia	10
Spain	10
Taiwan	9

Source: www.Infoplease, com/ipa/0/9/0/8/1/8/a0908185.phtmal Accessed on 21, November, 2003.

The "digital divide" has posed another kind of social segregation between those who are information-rich and who are information-poor on both individual and societal basis. Given the limitation of basic telecommunication infrastructure, it might take more time for ICT to be fully operated in the context of e-democracy in India. In the near future, those who will be the direct beneficiary of the ICT will be those who have access to politics and they are in a small minority-young, affluent, politically oriented and constantly online.

Contemporary Indian Political Culture as a requisite for E-democracy

Although, the percentage of Indian people to exercise their voting rights has increased significantly, Indian political culture has not changed much. Until recently, most political scientists' researches on Indian political behaviour have led to similar findings about "mobilized" participation rather than "voluntary" participation of citizens in the democratic process.

A prerequisite to E-democracy is increasing participation of citizens in the politics of the nation. Broad-based participation in politics may enhance the control of government by the people. Although ICT may enable people to be involved in and affected by governmental decisions, it also requires the participants to be active and rational. If citizens are being too passive and ignorant, it will lead to a reversal in the pattern of relationships. ICT is like a double edged sword that can be used either as a tool for public access to governmental decisions or as government's tool for political marketing, propaganda and domination. In addition to active civic participation, other prerequisites for the application of e-democracy (of any kind) include mechanisms for peaceful conflict resolution, a political culture of tolerance and consensus and wisdom of leadership among the citizens.

Conclusion

In the contemporary society, ICT has become part of our way of life whether we like it or not. In the domain of politics, it may lead to both favourable and unfavourable impacts. The advantages and disadvantages of ICT to a democracy depend partly on how well the people are prepared to take on the technology and partly on their political mindset. When dealing with the issue of e-democracy, most academia and practitioners always treat ICT as an independent variable and the changing status of democracy as a dependent variable. However, since ICT has penetrated most areas of the world, it is meaningless to ask the question what benefits will it bring to a particular society. On the contrary, a more relevant and important question that must be asked is how can the potential of a particular society be adapted to fully utilize ICT at the maximum level?

Online activists, special interest groups, and interested citizens and politicians alike also use e-democracy tools to enhance democracy within their own groups and amongst themselves. Thus, we see a culture of different forms of traditional democracy emerging outside the sphere of government circles whereas governments make tentative steps to move into the arena. Governments are traditionally conservative and slow to move towards change due to the nature of their organizations and the duty to take all the interests of society into consideration when undertaking change. At present a wide gap exists between what individuals and groups are doing online, and what governments are currently capable of doing online, especially in their relationships with the public.

To conclude, if the negative impacts arising from the use of ICT on the governance of human society are to be averted, it is of utmost importance to exercise extreme vigilance and guarantee equal access to all people in order to ensure that the electronic revolution integrates society more than it divides it. The quality of democratic governance can be enhanced to a great-extent by ICT providing the citizens with relevant and timely information to actively participate in the process of making decisions affecting their life and the nation.

REFERENCES

DeSario, Jack and Stuart Langton, *Citizen Participation in Public Decision Making,* Connecticut: Greenwood Press, 1987.

Dertouzos, Michael L, *What Will be: How the New World of Information will Change Our Lives,* New York: Harper Collins Publisher Inc., 1997.

Hagen, Martin, *A Typology of Electronic Democracy* http://www.unigiessen.de/fb03/vinvi/laboure/netzhag_en.htm, Accessed on 15.09.2003.

Haywood, Trevor, *Info-Rich, Info-Poor: Access and Exchange in the Global Information Society*, London: Bowker-Saur, 1995.

Joson W. Dennis, "The Cyberspace Election of the Future": in Bruce I Newman (ed.), *Handbook of Political Marketing*, London: Sage Publication Inc, 1999.

Kakabadse, Andrew, Nada K. Kakabadse and Alexander Kouzmin, "Reinventing the Democratic Governance Project Through Information Technology? A Growing Agenda for Debate" *in Public Administration Review, January-February 2003.*

Laudon, Kenneth C., *Communications Technology and Democratic Participation*, New York: Praeger Publisher, 1977.

Martin, William J., *The Global Information Society*, Hampshire: Aslib Gower, 1995.

Martinussen, John, *Society, State and Market: A Guide to Competing Theories of Development*, London: Zed Books Ltd, 1999.

Michalski, Wolfgang, Reil Miller, and Barrie Stevens, "Governance in the 21st Century: Power in the Global Knowledge Economy and Society" in Organization for Economic Cooperation and Development, *Government in 21st Century*, Paris OECD, 2001.

Ogden, Michael R., Politics in a Parallel Universe; Is there a Future for Cyberdemocracy? *In Futures*, 1994, 26.

Schalken, Kees, "Internet as a New Public Sphere for Democracy?" In I.Th.M. Snellen and W.B.H.J. Van de Donk (ed.) *Public Administration in An Information Age: A Handbook*, Amsterdam: ISO Press, 1998.

Tarschys, Daneil, "Wealth, Values, Institutions: Trends in Government and Governance in Organization for Economic Cooperation and Development, *Government in 21st Century*, Paris: OECD, 2001.

Verba, Sydney and Norman Nie, *Participation in America, Political Democracy and Social Equity*, Chicago: University of Chicago Press, 1972.

14

Public Administration and ICT Paradigm

Dr. Y. Pardhasaradhi, Dr. K.V. Ramesh Raju and Mr. T.V. Venkatamallu

Introduction

The theory and process of Public Administration has undergone tremendous changes in the last decade. These changes represent a paradigm shift from bureaucratic model of administration to a market model of management closely related to private sector. The rigid, hierarchical, bureaucratic form of public administration, which has dominated for most of the twentieth century, has changed in favour of a flexible, market based form of public administration. This is not simply a matter of reform or minor change in management style, but a change in the role of the government in society and relationship between government and citizen, market and government, government and bureaucracy and bureaucracy and the citizen. Traditional public administration has been discredited theoretically and practically, and the adoption of New Public Management focuses on management, not policy and on performance appraisal and efficiency.

New Public Management involves much more than mere public service reform. It means changes to the ways the public service operates, changes to the scope of governmental activity, changes to time honoured processes of accountability and changes to the academic study of the public sector. The main change is one of theory, one of paradigm. The effect of managerial change is not only on the public sector but also on the entire political system. A large number of philosophers, academicians and public functionaries have been discussing ways and means of governing societies. They have advocated different forms of political and administrative systems and methods of governance to reconcile the interest of the citizens with that of the role of the state. Governance is about new methods and forms in governing and ultimately is about a change in the meaning of government.

The World Bank report of 1992 added a new dimension to the whole issue of governance and administration. Governance is a broader concept, which subsumes public administration and management. Concept of Good Governance has suddenly entered the vocabulary of public administration since the 1990s. Good Governance is not simply something that government can achieve or do by itself. It depends upon cooperation and involvement of large number of citizens and organizations.

E-Governance is considered as an important tool of Good Governance. The use of Information Technology (IT) in government has led to e-Governance or e-Government. E-Governance is sometimes known as digital governance, as the new system uses internet as the gateway or the means by which people and government get connected with each other. The new technology facilitates the government's capacity to respond more effectively to the needs of the people. It also facilitates better interface between people and government and more transparency in operations of public organizations.

ICT and Governance

Full and effective participation in the emerging global information network is of fundamental importance for any country that wants to avoid marginalization from the globalization process and it is also essential for the full participation of its citizens in all spheres of life. Information and Communication Technology (ICT) can contribute to integration of developed and developing countries in the world economy, and it can create the conditions for information and knowledge exchange and utilization. ICTs offer tremendous potential to raise standards of living and enlarge opportunities for individuals, communities, countries and regions. While many in the world still remain directly untouched by the information revolution, one cannot deny the transformative effect they already had on our global society. Governments are confronted with a new reality and changed imperatives as a result of the diffusion of ICT throughout the world and within their nations. The advent of the information society is creating unprecedented conditions for exercising this function. Through ICT and e-government applications, communications between administrations, citizens and businesses can be enhanced to improve governance and public sector management, access economic and social opportunities and bridge the digital divide within a society and between countries.

E-government can transform the existing government system and consolidate the establishment of an inclusive governance system through digital means that is capable of exercising its powers and functions more efficiently and effectively *i.e.* it can pave the way for a governance system that is committed to working with civil society in a transparent and accountable way to reduce poverty, safeguard the environment, redress inequality, foster security and fulfill social, economic, cultural, civic and political rights. E-government supports broad public sector reforms and good governance through the introduction of innovative and sustainable applications of ICT both within government administrations, as well as in their interaction with citizens and the private sector.

Efficiency of E-Governance

Lack of uniform and consistent approach, openness and easy accessibility of government systems hamper efficient and transparent governance today. Use of It in governance backed by a networked and digitally enabled government can mitigate this handicap to a large extent. It based electronic governance will have wide impact not only upon its ability to bring economic benefits to the society, but also upon issues related to social, cultural, technological and financial aspects of the community. This will bring forth solutions to the problems related to human and material resources, trained manpower, spread of education and linkages with the operating aims of the government at all levels. It enabled government will facilitate disbursement and utilization of scare resources more equitably.

E-Governance refers to the use by government agencies of IT that have the ability to transform relations with citizen, business, and other arms of government. E-Governance implies upgrading efficiency and effectiveness of administrative machinery through the combination of IT and sophisticated multimedia to deliver better, cost effective and speedy services to the citizens. It will improve the image of the government as 'friend of the people'. It will create more effective linkage between the government and the citizens and increase transparency and accountability in government business. Public sector is increasingly seen as the main engine to bridge the digital divide at country level. Public agencies can start acting as model users of ICT and be catalysts for others to follow. The public sector tends to be the biggest provider of local content and it can nurture and foster the further development of the local ICT industry.

Conventional use of the prefix 'e' suggests that an activity is 'electronic' or digital in nature. Thus, e-government would simply refer to the use of electronic information and communication technologies in undertaking all kinds of government activities, in education, health, agriculture, governance, customs, etc. However, this does not reflect the value that the use of ICT can actually add to government's ability to foster development.

The key word in e-government is not electronic, but government. E- government should be regarded as an alternative and complementary approach to government administration and service delivery, as well as a means to redefine the way it interacts with citizens and the private sector, In this sense

E means efficiency: Governments should use ICT to minimize transaction costs and streamline their bureaucratic procedures, making their operations more efficient, freeing resources that enable them to deliver services in a better-organized and economical manner.

E means effectiveness: Governments can achieve better results and meet development goals by using ICTs to increase the relevance of the policy formulation process by increasing participation, improving the process of resource allocation, responding timely to citizen's needs and increasing the coverage and quality of their services.

E means empowerment: ICTs can support increased interaction between citizens and their government, and enable citizens both to participate in the decision-making process and to become more aware of their personal and community development.

E means economic and social development: Besides the economic benefits that accrue to the government due to efficiency and effectiveness in its operations, the use of ICTs in government's interactions with the business community and citizens can create new businesses, attract investments and generate employment. In other words, appropriate e-government initiatives can create and strengthen the conditions essential for good governance. Development of e-government is, therefore, not merely a technical issue but also a political one.

ICT and Decision Making

Economic processes demand the effective spread of the use of IT and associated services. But the fact remains that we have still not realised the full potential of our teeming millions in maximizing economic growth. To ensure opportunity for all in a world of technological change, governments need to be more citizen-centred. Technology is a tool in this effort. Around the world governments are emphasizing e-Governance. Government bodies are now giving out critical information online, automating once cumbersome processes and interacting electronically with their citizens. E-Governance, or the use of IT by the government to deliver better services to its citizens, helps bring in transparency, accountability and efficiency. Automated processes also help alter citizen perceptions about government. The delay in taking a decision and its communication can be reduced and even eliminated altogether with the help of IT. Quick decision-making process is an indicator of development whereas delay denotes underdevelopment.

E-Governance is more about transformation of government processes than merely putting information on the net. It involves re-engineering of the entire processes of the government before information put on the Internet. Technology is only a tool in this effort. E-Governance means the total restructuring of the processes that encompass government to government (G2G), government to business (G2B), government to citizen (G2C) transactions. Currently, there is a huge scramble to put information on the Internet in an effort to achieve an early bird status in this trend, but one should take more holistic look at e-Governance. Processes have to be streamlined and seamlessly linked between government bodies to ensure smooth functioning.

Paperless Administration

Advance of IT is affecting various aspects of life, including public administration. Concepts, structures and processes of management are already under going significant changes due to the impact of IT. Managerial development has been accompanied by the increasing use of computer and information technology in public administration. Computers, of course, are not a new phenomenon. They have been used in public bureaucracies in many parts of the world. Development of small, reliable and relatively cheap mini and macro computers has made it possible to install the computer technology throughout parts of the public sector/public bureaucracies.

IT systems are today an essential part of day to day work of most public service organizations, as it provides a powerful stimulus to the introduction of performance measurement scheme by providing the capacity to store, analyse and provide the data, whenever it is needed. The use of IT can bring about changes in organizational structure, break down the hierarchy, increase coordination of activities and reduce the tendency towards bureaucratic organisation. The potential of IT for decentralization has implications not only for the bureaucratic pattern of organisation, which characterizes public administration, but also for accountability and equity.

All these developments in IT can have a dramatic effect on the overall organisation structure and job design of individual employees. IT will lead to flattening and down sizing of today's organizations, eliminating the need for levels of bureaucracy and a long chain of command. That is to say, organizations, become flatter and less hierarchical. The need for "information-keepers", "number crunches", and "paper (file) pushers" is also eliminated.

When IT is installed in an organization, people working there will be replaced by the machines (computers) resulting in what is called downsizing or rightsizing of the organization. The impact of IT is felt mainly at the middle management level. In the traditional administrative process, the middle management level constitutes the mainstream of bureaucracy. Downsizing of government departments and directorates would create a new administrative culture by ding away with the middle management.

IT leads to paper less administration because the official business and documents will be digitalized under the system and this will enable more prompt and precise administrative procedures and prompt productivity and efficiency. In addition, information network will be established to unite citizens and government, so that both parties can communicate regardless of time and place.

Skills

E-governance demands a range of skills that may not be present initially in government agencies. The areas of expertise the government needs to possess in order to go digital are the following:

IT systems development: The era of stand alone mainframes requiring specialized personnel capable of writing proprietary software has virtually ended. Standardization in programming code and the use of object programming have accelerated the development of new software. This service can be supplied through specialized IT companies. Government still needs in-house capacity to decide what kind of systems and e-government applications it wants and can engage in.

Programme management: E-government initiatives tend to be complex, since they not only call for a particular agency specific IT application to be developed, but also require the services of many different agencies and their role players. These e-government initiatives also refer to other interventions needed in the overall system for the applications to work. Managing the implementation of an e-government initiative, coordinating among different agencies and other stakeholders, and focusing on deadlines and results while keeping a keen eye on process, require program management skills that are generally not abundant in government.

Change management: E-government is accompanied by organizational reform and human resources will have to be re-skilled and redeployed internally or elsewhere lest they will be laid off. In this context, resistance to change can be fierce. Change management skills are required to guide government institutions through this process of organizational restructuring.

ICT procuring and outsourcing management: Government needs to be an 'intelligent buyer' of ICT infrastructures and services, capable of specifying its needs, managing the procurement process, and managing vendors.

Case Studies

Two case studies from Andhra Pradesh are presented below in the light of the above analysis. Andhra Pradesh has recently emerged as one of the leading states in India in e-government applications. The state government has been implementing a comprehensive plan to utilize IT for better services to citizens. Guiding Coalition is very important for effective deployment of IT in government. Andhra Pradesh has attempted to create a guiding coalition by adopting a two-track approach. Firstly, awareness and training programmes have been organized for Ministers, Secretaries and Head of Departments. Secondly, an attempt has been made to build up a team of officers with the knowledge of and understanding of IT and its attendant change management issues. The research has been undertaken on two important programmes of the state government *i.e.*, CARD and E-Seva.

CARD

The first department of IT amongst the states in India was formally established in Andhra Pradesh in 1998 and the first department selected by the A.P. Government for computerization of all its operations was the Registration Department. Known as CARD (Computer Aided Registration Department), this is the first major IT project of the A.P. Government. It opened the gateway for the introduction of e-governance in the state. It is admitted that building up a whole new system based on a highly sophisticated technology for the first time is a real challenge. Therefore, the Government took the first step to impart IT skills to all the employee of the registration department as part of the CARD project.

For this case study CARD was selected by the researchers in order to explore the impact of computerization of all the operations of a department on the Government and the people/clientele. The study explored the administrative restructuring of the Department and the degree of satisfaction of the people after the introduction of IT. The study found that the process of registration of property which used to be a very complex, tedious and time-consuming task in the past became simple, straight, transparent and quick thanks to the simplification of the whole process of registration brought about by the CARD. The study also found that the citizens/clientele of the CARD also expressed their satisfaction and happiness over the significant changes that were introduced in the service delivery by the Department. Another lesson learnt from the study is that the CARD project is a good example of success story in several areas of public administration, like use of IT in improving the quality of delivery mechanisms, project management and administration, training and motivation. This project has already become a role model for several other departments in Andhra Pradesh.

Conducting an impact study on CARD, 100 per cent approved for CARD system as time taken is very negligible as compared with the manual system. After introduction of IT, the valuation of property is 12-18 minutes; market value assistance is 10-15 minutes; sale of stamp paper is 18-25 minutes; document writing is about 1 hour; registration is around 1 hour; encumbrance certificate is 15-20 minutes; and certified copies of document is 45 minutes. Under manual system the average time taken for valuation of property is 30 minutes—1 week, sale of stamp paper is 1-2 hours, document writing is 3-4 days, encumbrance certificate is 5-10 days, certified copies of document is 10-15 days.

e-Seva

The state has taken a number of steps to launch Andhra Pradesh into the digital age. The state government has launched a number of applications in different departments as part of its 'SMART' government initiative. e-Seva is one of the major IT projects undertaken by the Government of Andhra Pradesh as a part of e-governance. As citizens had to run around various departments and spend long hours to pay the utility bills, Government of Andhra Pradesh has taken a vital leap in providing citizens with convenience and comfort in all transactions with the government.

e-Seva is the first kind of service in the country, providing a wide spectrum of citizen friendly services that will save citizens from wasting time in running around various departments. e-Seva is built on the success of TWINS (Twin Cities Network Services) pilot project, which was launched in December 1999 in Hyderabad, the state capital. It is designed to provide citizens of Hyderabad and Secunderabad 42 services pertaining to six departments for delivery under one roof (on a one-stop mode). Services range from utility bill/tax payment, issue of certificates, to provision of information and facilitation.

e-Seva is a citizen service system with a difference, in that it provides service by a clean, transparent, efficient and effective administrative system through state-of-the-art electronic technology. Citizens are benefited by the direct interface with the government, which saves their time, energy and money and gives them hassle free dealings with the administration. All the administrative departments providing public services come to the customer under one roof for offering the citizen a wide range of citizen friendly services.

The paradigm shift in the delivery of citizen services by the Government through e-Seva enhances accessibility, convenience and speed. e-Seva is serving over a million customers across the twin cities of Hyderabad and Secunderabad. Internet services like Internet-enabled electronic payments, downloading of forms and government orders and filing of applications on the Web are also offered.

The e-Seva centres will function seven days a week and the services would be provided across the counter and also on the Internet. User charges will be collected for some of the services to sustain the project, which is using high-end technology. In a novel step to further citizen convenience, the Andhra Pradesh government's e-Seva, has joined hands with HDFC Bank to launch a co-branded credit card enabling hassle-free payment facility for utilities in the state.

E-Governance Outcomes and Performance Indicators

- Greater accountability and transparency in public Administration and government business processes are open to the public (tendering, procurement, recruitment, etc.).
- On-line availability of governments' budgets and expenditure reports.
- Accessibility on-line to government reports and documents, organizational structure, contract information, etc.
- Better coordination and cooperation between government agencies.
- Integrated government information and knowledge sharing network.

- Sharing of government data and information across agencies.
- Accessibility to government information (data, statistics, documents) and ability to interact/transact with governments.
- Number of IT related public-private partnerships established.
- Improved communications and public relations.
- Timely response by government to queries.
- Improved perception of government by people and business community.
- Increased awareness of rights of civil society and obligations of government.
- Accessibility to government legislation and regulatory information.
- Availability of on-line appealing and e-ombudsman.
- Higher awareness levels of principles of good governance among citizens.
- Greater public participation in governments' affairs.
- Posting policy drafts on-line for public participation in policy development process.
- Availability of on-line intervention on government decision-making and policy development (participatory budgeting, participatory legislative processes, etc.).
- Streamlined government structure and business processes.
- Decentralization and redefined role of local government.
- Availability of and accessibility to government data and information for local governments.
- Increased capacity of local governments to manage government administrative processes and service delivery operations, through integrated IT systems.
- Increased monitoring and evaluation capacity of state and central governments on local governments' performance.
- Increase in number of government operations performed by local governments.
- Increase in the delivery of services.
- All legislations available on-line, with explanatory notes.
- Legislation in place to deal with e-documentation,

e-record keeping, e-authentication, e-signature and e-transactions.

- Legislation in place concerning e-protection, privacy, and cyber crime.
- Enabling policy and regulatory frameworks. Policies and regulations available on-line.
- Guidelines and regulations available on-line concerning governments' e-interference.

Conclusion

Due to induction of IT there have been improvement in the efficiency and effectiveness in delivery of services to the citizens. It also enables the citizen from having access to passive information to active participation in government activities. It has been found to facilitate innovative use of information, collected and maintained by the government in the form of innovative and imaginative information linkages and information sharing at all levels of the government. IT is particularly helpful in establishing a two-way information-communication network both vertically and horizontally across the public and the administrative system and in reinforcing people's faith in the credibility of the government. Efficiency of e-Governance can be gauged from the standpoint of (*i*) empowerment that the citizen enjoys in accessing and making choices about government information system and services (*ii*) Increase in the transparency and accountability in government business and (*iii*) dismantling of administrative hierarchical structure.

Accessing of information by all citizens equally leads to e-Democracy; e-Governance is really enabled government, E-ffective government and E-xcellent government. E-Government is government 'any time, any where'. The future is e-homes with e-services at the doorsteps.

REFERENCES

Bedi, K.S., Parminder, J., Srivastava, S., *Government @net*, New Delhi, Sage, 2000.

Bellamy, C. and Taylor, John. A., *Governing in Information Age*, Bunckingham, Open University Press, 1998.

Bhatnagar, S., 'Productivity in Public Administration through Computerization: Manpower Bottlenecks', *Indian Journal of Public Administration,* 34(2), April-June 1998, pp. 284-93.

David Farnham and Sylvia Horton, Ed., *Managing the New Public Services,* London, Macmillan Press, 1996.

Dunsire, A, 'Administrative Theory in the 1980's', *Public Administration,* 1995, 73:1-15.

Garson G.D., *Information Technology and Computer Applications for Public Administration, Issues and Trends,* London, Idea Group Publications, 1999.

Garson, G. David, 'Micro Computer Applications in Public Administration', *Public Administration Review,* 43(5), September-October, 1983, pp. 453-58.

Garson, G.D., *Hand Book of Public Information System,* New York, USA, 2000.

Gosling, P., *Government for Digital Age,* London, Bowerdean, 1997.

Greenwood, J and Wilson, D., *Public Administration in Britain Today,* London, Mac Millan, 1989.

Hughes, O., *Public Management and Administration,* New York: St. Martin's Press, 1994.

Hughes, Owen E., *Public Management and Administration,* London, Mac Millan, 1998.

Massey, A., *Managing the Public Sector,* Aldershot: Edward Elgar, 1993.

Regan, Priscilla. M. Privacy, 'Government Information, and Technology', *Public Administration Review,* 46(6), November-December, 1986, pp. 629-34.

Rogers W'O Okot-uma, *Electronic Governance: Reinventing Good Governance,* London, Commonwealth Secretariat.

Taylor, J. and Williams, H., 'Public Administration and the Information Polity', *Public Administration,* 1991, 69:2-21.

World Bank Report, *Governance and Development,* World Bank, Washington D.C., 1992.

WEBSITES

www.andhrapradesh.com Accessed on 13.11.2003

www.coir.com Accessed on 29.10.2003

www.open-gov.uk Accessed on 4.11.2003

www.london-research.gov.uk/LBISN99 Accessed on 10.10.2003

www.worldbank,org/publicsector/egov/definition.Itm Accessed on 15.10.2003

www.egov.mit.gov.in Accessed on 22.10.2003

www.ap-it.com Accessed on 20.10.2003

CHAPTER V:
Good Governance and Public Administration

15

Good Governance at the Grassroots Level

Prof. S.C. Arora

Good governance generally means looking after the welfare of all in all respects. It may refer to high level of organizational efficiency and effectiveness and a responsive and responsible behaviour on the part of rulers in order to obtain pre-determined desirable goals for the society. To have a comprehensive understanding of the concept of good governance it would be desirable to take into account the parameters given by various scholars and institutions from time to time. Kautaliya, a great Indian philosopher, in his famous treatise *'Arthashastra'* has dwelt upon several indicators of good governance. They include: merger of the King's individuality with duties; properly guided administration; disciplined life with a code of conduct for the king and ministers; fixed salaries and allowances to the king and public servants; maintenance of law and order as the chief duty of the king; theft loses to be made good from king's salary; carrying out preventive and punitive measures against corrupt officials; replacement of bad ministers by good ones by the king and emulation of administrative qualities.[1] The gist of these indicators drives one to conclude that the main objective of good governance is to maximize the well-being of the people. As regards their relevance in the present day world, they still hold good.

Presently the concept of 'good governance' is being used in modern-western sense which is broadly conceived by the World Bank and Organization for Economic Cooperation and Development (OECD). It emphasizes political and bureaucratic accountability, as established legal framework based on the rule of law, independence of judiciary, freedom of expression and information, sound administrative system and cooperation between the government and the civil society organizations. Evidently, good governance implies utmost concern for people's welfare wherein the government and its bureaucracy follow policies and discharge their duties with a deep sense of commitment; respecting the rule of law in a manner which is transparent, ensuring human rights and dignity, probity and public accountability.[2]

There is no denying the fat that the indicators of good governance mentioned above are more or less applicable at the local level also. Besides, certain other factors such as committed political will for decentralization, non-hegemonic bureaucracy, constructive role of mass-media and non-governmental organizations, enlightened dutiful masses and their active participation and cooperation need special attention in this regard. All these together would determine the state of affairs of good governance at the grassroots level of administration.

The need for good governance, in India, has always been indispensable for delivering goods and services to the masses. However, its indispensability has assumed utmost significance considering the present changed national and international scenario. From the point of view of levels of government its urgency and need is all the more important at the grassroots level because of its proximity with the people. Further, it is this level which provides the foundation to a democratic super-structure. Keeping this in view, the Indian Government, since independence, has made numerous efforts in this direction.

In order to understand the efforts made by the Indian Government to ensure good governance at the local level one has too peep into the historical developments in this regard. Local self-governing institutions, both rural and urban, as an expression of democratic decentralization existed in one form or the other in ancient India. However, the credit of laying down the foundations of modern system of local self-government goes to British rulers particularly after the transfer of power system of local self government goes to British rulers particularly after the transfer of power from the East India Company to the Crown in 1858. Lord Mayo's Resolution of 1870, Lord Ripon's Resolution of 1882,

Recommendations of the Royal Commission on decentralization 1909 and Government of India Acts 1919 and 1935 are the pointers in this direction.

After independence, comparatively more attention was given to the development of rural areas and Panchayati Raj Institutions (PRIs) were visualized as potential agencies for bringing about socio-economic transformation by empowering rural masses. Accordingly, Indian Constitution, under one of the Directive Principles of the State Policy provided that 'the State shall take steps to organize village panchayats and endow them with such powers and authority as may be necessary to enable them to function as units of self-government'.[3]

However, prior to the establishment of PRIs, Indian Government launched Community Development Project and National Extension Service to bring about socio-economic development of rural India. But these twin efforts failed to achieve the desired objective for want of people's participation. Consequently, a Study Team under the Chairmanship of Balwant Rai Mehta was appointed to examine and report upon the mechanism to be evolved through which the active participation of the rural masses could be ensured. The Study Team recommended a three-tier system of panchyati raj *i.e.* Gram Panchayat at their village level, Panchayat Samiti at the intermediate level and Zila Parishad at the District Level with genuine transfer of powers and adequate resources to these bodies. It also recommended that all developmental schemes for rural areas should be routed through the PRIs. Accepting these recommendations, the panchyati raj system was introduced in several states of India. Unfortunately, the system would not make much headway even after a long trial for want of its implementation in the true spirit and desired response from the political masters, bureaucrats and rural masses.

Another attempt to revamp the Panchayati Raj system was made by the Janata Government in 1977 by appointing a committee headed by Ashoka Mehta. Its main recommendations were: two tier system of panchyati raj *i.e.* Mandal Panchyat (consisting of a number of villages have a population between 15 to 20 thousand) and Zila Parishad at the district level; regular elections of these bodies; establishment of Nyaya Panchayat; party-based elections of PRIs; reservation of seats for weaker sections and women;

provision of adequate financial resources; no suppression of PRIs on partisan grounds; people's participation in the developmental activities through PRIs and appointment of a Minister for Panchayats in the State Council of Ministers. These recommendations could not be implemented because of the fall of the Janata Government in 1980. However, they succeeded in initiating debates and discussions throughout the country for improving the health of PRIs.

Post-independence era has also witnessed numerous impressive attempts for reform at the level of local urban government. Some of the most important steps in this direction include the Local Finance Inquiry Committee (1949), The Taxation Inquiry Committee (1953) and the Rural-Urban Relationship Committee (1963). However, most of the thinking on municipal reforms remained confined to augmenting the financial resources only. As a consequence, they failed miserably to deal with the dynamic growth created by the process of steady urbanization and urban growth. Simultaneously, most of the functions of urban local bodies especially the developmental, were transferred to specialized agencies created for the purpose.

Thus the need to revamp the local bodies both in rural and urban areas remained alive and became an issue of debates and discussions, both inside and outside the parliament, during the eighties and various steps have been taken in this direction. Due to expansion of anti-poverty programs and creation of DRDA and other organizations for rural development at lower levels, it was required to integrate the PR system with development programs. As a result, a Working Group on District Planning was set up in 1983 under the chairmanship of C.H. Hannumantha Rao. The Committee emphasized the need of decentralization of planning process and recommended the district as a unit of decentralized planning. Likewise, the complexities that arose due to increasing urban population and the growing demand for qualitative and efficient civic services made it imperative to set up a National Commission on Urbanization in 1985. The Commission gave detailed recommendations about the measures required for strengthening the management and administration of urban local government institutions in the country. In the same year G.V.K. Rao Committee was appointed to review the existing administrative arrangements for rural development and poverty alleviation programs. In the very next year, a Committee headed by L.M. Singhvi, was appointed to prepare a concept paper on PR. Apart from these, Workshops of Collectors/District Magistrates on Responsive Administration (1987-88), Panchayati Raj and Nagar Palika Sammelans (1989), the Chief Ministers and Chief Secretaries' Conferences (1989) and introduction of 64th and 65th Amendments Bills also dealt with local self-governing institutions. All these efforts culminated in the passage of the 73rd and 74th Amendment Acts dealing with PRIs and municipalities respectively in the early Nineties.

The two Amendment Acts have provided a constitutional status to PRIs and municipalities for the firs6t time; also brought about a sort of uniformity in local governance by introducing the three-tier system of rural and urban local bodies for the entire country; and injected a new life into these institutions by making them more representative ones by widening the scope of direct elections. Besides, their security of tenure for five years has been ensured by restricting the powers of the State Governments to supersede them and holding of the elections mandatory on the part of the respective state governments. Moreover, the Acts have also facilitated people's participation in their local affairs by introducing Gram Sabha and Ward Committees in rural and urban areas respectively. A provision has also been made for constituting a District Planning Committee to consolidate the plans prepared by the panchayats and municipalities in the district and to prepare draft development plan for the district as a whole.

Further, the Amendment Acts have reduced the domination of the socially privileged sections in the power structure at the grass-roots level by providing adequate representation to persons belonging to Scheduled Castes/Scheduled Tribes and Backward Classes in both the rural and urban local bodies. Likewise, these have offered an opportunity to women who constitute about half of the country's population to play a decisive role in the administration of their local affairs by making provision of reservation of not less than one-third of seats for them and that too without any time limit. The same benefit has been extended to them along with persons belonging to SC and ST categories with regard to positions of chairpersons of local self-governing bodies at various levels. The Amendments Acts have also provided for setting up of State Election Commission on the lines of central

Election Commission to conduct free and fair elections to the local bodies. Last, but not the least, they have provided for the setting up of State Finance Commission after every five years to ensure that financial health of the local bodies is not left to be decided on ad-hoc, arbitrary and whimsical manner.[4]

Thus, the main objective of these Amendment Acts was to take the government to the people, to make the administration accountable to the people and to ensure people's participation in the administration at the grass roots level. Besides, they also aimed at enhancing the capabilities of the people to involve them in the planning process with according to their priorities. Further, these envisaged decentralization of the execution of all types of developmental activities with the active participation of the masses. In brief, the purpose of these Amendments was to bring good governance at the grass roots level of administration by strengthening and streamlining the functioning of rural and urban self-governing local bodies which may be regarded as a welcome step.

Nevertheless, their in-depth analysis reveals some inherent ambiguities. The most important one is the lack of clear cut demarcation of functions (29 in the XI and 18 in the XII Schedule relating to Panchayati Raj and municipal bodies respectively) amongst the three tiers of rural and urban administration. At the same time the powers and functions of Gram Sabha have not been specified under the 73rd Amendment.

To give effect to these Amendment Acts, the states began enthusiastically to incorporate the provisions contained in them, in their respective Panchayati Raj and Municipal Acts and by now most of the states have held two rounds of elections with reservation of seats to women and other weaker sections of the society under the supervision of their State Chief Election Commission. Consequently, local bodies, both in rural and urban areas, came into existence throughout the country in the true spirit of these Amendments. Further, several states have appointed Finance Commissions (some states twice) also for improving the financial position of these bodies. But in so far as the actual devolution of powers-both administrative and financial is concerned, no desirable change has been observed as they continue to be as poor as they were in the past. It goes without saying that in the absence of these powers, envisaged under the Amendments, the cherished goal of making grass roots level bodies truly self-governing units would remain a distant dream and good governance at this level a distant reality.

Again, to facilitate people's participation in civic affairs Ward Committees were provided under the 74th Amendment Act but so far these have remained only on papers in most of the states. The same is the case with regard to the setting up of District Planning Committee. Likewise, under the 73rd Amendment Act, an effort was made to revamp the Gram Sabha by according it a constitutional status and it was hailed as Lok Sabha of the village people. The purpose of this moves was to bring transparency in the functioning of the village panchayat and make it accountable to the villagers, besides ensuring their active participation in its working. However, the experience of the last decade shows that it is still a non-functional body mainly because of the lack of faith of the rural people in its effectiveness resulting in their indifferent attitude towards this body.

As far as the emerging political leadership in rural-urban local bodies is concerned, it does not seem to be of a better quality. While this may mainly be attributed to the degenerating petty party-politics dominating the elections, other contributing factors are the influential role of money and muscle power, and considerations of caste, class, clan, religion and region during elections. No doubt, one-third reservation has been provided to women in local bodies, but the experience so far shows that they have failed to play their expected role independently and still seem to be puppets in the hands of male members of their family. At the same time, the leadership in these bodies has yet to reach the common people as it is still in the hands of the elites. Moreover, a close look at the functioning of the local bodies reveals that it is marred by petty politics and suffers from domination ¾ both political and bureaucratic, and caste religious considerations which is far from the ideal of good governance.

On the basis of the preceding discussion, it may be observed that the implementation of the 73rd and 74th Amendments during the last decade has yet to exhibit a qualitative improvement in the governance of local bodies in India. It is mainly because of the fact that certain essential pre-requisites such as revamping the gram Sabha, constitution of Ward Committees in municipal areas, financial viability, political will for decentralization, attitudinal and behavioural changes on the part of both politicians and bureaucrats, enlightened masses, committed and dedicated representatives and office-bearers etc. have not been given due attention. Hence, corrective measures must be taken immediately to facilitate the self governing units to function in such a way as to send signals of good governance to the masses.

In order to ensure good governance at the grassroots level, first of all, the ambiguity regarding the distribution of the subjects contained in the XI and XII Schedules amongst the PRIs and municipal bodies needs to be done away with so as to demarcate the role of each tier to pin down its respective responsibility.

Secondly, powers and functions of the Gram Sabha have also to be specified and at the same time, it must be reinvigorated in actual terms to enable it to perform the role of a mini parliament at the village level. This will certainly ensure transparency, accountability and people's participation¾the essential components of good governance. Likewise, to elicit active participation of the urban masses in the conduct of their civic affairs, Ward Committees be constituted without any delay.

Thirdly, political masters ought to exhibit their will to transfer the powers and functions in the true spirit of the Amendments to achieve the desired objective of democratic decentralization which ultimately contributes to good governance at the grass-roots level.

Fourthly, considering the fact that financial viability of any administrative system is the sine-qua-non for its effective functioning, the financial health of local bodies needs to be improved and strengthened. Here too, the political masters have to show the spirit of magnanimity in making them financially self-sufficient. At the same time, these institutions should come up with the strong will power to generate, mobilize, tap and augment their own financial resources, shedding their populist approach.

Fifthly, the office-bearers, who are the actual actors in the local administrative system must be men of vision and integrity, fairly educated, committed and dedicated to serve the masses. But this can hardly be expected in the given socio-economic and political set-up of the Indian society particularly in rural areas. So, what is needed is a radical change in such a set-up in which electoral process encourages righteous and awakened people to come forward to serve the masses. It should be conducted in a such a manner as to leave little scope for party-politics and considerations of caste, class, religion, region etc. The best alternate could be the election of representatives through consensus who, in turn, would function in the spirit of accommodation.

Sixthly, keeping in mind the famous dictum that 'people get the type of governance they deserve,' masses must be an awakened lot, understanding their rights, duties and responsibilities under the newly evolved decentralized system. It is they who can ensure efficient and effective functioning of the system embedded with accountability, transparency and probity.

Seventhly, to provide good governance at the cutting edge level of administration, the bureaucracy must be inclined to play the role of friend, philosopher and guide to local bodies since the general impression at present is that it continues to play a hegemonic role in its formal characteristic way. Hence, what is required is the necessary attitudinal and behavioral changes in its style of functioning, so as to make it change-oriented, result-oriented and people-oriented to enable the rural-urban local bodies to flourish as truly self-governing units. The same applies to political masters as well as they are expected to play the róle of big brothers and faithful guides so as to allow these bodies to function as effective units of participatory democracy.

Lastly, impediments to good governance like constitution of parallel bodies (Gram Vikas Samitis in Haryana) and postponement of timely elections of local bodies which are raising their ugly heads here need to be curbed immediately with an iron hand.

To sum up, if all the above mentioned remedial measures are properly taken care of, good governance at the grass roots level which hitherto has been an elusive dream could become a hard reality.

REFERENCES

1. L.N. Sharma and Susmita Sharma, 'Kautilyan Indicators of Food Governance,' *Indian Journal of Public Administration*, New Delhi, Vol. XLIV, No. 3, July-September, 1998, pp. 265-70.
2. Peter Blunt, 'Cultural Relativism, Good Governance and Sustainable Human Development', *Public Administration and Development*, Vol. 15, 1995, pp. 5-7.
3. Article 40 of the Indian Constitution.
4. The Constitution Seventy-third and Seventy-fourth Amendment Acts, 1992.

16

Good Governance for Sustainable Development: A Study of People's Institutions in Rural Andhra Pradesh

Dr. T. Satyanarayana

Governance as a strategy in the context of managerial reforms assigns a steering and regulating role to the government vis-à-vis the private sector and forges productive partnerships between the government and social organizations. The task of public policy formulation and implementation has now assumed the nature of cooperative endeavour of governmental organizations, state institutions, social groups, NGO's and private institutions. We are moving towards a framework of multi-actor and multi-level governance. In this context, the study of governance of people's institutions, which, in service of multiple organizations perform multi-activities and cater to the needs of multiple groups and areas at the grass roots level, assume considerable importance. The present study is divided into 4 Sections. Section I is devoted to present the context, key determinants and components of good governance and also its relevance to sustainable development which would provide greater insights into the phenomena. Second II deals with the governance and development paths in India. Section III analyzes the governance of people's institutions

---

The author is grateful to Prof. Ch. Bala Ramulu, Department of Public Administration and Prof. M. Raja Gopala Chary, Principal, University P.G. College (K.U.), Nirmal, for their suggestions on this article and continuous support in all his academic activities.

and their role in policy formulation and implementation of developmental programmes in Andhra Pradesh. Section IV presents the conclusion of the study.

Context of Good Governance

Issues relating to the state and government have attracted the attention of the best minds (Plato, Aristotle, Thomos Hobbes, Kautilya, John Rawls) over space and time throughout history. But, the debate on Good Governance (GG) or New Public Management (NPM) is gaining momentum world over in the recent past. In the 1980s a number of factors in the objective situation all over the world have indeed drawn sharp attention to various aspects of governance. The social, economic, political and administrative factors have brought the issue to the forefront. The World Bank (WB), International Monetary Fund (IMF), Organization for Economic Cooperation and Development (OECD), bilateral donor agencies (like ODA, DFID–UK), Multi-National Corporations (MNCs) and Non-Governmental Organizations (NGOs) have brought the approach of GG to manage public institutions to the main agenda of the governments in the 21st century. The concern of the WB is to improve the capacity of borrower governments to efficiently implement the projects and programmes assisted by it for sustainable development.

The WB first raised the issue of governance in the 1980's in the context of:

- (*i*) collapse of command-and-control economies in the former Soviet Union and East European countries;
- (*ii*) fiscal crisis of the welfare state in most of the established industrial economies;
- (*iii*) important role of the state in the miracle economies of East Asia; and
- (*iv*) collapse of states and the explosion of humanitarian emergencies in several parts of the world.

World Bank on Good Governance

WB advocated NPM/GG to meet the challenges of new millennium.[1] GG has become a critical issue today in the context of an increasingly borderless world, and the growing presence of multi-nationals. In India the discourse on good governance has been gaining momentum since the adoption of New Economic Policy (1991) and it has become inevitable for the Indian state to compete with international market forces in the 21st century.

WB's conception of Good Governance entails reforms in four areas:

First, an economic role of the state which includes budget restraint, reducing bureaucracy and accent on results, both in planning and in evaluation of programmes and people, investment in basic social services and infrastructure, protecting the vulnerable, protecting environment, service to the public, with a special concern for quality and citizens as client.[2]

Second, a set of specific policies or policy reforms viz., fiscal consolidation, reduction and redirection of public expenditures, reform and reduction of taxes, maintenance of competitive exchange rates, financial, trade and investment liberalization, overall deregulation, and privatization of state enterprizes.[3]

Third, the non-economic aspects of the government, which include: electoral democracy, transparency, accountability, participation, responsiveness in the processes of government, the assurance of safety and security to citizens, the non-arbitrary rule of law, effective enforcement of contracts, protection of human rights, reduction of military expenditure, private sector techniques for motivating employees such as merit pay, mission statements and quality circles.[4]

Fourth, GG in WB's perception also involves notions like corporate management, corporate culture and bottom-driven rhetoric.

The studies[5] *reported in the Indian Journal of Public Administration* (IJPA) 1998 by (O.P. Minocha, Mohit Battacharya, Subash C. Kashyap, Asok Mukopadhyay, Bata K. Dey, R.C. Sekar, Yatish Mishra, 1998 and Madhav Godbole, 1997, Pardeep Sahni, 2003, V.S. Prasad, 2003 and Haragopal G., 2003), point out the following as main components of GG at all levels (Central, State, Local) of government. They are (*i*) mobilization and utilization of natural resources for betterment of society, (*ii*) maintenance of macro-economic stabilization, (*iii*) providing suitable living environment, (*iv*) interaction among the government, civil society and private sector, (*v*) respect for democratic institutions and human rights and values, (*vi*) citizen caring and responsive administration, (*vii*) providing safety and security to the people, (*viii*) control of corruption and corrupt practices, (*ix*) emphasis on organizational effectiveness, (*x*) capacity building of the communities, (*xi*) ensuring peoples participation, (*xii*) satisfying the expectations of all the stakeholders—including customers, employees, suppliers, (*xiii*) compliance of standards set by the investors, (*xiv*) maintenance of honesty and ethics rather than imposition of legislation forcefully in the societal organization, (*xv*) organizational pluralism-state, market and societal organizations for governance, (*xvi*) transparent administrative system, (*xvii*) competitive government, injecting competition into service delivery, (*xviii*) performance partnership between government, NGOs and private agencies, (*xix*) E-governance.

All these factors are important for achieving sustainable development in any society.

Governance for Sustainable Development

The issue of sustainable development is concerned with enhancing human wellbeing through time. What constitutes a good life is highly subjective, and the relative importance accorded to different aspects of wellbeing varies with individuals, societies and generations. United Nations Development Programmes (UNDP) has observed that eliminating poverty, creating jobs and sustaining livelihoods, protecting and regenerating the environment and promoting advancement of women are the most critical elements of sustainable development in the 21st Century.[6] World Development Report 2003, adopting a longer time horizon of 20 to 50 years argued that ensuring sustainable development requires attention not just to economic growth but also to environmental and social issues. The report takes a comprehensive, longer term and dynamic view of sustainability with a clear focus on poor and backward areas.[7]

But, for sustainable and equitable development institutions which are stable, capable of changing and adapting and emergence of new institutions are essential. When they function well, they enable people to work with one another to plan a future for themselves, their families and their larger communities. But, when they are weak or unjust, the result is mistrust and uncertainty.[8]

Therefore, development in any country mostly depends on the nature and functioning of governance of public institutions – both at **macro** and **micro** levels. Governance for development ought to be accountable, participatory, responsive, effective and efficient for promoting the rule of law, safe guarding the interests of citizens, and marching towards a holistic development.

The changing concept of development, globalization and growth of new technologies, changing perception of role of the state/government etc., are some important factors influencing the nature and process of the governance of public institutions. The WB document (1997) envisages a more effective state by restricting its activities to match its capabilities an also advocates improving the state's capabilities by re-invigorating public institutions. In the context of globalization the GG is expected to integrate the roles of the state, the market and the civil society in development process.[9] Further, GG is also considered as the deliberate and conscious management of regime structures for enhancing the public realm. Such conscious management could be done through different sets of tools including code of ethical behaviour; outcome-based performance assessment; result-based management; outcome-measurement; balanced scorecard; social auditing; sharing best practice; information retrieval; competencies profiling; knowledge discovery; sharing and development; learning after action review; learning logs; decision diaries; intellectual capital measurement systems; interrogatory knowledge management studies and so forth.[10]

The WB (1992) defines 'governance' as: "The manner in which power is exercised in the management of a country's economic and social resources for development" and 'good governance' as: "The one epitomized by predictable, open and enlightened policy making, a bureaucracy imbued with professional ethos acting in furtherance of the public good, the rule of law, transparent processes, and a strong civil society participating in public affairs".

R.A.W. Rhodes (1996) has presented six categories of governance perspectives:

The Minimal State, Corporate Governance, New Public Management, Good Governance, Socio-cybernetic System and Self-Organizing Network.

John Healey and Mark Robinson define GG as: "A high level of organizational effectiveness in relation to policies actually pursued, especially in the conduct of economic policy and its contribution to growth, stability and popular welfare".

Governance and Development Paths in India

India's development experience during the last five and a half decades has thrown up several challenges to the development debate itself as well as to governance. Development, initially aimed at rapid growth, with a dose of distributive justice. This did raise the levels of expectations of the classes and masses of society. The classes were expecting greater share in the wealth generated from rapid growth and the masses were hoping for a better life through distributive justice. Thus, they provided the context and the support base for the government, political stability and legitimacy of the system in the first two decades of independence. It was from the nineteen sixties that signals of restlessness started appearing, rendering governance difficult. The state, in the process of reacting to these signals, responded through both responsive as well as repressive forms. Responsive measures included land reforms and anti-poverty programmes. The repressive steps included arbitrary laws, restrictions and regulations, more powers to police and para-military forces.[11]

In the 1990s this model of development underwent metamorphosis and became a techno-managerial model with exclusive emphasis on growth. The concern for justice almost came to be abandoned under the structural adjustment programme. The LPG (Liberalization Privatization and Globalization) approach to development started de-recognizing the role of the state. This led to the closure of several public undertakings managed earlier by the state, retreat from the welfare domain including public distribution system, abandonment of agrarian reforms and relaxation of laws meant for protecting the industrial labour. All this was done with a single argument that the state was incapable of performing the role of producer of wealth or even of a distributive agent to effect "efficient allocation of values". The whole emphasis on privatization led to downsizing the bureaucracy, confining government's role to only maintenance of law and order, through the rule of law.

The second stage economic reforms emphasize participatory development through semi-public, NGO's and private institutions and application of Information Technology for stimulating economic growth in the country. In the last few years privatization has been significantly promoted in all the sectors. This paradigm is based on the premise that by narrowing down the scope of government activities, an efficient, transparent, effective and accountable governance would appear. The rationale appears to be that with fewer bureaucratic structures there would be only a few bureaucratic problems. This approach is also designed to minimize the role of welfare state by reducing expenditure in many essential areas and allowing market forces to take over. But, markets are ruthless and market approach to empowering the people will increase exploitation and oppression of the weak. It will manipulate democracy, curb local initiatives and involvement of people while promoting individualism.[12]

An examination of Governance in India reveals that factors such as multiple agencies for governance with different frameworks of operations, centralized power structures, increasing public expenditure, market imperfections, wastage, inordinate delay and corrupt management, lawlessness, deligitimisation of process, political interventions, etc., have resulted in challenges to governance. Further, studies also reveal that people's institutions and their role in the policy formulation and implementation have been reduced to that of recipients, and not creative agents. The development model did warrant mobilization strategies by strengthening the existing institutions (73rd Constitutional Amendment Act, 1993). But, these measures mostly contributed to accommodate the rural elite in the structure of governance without substance of power. In a conflict-ridden society, participation should include increasing the capability of collective bodies to resolve conflicts. But, in practice as people's institutions have become passive participative institutions, conflicts get accentuated, as distribution of resources is done on the basis of given power structure. All these and other factors are resulting in growing unrest all over the country raising new issues and posing challenges to governance.[13] It is in this context an attempt to analyze the performance of people's institutions at the grass root level in Andhra Pradesh is considered relevant to the present discourse on GG. The Andhra Pradesh (A.P.) government during the last one decade, has been heavily relying on these institutions for stimulation of development process and politics of accommodation of ruling party members. Therefore, it is time to evaluate the performance and future of the people's institutions in the State.

People's Institutions in Andhra Pradesh

If institutions denote rules, organizations and social norms that facilitate coordination of human action or behaviour, their key functions are: generating information, giving citizens a voice, responding to feedback and fostering learning; balancing the interests of different groups, avoiding stalemates and conflicts and executing and implementing laws, policies and programmes. Civil society institutions are particularly important for promoting environmentally sound development strategies and growth processes which can contribute to people's wellbeing on a sustainable basis.[14]

There are different kinds of people's institutions in AP. They include: (1) Panchayat Raj Institutions (PRIs); (2) Water Shed Committees (WC); (3) Water User's Associations (WUAs); (4) Vana Samrakshana Samithies (VSS); (5) Development of Women and Children in Rural Areas (DWCRA); (6) Development of Women and Children in Urban Areas (DWCUA); (7) Chief Minister's Empowerment for Youth (CMEY); (8) Mothers' Committee (MC); (9) Vidhya Committee's (VC); (10) Village Tribal Development Committee's (VTDC); (11) Janmabhoomi Habitation Committee (JHC); and (12) Hospital Committees (HC). In all these institutions nearly 174 lakh people (nearly one third of the total population of the state) are expected to participate in the development process and ensure GG to the people.

In the context of development, people's institutions are expected to facilitate "active participation" of the public by involving people in actions which enhance their wellbeing, income, security or self-esteem by involving them in planning including assessment of local needs by collectively organizing and continuing efforts by the people themselves in setting goals, pooling resources together and taking actions which aim at improving their living conditions and ensuring participation of people with no class dominating the others. On the contrary, "passive participation" involves the people in actions that have been throughout, designed and controlled by others.[15]

The main objectives of peoples institutions are: proper utilization of natural and human resources; creation of infrastructural facilities; providing employment and income to the people; ensuring transparency in the implementation of government programmes and accountability for the development programmes; ensuring power in the hands of people to manage their affairs collectively; to develop confidence among the members of the groups and improve their socio-economic conditions; and to contribute to the economic growth.[16]

Performance of Peoples Institutions in AP

(*i*) *Panchayat Raj Institutions (PRIs)*

The Government of Andhra Pradesh amended the PRI Acts, time and again to strengthen the PRI's. At present these institutions are governed by AP PR Act, 1994 which provides constitutional status to the institutions. Unlike the earlier Acts, this Act is providing an opportunity for 2,47,375 persons to occupy leadership and other positions in the panchayats with the representation of STs, SCs, BCs and women being 8per cent, 18per cent, 34per cent and 33.3per cent respectively. These members are expected to prepare plans on 29 subjects and take part in decision-making and implementation of the development programmes. But, the major problem of PRIs is that they have no sufficient powers. The state government is scuttling the powers of these institutions covertly and overtly. Absence of conscious political support to local leadership from rural people, particularly from the poor, privatization of public services like health, education, agriculture, animal husbandry, etc., which are to be performed by the PRIs, non-release of grants by the State Government, inadequate financial resources to local bodies, creation of SHGs and assigning them the developmental programmes by neglecting PRIs etc., have collectively reduced the Panchayats into 'decorated statues', 'ornamental pieces', 'children born without parents' and weakened the PRIs in the state.[17]

The experience with the 73rd Amendment—a landmark in the history of grassroots institutions—is qualitatively, no different.[18] PRIs have come under severe attack by the Government in AP essentially in two manifest forms: a parallel set of institutions have been built around Janmabhoomi programme in the name of making people the center of development but ironically, without any representative character, and drying up of the financial resources of Panchayats and strengthening of the hands of local bureaucratic machinery in disbursing the funds under the scheme. Besides, the government of AP has transferred only 16 items, mostly insignificant, as against 29 items that 73rd amendment prescribes to Panchayats. The resultant crisis has manifested in Panchayat Raj leaders organizing themselves cutting across all party lines to launch a statewide agitation and also filing suits against the State government in the court. The undermining role of Janmabhoomi vis-à-vis PRIs must be seen as concomitant to the logic of reforms initiated in the state.[19]

(ii) Self-Help Groups (SHGs)

People's participation is sought through SHGs to collectively harness the opportunities from government schemes, resources, services and laws meant to help the people. They focus on organization of people into groups to foster the collective approach to their problems in order to improve their lot by enhancing their bargaining power and to resist exploitation. These organized groups are expected to draw many of the resources of the government programmes into the village coffers for their benefit. In Andhra Pradesh, there are 11 types of SHGs, consisting of 5,85,501 committees and 171.05 lakh members with financial transactions worth Rs. 28,79,880 crore.[20]

An examination of government reports and other studies on the functioning of SHGs unfolds that these institutions are organizing different groups of people–mainly women, farmers, tribals, parents, poor and unemployed persons to increase their empowerment.

The following are the some of the achievements of SHGs:

(*a*) **Development of Women and Children in Rural and Urban Areas (DWCRA and DWCUA):** International recognition has been accorded to DWCRA groups, establishment of banks, minidairy, marketing centers, shops, industry etc., under mutually aided co-operative society. Significantly, the Women Dairy Co-operative

Leadership Programme (WDCLP), a major component of EU (European Union) funded special project has shown that village dairy co-operatives can become effective instruments for women's empowerment since more than 90,000 women farmers actively participate in the affairs of around 2000 milk co-operatives in India.[21] The Co-operative Development Programme (CDP) of National Dairy Development Board (NDDB) is specially designed to encourage women to join the white revolution. Clearly and apparently, CDP seeks to promote self-reliance and create conditions for the formation of autonomous women owned milk co-operatives. It lays stress on women's education and development of leadership, formation of a corpus fund to the tune of Rs. 825 crore, establishment of DWCRA bazaars in all the districts of the State, setting up of 826 banks exclusively for women at Mandal level, distribution of loans worth 30 crore per year from different financial institutions to the members, improvement in the income levels of the groups ranging from Rs. 250 to Rs. 2000 per year, improvement in the social status of the women, good response from women to family planning literacy, environment, food and nutrition programmes and thereby enlightening them on modern science and technology. There is also appreciable improvement on the following parameters: sending the girl child to school, reducing family size and increasing working days. While there is increased role of women in decision making in their household affairs, the male dominance continues in some areas. Women power has stepped up its involvement in solving community problems. 93per cent of women representing 19-35 years of age group which constitutes 56-85 per cent of DWCRA groups have undergone family planning and this has also led to the enlightenment of others. Elimination of social evils like dowry, prostitution and other atrocities committed by male members, husbands, criminals etc., insurance benefits to the members of DWCRA, giving awards to the person who worked for the welfare of women etc., are also the achievements of women groups.

(*b*) **Vidya (Education) Committee:** 1,36,132 Vidya Committees have been formed providing employment to more than 50,000 persons as Vidya Volunteers at Panchayats, Mandal and Municipal levels. Further, 25,000 school buildings have been constructed under the supervision of Vidya Committees and enrolment of students (Drop outs) has taken place.[22]

(*c*) **Mothers Committees:** 36,436 mothers committees are constituted and assistance is extended to about 10 lakhs mothers and 29 lakh children from Integrated Child Development Scheme (ICDS).

(*d*) **Forest Conservation Committees (Vana Samrakshan Samithies):** 6,705 Vana Samrakshana Samithies have been formed and tree plantation and development of forests in 20 lakh hectares of land has taken place under the management of VSS, generating employment and income to the female members and arresting migration of poor tribals.

(*e*) **Watershed Committees:** 6,340 Water Shed Committees have been formed in 12 districts with a financial outlay of nearly Rs. 11,000 million leading to cultivation of 4,840 lakh hectares of land.

(*f*) **Water Users Associations (WUAs):** It has come to light that more than 14,000 water users associations have been set up with the financial support to the tune of Rs. 4,994 crore under AP Economic restructuring Project (Irrigation component) for strengthening the WUAs, enabling farmers to get water to tail-end areas and increase the production of paddy yields from 2.5 to 3.5 tonnes per acre, and increase revenue collection by 20per cent.[23]

However, the functioning of SHGs also reveals that these institutions are in no way different to that of any other government or Panchayat Raj Institutions (PRIs). The major problems faced by these groups are:

(1) The SHGs are guided and controlled by the government and they do not have autonomy in preparing the plans and implementation of the programmes. These groups also have to execute the government schemes and follow the rules and regulations prescribed by the government.

(2) The persons, who are not directly connected or have no knowledge about the activities of the SHGs are becoming the Chairman/Members of the groups. For instance, a non-agriculturist is becoming the Chairman of Vidya Committees through back door method.

(3) Undemocratic tendencies like money, muscle power, caste, liquor etc., are dominating the elections of the members/chairman of the SHG committees. Recently the government has conducted the elections to the village and mandal level Vidya Committees in which the candidates spent amounts ranging between Rs. 20,000 to Rs. 2 lakh and resorted to different undemocratic practices like threatening and threatening and kidnapping of voters, use of caste, religious affinity and violence. All these tendencies undermine the democratic process and adversely affect the functioning the SHGs. An important dimension of these institutions is that elections are fought on party basis and rich farmers and vested interest groups have occupied these institutions. Thus, these institutions have not been made fully democratic and accountable. Unlike the general elections, these group elections are disturbing the minds of children and also academic atmosphere.

(4) Another major problem in the functioning of SHGs is involvement of the institution of contractor. As per the statutes the works have to be carried out by the members of the SHGs, but in practice, they are being assigned to contractors. In certain cases contractors with the support of political leaders and NGOs, have swallowed the amount without constructing check dams or undertaking works on temporary basis (spread of clay) on the existing percolation tanks, or using low quality material, or undertaking the works where it is not useful to the members or using machinery in completion of works. The outcome of these practices is that the local people are denied employment and income defeating the very purpose of creation of SHGs.

(5) Frequent changes in the guidelines, lack of coordination between Central and State governments, and between government department and financial institutions, lack

of commitment and understanding on the concept of SHGs on the part of the authorities concerned, inordinate delay in taking decisions, non-utilization of funds etc., are weakening the initiative of people's institutions.

(6) The performance of SHGs (WUAs) in backward region has paved the way for widening gap between the canal irrigated areas and also between the better endowed farmers and poor farmers. As per the AP Farmers Management Irrigation System Act, 1997, the WUAs are expected to collect contribution (15 per cent of cost of the works) from the water users for organizing and maintenance of the works. The government gives priority in allocating works/finance to those WUAs, which complete the work in time. WUAs, representing the coastal Andhra region and medium and major irrigation projects, are availing themselves of the facilities offered by the government and are deriving benefits from the completed works.

(7) The socio-economic background of the Presidents/ Chairman and members of the SHGs reveals that majority of them belong to the upper caste, backward classes and middle and lower middle classes. The representation and participation of the poor and lowest caste people is nearly one-third of the members of the SHGs. This situation would pave the way for widening the inequalities among members of groups. The SHGs have become rehabilitation centers to the contractors, party workers and unemployed persons. These are instances where the contractors have undertaken the works without proper estimates. In some cases the political executives of the SHGs have withdrawn the amount from the bank and used it for personal purpose. They also have not prepared the plans so as to reach the benefits to the poor and the needy. The political parties are using the SHGs to accommodate the persons who are politically unemployed. Most of the Chairmen and members of SHGs committees at all levels (village, mandal, district) belong to the ruling party.

(8) The government with the co-operation of NABARD and other financial institutions, is expected to form Mahila

Banks to improve the economic conditions of women. Though several lakhs of DWCRA groups are formed more than two decades ago, many of them are not financially viable. The SHGs are becoming non-viable due to lack of forward and backward linkages. There is no required support and encouragement from the government and financial institutions. The SHGs have mostly remained as the agency for distribution of loans and are slowly withdrawing their interest on loan, and improving the skills and productivity of the members (Government of A.P. report: 2001).

(9) Presidents and members of SHGs, (VSS) are expected to protect the forest and environment. But, in practice they are doing timber business by cutting the trees and causing environmental imbalance. In certain places the land allotted for tree plantation is being used for commercial crops by the relatively rich farmers. The authorities concerned are ot taking interest in afforestation.

(10) The objective of CMEY, a SHG is to assist the unemployed youth groups (consisting of 5-10 members) and enable them to improve their socio-economic conditions and participate in the elimination of social evils and in nation building. But, there are several instances where the groups used up the amount without establishing the industry, or diverting the amount for other than the intended purpose. The authorities concerned have not taken into account the skills, interest o the groups and feasibility of the schemes etc., while granting the scheme/s. In many cases, the names of groups and grounding of the schemes is confined to paper work. The relatively better-off sections or families have influenced the officials and cornered the benefits for the poor and the unemployed.

A major outcome of this approach is that the operations of SHGs are marginalizing PRIs and appear to be conducive to the economic reforms. The funding agencies like World Bank/ DFID find it more convenient to push the economic reforms through SHGs rather than PRIs in the State. DFID in its report in Andhra Pradesh speaks encouragingly of stakeholders running SHGs and hails it as genuine decentralization.[24] The Chief Minister of the state Sri N. Chandrababu Naidu also speaks about these institutions and calls for people's direct participation in governance. The implicit assumption, in the emerging notion of governance being associated with the so-called second phase of reforms is that institutions must be shaped to facilitate the reforms. The idea of people's direct participation through SHGs shifts the responsibilities on to the people themselves while undermining their substantial rights towards sharing resources. This approach to development calls for consumer like individual (a user of resources) who is to act more like the man in the market.[25] More than the government, NGOs are actively involved in forming SHGs to operationalize the development programmes and also help the MNCs to expand their market in the State. For instance MART (Marketing and Research Team), an agency with vast experience in Mahaboobnagar district of A.P., organized meetings of women of the SHGs, the potential customers, and explained about the benefits of PRESTIGE pressure cooker brand. The Prestige company with the active innovative techniques of MART not only sold its products but also over a period of time established its base in rural areas. Further, the company established rapport with the department of women empowerment, Government of A.P. and spread its business activities in other districts of the State[26] (George, K.G.: 2003).

Multi-National Companies (MNCs) are also adopting new distribution model through their own projects and SHGs in the State. For instance, Hindustan Lever Ltd. (HLL) launched a project called "SHAKTI" in Nalgonda district in 2000 and later expanded it to other districts. The Shakti idea essentially is to avail micro-credit from government/bank for SHGs; provide income generation activity offered by HLL; and make women SHGs to operate like rural sales distributors for HLL products.

The SHGs or Women Entrepreneurs who are spread over in several districts mostly sell the products of HLL like Life-Buy, Lux, Wheel, Ponds, Pepsodent, Annapurna Salt, Clinic Plus Shampoo and Three Roses Tea Powder to the members of SHGs. Though the SHGs are earning a profit of Rs. 750 to Rs. 2000 a month, the profit of HLL is manifold.[27]

Conclusion

Following Government of India's new development strategy based on empowerment of people during 1990s by either strengthening the existing grass-root level institutions or creating new ones for sustainable development, Andhra Pradesh has also created several new institutions such as Self-Help Groups and Community Based Organizations, and introduced reforms in the existing people's institutions with a view to involving the people to participate in decision-making and implementation. But, the analysis unfolds that these measures mostly contributed to accommodate the rural elite in the structure of governance without substance of power. People's institutions have become passive participative bodies and the distribution of resources is based on the given power structure. Further, the study reveals absence of conscious political support to local leadership particularly from the poor, privatization of public organizations, inadequate financial resources, creation of multiple and conflicting organizations, involvement of contractors in the decision-making and implementation of programmes, frequent changes in the guidelines, lack of coordination between central and state government, lack of forward and backward linkages, cornering the benefits intended for the poor by upper castes etc. These have weakened the functioning of people's institutions and defeated the very purpose of their creation. In short, the Andhra Pradesh experience with the reforms in people's institutions has reduced them into "rehabilitation centers" to contractors, party workers and unemployed persons.

REFERENCES

1. World Bank, *The World Bank Development Report*, Oxford University Press, Washington, 1997.
2. Dwivedi, O.P., "The Challenge of Cultural Diversity for Good Governance", *IJPA*, Vol. XLVIII, No. 1, January-March, 2002.
3. Guhan, S., "World Bank on Governance—A Critique", *EPW*, Vol. XXXIII, No. 4, January 24, 1998.
4. World Bank, *The World Bank Development Report*, Oxford University Press, Washington, 1994 and 97.
5. See the following articles in the *Indian Journal of Public Administration*, Special Number on "Good Governance", Vol. XLIV, No. 3, July-September, 1998.

O.P. Minocha, "Good Governance: New Public Management Perspective";
Mohit Bhattacharya, "Conceptualizing Good Governance";
Subash Kashyap, "Towards Good Governance: Need for Political Reforms";
Asok Mukopadhyay, "Reinventing Government for Good Governance".
Bata K. Dey, "Defining Good Governance";
Sekar, R.C., "Ethics the other name for Governance";
Yatish Mishra, "Extra Governmental Organizations and Good Governance";
V.S. Prasad, "Governance for Development: Key Concerns", in Pradeep Sahni and Uma Medury, Eds., *Governance for Development: Issues and Strategies*, Prentice Hall of India Pvt. Ltd., New Delhi, 2003.
Hara Gopal, G., "Governance through Participative Development: The role of People's Movement", edited by Pradeep Sahni and Uma Medury in *Governance for Development, Issues and Strategies*, Prentice Hall of India Pvt. Ltd., New Delhi, 2003.
Madhav Godbole, "Administrative Reforms", *The Hindu*, July 7, 1997 and K.A. Chandrasekaran, Hindu, September 23, 1997.

6. Pradeep Sahni and Uma Medury, *op. cit.*
7. World Bank, Sustainable Development in a Dynamic World, Transforming Institution Growth and Quality of Life, *World Bank Development Report*, Oxford University Press, Washington, 2003.
8. *Ibid.*
9. World Bank *Development Report*, Oxford University Press, Washington, 1999-2000.
10. Sahni and Uma, *op. cit.*
11. Haragopal, G., "Governance through Participative Development: The Role of People's Movement", *op. cit.*
12. Ramaswamy, P.R., "The Challenge of Globalization for Civil Servants", *IJPA*, Vol. XLVIII, No.1, Jan.-March, 2002.
13. Haragopal, G., "Governance through Participative Development: The Role of People's Movement, *op. cit.*
14. The World Bank, *Sustainable Development in a Dynamic World, Transforming Institutions, Growth and Quality of Life, op. cit.*
15. Bala Ramulu Ch., "Participatory Development: The Experience of Andhra Pradesh", *IJPA*, Vol. XLVIII, No. 4, October-December, 2002.
16. *Ibid.*
17. *Ibid.*

18. Haragopal, G., "Governance through Participative Development: The Role of People's Movement, *op. cit.*
19. Krishna Reddy G., "New Populism and Liberalization: Regime Shift under Chandrababu Naidu in A.P.", *Economic and Political Weekly*, March 2, 2002.
20. Bala Ramulu Ch., "Participatory Development: The Experience of Andhra Pradesh", *op. cit.*
21. Radhakrishna Rao, "Women in Dairy Co-operatives", *Social Welfare*, Vol.50, No.2, May, 2003, New Delhi.
22. *Eenadu*: Daily News Weekly, Hyderabad, 2001-02.
23. Bala Ramulu Ch., "Participatory Development: The Experience of Andhra Pradesh", *op. cit.*
24. Department of International Development of UK, *Andhra Pradesh State Strategy Paper*, May, 2001.
25. Krishna Reddy G., "New Populism and Liberalization", *op. cit.*
26. George, K.G., "A Matter of Prestige", Case Study, Praxis, Business Line's, *Journal of Management*, Vol. 4, Issue 2, July, 2003, Chennai.
27. Vinay Kamath, "HLL's Rural Shakti on Creating a New Distribution Paradigm", Praxis (Business Line's *Journal of Management*), Vol. 4, Issue 2, Chennai, July 2003.

17

Delivering Social Services: A Case Study

Prof. Renuka Garg and Dr. Priti Garg

The Government by and large remains the major agency to design and deliver social services like education, health, sanitation, water, energy and others. Though, there have been massive investments in these areas by the government, the results are far from satisfactory. Various reasons are responsible for this state of affairs. The services in the social sector are highly subsidized. As such, the beneficiaries fail to identify with the programmes, as they have no stake. The lack of voice of he clients leads to lack of accountability on the part of the policy-makers or/and the providers, leading to low quality services. The government staff members also fail to identify with the programmes as the commitment, many a time, is missing. Lack of motivation on their part makes the implementation ineffective. Bureaucratisation leads to lack of flexibility to adapt to ground realities and monetary leakages are responsible for optimal results not being attained. The interventions require financial, institutional, human and technological sustainability, which at times is missing. The providers, many a time do not know the threshold level of service outputs required by the various stakeholders, act as all knowing and push for achieving physical targets without assessing the demand; fail to align resources (man, material, machine, information, and money) and organization to critical processes; and given less emphasis to improving processes.

Sanitation, water, health, and education are key Human Development priorities for India. However, the availability of potable water, and latrine facilities has not shown significant improvement as is evident from comparative figures of Census 1991 and 2001. In terms of drinking water availability, there has been a significant increase in the households using tap water-from 49 million in 1991 to 70 million in 2001 (an increase of 44.55) yet, the tap served only 36.7 per cent or roughly one in three households as source of drinking water in 2001 at the national level. It is worth noting that about 39 per cent households in the country in 2001 had drinking water facility of any kind available within premises, 44.3 per cent had drinking water facilities near the premises, while, for 16.7 per cent of the households it was far away from the premises. The Census figures also show that "more than 3 out of 5 households in 2001 are bereft of availability of laterine within the house". The figures show that at the national level, there was an increase in the number of households having laterine within their holes from 36 million in 1991 to 70 million in 2001, an increase of 95 per cent. However, the number of households where laterine facility is not available also increased from 115 million in 1991 to 122 million in 2001 (TOI, April 20, 2003).

Generally, the reasons often put forward for the lack of progress on improving sanitation, water supply and hygiene are shortage of water, government not having sufficient funds, people too poor to pay, lack of technology, and rapid population growth. In September 1994, Surat in the wake of the plague, had earned the dubious distinction of being one of the dirtiest cities in the country and faced nearly all the problems listed above. In spite of all odds—a growth in population from 1.49 million in 1991 to 2.45 million in 2001—a decadal growth rate of 62 per cent, on area of 112.27 sq. km., and a large floating population due to burgeoning trade and industry, within a short span Surat has earned the distinction of being the second cleanest city in the country. The transformation has led to its being a role model for various Municipal Corporations.

The paper highlights the efforts made by the Surat Municipal Corporation in meeting the needs of its stakeholders in the areas of water supply and sanitation in the city of Surat. The term Sanitation has been used in its broader sense to include human waste disposal, waste-water disposal, solid waste disposal, control of vectors of diseases, personal and food hygiene, and housing.

Framework Used to Study the Efforts Made by the Surat Municipal Corporation

In order to study the efforts of the Surat Municipal Corporation (SMC) in the area of delivering social services like water and sanitation, one could raise issues like: (*a*) provision of water and sanitation facilities and investments made, (*b*) organizing waste collection and investment made, (*c*) providing basic amenities to slums and protecting wider environment, (*d*) the partnerships of Corporation with Community, NGOs and Private sector, (*e*) regulating and reviewing outsourced work to contractors, other private companies, and NGOs, (*f*) revenue generation, and (*g*) achieving efficiency, financial self sufficiency and accountability (adapted from the Sulabh WASH Campaign, Sulabh International Social Service Organization).

Provision of Water and Sanitation Facilities

Water

The area of Surat City is 112.27 sq. km. The length of the water pipeline laid is 2400 km. There are 2,57,000 water line connections (2,54,977 for households, 273 for industrial and 1750 for commercial establishments). Presently 520 MLD water is provided per day. Per head requirement is 135 litre of water per day against which 195 litre of water per day is provided. There is capacity to cover 100 per cent population and to cater to the needs of population till 2020. 97 per cent area is covered by water pipeline. The remaining 3 per cent is not covered due to illegal constructions and lack of awareness among the people. The SMC spends Rs. 27 crore in electricity consumption and a total of Rs. 50 crore including maintenance expenses to provide water to the city. Surat is the first city to have alternative pipelines for water supply stations so that if there is any problem, that area will not remain without water.

Water works are situated at 4 places through which water is provided to 9 distribution stations with a total storage capacity (underground tanks) of 3015 lakh litres and 3 other distributions stations with overhead tanks with a storage capacity of 67.5 lakh litres. An overhead tank with a capacity of 15 lakh litres is under construction. The Hydraulic Department in the year 2002 completed various projects at the total cost of Rs. 4734.21 lakh. The various works undertaken were construction of the intake well, water purifying plant, underground tank, construction of chlorination building, for mechanical and electrical works, laying of transmission line for distribution, construction of overhead tank, and for creating distribution network. For the year 2003, the budgeted figures are largely for laying the distribution network at a cost of Rs. 606.00 lakh.

Drainage

In 2003, the population covered by sewage line is 95 per cent, whereas in 1995 it was 40 per cent. Area presently covered is 92 sq. km whereas it was 26.29 sq. km in 1995. The number of connections provided in different Zones are-Central: 66711, East: 163, West: 37204, South: 162, and South-West: 717. The capacity of Public Pay and Use toilets is—Toilets: Male-872, Female-783; Baths: Male-192, Female-174; Urinals 410. The total budgeted figure for the work-in-progress or completed works under the drainage department for the year 2002-2003 is Rs. 9747.00 lakh, and the projected figure for the year 2003-2004 for the drainage department is Rs. 6430.00 lakh. These investments cover costs for sewage networking, change of drainage lines, constructions of pumping station, and augmentation of the sewage treatment plant (SMC Diary, 2003).

Organizing Waste Collection and Investment

Solid Waste

Some of the major objectives of the SMC for Solid Waste Management are "to devise a system of waste and segregation of recyclable waste at source; to improve the system of primary collection of waste; to device more efficient system of day-to-day cleaning; and to device a system to eliminate practices of throwing garbage on the road causing nuisance and health threat".

In order to achieve these objectives the "Micro Planning" approach has been adopted for sanitation, collection, transportation and disposal of solid waste. There is decentralization of administrative and financial powers at the zone level. The city had been divided into 6 zones and 56 ward offices. Ward-level planning is done and special care taken of areas like vegetable markets, eateries, and congested areas with heavy traffic flows. Methods of garbage collection vary with regard to each of these areas/functions. If we trace the history we find that in 1973 bullock carts were used to carry solid waste for disposal. In 1980, motorized vehicles were used for the purpose. In 1983 the SMC gave the contract to a private party for solid waste disposal at the disposal site. Surat was the second city to do so in the country. SMC daily manages 900 to 1000 metric tonnes of solid waste. The SMC spends Rs. 5 crore annually for solid waste disposal. 'Door-to-Door Garbage Collection Scheme' is going to be implemented soon. This is to prevent littering by some citizens who fail to throw waste in garbage collection containers. It will be compulsory for the citizens to put garbage into particular kinds of bags. Already door-to-door collection has started in the Varaccha area. Industrial waste management is the responsibility of the industrial units.

Bio-medical waste

One tonne bio-medical waste is being treated at the bio-medical waste treatment facility at Bhatar. Earlier this was treated as solid waste. A private company is now responsible to handle the bio-medical waste on the BOOT contract basis. There are 1180 members including hospitals and doctors who have to pay Rs.10 per kilo for bio-medical disposal (Gujarat Mitra, August 22, 2003).

Liquid waste

For the liquid management, there is an approximately 100 km. long drainage line. There are 31 drainage-pumping stations that collect (suck) the liquid waste and take it to 6 sewage treatment plants. After primary and secondary treatment, the treated water is then disposed. The existing total capacity of the 6 treatment plants is 562 MLD. As against this, presently the liquid waste is 450 MLD.

Providing Basic Amenities to Slums and Protecting Wider Environment

There are 306 slum pockets in the city. The number of slum households is 1,16,663 and the slum population is 4,90,305. SMC has a Slum Up gradation Cell which functions towards Slum Upgradation, whereby the existing slums are provided various amenities and their environment is sought to be upgraded to a hygienic level; and Slum Rehabilitation whereby they can avail of readily available built houses. Efforts are being made for 100per cent population coverage for water and sanitation. Wherever provision of individual facilities is not possible, public toilets, urinals and baths are provided. This could be at the instance of the SMC employees or the councilor of the area or the community.

The Health and Sanitation Department is engaged in preventive, curative and promotional activities. Various measures being undertaken to minimize the incidence of malaria, and filarial are: (*a*) Anti-larval measures include para domestic work, intra domestic work and biological measures, (*b*) anti-parasitological work which includes parasitological measures, night survey and filarial day, (*c*) Anti-adult measures which include insect collection, indoor residual spraying, fogging and training programme, (*d*) Health education, and (*e*) Legislative measures. To control the incidence and spread of diseses, health related statistics are collected on a daily basis from various hospitals and major clinics for monitoring and comparison purposes. The Food Inspection branch undertakes food inspection and takes punitive action against the errant establishments. According to an estimate, there has been a reduction of 67 per cent in the incidence of diseases after 1995 (outbreak of plague in 1994).

The results of the various efforts are indicated through the statistics showing the incidence of and death due to some diseases.

Name of Disease	*Incidence (in no.) Years*		*No. of Deaths Years*	
	1995	2001	1995	2001
AR	392	37	14	00
Viral Hepatitis	504	600	13	00
Enteric Fever	276	135	00	00
Gastroenteritis	1678	2043	10	01

* Population in Surat City (1991): 1.49 million
(2001): 2.45 million

* Infant Mortality Rate: 19.21

* Maternal Mortality Rate: 0.61

Source: www.suratmunicipal.org

Partnership-Working with the Community, NGOs and Private Sector

The SMC seeks the support of the citizens of the City in maintaining a responsive, and transparent administration through its Grievance Redressal System. A major mechanism for self-correction is feedback. The SMC has a Grievance Handling System for which it has bagged the award for the best managed Municipal Corporation in Gujarat by the City Manager Association. The SMC facilitates the citizens to air out their complaints through all possible modes-writing, paging, dialing or e-mailing the complaint. The SMC's complaint redressal system is as under:

The complaints received are categorized into white card or red card. White card category complaints are answered within 24-48 hours and deal with "14 categories of sanitation and public health related complaints". 13 PHE related complaints are given red cards and are answered within 3-7 days. 96 per cent of the complaints are attended to within the specified time.

The SMC has adopted a three-pronged strategy to resolve the problem of cleanliness. Positive involvement of the public, penalizing the culprits and creating public awareness are the planks on which the cleanliness drive is maintained. In order to maintain cleanliness the SMC spends Rs.1.25 crore for scrapping and brushing the city clean. Approximately, 810 workers work from 10.30 p.m. to 4.00 a.m. to sweep the city clean. On the main roads machines are also used for cleaning. In order to get the contributions of the citizens in keeping the city clean, educational campaigns have been launched to persuade the housewives to pack the garbage and dispose it off in the designated bins. "Jan Jagriti Abhiyan" is also undertaken. All shops are required to have dustbins; and restaurants and hotels have to maintain separate bins to dispose off waste at designated disposal sites. There is litter patrol and punitive action is taken against that litter, through on the spot administrative charges. Regular checking is done of the hotels, restaurants, lari and galas; and of their food items for hygiene and sanitation purposes.

Consultants like AIC Watson, Tata Consulting Engineers, Multimedia, CRII, School of Planning and Architecture-New Delhi, S.V.N.I.T-Surat, Price Waterhouse-Coopers have been hired to provided expertise.

For its Slum Rehabilitation and Slum Upgradation Projects

funds have been provided by HUDCO on loan basis. Certain projects have also been funded by multilateral funding agencies likes the World Bank.

Regulating and Reviewing Outsourced Work to Contractors, other Private Companies and NGOs

Much of the work is outsourced by the SMC. Works like garbage collection, cleaning of roads, transportation of municipal refuse; construction of public toilets have been outsourced. The cartel of contractors has been broken. Monitoring of projects is done on a weekly basis. To ensure execution of the projects as per the contractual arrangements 'third party quality inspections are undertaken. A six-month time limit is set for all projects. The exceptions are thoroughly reviewed. In case of non-performance, fine is imposed. Contractors are blacklisted. Review of contractual terms is undertaken. Initially NGOs were involved in constructing and maintaining public toilets for a 30 years period. The SMC had to provide land and bear the water and electricity charges. Now contracts are given to contractors and only land is provided by the SMC.

Revenue Generation

The SMC has the highest revenue collections in Gujarat. The per capita collection has increased by 72 per cent since 1994-95. Presently it is to the tune of Rs.1579 per capita. Attempts are being made to shift the overdependence on Octroi as the revenue earner to Property tax and User charges (www.suratmunicipal.org). Rebate is provided to citizens if they pay their tax bills in the month of April. The Commissioner Shri G.R. Aloria is planning to provide incentives to people who bring to the notice of the corporation incidence of tax evasion. Necessary action is to be taken against employees who fail to achieve the required target.

Water is supplied on metered basis to the commercial, industrial and educational institutions according to the nature of business and location site—whether situated within or outside the city limits. Charges vary from Rs. 8 to Rs. 25 per 1000 litre within the city. Supplying water on metered basis to households is also being mooted. Each household presently has to pay a tariff of

Rs. 240 annually. There is a proposal to hike the Water Supply tariff and user charges.

Safai charges are lived on the basis of the type of property, which is categorized as A, B and C. The charges are 6 per cent, 12 per cent and 24 per cent respectively, subject to a minimum of Rs. 72 for Category A, and Rs. 96 for Category B and C annually. For gutter connection the charges vary according to the type of residence-high-rise buildings, tenements, bunglows from Rs. 500 to Rs. 1000. Charges for processing houses, hotels, lodging, boarding, factory/industrial/commercial establishment for connection vary from Rs. 1000 to Rs. 10,000+Rs. 3 per sq. feet (SMC Diary, 2003).

Achieving Efficiency, Financial Self-Sufficiency and Accountability

The measures adopted for efficient delivery of services, financial self-sufficiency and accountability are many. They include: Profit centred approach; micro-planning for alignment of resources-men, materials, machine and money and organization with critical processes; incentives to employees who perform and disincentives to non-performers; IT enabled processes-GIS, Project Management, CAD Software, Civic Centres for online information gathering, filing complaints, payment of taxes, getting various forms/certificates etc. and bringing services to the doorsteps of the citizens; Supervisory Control and Data Acquisition system (SCADA) for drainage and water supply network, and information about the amount of water distributed or whether the distribution is in progress for a particular water supply station can be found out from any place at the keys of the laptop; Cost Benefit Analysis; switch-over from traditional Receipt and Payment Accounting System to Double Entry Commercial Accounting System.

A 5-point reform package has been prepared which includes installing leak detectors to prevent water leakages at the consumers' end as also in the distribution system; controlling the use of water during peak hours; installing a flow meter for water procured from river Tapi; and energy audit to bring in efficiency in operations. In the words of the Commissioner "there's a limit to raising taxes, so we are imposing restrictions within the house so that money of the tax-payers can be put to better use". Energy audit is undertaken to evaluate the efficiency of various electrical equipment at the drainage, sewerage, and community service departments. Energy Bill Monitoring System has been set up to keep a tab on whether the SMC is paying the right tariff for power consumption (TOI, November 24, 2003).

Some Major Future Plans and Tasks Ahead

The Standing Committee has approved a project of Rs. 113.50 crore for conservation plan for river Tapi. This project will attract 50 per cent grant from the Central Government (Gujarat Mitra, October 10, 2003). Steps are being taken to apply for ISO 9000 Certification for water quality. Plans are being made to provide water for 24 hours (Gujarat Mitra August 1, 2003).

"Waste to Power" project has been approved by the Standing Committee to produce 24 Megawatt of electricity from 850 metric tonnes of solid waste using Incineration S.F.B.C. technology at a cost of Rs. 160 crore, in partnership with a private firm. Land, solid waste are to be provided by SMC (Gujarat Samachar, October 5, 2003).

It has been observed that in certain areas of the city the ground water level has decreased substantially. One of the major reasons has been the indiscreet extraction of water by private water suppliers using submerged pumps that can extract 60,000 to 70,000 litres of water per hour. This water is supplied to the industrial belt, where the SMC provides metered water connections. The SMC needs to be more vigilant to stop these practices (Gujarat Mitra, November 21, 2003). Remedial measures like recharging need to be taken up and the public must be made aware of the consequences to be faced in future if conservation, and preservation measures are not adopted. Provision of public toilets, urinals, and bath is not sufficient. They have to be maintained, kept clean and in hygienic condition. People at times fail to use toilet facilities due to their poor condition. More efforts need to be made to create awareness in the public for the proper use of toilets and to inculcate good hygiene practices. The Corporation requires help from various other quarters like the media, non-governmental organizations and educational institutions in these efforts.

Lessons to be Learnt

From the experiences of SMC certain determinants for success can be identified. These are: a shared vision and clarity of goals; continuous improvement in systems to bring about efficiency, financial self-sufficiency, and accountability; administrative and financial decentralization; harnessing traditional knowledge as well as state of the art technology; major strides towards e-governance; dedicated and committed team including professionals and a dynamic leadership; a learning attitude using the tool of bench marking; change of working style from air conditioned rooms to daily chores ("AC to DC"); sensitivity when dealing with civic problems with the delivery mechanism being adaptive to the specific needs of the citizens by adopting flexible work methods; gaining credibility through demonstration-a sea change in the city from 1994 to 2003; sustainability-financial, institutional, technical, and operational; cooperation of and partnership with various agencies; model being replicable—various other municipal corporations have come to study the efforts; and ongoing research to make continuous efforts towards "Bahujan Hitaya, Bahujan Sukhaya"—its motto.

To Sum Up, the efforts of the SMC in the area of providing good sanitation, drinking water, and drainage system has led to the reduction in the incidence of diseases and infant mortality rates, indicators of good hygiene practices. This could be achieved among others, through the creation of infrastructure facilities, demonstration effect, penal action, "top down" approach for regulation and "bottom up" approach for development, social auditing, innovative management practices, political will of the elected representatives, vigilant public and committed team led by dynamic leadership. The result is efficient, responsive, and transparent administration and clean, green and quenched Surat.

REFERENCES

1. Chanda Rupa, 'General Agreement on Trade in Services: Implications for Social Policy-Making', *Economic and Political Weekly*, April 19-25, 2003, pp. 1567-78.
2. Rao S.R. *Change Management In Indian Context-Lessons From Surat*, (www.worldbank.org/wbi/urban/paperhyderabad.htm)
3. *Surat Municipal Corporation Diary*, 2003.
4. www.suratmunicipal.org

18

Public Grievance Redressal System in India

Dr. Inderjeet Kaur

In a democratic country public administration works for serving the public interest by providing various services. The standardized supply of public services needs to be provided on time, in proportion to the needs of people, in an honest manner and without any kind of harassment to the people. Successful delivery of services to the public can also be measured in terms of the rate of satisfaction of people/consumers. Dissatisfaction of the people due to non-delivery of service, delay, or bribery or harassment, may lead to grievances and complaints.[1] The lower the rate of satisfaction of the public the higher will be the rate of public grievance (PG) and vice-versa.

Barnabas in his pioneering work entitled **Citizens' Grievances and Administration** has adopted a broader meaning of the world grievance. In his opinion, it refers not only to any real or imaginary feeling of personal injustice the citizens may have, concerning their relationship with administration, but also their feelings, again real or imaginary, of injustice in regard to the delay in the provision of services which they expect.[2] 'The grievance procedure', according to Barnabas means, 'a formal remedial system through which dissatisfied citizens can take their discontent or complaint for redressal to successively the highest levels of administration'. In fact public grievance stands for the gap between services being provided by the administration and the public needs both real and expected. In other words PG expresses the dissatisfactory relationship existing between the citizen and administration. The failure of the administration gives rise to the grievances.

Relationship between administration and citizens has undergone tremendous change. The state has become more complex while democratic expectations have heightened. The intervening period has witnessed large institutional changes which include the attempt to make the government more accountable to the citizens. Human rights have become almost universally accepted along with new court structures, commissions and investigative mechanisms, Freedom of Information legislation has come into its own.[3] The citizens have become more aware about their entitlements. All these together vindicate the urgent need of redressing PGs. An unconcerned government about public grievance may put itself into trouble by inviting the public outbursts in the form of strikes, demonstrations, etc.

Public grievance is an universal phenomenon irrespective of the level of the development of the particular administration or of a country (fully developed or undeveloped) because no administration is complete to match the expectations of the people. In fact, this is a well established fact that if needs of one level are satisfied the needs of other levels grow (hierarchy of needs). Likewise a new set of expectations comes into being on the fulfillment of the existing ones. Hence it is difficult to think of a situation where there will be an end to PG. The major difference about PGs of developed and underdeveloped countries lies in the mechanism of redressal of PGs. There exists a systematic and powerful public grievance redressal system (PGRS) in the former which not only makes it more accessible for the citizens for any kind of grievance but also ensures its sure and short redressal. A good PGRS entails:

- People, irrespective of their caste, colour and creed enjoy equal access to approach the administrators even at the highest level;
- Clear indication of the persons in charge for specific grievances;
- Specified time limit for redress of a grievance; and
- Preventive measures besides remedial measures.

Some prerequisites essential for an effective PGRS are:

1. a well established grievance redressal structure;
2. the level of awareness of the people;

3. the concern of the officers for PGR, *i.e.* only a people-oriented attitude of the employees can ensure the redress of PG;
4. only genuine PG, supported by evidence or PGRS authentication can create real pressure on the authorities;
5. easy accessibility through modern means of communication; and
6. clear cut and simple procedure.

This paper based on secondary data on the PGRS in India focuses on its evolution, structure, procedure, and environment (particularly in the context of Good Governance and IT developments).

Reasons for PGs

The following factors may cause PGs:

- Wrong policy/policies overlooking the general interest of the public itself can be the main reason for PG.
- Non or inadequate supply and supply of poor quality of desired services by administration, *e.g.* contaminated water, short supply of electricity, release of pension, etc.
- Delay or non response from administration to applications for license for industry, water connection, etc.
- Infringement of citizen's right because of wrong administrative actions.
- Unethical practices adopted by officials to serve their own interest with adverse effects on people.
- Misappropriation of money or goods by officials allocated for the people, *e.g.* ration for the people, seeds for the farmers, stipend for the students, etc.
- Non information or misinformation about Government's decisions.
- Discourteous and insolent behaviour towards citizens visiting public offices.
- Apathetic attitude towards the clients, *e.g.* People keep standing in the queue at time in the scorching sunlight and officers either keep gossiping or sipping tea or smoking.

- Over charging for the services and inflated bills, etc.[4]

Public Grievance Redressal System in India

Since, complaints usually pertain to the managerial, procedural and human aspect of the administration, a multi-pronged strategy is required to manage or redress the PGs. Keeping this fact in view the Government of India constituted in 1964 the Department of Administrative Reforms and Public Grievances (DOAR&PG) as the nodal agency 'for administrative reforms and redressal of public grievances relating to the States in general and grievances pertaining to Central Government agencies in particular[5] which became an integral part of the Ministry of Personnel, Public Grievances and Pensions in 1985. Its various dimensions are:

1. Improvement of Government structure and processes
2. Citizen-friendly initiatives including redress of the public grievances
3. Documentation, and dissemination of the best practices
4. Codification and simplification of procedures
5. Networking with various agencies.[6]

The 20-point Programme of the Rao's Government with a view to make the administration responsible and accountable emphasized the following reforms:[7]

1. simplification of rules and procedures
2. delegation of authority
3. enforcement of responsibilities
4. evolving monitoring system at various levels of the administration and
5. redressal of grievances.

To implement this programme those governmental, semi-governmental and public sector enterprises were identified in respect of which expedient action can be taken by the concerned ministries and departments.[8]

A Conference of Chief secretaries of States and Union Territories was convened on November 20, 1996 to discuss the issues of making administration responsive, accountable, effective, and ensuring its adherence to constitutional principles. After eliciting views from a wide cross-section of people the Conference of Chief Ministers on May 24, 1997 recommended a concrete Action Plan (AP) which emphasized.

1. Accountable and citizen-friendly Government
2. Transparency and Right to Information
3. Improving the performance and integrity of the Public Services.

An Implementation Committee comprising chief secretaries of various states and secretaries of the major ministries and Directorate General, National Informatics was constituted to effect the reforms.

In April 1998 Point-24 of the National Agenda adopted by the Coalition Government of Atal Bihari Vajpai provided for the appointment of the Lokpal to make the administration accountable and for the Right to Information to citizens to bring transparency in the government. This shows the serious concern of the government about the PGs. The introduction of the Lokpal Bill, 1998 in the Lok Sabha on August 3, 1998 lapsed like previous bills. Till this date it could not be passed.[9] One of the most commendable developments in the post Independence India had been the emergence of a strong media, a fleet of NGOs etc. which are playing crucial role in both highlighting and solving the citizens' grievances.

The Public Grievances Redressal System in India is very complex and democratic. It provides space for government agencies, media and non-governmental bodies. While (1) Government machinery for the redressal of public grievances, (2) administrative procedure reforms, (3) attitudinal change, (4) Legislaltive, (5) commissions, and (6) courts are sub-systems of the PGRS, media, and NGOs, constitute the non-official parts of the system redressal mechanism.

1. Machinery for the Redressal of Public Grievances

Prime Minister's Office

At the apex of the redressal mechanism stands the Office of the Prime Minister. The Prime Minister's Office performs monitoring role in redressal of PG received by it. The PM himself attends to the PGs. The 'Khula Darbar' (Open Session) at PM's residence in the morning has become a regular feature in which he hears complaints pertaining to all levels. Nowadays, Ministers/Dy. Ministers and their officers hear the complaints on particular day during the hours fixed for the purpose in the centre.

Public Grievance Redressal Unit/Officer

At the internal level there is a PGR unit/officer of the rank of Joint Secretary in each Ministry/Department of the Central Government. Each office observes Wednesday as Grievance Redressal Day when people can visit the Grievance Officer between 10 a.m.-1 p.m.

Department of Administrative Reforms and Public Grievances (DOAR&PG) is the nodal agency which monitors the other ministries and departments. Its functions are manifold:

- To assist in the formulation of the policy making function;
- To assure speedier and prompt action at the secretarial level;
- To issue directives or provide guidance for the execution of policy;
- To coordinate all efforts pertaining to action;
- To conduct study pertaining management and to identify where the number of PGs are found more and works for remedial action in such cases; and
- To conduct research studies to find out new ways and means for improving quality of Public administration. It brings out two publications (*i*) Management in Government and (*ii*) Civil service News.

PGR Directorate

PGR Directorate is another such external agency which takes action for longstanding complaints pertaining to railway, postal, telephone, financial institution, air ways, transport, urban development etc.

Core Group

A Core Group under the chairmanship of Secretary (Personnel) has been formed for monitoring the formulation of Citizen' Charter by identified Ministries/Departments. In this connection the DARPG has been coordinating the entire exercise with the involvement of consumer groups.

Information and Facilitation Counters (IFCs)

Information and Facilitation Counters (IFCs) are set up to provide information about schemes and procedures of the concerned organs, and assistance to the public. Information is disseminated through printouts, brochures, booklets, display boards and sometimes through telephone too. The DARPG has also coordinated the setting up of 75 IFCs including 24 **May I Help You** counters in various Ministries/Depts (2002:78) These counters also undertake the task of acknowledgement and status report of individual application and grievances.[10]

Efficiency Unit

An Efficiency Unit has been constituted as a part of the Cabinet Secretariat in order to undertake an overall assessment of the functions of various ministries/depts. and agencies of the Central Government in the light of the recommendations of Fifth Central Pay Commission and to examine various measures for procedural and legal change for greater accountability and speedier decision making. The unit is located in the DOAR&PG under the charge of an Additional Secretary (Administrative Reforms & Training). No extra staff has been provided for the unit. It is expected to drawn upon consultants and resource persons for detailed studies.

Hence, the existing administrative machinery for redressal of public grievances has been considerably strengthened.

At State Level

Similar arrangements exist at the **State level** as well. In each department there exists a complaint cell/officer as internal arrangement and separate grievance department as external arrangement. In some states a Public Grievance Commission has also been constituted. The rank of the complaint officer differs from state to state. While he is off the rank of Assistant Secretary in Andhra Pradesh, it is Deputy Secretary in Gujarat, Kerala, West Bengal, and Tamil Nadu and Gazetted Officer in Karnataka, and Under Secretary in Punjab. In some states there exists PGR Directorate as well. In some other states there exists a Central Reception Officer in the Secretariat and each department has Public Relations Officer and Cell for assistance to the public.

At the **district level** in various states a senior magistrate or officer of his level is appointed for hearing public grievances. In some states public cells have been created and in others we come across complaint committees. In Madhya Pradesh there are two kinds of committees-one comprising non-official members *i.e.* only MLAs in which ministers are not entitled for its membership and the other of official members. Some members from outside the government are also appointed. The committee works under the chairmanship of the Collector.

In Punjab the Public Relations and Grievance Committee comprises departmental heads, MPs, MLAs, Chief of the district Congress and secretaries, Chief of leading NGOs and representatives of businessmen and farmers.

2. Administrative Procedural Reforms

In India the root cause for most PGs lies in cumbersome administrative procedures, hierarchical structure of the organization, obsolete approach to work, rigidity of rules and regulations, etc. Hence it is essential that reforms should be undertaken to improve the system. The Department of Administrative Reforms and Public Grievances is a central agency to take up the administrative and structural reforms.

Administrative reform process has been continuous in India since the adoption of the Constitution. Nevertheless, the years 1991-1996 can be called the watershed years in the reforms process. During this period the policy of liberalization and globalization adopted by the Narasimha Rao's Government heralded an era of new reforms which emphasized the following elements of good governance.

- Decentralization of administrative authority
- Simplification of rules and regulations
- Elimination of undesirable controls
- Strengthening of monitoring system at various levels of administration
- Making government transparent and open and
- Modernization of administrative offices.

Modernizing Process

The casual and obsolete work procedures of the offices have been identified during various drives for reform of the administration. In 1987-88 a modernization plan was adopted for the offices in India to improve the functional environment through modern office aids, reduction in paper work, minimizing levels of considering in the disposal work, fixation of time limits as well as records management.[11] Under this plan one section or unit of a Department is selected for modernization and other parts and sections are accordingly modified. The DOAR&PG laid emphasis on the use of modern machines and equipments so that performance could be improved and the quality of the service be enhanced. In this context, adoption of Information Technology (IT) an important component of the National Agenda aims at the transformation of India into a Software Super Power under the National Informatics Policy. For this purpose the Government of India constituted a National Workforce (NWF) in May 1998 to formulate the National Policy for IT. It submitted the Information Technology Action Plan consisting of 108 points. Its principal aim is to make available information technology at all levels of Education and building India into technologically the best nation. The development in this field will definitely empower the people by making available any desired information. This will serve twin objectives: one, it will empower the people and two, by making governance more transparent it will check the arbitrary functioning of administration.

E-Governance

In this context another notable step taken by the government is introduction of the concept of e-Governance. The Minimum

Agenda for e-Governance has been drawn up by the IT Managers designated in various Ministries/Departments on the line of Grievance Officers and Vigilance Officers. **This Minimum Agenda includes making available PCs, setting up of LAN, training and capacity building in IT, redress of grievances using It, setting up of websites, making available forms on the websites, enabling the submission of forms online, electronic publication of information in public domain including Acts and rules.** This programme is being thoroughly monitored and enhanced through various Conferences. So far 73 Central Ministries/ Departments have appointed IT Managers. About 66per cent of the reporting Ministries/Departments have been provided PCs and have initiated action. Likewise about 1/3 of the Ministries/Departments have made significant achievements in making available forms on website, submission of forms on-line and on line delivery of services.[12]

Right to Information

The Bill for Freedom of Information drafted in accordance with the Report of working Group under the chairmanship of Shri H.D. Shourie has became law in Dec. 2002. The Act ensures both freedom of information and transparency in governance.

Review of Laws

Further, in this direction a Commission was constituted in consonance with PM's desire in May, 1998 to review the existing laws to make recommendations for repeal/amendments of laws, regulations, procedures, legislative processes with a view to improve service delivery and transparency in the functioning of government. The Commission so far has reviewed 2500 laws. It has suggested the repeal of 1382 laws of different categories on the ground that these have become either irrelevant or dysfunctional.[13] It is expected that due to this review of laws the number of the PGs is going to be effected downward.[14]

Committee on Procedural Reforms

Four Committees were constituted on July 30, 2000 to conduct studies and suggest measures for procedural reforms. These are:

1. Committee on Appointments at Senior Positions
2. Committee on Vigilance procedure
3. Committee on Service Litigations
4. Committee on Reforms in Recruitment Rules.

All the committees have submitted their reports and further action is in progress.[15]

Citizen's Charters (CCs)

DOAR&PG constituted a Core Group under the chairmanship of the Secretary (personnel) for making the administration people-oriented in 1998. This group is monitoring the work of Citizens Charters being adopted by various ministries and departments. These Charters publicize the commitment of the organization, the expected standards of service delivery, timeframe, and grievance redress mechanism. The department also coordinates the efforts of formulating and operational zing Citizens Charters in various States and UTs. So far 69 Charters of Central Ministries/Depts./ Organizations and 367 Charters by various States/UTs have been adopted.[16]

Interactive WEB-enabled PGR and Monitoring System

The system has been developed in collaboration with National Informatics Centre (NIC). The system was installed and commissioned in the DOAR & PG on September 1,2001. It has also been installed in 19 other Central Government Ministries and Departments including the Directorate of Public Grievance, Cabinet Secretariat, so far.[17]

Wide Publicity

The Departments give wide publicity annually to the names, addresses, telephone, FAX, E-mail addresses of the Grievance Officers and hours set apart to hear and received PGs. Ministries/ Depts. Have been asked to give wide publicity to their PGR Machinery, CCs, and Information Facilitation Counters. A compilation of the Guidelines for PGR has been issued by the Dept. and is made available on demand.[18]

3. Change of Official Attitude

It has been invariably observed that the genesis of various PGs lies in the human factor. Some of its manifestations are officials taking bribe, rude/misbehaviour towards citizens who are now considered as clients or customers, lack of cooperation with colleagues, abuse of their power and neglect of their duties. Its solution lies in changing the attitude of officials so as to have courtesy and concern for the people and commitment to public service. This can be effected by adopting a rigorous training programme and creating role models. In this regard, the DOAR&PG has conducted short duration training on gender sensitization, interactive skills, team and capacity building, and integrity in the employees. In this context the Dept. proposes to set up a **National Institute of Smart Government** As popularized by Chandra Babu Naidu SMART is an acronym which stands for **Simple, Moral, Accountable, Responsive, and Transparent Government.** "The Institute will be autonomous and will function as think tank for exploring new and effective solutions for fulfilling societal commitment and assist the government depts. In providing innovative and quality delivery of service to citizens."[19] The Department has also brought out a monograph titled 'Quality Management in Government: Theory and Practice'.

The Department has also been organizing a lecture series on **"Ideas that have worked"** since March 2000. The speakers were selected from both public and private sectors who have made real difference in their fields and achieved excellence (a few of these distinguished personalities who were invited: Dr. A.P.J. Abdul Kalam, Shri E. Shredharan, Shri M.D. Ambani, hri R.N. Tata, etc.[20]

The Department has introduced **an Incentive Scheme for Model Behaviour** in the Department on a pilot basis w.e.f. June 1. 2001. The parameters on which the rating will be based include Observance of 3Cs-clearing, cleanliness and categorization; KAIZEN-innovative efforts made to improve the work in qualitative and quantitative terms; and Adherence of Discipline-punctuality, availability and maintenance of office decorum.

Improvement of Office Environment

The 5th Pay Commission after observing various offices found that these were marred by lack of proper light, drinking water, proper toilets, etc. hence, in its report it has strongly suggested to improve the environment of offices. Underlying feeling in this suggestion was that there is impending need to remove the grievance of those officers who are taking care of the public grievances. The satisfied and contented official can render satisfactorily.[21]

4. People's Representatives and PGs

Parliament and State legislatures are the constitutional mechanisons to air, discuss, debate and solve public grievances. Various devices are available to legislators to draw the attention of the Government to public problems and grievances. These include: the debate on the President's/Governor's Address, Budget discussion, adjournment motions, censor motions, call attention motions, half an hour discussion and the Question Hour. The Opposition not only criticizes Government policies but also exposes the failures of various departments.

A common man having more confidence in the representatives generally takes their problems—both general and particular such as choking of gutters or drains, dark lanes or getting electricity connection for one's house (particularistic). In such cases the representatives are instrumental in redressing the grievances of their constituents by approaching the right official(s) and urging them to solve the problem. A heavy weight representative can possibly ensure speedier action from the administrators. Usually people are found to flock to the houses of Councilors/MLs/MPs in the morning visiting hours. The more serious minded representatives, gather people's grievances by regular visits to their constituency and take pain to attend the same. Pre-election assessment of representatives carried out by media-TV and newspapers in various states revealed that redressal role of the representative is a determinant factor for the reelection of the person. Mostly Election Manifestos of various political parties reflect macro level PGs. The political parties make high promises to address the same to woo the voters by highlighting the prospective remedial measures.

5. Law Courts, Lok Adalats, Open Adalat and Open Session (Khulla Darbar)

It has been a general practice to move the courts to get relief against the adverse effects of administrative action or inaction. However, this is a known fact that legal procedure of the ordinary law courts has become so time-consuming arduous, dilatory and costly that the common citizens in most of the cases do not get justice, hence the practice of **Lok Adalat** (People's Court) is in vogue as an alternative in various states. Its informal way helps in resolving the matter speedily. Their successful functioning has led to the establishment of Lok Adalat on permanent basis in New Delhi, Patiala Court since November 1999. Besides these adalats, various Depts. having more public dealings have been organizing **Open Sessions** for redressing (such as Departments of Communications, Railways, Electricity, Food and Supply) long pending and other intricate grievances in which the highest officers take part personally and resolve the same at times applying the established rules and regulations flexibly. This has become a popular way tc redress the maximum problems in minimum time-frame.

Lokayukta

The office of the Ombudsman has long emerged as the most effective redressal mechanism in many countries. Ever since the Central Administrative Reforms Commission recommended the Indian version of the Ombudsman-the office of Lokpal and Lokayuktas in the 1960s,Central government could not go beyond the stage of introduction of the bill for instituting the office of the Lokpal. Office of the Lokayukta exists in a good number of states.[22]

The Lokayukta and Uplokayukta Acts provide a forum for attending to complaints against public functionaries of corruption, favoritism, abuse of position and power. The Acts, invariably, take within their ambit the Ministers including the Chief Minister, Members of Legislative Assembly Secretaries, Members of Municipal Corporation etc.

Administrative Tribunals

The Central Administrative Tribunal constituted on Nov. 1985 under Administrative Tribunals (AT) Acts, 1985 in consonance with Article 323-A of the Constitution of India. has 17 regular Benches. Likewise, Ats are operating at he State level also. The Tribunals are entitled for adjudication of disputes and complaints with respect to recruitment and conditions of service of persons appointed to the public services and posts in connection with the affairs of the Union and the State. The distinguishing feature of these tribunals is that procedure of rendering justice is simple and free from shackles of technicalities. The aggrieved person can also appear before it personally. Only a nominal fee of Rs. 50 is charged for filing the application. Thus the objective of the tribunal is to provide inexpensive justice to the litigants.

6. Commissions

Various commissions such as National Human Rights Commission, Commissionsfor Scheduled Castes and Scheduled Tribes, Commission for Minorities, National Commission for Women etc. exist for the protection of interest of general masses and marginalized classes such as SC, ST, OBCs and Women. They are also performing the grievance redressal role as intervener, facilitator, and policy advisor.

The Regulatory Commissions are new agencies which are taking care of the market forces which have emerged as service providers in the area of power, telecommunication, etc.

Consumer Disputes Redressal Commission

Since the advent of the era of globalization and liberalization the notion of citizen as receiver of administrative services has undergone a qualitative change. Now he is being considered as customer/client whose satisfaction is one strong parameter for evaluating the administrative performance. For the consumer the forum available to him is Consumer Disputes Redressal Commission. There is District Forum for each District, State Commissions for the state and National Consumer Disputes Redressal Commission at the Centre as envisaged in **The Consumer Protection Act, 1986**. The commission is an independent body responsible for speedy redressal of complaints relating to acts of omission or of commission. It can also take up suo-motu action, where required.

The Act has been enacted with a view to provide speedy and in-expensive remedy to consumers and is aimed to protect the consumers from exploitation by traders and service providers.

A complaint can be filed in writing if:

(*a*) Consumer has suffered loss or damage as a result of any unfair Trade Practice.
(*b*) The goods purchased suffer from any defect.
(*c*) The trader has charged a price in excess of the price displayed or fixed by any law for the time being in force.
(*d*) The goods hazardous to life and safety are being offered for sale to public.
(*e*) The services hired or availed of, suffer from any deficiency.

The Act further provides that complaints can be filed by:

(*a*) A Consumer.
(*b*) Any registered Voluntary Consumer Organization.
(*c*) The Central or State Government.
(*d*) One or more consumers on behalf of numerous consumers who are having the same interest.

The consumer has been defined as:

"Any person who buys any goods, hires any service for a consideration which has been paid or promised or partly paid and partly promised or under any system of deferred payment, comes within the definition of consumer. A person will not be within the definition of consumer if he purchases goods for commercial purpose or for resale. However if he purchases goods for the purpose of earning his livelihood by means of self employment, he will be a consumer."

It has been observed that the citizens have been using these forums quite often not only for complaints against private agencies for claiming damages for the aforesaid reasons but also against the Government Departments and Agencies. Nevertheless, the number of cases filed against the latter has been found to be comparatively low.

Procedure for Redress of PGs

The following steps are involved in the process of redressing the grievance:

The acknowledgement of the petition/complaint letter. It involves registering the complaint with date. The strict directives have been issued to all offices both at centre and state levels. The complaints are not registered in the following cases:

1. If the complaint is concerned with a subject which is sub-judice. Complaint pertaining to subjects about which the complaint can be made in the courts
2. If the Complaint is related to a subject about which the government has already decided and no new developments have taken place thereafter.
3. When complaints are sent without name or wrong names. Such complaints are entertained only when charges made there but can be properly authenticated.

- The time limit for redressing the complaint has been fixed in various Departments.
- About the PGs an inquiry is made from the representatives and they are handled through the specified procedures and directive.
- The officers who go for inspection visits are directed to attend various grievances which they come across during visits.
- Complaints pertaining to corruption are handled at different levels by different agencies. Anti-corruption Committee, Anti-corruption officer, Crime branches of C.I.D., Vigilance Commission/Dept. are entitled to take special action about these complaints.
- In different states a handbook is issued for the people informing the GR procedure.
- If the application carries a substantial evidence to testify its authenticity the decision is immediately taken by the concerned officer about the same or in a case lacking substantial evidence the proper inquires are conducted. In case of implication of a particular officer in a complaint then the inquiries are

made by other officers. After ascertaining all the facts the case is resolved.

Non-Governmental Organizations and PGs

The NGOs are also playing crucial role in redressing various PGs. They perform this role either at the behest of the administration or on behalf of citizens. In the case of the former their role can be more preventive in nature while in the latter capacity, they work as forum through which the citizen's grievances are presented before the appropriate authorities either in the form of petitions for public interest litigation (PIL), or memos/articles in newspapers. In their former role they perform three functions: (*i*) dissemination of information to the public; (*ii*) work as watchdogs on administrative agencies providing various services so that no injustice is done to any individual; and (*iii*) work for securing the best service from the administration *e.g.* by representing in administrative committees, legislative committees, local/area committees of fair prie shops, electricity distribution circle/regional committees, etc. In their latter capacity they make representation on behalf of aggrieved party/parties in the legislative and administrative committees, highlight PGs through the media, organize public meetings and demonstrations, etc. The notable NGOs working for citizens' cause are Common Cause (CC), Citizens Civil Society of India (CCSOI), Campaign for Electoral Transparency, Parivartan ational Campaign for People's Rights etc. If the CC forum is recognized for taking PGs to the court in the form of PIL, CCSOI, like others is working to create more and more awareness among the citizens about their rights/entitlements and the procedure for redressal of their grievances. A recently published **Handbook for Empowering Citizens** is available on its web-site.[23] This is the latest step taken by this organization.[24]

Media and PGs

In a democratic polity like India, media has an important role in public life. Media serves twin purposes. On the one hand, the government disseminates information pertaining to public interest through newspapers, radio, television and lately through the internet while on the other, people make use of these medium to express their complaints/problems/grievance. If the administration can prevent the occurrence of the PGs by use of the media to provide timely and accurate information to the public, its (media) use for ventilating the grievances of the public makes the administration more alert, responsible and accountable. It will not be an exaggeration to say that media provides a formidable link between administration and citizens. 'Citizens' Column'/ 'Action Taken' are designed to provide space to Public Grievances in the daily newspapers; 'Janata ki Awaz', 'Living at Edge', 'Ghoomta Ayina' and such other programmes on TV and radio also serve as the fora for the people to present their grievances forcefully and force the administration to take immediate action.

Conclusion

An overview of the PGRS reveals that the administration in India has taken commendable steps towards expanding, strengthening and modernizing the system which is an assurance for good governance in the future. The system can also be applauded for adopting an integrated approach to tackle the problem. However, given the complex character of the PGs, unwieldy size of population, rising expectations with growing awareness, and media exposures, PGR will remain a gigantic task. The number of the grievances being received by the Department are just the tip of the iceberg. The grievances received by various agencies, if taken together, will be too large to handle. Besides, the registered grievances, many are never registered either because of the complacency of the aggrieved citizens or their loss of confidence in the ability of the system to remove them. These are related basically to scanty services in various basic areas. The Government, therefore, need to work for **Public Grievance Preventive System** since **"Prevention is better than cure."** The Government both at central and state levels, should work for generating more resources and adopting high speed programmes to enhance services by itself or with the participation people.

In India the need of the hour is to improve and strengthen the public service delivery mechanism which is marred by inefficiency, non-performance, non-utilization misuse and embezzlement of funds, biases, favouratism, lack of courtesy, concern and commitment on the part of officials. The reports of the Ministry of Implementation and Office of the Comptroller and Auditor lend credence to these facts.

Indeed, the idea of creating of interactive Web-Site and programme of e-Governance is quite fascinating but it will remain a rhetoric in the context of the digital divide—the availability of IT facility to a very small number of people in India, and glaring rate of illiteracy in the country. The day illiteracy is wiped out from the country and the entire citizenry becomes a literate community can the benefits of good governance/e-governance become real.

REFERENCES

1. The cause of dissatisfaction as described shows the malfunctioning of the officials in one form or the other. This malfunctioning has been ascribed by Victor A. Thomson in Modern organizations to many conflicts and dilemmas. For instance organizations come into being for achievement of certain specified goals but in actual practice the organizational goals tend sometimes to get subordinated to the personal goals of the men in them: organization procedures also tend to masquerade as ends, rather than serve as means to an end. Quoted in Jagannadham, V and Makhija, H.R., **Citizen Administration and Lokpal**, S. Chand & Co., 1969, p. 5; Likewise Robert Presthus '...As size increases, morals decreases... lower productivity and absenteeism are also associated with organizational size' **The Organizational Society: An Analysis and Theory**, New York, Alfred A. Knopf (1962), pp. 30-31.
2. Supra No. (i).
3. Lewis, Norman and Singh S.S., (eds), *Ombudsman-India and World Community*, British Council Division, 1995, p. 1.
4. *Jagnnadham, v. and Makhija H.R.*, cit.ab., pp. 14-16.
5. Annual Report (AR), Ministry of Personnel, Public Grievances and Pensions (MOPPP), GOI, 1997-98, p. 65.
6. AR, MOPPP, 2001-2002, GOI, p. 70.
7. Quoted by Barnabas, cit. ab., p. 110.
8. India, GOI, 1991, p. 49.
9. Lewis and Singh opine that freedom of Information legislation has come into its own, administrative tribunals have been established and extended, Administrative Procedure\Acts have proliferated but perhaps above all the dominant accountability mechanism of the second half of the century has been the Ombudsman or citizen's

defender', p. 1. In this context it will also be interesting to know that Administrative Reforms Commission constituted in on 6th January 1966, in its special report submitted in Oct. 1966 gave highest priority to the question of citizens' grievances. Its main finding was that the district channels of the redress were too much loaded against ordinary citizens in securing prompt and fair redress of their grievances. The Commission for the first time to suggested that the Ombudsman-type of the institutions of Lokpal and Lokayukta was a "must" for developing the people's confidence and faith in the capability of the administration to deliver the goods. The first time to the Lokpal and Lokayukta Bill to that effect was introduced in 1969. However, the Bill lapsed due to the dissolution of the Lok Sabha which preceded the mid term general election of March 1971. Since then the Bill has been introduced several times but its fate always remained the same. The last attempt is again made on 14.8.2001 when a new Lokpal Bill was introduced in the Lok Sabha. At present the bill has lapsed with dissolution of the Lok Sabha.

10. AR, MOPPP, 1997-98, p. 67.
11. *Ibid.*, p. 73.
12. AR, MOPPP, 2001-2002, p. 65.
13. *Ibid.*, p. 72.
14. Jha, *IJPA*, 1999, p. 244-45.
15. AR, MOPPP, 2001-2002, p. 73.
16. AR, MOPPP, 2001-2002, p. 77.
17. *Ibid.*
18. *Ibid.*, 78, For the list see my book, Lok Prashashan, Sahitya Bhavan, 2001, Appendix 4.
19. *Ibid.*
20. AR, MOPPP, 2002, p. 66.
21. *Report of the Fifth Pay Commission*, GOI.
22. The office of the Lokyukta exists in Maharashtra, Bihar, Rajasthan, Uttar Pradesh, Madhya Pradesh, Andhra Pradesh, Himachal Pradesh, Karnataka, Assam, Gujarat, Delhi, Kerala and Punjab. Orrisa was the first state to establish (1970) the office and abolish it in 1993.
23. See www.ccsindia.org
24. Swaminathan SAA Aiyer, Swminomics, TOI, 16 November 2003, p. 12.

CHAPTER VI:
Decentralized Governance and Development Administration

19

Glocalization in Mumbai

Dr. Marina R. Pinto

The 1990s have seen a twin development in India. In 1991, the country embarked on a course of liberalisation, privatisation, and globalisation. In 1992, the Indian federal system was restructured through a Constitutional Amendment, to make it three tiered and to empower the local state. While globalisation can act in ways that make the market supreme, democratic decentralization can serve as a countervailing factor in that it empowers the people at the grassroots. Also, the global and the local could be seen as interdependent elements in a universal process, best exemplified as "glocalisation". How far these two processes have impacted Mumbai's governance is the concern of this paper.

The study highlights how Mumbai is yet to function as a global city though it is a mega city with global connections. Decentralization has affected to some extent the Municipal Corporation of Greater Mumbai [MCGM] which is the urban local body administering an area of 437.71 sq. kms. that includes the island city of Mumbai and its extended suburbs. Neither of these processes has gone far enough to make major, massive changes in city management. Much is in the pipelines; the systemic churning is bound to gather momentum and the shape of things to come will only unfold over a period of time.

Theoretical Frame

In the era of globalisation, the state is undergoing a transformation.

Nation-states function not only as political agencies in a complex system of power from world to local levels, but they have centrality because of their relationship to territory and population. If 'sovereignty' is of decisive significance, it is because the state can legitimately transfer power or sanction new powers both 'above' it through agreements between states to establish and abide by forms of international governance and 'below' it, through the constitutional ordering within its own territory in respect of the relationship of power and authority between levels of governments and civil society.

Governance is a function that can be performed by a wide variety of public and private, state and non-state, national and international institutions and practices. Governing powers cannot simply proliferate and compete. The different levels and functions of governance need to be tied together in a division of control. They need to be 'sutured' together into a relatively integrated system and in this, the nation-state assumes critical salience.

Viewed differently, the nation-state has become both—too big and too small. It is too big to cater to a citizen's needs and hence the need for decentralization which spells more autonomy to local bodies. It is too small to deal with global trends. The state now plays the role of a facilitator or enabler, permitting localities to become arenas for testing, experimenting and working out policies. Localities, therefore, have become significant sites of action. Local policies and strategies are formulated not only to revitalize local structures, but also to cut a positive image of cities to find a place in global ordering. Hence, there is a double movement, of globalisation on the one hand and devolution, decentralization and localization on the other, which has been termed as "glocalisation".[1]

When globalisation is modified by its contact with the local, new forms of interaction, making for interesting fusion and creativity arise, resulting in a transformation of political and social life at the local level. Here, non-state, voluntary bodies play a significant role in the expanding political space. In fact, this is seen as 'double democracy' of government and political life at both the global and local levels, forging authentic alternatives for the people. This kind of thinking is reflected in the debates of the General Assembly of the United Nations which recognized the importance of the local in the era of globalisation.[2] The World Development report, 1999-2000 also focuses on globalisation and localization and indicates that they raise new challenges as well as new opportunities for revitalizing the local realm. Localization, it asserts, can lead to decentralized government which can make for more responsive and efficient local government.[3]

In the context of localisaiton, mention must be made of the new wave of theoretical development described as New Localism. It is identified with the new local state and local activim. It concentrates on political-cum-administrative restructuring taking place, vertically in terms of Centre-state-local relations and horizontally though a re-definition of responsibilities between the state and orgnizations of civil society, between the public and private sectors at the local level. Horizontal restructuring looks at the participatory, facilitative, regulatory and adjustive roles that local governments can play in respect of the market. Looking at Mumbai in terms of glocalisation, would mean to put the spotlight on the emerging political architecture keeping New Localism in mind.

Mumbai: A Global City?

Globalisation is a process generated by the world wide interplay of capital flows and communication flows, enabled by new technologies which connect countries, societies, cities, firms and individuals. It has brought in the global cities, which are command points in the organisation of the world economy; key locations and market-places for leading industries and also major sites of production for these industries. Hence they become sites for immense concentrations of economic power as also for the advanced services and telecommunication facilities necessary for the implementation and management of global economic operations. Although in the past, there has been a world economy and an international economic system, the current system is different in that one sees the formation of transnational spaces for economic activity where governments play a minimal role, even though these spaces are located in national territories under the rule of sovereign states. Thus, 'the global city represents a strategic space where global processes materialize in national territories and global dynamics run through national institutional arrangements.'[4]

Mumbai is not a global city in the way London, New York and

Tokyo are, for it does not represent the 'endogenising of key dynamics and conditionalities of the global economy.'[5] But it is a mega-city with global linkages. It is embedded in a global network of cities and functions as a centre of economic, technological and social dynamisms in respect of India and on a global scale. It functions as a gateway to the global economy, as a centre of cultural and political innovations and as a connecting point to global networks of all kinds.

In respect of Mumbai, in the context of liberalisation, privatisation and globalisation one has to keep in kind the two-pronged strategy of the state in that it makes way simultaneously, for NGOs and market forces. The former is intended to support a greater role for the voluntary sector, decentralization and people's participation and the latter, to satisfy the demands of global capital and transnational corporations. Hence, to see how it functions on the ground, one has to look at local activism which is the defining feature of new localism and which, among other things, manifests itself in public-private partnership that have been encouraged by the state.

In 1995, the Government of Maharashtra launched the New Industry, Trade and Commerce Policy which accentuates the role of the private sector in development. In various sectors like power, roads, ports and telecommunications, the State Government, in keeping with the Central Government policy for privatisation has taken its own initiatives. In 1991, the Central Government opened the doors to privatisation and foreign participation in the power sector. In 1996, the State Government announced its own power policy, in line with that of the Centre. For instance, it provides several incentives to developers setting up power projects using non-conventional sources of energy as also assistance in identification of feasible sites for wind power through the Maharashtra Energy Development Agency (MEDA). In 1994, the Central Government announced a package of measures, including the declaration of the road sector as an industry. The private sector can now undertake road projects on a BOT basis for which tax concessions are available. The Government of Maharashtra has also permitted private sector participation in the construction and operation of roads and bridges and has formulated a Road Development Plan (1981-2001). Furthermore, in 2001, the Water Supply and Sanitation Department of Government of Maharashtra issued guidelines for private sector participation for sewerage work in Municipal Corporations and 'A' class Municipal Councils.[6] Many such moves are in the pipeline. There is also the effort to promote a Special Economic Zone (SEZ) in Navi Mumbai which will attract direct foreign investment and will be a joint sector venture with private partnership. SEZ is considered a foreign territory within a country and local laws and levies do not apply. But this would mean that the area will have to be demerged from Navi Mumbai Municipal Corporation which stands to lose much revenue.

Civil society is seen in action and initiatives are being taken to form new partnerships of all kind. The State Government has committed itself to 'empowerment of the people at all levels'. The traditional approach of dependency and centralization of authority is sought to be replaced by dynamic empowerment. This implies a shift in its role from controller to facilitator in the process of all-round development. However, this has yet to be reflected in ground realities in a big way. In Mumbai, initiatives for formations of new partnerships are under way. Communities have organized themselves, especially the downtrodden and disadvantaged, like slum and pavement dwellers and in concert with NGOs and Government have worked on their problems.[7] To mention a few of the citizens' initiatives, there is the case of Pratham, a public charitable trust, initiated in 1994 by UNICEF, MCGM and some citizens to achieve universal pre-primary and primary education in the city. Pratham represents triangular partnership between citizens, local government and the corporate sector.

Advanced Locality Management (ALM) is a partnership of citizens and MCGM which works on the basic principle of self-governance for creating infrastructure and spreading awareness. It was the idea of Viren Merchant and the Additional Municipal Commissioner Ratnakar Gaekwad. To begin with, AML was restricted to management of garbage, but is now expanded to include all civic services in the localities. There are over 700 ALMs doing useful work. The MCGM constitutes a nodal agency in each ward to collaborate with the ALM and appoints one Special/Nodal Officer who visits the locality on a regular basis to liaison with the local community.[8] The ALM movement has had a snowballing effect. For instance, Chembur's 60 ALMs have now formed their own network ALMANAC which strengthens the movement considerably by helping to create more ALMs. Then there is Action for Good

Governance and Networking in India (AGNI) that works with various NGOs to build citizen awareness. It is self-help network of volunteers, which started out by focusing on civic services. Its Joint Area Action Groups (JAAGs) in municipal wards establish local priorities, mobilize resources, conduct activities and help interaction among citizens, administration and elected representatives. They co-ordinate with NGOs like the Dignity Foundation, Police-Public Mohalla Committee and Bombay First to tackle intractable problems. Mention must also be made of Bombay First, an organisation dedicated to improving the economic and social infrastructure of the city, making it globally competitive and raising the quality of life of its citizens. Bombay First is an initiative to make the city a better place to live, work and invest in. It aims to serve the city with the best that private business can officer. It believes in working through partnerships with government, business and civil society. It made possible the McKinsey Study on 'Transforming Mumbai into a World Class City.'

Heightened citizen awareness has at times made for confrontation, especially when genuine needs are ignored or are trampled upon. For instance, the plan of the Slum Rehabilitation Authority (SRA) to provide free houses to slum-dwellers has backfired. Citizens have joined hands to fight builders who have cornered slum plots in prime localities and are-re-devloping them while their lives and properties are at risk. Citizens have formed area-wise organizations and networked to challenge development plans of Government agencies.[9] Citispace, an NGO that is fighting to preserve the few remaining open spaces in the city has got a High Court Order that prohibits SRA from sanctioning any slum scheme on land reserved for public purposes.

Municipal Corporation of Greater Mumbai (MCGM)

A study of the city's governance must begin with the Municipal Corporation, which is the urban local body administering the city and its suburbs. With a history older than that of the State or Central Government, it is governed by the Bombay Municipal Corporation Act of 1888, and is believed to be powerful and autonomous. The MCGM, the richest Municipal Corporation in India, is virtually a state within a state. It has a huge budget but is often in the red due to financial mismanagement. The Tinaikar Report has shown how 'in order to display a formal compliance with MMC Act, the Budget Estimates were artificially framed to show a saving of a statutory cash balance at the end of the year, by a pretentious covering of past deficit, and the future estimated high expenditure by showing hug estimate of Income, which it was impossible to realize'.[10] State Government is also to be blamed as it permitted heavy withdrawals from the Provident Fund and other irregularities.

The Tables below show the Revenue Income and Expenditure of the MCGM from 1998-2001. State funding is not of a high order and is mainly limited to primary education. Most of the income is drawn from Octroi and Property Taxes.

MCGM Revenue Income

Budgets A, B and E (excluding inter-budget contributions)
Rs. in crores

Source of Income	*Actuals 1998-99*	*Actuals 1999-00*	*Actuals 2000-01*
Opening Balance as on 1st April	-360.47	-545.56	-644.96
Budget A (Revenue) Octroi (Net)	1138.54	1309.75	1613.17
Taxes	287.57	318.13	367.92
Fees and Charges, etc.	253.93	305.68	373.64
Recoveries from Govt. of Maharashtra	39.11	12.65	40.32
Total Budget A	1719.15	1946.21	2395.05
Budget B (Slums, etc.)	15.79	23.52	16.89
Budget E (Education)	101.72	88.16	187.47
Net Income Budgets A, B & E	1836.66	2057.89	2599.41
Net Expenditure Budgets A, B & E	2021.75	2157.29	2170.40

MCGM Revenue (Expenditure)

	1998-99	*1999-00*	*2000-01*
1. Water Supply & Sewerage	566.81	547.04	617.43
2. Primary Education	352.29	349.09	371.38
3. Improvement/Slums	61.93	66.70	64.34
4. Public Health, Medical Relief & Education	400.78	410.05	467.81
5. Solid Waste Management	288.82	284.48	350.02
6. Traffic Operations, Roads & Bridges	230.37	254.24	288.14
7. Storm Water Drains	54.91	69.97	30.52
8. Others, Pensions, etc.	632.65	722.76	598.19
Total	2588.56	2704.33	2787.83

Source: MCGM

The MCGM has an impressive list of functions. The obligatory ones include construction and maintenance of drainage system, water supply, sanitation and health, primary education, public hospitals, public street lighting, fire fighting services, urban forestry, environment and ecology and importantly, planning for economic and social development. The discretionary functions include not just survey of buildings and lands and maintenance and libraries, museums, parks and gardens, but also slum improvement and upgradation and urban poverty alleviation. Thus, all the 18 functions in the Twelfth Schedule of the Constitution are devolved to the MCGM.

In the MCGM, the Corporation, an elected body of 277 members is the deliberative wing, which lays down broad policies, frames bye-laws, sanctions the budget and oversees the administration. But the entire executive authority is statutorily vested in the Commissioner, who, along with the Corporation and the Standing Committee constitute the three co-ordinate authorities of the MCGM. Given a large heterogeneous council and many committees, the locus and focus of authority is indeterminate. Decision-making suffers and delays abound. Despite structural dysfunctionalities is still works, given the numerous checks and balances.

The whole system revolves around the Municipal Commissioner who is all-powerful and has wide-ranging administrative, discretionary and emergency powers. Being appointed by the State Government, he could as well function as the eyes and ears of the State Government. He is indeed the link between the two wings of the Corporation as also between the Corporation and the State Government. His role is a difficult one. Pressure, political or otherwise build up. He has to face pulls and counter-pulls from local functionaries, government authorities, voluntary agencies and citizen groups while discharging his responsibilities to the ruling parties in the MCGM, the State Government and the people at large.

Politically speaking, the MCGM has been the preserve of the Bharatiya Janata Party and the Shiv Sena, while the State Government is controlled by the Congress combine. This skews state-local relations and has made for inroads into the local body's autonomy. Given the level of corruption, mismanagement and inefficiency, the State Government's intervention can be legitimized, but the political factor cannot be ignored. The opportunity to change structurally from the Commissioner-type to the Mayor-in-Council[11] that is more people-oriented was lost as the 74th Constitutional Amendment Act, 1992, did not address this issue. If local governments are to be strong, self-governing bodies, such a change was certainly warranted.

Impact of the 74th Constitutional Amendment Act (CAA), 1992

The CAA has undoubtedly devolved a status on local bodies for the first time in the history of India. It has sought to make urban governance responsive and closer to the people and strengthened it as the 3rd tier in our multi-level democracy. To-day, there is far too much power at the Centre and not much less in the states. But there is virtually none at the local level where the people are. This is sought to be corrected by the 73rd and the 74th Constitutional Amendment Acts. Hence, the attempt is to empower the people and also re-define state-local functional and fiscal relations.

In pursuance of the 74th CAA, the Bombay Municipal Corporation Act has been amended in 1992 to provide for 5 nominated councillors, reservation of seats for women, Scheduled Castes and Scheduled Tribes, and backward class citizens and reservation of the Office of Mayor by rotation for the members of these categories. The State election Commission is in place and has conducted the elections in 1997 and 2002. The right to exist is ensured, for, in the eventuality of dissolution, fresh elections must be held in six months. Though some 16 Ward Committees have been constituted, all is not well with their functioning. Either there is no NGO representation or the nominated social workers have no institutional backing, are not really aware of citizens problems and often clash with councilors. Also, the functions assigned to these Committees include mundane matters like repairs to roads, schools, markets, footpaths, maintenance of municipal dispensaries and hospitals and verminculture schemes, all within a total financial allocation of Rs. 5 lakh per project. A view expressed is that with more empowered Ward Officers, devolution of civic services and creation of Ward Committees, ward administration has opened up. Nonetheless, it is feared that these committees can fuel the engine of corruption. The Ward Committees in terms of their constitution and functions have not yet got off the ground. Undoubtedly, empowerment of the people has yet to be realized.

The Amendment requires the constitution of a State Finance Commission that looks into the finances of local bodies by laying down principles for tax assignments, sharing of taxes and grants-in-aid. Federal transfers are also on the cards. Through an amendment of Article 280 of the Constitution, the Central Finance Commission is now required to suggest measures needed to augment the Consolidated Fund of a state, and to supplement the resources of municipalities on the basis of the recommendations of the State Finance commission. Even so, the financial position of urban local bodies remains precarious. In the case of Maharashtra, it is not only a reflection of the difficult financial situation at State level but also of the lack of interest in the State Finance Commission reports that are not acted upon in the required timeframe. For instance, the first State Finance Commission, appointed in 1994 for 5 years, only made tax specific recommendations.[12] Besides, there was not much time for the actual implementation of the accepted recommendations as the Action Taken Report was tabled by the Government only in March 1999.

As per the requirements of the Act, Maharashtra has passed the Metropolitan Planning Committee (Constitution and Functions) Act, 1999[13] but these Metropolitan Planning Committee (MPCs) have yet to be constituted in practice. This is because the State Government is in a fix. It has not only to co-ordinate the functioning of the MPC with the MMRDA perhaps by making the latter the technical arm of the former, but also it has to find a place for the MPC plan and its implementation, when it already has its own Master Plan under Town Planning Legislation. All said and done, the CAA has not looked into relationships between urban local bodies and statutory State-level agencies. The bone of contention is that every development expenditure makes a corresponding impact on recurring expenditure on maintenance of works and the municipal bodies resent an increase in the latter because they are concerned with maintenance and therefore, have to cope with the additional financial burden.

The Amendment has not re-structured municipal bodies, nor examined the need for a strong and professional municipal service or even a local list in the Constitution which would further strengthen local self-government at the base. Thus, while the CAA wants vibrant urban local bodies, ground realities belie the fact. Barring the functioning of the State Election Commission and the State Finance Commission, with the latter having a long way to go, the status quo ante continues. Unfortunately, the CAA has not gone far enough and has left too much to the discretion of the State Government.

Quasi-Governmental Organizations

Mention must be made of several parastatals that are state-appointed, nominated bodies—both uni-functional agencies as also area development authorities. This is because the state government has progressively pruned away powers and functions of municipal bodies and grafted them on to administrative structures more directly accountable to itself. The chart below shows those parastatals that relate to Mumbai.

Administrative and Planning Organizations in Mumbai

Among the few parastatals discussed here, the **Mumbai Metropolitan Region Development Authority (MMRDA)** needs special mention as it was set up, not as the planning and coordinating agency of the city or the entire state but of the Metropolitan Region[14] of which the Mumbai Municipal area is only a part. The region is a vast area of 4,350 sq. kms. It covers Municipal Corporations of Brihan Mumbai, Thane, Kalyan, Navi Mumbai, Ulhasnagar, Bhiwandi and Mira-Bhayandar, 13 Municipal Councils, parts of Raigad and Thane districts and over 900 villages. It has therefore to plan and develop the region in a multi-municipal jurisdiction. Though not a part of the municipal structure, it has to work in patently municipal functional areas. It brings together the Central and State Governments to jointly fund urban development and relates to their agencies that operate in the region.

MMRDA has friction points with the MCGM. This is because of Section 17 of the MMRDA Act which specifically prohibits it from undertaking any work which falls under the obligatory or discretionary functions of the MCGM and Section 16 which stipulates that the MMRDA should undertake the execution of any work only with the sanction of the State Government which should satisfy itself that there is no other authority competent or willing to do so. MCGM also fears its political clout more than Section 14 of its Act which gives it over-riding power to direct any local authority. In fact, when the State Government permitted MMRDA to undertake infrastructure projects in Mumbai, there was so much opposition from the MCGM that it had to modify its stand and the Maharashtra Ordinance No. XV of 2002 stated that MMRDA's actions would be in consultation with the Municipal Commissioner.

When MMRDA came into being in 1975, the emphasis was on central planning and coordination. The Regional Plan of 1973 was upheld and it was essentially a land use plan. But the picture is very different in the 1990s as emphasis has shifted to decentralization and participation. Its draft Regional Plan 1996-2011 takes into account not just land use, but provides a policy framework for the overall growth of the Region. In keeping with the 74th CAA it seeks to promote effective citizen participation in the process of development. This is very significant, as MMRDA has to interact with new Municipal Corporations in the region.

MMRDA has been successfully playing the coordinating role in project work where external finances are involved. It played the lead role in the Mumbai Urban Development Project (MUDP) financed by the World Bank. There is also the World Bank funded Mumbai Urban Transport Project (MUTP) whose cost is Rs. 4,526 crore. It has a Rail component, a Road Transport Component and Rehabilitation Programme of 19,128 households affected by MUTP with active involvement of NGOs and community participation. Implementing agencies are MMRDA, MCGM, Maharashtra State Road Corporation (MSRC) and Mumbai Traffic Control System. The project implementation period is 2002 to 2008. Mention must also be made of the ambitious Rs. 2,648 crore Mumbai Urban Infrastructure Project (MUIP). Its master plan is sanctioned by the MMRDA and the entire project is executed without the help of any external agency. MMRDA, MCGM, MIDC and the State Government will jointly fund the project.

To ensure balanced development and to arrest further concentration of offices and commercial activities in South Mumbai, MMRDA is creating new growth centres like the Backbay Reclamation area, Bandra-Kurla complex which will even house an International Finance and Business Centre and the Oshiwara Centre. Though elsewhere, MMRDA is a deemed local authority, in all these areas, it is the Special Planning Authority.[15] MMRDA has also accepted the responsibility for strategic environmental planning and should assist Municipal Councils to discharge their new legal responsibility of preparing environmental status reports.

MMRDA, funded by the Central and State Governments is an umbrella organization that can plan, formulate and implement projects. Given its wide-ranging intersectoral mandate, it is more than a think-tank for the region. It has to coordinate its activities with other functional agencies like MHADA and municipal bodies like MCGM. MMRDA's work necessitates interaction with the Collector who is the revenue authority o the city and holds jurisdiction over the Titles and Deeds in respect of ownership of land. MMRDA has also to handle centrally sponsored schemes. A good example is the Mega City Scheme introduced by the Planning Commission and Ministry of Urban Affairs and Employment in the Eighth Plan (1993-98) for infrastructure development. It has executed by MCGM, CIDCO, Thane Municipal Corporation, Navi Mumbai Municipal Corporation and MMRDA and the Government of India has released Rs. 165.02 crore for it, up to 31st March, 2002.

Many fear that the MMRDA functions more as a line agency under the Urban Development Department and not as a nodal body. Its Executive Committee chaired by the Chief Secretary does not give representation to concerned departments like Industries and Environment or to municipal corporations other than the MCGM. The MMRDA has still to emerge as a strong coordinating body of the Mumbai Metropolitan Region.

In the housing sector, the main State-appointed agency is **Maharashtra Housing and Area Development Authority (MHADA)** set up under the Maharashtra Housing and Area Development Act, 1976, to make available houses to the poor and needy at affordable rates. Due to acute shortage of housing after World War II, it was felt that a comprehensive and coordinated approach to housing was necessary and so the four existing Boards were amalgamated in **MHADA**.

MHADA is an entirely nominated body, with all its members appointed by the State Government, a quasi-Government organization under the Housing and Special Assistance Department. It works through nine Regional Boards, three of which directly relate to Mumbai. They are: (1) Mumbai Housing and Area Development Board for the city and its suburban district only, wherein it interacts with MCGM as the civic body has to maintain the facilities it creates. (2) Mumbai Building Repair and Reconstruction Board which confines its activities to the island city only. Its task is colossal as it has to undertake structural repairs or even reconstruction of old cessed buildings which in 2002 numbered 19,642.[16] The Board repairs private buildings at virtually State Government's cost, a unique activity not seen anywhere in the world. (3) Mumbai Slum Improvement Board for the city and its suburban district only. Under the Slum Improvement Programme (SIP), MHADA adopts a cafeteria approach and provides basic civic amenities like common toilets, roads/pathways, water taps, storm water drains and streetlights in slum pockets on Government or private lands.

In 1991, the State Government had permitted redevelopment of slums where structures and inhabitants figured in the electoral roll of 1985. It subsequently took a policy decision to provide free houses to 40 lakh (4 million) slum dwellers in Mumbai. A slum family, having its name in the voter's list of January 1st 1995 was eligible to get a free house. In order to implement the scheme, the Maharashtra Slum Areas (Improvement, Clearance and Redevelopment) Act, 1977, was amended to set up the **Slum Rehabilitation Authority (SRA)** in 1995. It is seen as a very powerful body as the Chief Minister of Maharashtra in Chairperson, a Senior IAS officer is full-time CEO and 14 other members, mostly ex-officio, constitute the Authority. The SRA has the status of corporate entity from 1997. By amendment to the MR&TP Act, 1966, it has been declared as a planning authority, to function as a local authority for the area under its jurisdiction. It can survey slum areas, formulate schemes for slum rehabilitation and get them implemented. For any other scheme, the developers have to approach various departments of MCGM for development permission, which is cumbersome. For the SRA scheme, the procedure has been simplified and all approvals are issued by SRA by providing a single window clearance. All said and done, the MCGM perforce has to grant permissions, MHADA is under pressure to provide transit tenements, builders are not that enthused to put up structures and citizens are ready to fight legal battles as they fear the new tall buildings will result in civic facilities breaking down.

Maharashtra Water Supply and Sewerage Board had its

origin in a Government Department. Water supply and sewerage schemes involve large capital investments, which require loan finance, which used to be provided by the Life Insurance Corporation (LIC). Since LIC could not trust the municipalities to make repayments, each loan involved making a tripartite agreement between the LIC, State Government and the concerned municipality. This was a very cumbersome procedure. Now the Board could be the body to negotiate the loan amount with the LIC, pass it on to individual municipalities and be responsible for collection of interest and repayments. In 1979, government decided to convert the Board into a functional organization to manage water supply, sewerage and sanitation schemes.

There have been drawbacks in the functioning of the Board like when the loan fixed for one local body was diverted to meet the needs of another. Moreover, the State Government does not want to stand guarantor for loans anymore especially after its property was sought to be attached at the instance of the court. It has now permitted the local bodies to undertake work through the Board or private sector agency. Hopefully, this will generate healthy competition and improve the Board's performance.

Maharashtra Pollution Control Board (MPCB) comes under the Environment Department set up in 1970 under the Maharashtra Prevention of Water Pollution Act, 1969. In 1981, the State Government repealed this Act and brought into force similar Central legislation as it was advantageous for it to do so. From 1983, with the Cess Act, 1977 of the Central Government being made effective in Maharashtra, the Board levies a cess on water consumed by an industry or local authority. The amount however is remitted to the Government of India, which makes over a specified share to the State Board. The Board is tight on finances as it does not get its fair share from the Centre and this is further curtailed by the State Government.

To develop a twin city of metropolitan size, across the harbour, as a counter magnet to Mumbai, the state government set up **City and Industrial Development Corporation of Maharashtra Ltd. (CIDCO)**, a company which was a subsidiary of the State Industrial and Investment Corporation of Maharashtra (SICOM). CIDCO comes under the Urban Development Department. It is a New Town Development Authority for Navi Mumbai.

All these parastatals have a significant role to play. They meet technology needs and have the required level of professionalism. They also make for economies of scale, have state wide jurisdiction and above all help the state to discharge its Constitutional responsibilities development. Each has a history and logic of its own which can justify its existence. Nevertheless, these agencies are highly bureaucratized and lack direct public accountability. They not only weaken the MCGM, but also give rise to problems of overlap of civic and urban functions. There is no integration of their activities in the field as each is linked to its parent department at the state level. Often functional autonomy is reduced because of state controls and statutory constraints.

Conclusion

Globalization in Mumbai presents a complex and confusing picture of city governance. There is a plethora of quasi-governmental organizations that interact between themselves and with the NCGM making for overlapping competencies and conflict areas. While the process of globalization could make the market supreme, it need not work to the detriment of the people as the simultaneous process of democratic decentralization through the 74th Constitutional Amendment empowers them at all levels. Political decentralization provides for a more durable rational-legal frame that makes decentralization meaningful and fruitful. Yet, what ground realities indicate is that the state government drags its feet when it comes to the implementation of the Amendment in toto, both in letter and spirit and much headway has to be made in respect of the working of bodies like the Finance Commission and Wards Committees. May be, a further amendment is called for.

What its economy growing at a steady rate, India is poised for super power status in 2050. A Goldman Sachs study says that India may be the third biggest economy after China and the USA by that time and in this Mumbai is expected to play the lead role. It is a much happening city. There is growing foreign direct investment and worldwide interest in the Indian market. Public-private partnerships, joint ventures and the like are picking up. The churning process is on and New Localism is manifest through dynamic inter-governmental relations, an alert local state and growing citizen awareness.

REFERENCES

B. Mohanty, (ed.), *Urbanization in Developing Countries,* Concept 1993.

Brihanmumbai Mahanagarpalika Year Book 2002.

Database on Municipal Governance in Some Major States, Nagar Palika Network, All India Institute of Local Self Government, New Delhi, 2002.

E.G. Goetz, Susan E. Clarke, (eds.), *The New Localism,* London, Sage, 1993.

Guidelines for the Implementation of Slum Rehabilitation Schemes in Greater Mumbai, Slum Rehabilitation Authority, Housing and Special Assistance Department, Government of Maharashtra, 1997.

Implementation of 74th Constitutional Amendment Act, Paticipatory Strategies of Indian Municipalities, Report by All India Institute of Local Self-Government, Mumbai 2002.

Maharashtra Housing and Area Development Authority, *Activities and Achievements (Year-2002).*

Maharashtra Ordinance No. XV of 2002, dated November 15th 2002.

Marina R. Pinto, *Metropolitan City Governance in India,* Sage Delhi, 2000.

M.B. Maduskar, Municipal Administration in Mumbai, *Quarterly Journal of the All India Institute of Local Self-Government,* Vol. LXVII No. 3, 1996.

M.D. David, *Urban Explosion of Mumbai,* Hamalaya Publishing House, Mumbai, 1996.

R.N. Sharama, K. Sita (eds), *Issues in Urban Development: A Case of Navi Mumbai,* Rowat Publications, Jaipur and New Delhi, 2001.

S.S. Gadkari, A.S. Kharkar, V.V. Velankar, *Organization of the State Government in Maharashtra,* Himalaya Publishing House, 1992.

The Constitution (Seventh-Fourth Amendment) Act, 1992.

The Mumbai Metropolitan Region Development Authority Act, 1974.

Saskia Sassen, *Losing Control? Sovereignty in an era of Globalisation,* Columbia University Press, 1996; *Cities in a World Economy,* 2nd edition, Pine Forge Press, Thousand Oaks, London, New Delhi, 2000; *The Global City,* 2nd edition, Princeton University Press, Princeton and Oxford, 2001.

Elmar Reigar and Stephan Leibfried, *Limits to Globalisation,* Blackwell Publishing Ltd. Cambridge, 2003.

NOTES

1. Ash Amin (ed), *Post Fordism: A Reader,* Oxford and Cambridge, Blackwell 1994, p. 282.

2. *Agenda 21 Programme for Action for Sustainable Development,* United Nations, New York, 1993.
3. *World Development Report 1999-2000,* New York, Oxford University Press 1999, p. 173.
4. Saskia Sassen, *The Global City,* Princeton and Oxford, Printed in USA, 2nd Edition, 2001, p. 347.
5. *Ibid.*
6. Government of Maharashtra, Water Supply and Sanitation Department
   (*a*) Resolution No. UW5-100/CR410/WS-22, dated July 15th, 2000.
   (*b*) Government Resolution No. NAPAPU/1000/CR-419/PAPU-22, dated September 27th, 2000.
   (*c*) Government Circular No. NAPAPU-1001/503/PAPU-22, dated June 12th, 2001.
7. A good illustration is the Kanjur Marg experiment in slum resettlement. It was a partnership between the Railways (on whose land the slums existed) who gave the money, the Society for Promotion of Area Resource Centre (SPARC), an NGO that organized the slum-dwellers, especially the women and the SRA and the State Government Departments that coordinated the joint effort successfully.
8. The built-in work procedure is that on every fourth Saturday, two representatives of ALM societies from each Ward meet the Additional Municipal Commissioner along with NGOs for discussions and action.
9. In Mumbai, fearing that civic servicves will collapse because of huge skyscrapers being put up, citizens have joined their respective organizations in the four affected areas to form PACT. Their concerted pressure forced the State Government to appoint a committee to examine the grievances.
10. For details read Report of the High Power Committee (S.S. Tinaikar Report) on Financial Mismanagement of Municipal Corporation of Brihanmumbai resulting in heavy deficits in Budgets since 1995-96, set up by the Government of Maharashtra, August, 2001.
11. The system is a replication of cabinet government at the local level. The Mayor and his Council are drawn from the Corporation and accountable to it. Through an Amendment in 1998, the Mayor-in-Council was introduced for a while. Within 10 months, the experiment ended. The NCGM reverted to the Commissioner type, with the Commissioner emerging more powerful than before.
12. For the MCGM, the following were the recommendations of the State Finance Commission: Land revenue and non-agricultural

grants to be raised to 75 per cent of land revenue collected in the area; 25 per cent of entertainment tax collection in the region; 10 per cent of Profession Tax grant for local bodies of which, 80 per cent should be reserved for urban local bodies; slum improvement grant to be increased to Rs. 1,000 per capita; incentive grant of Rs. 1 crore ($ 0.22 million); primary education grant remain unchanged.

13. Out of 45 members of the MPC, 30 will be elected from amongst elected members of municipalities and Chairpersons of Panchayats in the metropolitan area; 4 experts and the rest ex-officio special permanent invitees from State agencies and Government of India organizations.
14. The Mumbai Metropolitan Region is bounded by the Tansa river in the north, the Patalganga river in the South, the Arbian Sea on the west and the Sahyadri ranges in the east.
15. Municipal bodies generally take care of maintenance of facilities created as these are civic functions; they are also planning authorities in their respective areas. The means that all permissions for any developmental activity has to be sought from them. Sometimes, this role is denied to them when parastatals are designated as Special Planning Authorities in specific areas as in the case of MMRDA and MHADA. MHADA is the Special Planning Authority for Dharavi.
16. It is reported in the print media in May 2003 that MHADA's guidelines are blatantly flouted by developers. MHADA has admitted to gross violations of rules by builders as well as its own officers in cases pertaining to the reconstruction of old buildings in the island city.

20

Urban Governance in Andhra Pradesh: An Appraisal

Dr. B.V. Chalapathi

Urbanization has become an inescapable feature of modern life. In the history of mankind the growth of urban life has given rise to striking development. Urbanization and technological changes following it have brought about transformation in the way of living or people, in their life styles, especially in urban areas.[1]

Urban areas are engines of growth, creating skills and wealth for the nation and generate employment for the millions of migrants from rural areas. In 1950-1951, the contribution of urban India to the net domestic product of the country was only 29 per cent.

That local self-government is of supreme importance to a democratic polity cannot be denied, although it is not always realized. This is especially true of developing countries like India which whose to become democracies, after liberation from prolonged colonial rule. Briefly state, local government ensures not only democracy survives but also functions properly. As local government is subordinate to the state government, which supervises and controls it, its jurisdiction is necessarily limited to a specific area.

Local self-Government in India operates in both rural and urban areas. It functions in rural areas through Panchayati Raj Institutions (PRIs) in the form of Zilla Parishads, Panchayat Samitis, and Mandal or village Panchayats. In urban areas local self-government is carried on by Municipal corporations, Municipal Councils, Notified Area Committees, Town Area Committees, and Cantonment Boards.

These institutions differ in their structure and organization in different states, although their functions more or less remain the same. According to the Census of India, 1991 there are 3252 municipal bodies in India classified into four categories, namely Municipal Corporations, Municipalities/Municipal Councils/ Boards and committees, Town Area Committees and Notified Area Committees. Town Area Committees are either fully or partially nominated bodies. Under the 74th Constitution amendment, the latter two categories in towns are designated as municipalities or major panchayats with elected bodies.[2] As Table 1.1 shows India witnessed a galloping increase in urban population from 25.8 million in 1901 to 78.9 million in 1961, from 109.1 million in 1971 to 159.4 million in 1981 and 217 million in 1991. According to the report of the Census of 2001, the total population of the country is 102,70,15,24, of which 53,12,77,079 are men and 49,57,38,168 are women.[3] It is seen-that the total population of the country increased from 844 million in 1991 to 1027 million by March 2001.

The phenomenal growth in urban population is a natural corollary to the process of industrialization, which the country embarked upon soon after independence.[4]

The table below also reveals that the percentage of urban population took a substantial jump after 1951. The percentage increased from 17.87 in 1961 to 25.72 in 1991. In absolute terms, the rise in urban population during the decades ending 1971, 1981 and 1991 has been 30.2 million, 50.3 million and 57.7 million respectively.

Table 1: Growth of Urban Population in India

Sl. No.	*Census Years*	*Total Population (Million)*	*Urban Population (Million)*	*Total*	*Urban*	*Decadal Growth Urban Population As Percentage of Total Population*
1.	1901	238.4	25.8	N.A.	N.A.	10.84
2.	1911	252.1	25.9	5.75	0.35	10.29
3.	1921	251.3	28.1	0.31	8.27	11.28
4.	1931	278.9	33.4	11.00	19.12	11.99
5.	1941	318.6	44.1	14.22	31.97	13.86
6.	1951	361.1	62.4	13.31	41.42	17.29
7.	1961	439.2	78.9	21.64	26.41	17.87
8.	1971	548.1	109.1	24.80	38.23	19.91
9.	1981	683.3	159.4	24.66	46.41	23.24
10.	1991	844.3	217.1	23.56	36.19	25.72

Field Investigation

Andhra Pradesh, which came into existence as a state in 1956 when states were reorganized, consists of three distinct regions viz., Coastal Andhra, which has nine districts, Telangana which has ten districts and Rayalaseema, which has four districts *i.e.*, Anantapur, Kurnool, Chittor and Chuddapah. The urban administration of this state is carried on by 109 municipalities and seven municipal corporations.

Locale and Objectives of the Study

The municipality of Proddatur, an important town and commercial centre in the Cuddapah district was selected for detailed investigation. Thus it constitutes the locale for this micro study. The objectives of the research are three fold:

(*i*) Studying the organization and performance of the municipality;
(*ii*) Identifying the problems it faces and the manner in which they have been tackled; and
(*iii*) Making some practicable suggestions to improve its operational efficiency.

Findings of the Study

1. *Problems Relating to Deliberative Wings*

According to the provisions of the amended Andhra Pradesh Municipalities Act, the municipal council is the policy making body. The role of the council is strictly confined to the formation of policies after detailed and objective discussion of the issues. But in Proddatur Council it rarely happens. The Study reveals that majority of the councilors are from the Reddy community and the Brahmins, and Vysyas are not represented in the council. Those elected to the council are middle aged and with poor educational background. Business or agriculture is their main occupation. The participation of the women councilors is confined to the wards, which are reserved for them. Decision-making in the council has never been smooth because of vested interest among the councilors and their ignorance of the laws and procedures of the Municipality. Irrespective of the caste, community or religion to which he belongs the elected councillor has to justify himself by fulfilling the responsibilities for which he is elected.

2. *Lack of Understanding of Rules and Regulations*

It is found that most councillors are quite ignorant of the various aspects of the functions of the Municipality. They do not make any effort to understand the municipal laws and procedures either. During their participation in the decision making process they act according to the opinion of their group leaders and rarely consider the merits or demerits of the issues involved. They also maintain lobbies. Some of them do not take interest in civic problems at all. They appear to have sought elections for gaining prestige and patronage.

The study also reveals that municipal councillors have a tendency to interfere in the day to day municipal administration, which invariably leads to conflicts and confrontations. Many a time tensions have prevailed and clashes occurred between the chairperson and ward members on the one hand and the municipal commissioner on the other. Political pressure is brought upon the bureaucracy to get things done according to their interest. As a result, the administration often fails to be impartial and effective. Personal rivalries, factionalism, favouritism, selfishness, irresponsibility, irregularities, illegalities and unparliamentary behaviour are more frequently manifest in the council meetings than honesty, civic consciousness and responsible behaviour amongst the members.

In the Proddatur municipal council, meetings turn into virtual battles between the Congress and Telugu Desam Party (TDEP). The male members are often locked in group combats forcing the panic-stricken female councillors to take to their heels. Chairs are thrown at each other and the members exchange blows making it a free for all Trouble started when the TDP councillors (Gurivi Reddy, Ramesh, Subramanyam, Lakshmi Devi) and a few others took strong exception to the presence of the co-opted members (V. Obula Reddy and Palle Savithri) in the meeting on the issue of debarring the co-opted members.

It is therefore, suggested that dynamic and enlightened leadership is needed to improve the state of affairs in the municipality. The need of the hour is to prescribe minimum period of training for councillors to equip themselves with the knowledge of municipal administration and to observe scrupulously the democratic values. In this connection, the services of the Regional Centre for Urban and Environmental Studies, Hyderabad can be tapped.

3. *Insufficient Powers to Chairperson*

At present the chairperson is directly elected. The powers and functions of the chairpersons of municipalities in Andhra Pradesh in general, and Proddatur municipality in particular, have been undermined inconformity with the legislation made in 1994. Introducing direct election of chairmen, curtailing their powers in signing contracts, making appointments, and in taking disciplinary action against erring municipal employees, have been found to be counterproductive.

It is therefore, suggested that this law needs to be modified. Once the people elect the chairperson directly he/she should enjoy full-pledged powers of control over all administrative units. To remodel, re-strengthen, revitalize municipal institutions, he needs to be given certain powers by the Government, which will provide dignity to the chairmen's office. Otherwise, the chairperson of the council has to play a balancing, and harmonizing role.

4. *Lack of Administrative Co-ordination*

The powers of the commissioner in municipal administration have varied from time to time in accordance with the Acts. The powers of the commissioner which were considerably reduced under the 1965 Act, have been restored in 1971, and in 1994, through amendments in the municipal laws.

The Commissioner of Proddatur Municipality is the most important official. He has the power to control the municipal staff. The study found that the Commissioner can misuse or arbitrarily exercise his powers. In the process professional integrity and administrative neutrality are sacrificed; the needs and standards of efficient municipal administration disregarded; and the interest of the people ignored for personal gains.

The study also reveals that the commissioner has problems in his relationship with other officers of the municipality such as the

Municiapal Engineer, Town Planning Officer, Sanitary Inspector and others. To put it briefly, their relations in the Proddatur Municipality is anything but cordial. Strictly speaking the other officers are expected to be co-operative with the commissioner and assist him in the exercise of the his duties as the chief executive officer of the municipal administration. The study reveals that these officers resent the commissioner's manner of functioning. They complain that he frequently behaves like a 'boss' rather than a 'leader' and does not consider the proposals submitted by them. As the chief executive of the municipality it is the duty of the commissioner to minimize friction and maximize the spirit of work culture in the eyes of the public as well as among the ministerial and other staff of the municipal office. Other officers too should respect the views of the commissioner in running the administration smoothly, properly understand the constraints under which he works, and co-operate with him.

Being the head of the civic body, the commissioner should take his colleagues into his confidence while discharging his duties in the different branches of the municipality. Thus, the commissioner should be not only a dynamic administrator but also a good Public Relations Officer.

In this connection, it is suggested that a separate post of public relations officer be created to promote co-operation and co-ordination among the officials and non-officials of the municipality and ensure liaison between the public and the municipality.

5. *Lack of Training Facilities*

Training is an investment, it can give dividends only if it is properly designed. Training is the well-articulated effort to promote competence in the employees by imparting professional knowledge. The study found that the present facilities for the training of municipal employees are grossly inadequate.

At present there are only two employees in the Proddatur municipality who have undergone training, one at Eluru, and the other in the All India Institute of Local-self Government, Mumbai. But the remaining staff have not been exposed to any training. It is the duty of the State government to provide training facilities at frequent intervals for all the employees, to enable them to work efficiently in a fast changing technological world.

6. *Problem Relating to Disciplinary Action*

The powers of the Proddatur council and the Commissioner to take disciplinary action against erring employees have been taken away by the Directorate at the State level. Now the Commissioner can only suspend them and initiate proceedings against them. The final action depends on the Heads of Departments in the Directorate. This results in lessening the Commissioner's control over the staff under him and he is unable to make them work properly. This has given rise to political interference which always obstructs smooth administration. Unless the Commissioner and the council are empowered to punish the delinquents, not arbitrarily but after proper inquiry, better work cannot be expected from the employees. This can be done if the commissioner is endowed with the power to take disciplinary action.

7. *Problem Relating to Provincialization of Municipal Services*

Another problem pertaining to municipal staff is the need to introduce provincialization of their services on par with the Panchayat Raj employees. The municipal employees from time to time, *i.e.* in 1989 and 1993 went on strike to get their services provincialised in order to improve their conditions of service. It has been observed that for months together the employees do not get their salaries. It is a frustrating and most disheartening experience for the staff. Under the circumstance how can they be expected to discharge their duties sincerely and effectively?

Since the issue involves both administrative and human considerations, it is necessary that the authorities concerned at the State level recognize the employees' needs and provincialise their services without delay, as there are so many developmental activities to be carried out efficiently and effectively in the municipality.

8. *Problem Relating to Property Tax*

The property tax is an important source of revenue for the municipality and much of its performance depends upon the interest and zeal with which the municipality collects it in time. The average receipts of the Proddatur Municipality are about one crore. There is a slight increase from year to year on account of new assessments. The system of arriving at hypothetical annual rental value was give up and a new system of arriving at the annual rental value based on measurements, type of construction, region, sub-region and use of the building was introduced from 1-10-1993.[5] However, the purpose with which the new system was introduced appears to have been defeated because no systematic and rational procedure has been adopted in notifying the regions in Proddatur to assess the tax properly. For example, the western and eastern side of the Gandhi road have commercial importance in Proddatur but they are included in two different regions where different rates of taxation prevail. Not only that, the town is divided into wards on political grounds rather then on rational considerations based on the taxation rules. No sub-regions have been notified, resulting in heavy recurring loss of revenue. Further there are glaring defects in classifying the regions. For example, a large portion of the residential areas on the west and east of the Gandhi road consist of commercial buildings and have high rental value. The owners of the adjoining residential areas which are distinct from commercial areas, are made to pay tax at the same rates as the owners of commercial areas. The procedure is illogical and incorrect. This anomaly has to be remedied.

A look at the general revision lists of 1993-94 during the field study showed that details noted against the assessments are incomplete. Who prepared the lists and supervised the work is not noted. The lists are not attested by any higher officer and the tax assessments are not certified. The present property tax demands of the municipality is based on the assessment lists prepared in 1993-94. As a result there is a heavy loss of revenue to the municipality under the most important tax item and source of revenue. One cannot but suspect that there has been manipulation by interested parties.

It is therefore, suggested that such type of irregularity is rectified at the earliest, in order that the municipal income goes up and public criticism is avoided.

Another unfortunate problem has come to our notice. It has arisen relating to the implementation of the new property tax rule since 1993. Generally property tax is revised once in five years. But, the State government did not allow the municipality to collect the tax under the new system. But tax according to the new system would be much less than the tax under the old system. As a consequence the town municipality lost nearly half of its property tax revenue.

Conclusion

To sum up: success of a municipal administration and the development activities carried out by municipal bodies depend on the interplay of several factors, such as political will, financial viability, social awareness, environmental conditions, and competent staff committed to municipal development and culture.

Problems and difficulties encountered by our municipalities in a way, reflect the characteristic features of a developing society. All that is required is a strong will on the part of the State Government to act with determination and clothe the municipalities with sufficient powers and funds and provide them with the required expertise. If these prerequisites are met, the Proddatur Municipality can also play a vital role in the planned development of the urban areas in terms of both quantitative and qualitative improvements.

REFERENCES

1. Deva Manikyam K. and Sujatha T.V., 'Administrative implication of 74th Constitutional Amendment Act in Andhra Pradesh [India]' in V.B. Singh, ed. *Revitalized Urban Administration in India,* Klpaz publication, New Delhi, 2002, p. 63.
2. Mukesh P. Mathur., *Municipal Finances in India: Present Status and Future Prospects,* Konrad Adenaur Foundation, Manohar Publications, 1998, New Delhi, p. 41.
3. Vejath, 'Competition', *Current Affairs,* Bandh Publication Bombay, 2002 p. 43.
4. Sreedharan, E. 'Rail-based urban Transport', The *Indian Journal of Public Administration,* July-September, 2001 Volume, XI-VII-No. 3, p. 303.
5. *The Hindu,* October 15th 1993, p. 1.

21

Gender Issues in Global Development

Dr. Lipi Mukhopadhyay

This paper attempts to analyze some of the Socio-Psychological issues in the present global economic restructuring process and their likely impact on gender, employment, human resource development and future prospects. Research studies confirm that women are at a disadvantaged position despite new opportunities and free trade system. According to the UN, seventy percent of the world's poor are women. Noble Laureate, Amartya Sen says -

"Within each community, nationality, and class, the burden of hardship falls disproportionately on women"

Introduction

The word *gender* refers to differences between men and women that are learned. It is not fixed but determined by social and cultural values. This means that gender differences between men and women vary across countries and regions and can be changed by education, policy interventions, media images and opinion leaders.[1] Why gender issues are important phenomena in global situation? The question needs to be looked at from the perspectives of equal opportunity for men and women, negative impact of gender based occupational segregation, and access to fruits of development. First, occupational segregation by sex has an important negative effect on how men see women as well as how women see themselves by reinforcing and perpetuating gender stereotypes. This, in turn, negatively affects women's status and empowerment in terms of mortality and morbidity, poverty and income inequality.

Second, the segregation of men and women into different occupations negatively affects the education and training of future generations.

Third, it has negative effect on labour market *efficiency* and *functioning*. When most women are effectively excluded from most occupations, human resources are wasted and consequently income levels are reduced, as many of the best suited and most skilled people are excluded from working in the occupation where they would be the most productive.

Fourth, it makes *labour market* rigid to respond to change. It is important to note that labour market rigidity in terms of occupations includes not only the exclusion of women from 'male' occupations but also the exclusion of men from 'female' occupations.

Fifth, occupational segregation probably keeps many women out of wage employment altogether. This has link with population growth.

Sixth, Sex segregation is a major *determinant* of male-female wage differentials. Most research findings on male-female wage differentials have confirmed that 'female' occupations have lower pay as compared to 'male' occupations. Some authors even go so far as to say that occupational segregation is mainly of interest as a subject because of its effect on the female-male pay gap.[2]

Seventh, the low pay and incomes for women workers that accompany occupational segregation are becoming an increasingly important *contributor* to poverty and *inequality* in society as a whole.[3]

It is important to keep in mind that a high percentage of households in the world are headed by women and that this percentage is increasing. It is also important to keep in mind that women generally spend a higher proportion of their income on children and family necessities as compared to men.[4]

Gender Theories and Other Explanation

The above phenomena may be understood by gender theories and social conditioning.[5] The basic premise of gender theories is that women's disadvantaged position in the labour market is caused by patriarchy and women's subordinate position in society and the family. In all societies, household work and child care are seen as the main responsibility of women, while men are seen as mainly responsible for bread earning.

This division of responsibilities and patriarchal ordering of society help determine why women tend to accumulate less human capital as compared to men, that is, why female children receive less education than male children, and girls are less likely to pursue fields of study which are relevant for the labour markets such as sciences and crafts.[6] It also explains why women acquire less labour market experience, on average, as compared to men—why many women withdraw from the labour force early.

Gender theory makes a valuable contribution to explaining occupational segregation by sex by pointing out how closely the characteristics of 'female' occupations correspond to typical stereotypes of women and their supposed abilities. Some common female stereotypes; are listed in Table 1.1. These are divided into three categories of stereotypes—Positive, Negative and others.

Positive Stereotypes—Five stereotypes—caring; skill and experience at household—related work; greater manual dexterity; greater honesty; and physical appearance are noted in table 1.1. It would seem logical to hypothesize that these characteristics, if true, would help 'qualify' women for the following types of occupations: nurse, doctor, social workers, teacher, typist, maid, housekeeper, cleaner, cook, waiter, weaver, etc.

Negative Stereotypes—Five negative stereotypes such as disinclination to supervise others; less physical strength; less ability to do science and maths; less willingness to travel; and less willingness to face physical danger and use physical force can be noted in Table 1.1.

Other Stereotypes—Three other stereotypes, such as greater willingness to take orders, greater docility and less likelihood to complain about work or working conditions; less likelihood to join labour unions, greater willingness to do monotonous/repetitive work; and greater willingness to accept lower wages and less need for income and greater interest in working at home are specified in Table 1.1.

These characteristics have a greater influence on the general characteristics typifying 'female' occupations, such as—low pay, high flexibility, low status, less decision-making authority than on qualifying or disqualifying women for particular occupations.

Table 1.1: Common Stereotyped Characteristics of Women and their Expected Effect on Occupational Segregation by Sex

Common stereotyped characteristics of women	*Effect on occupational segregation*	*Examples of typical occupations affected*	*Comments*
Positive			
1. Caring nature	Helps qualify women for occupations where others are cared for, such as children, the ill, older people.	Nurse, Doctor, Ayah, Social worker, Teacher, Midwife	Often felt to be biological (*i.e.* sex difference), because women are mainly responsible for child care in all societies. This is, however, a learned, gender-based difference. Note that occupations which require care but which also require greater authority, such as medical doctor, are often male-dominated.
2. Skill (and experience) at household-related work	Helps qualify women for occupation that are frequently done in the home (almost always by women), often as unpaid household work.	Maid, Housekeeper, Cleaner, Cook, Waiter, Launderer, Hairdresser, Spinner, Sewer, Weaver, Knitter, Tailor/ dressmaker,	Skills easy to learn (therefore, women's greater experience before entering the labour market should not be very important)
3. Greater manual dexterity (especially smaller, nimble fingers)	Helps qualify women for occupations where finger dexterity is important.	Sewer, Knitter, Spinner, Weaver, Tailor/ dressmaker, Typist,	Belief is partly based on: -Biological (sex) difference; and -experience (gender) differences in house before joining the labour market (also see stereotype 2). Skill is easy to learn.

(*Contd.*)

(Contd.)

Common stereotyped characteristics of women	*Effect on occupational segregation*	*Examples of typical occupations affected*	*Comments*
			Occupations often similar to those noted under household-related work activities (see stereotype 2)
4. Greater honesty	Helps qualify women for occupations where money is handled and/or trust is important.	Cashier/bookkeeper, Salesperson, Accountant,	Higher paying and higher status Occupations (such as accountant which is a professional occupation) are often male-dominated.
5. Physical appearance	Helps qualify women for occupations where physical appearance would help attract and/or please customers.	Receptionist, Salesperson, Shop assistant	This advantage is often thought to be combined with a more pleasant and accommodating personality of women (*e.g.* for receptionist or salesperson). Other times, sex appeal is sued to attract male customers (*e.g.* barmaid or prostitute). In certain cultures and countries where public interaction between men and women is frowned upon, this characteristic disqualifies/ excludes women from certain occupations (*e.g.* salespersons in the Middle East).
Other 6. Greater willingness to take orders Greater docility and less likelihood of	General characteristics which help qualify women for occupations and sectors of the economy where working conditions are	Note: These general characteristics (6,7, 8) `qualify' women for many jobs which are low paid, unskilled, unprotected	These stereotypes have been combined because they are similar in that all imply a subservient nature. These are archetypal learned (gender-type) characteristics.

(Contd.)

(*Contd.*)

	Common stereotyped characteristics of women	*Effect on occupational segregation*	*Examples of typical occupations affected*	*Comments*
	complaining about work or working conditions Less likelihood of joining trade unions Greater willingness to do monotonous/ repetitive work	poor, labour laws are not applied (*e.g.* informal sector) and work is routinized.	and repetitious in nature.	
7.	Greater willingness to accept lower wages/Less need for income	General characteristics which help qualify women for low-paid occupations and sectors of the economy.		Often related to (and often justified by) belief that women are secondary earners (*i.e.* not main `breadwinner'). -increase in incidence of female headed households; and -need of many families for multiple incomes. Often implies occupations which are in highly competitive industries, where cost considerations are very important. This often includes export products such as textiles. Low-paid occupations may be partly low paid because they are highly feminized.
8.	Greater interest in working at home	Helps qualify women for occupations and sectors of the economy where work is organized in a home-based `putting out' type of		Home-based work is usually poorly remunerated and often based on piece-work. Home-based work is easy to combine with household/child care.

(*Contd.*)

(*Contd.*)

Common stereotyped characteristics of women	*Effect on occupational segregation*	*Examples of typical occupations affected*	*Comments*
	production system.		`putting out' production system is often set up specifically to make use of the available cheap female labour. Home-based work is increasing in importance.
Negative 9. Disinclination to supervise others	Helps disqualify women for all types of supervisory and managerial occupations.	Manager (general; production; trade, catering and lodging) Supervisor (clerical; sales; production) Government executive officer and administrator Legislative official	This is in many ways the opposite of willingness to take orders (see no. 6). This often affects vertical occupational segregation (with lower level jobs for women)
10. Less Physical (muscular) strength	Helps disqualify women for occupations requiring heavy lifting and/or physical effort.	Construction worker Miner/quarrier Well driller	There is considerable overlap in the physical strength of individual women and men which means that many women are physically capable of doing this work. Becoming less and less important in today's economy.
11. Less able to do science and maths	Helps disqualify women for occupations where high levels of science and maths are required.	Physical scientist (chemist/physicist) Architect Engineer Mathematician Statistician	Gender discrimination here begins in school where girls are discouraged from majoring in maths or science. Some believe that this is a biological (*i.e.* sex) difference. If so, it is a small average difference with a large

(*Contd.*)

(*Contd.*)

Common stereotyped characteristics of women	*Effect on occupational segregation*	*Examples of typical occupations affected*	*Comments*
			overlap in the abilities of individual men and women.
12. Less willing to travel	Helps disqualify women for occupations where considerable travel is required.	Aircraft officer and worker ship officer and worker Transport Equipment driver/operator	Many women are willing to travel, as evidenced by, for example, airline stewardesses (who were originally sought for their physical appearance-see stereotype 5). Many drivers do not travel overnight.
13. Less willing to face physical danger and use physical force	Helps disqualify women for occupations where physical danger is relatively great.	Fire-fighter, Police officer, Security guard, Miner/ Quarrier	This is a learned gender difference. Many women are willing to do these occupations.

Notes: Many of these stereotypes overlap in their effects. While some stereotypes help reinforce sex segregation of particular occupations (*e.g.* greater manual dexterity and skill at household-type work for sewer), the effects of other stereotypes counterbalance each other (*e.g.* physical appearance and disinclination to supervise others for sales supervisors). Almost all examples of occupations are taken from two-and three digit ISCO-68 occupational classifications. Bidi maker (local Indian cigarette), which is the largest non-agricultural occupation for women in India according to 1981 census data, is almost exclusively a home-based industry.

Source: Author's impressions and Anker and Hein (1985; 1986).

That Sex Stereotyping plays an important role in affecting occupational segregation by sex is established in empirical studies carried out by ILO in several countries including India. In those surveys employers were directly asked whether they preferred men or women for certain occupations and types of work. Despite the direct nature of these questions, many employers indicated that a person's sex is an important characteristic affecting hiring and promoting decisions. In Lucknow, UP, roughly 60 per cent of the employers interviewed reported that women were unsuitable or less suitable than men for sales, production, service and executive/supervisory occupations.[7] It seems reasonable to assume that responses admitting sex bias represent only the tip of the iceberg.

In addition to female stereotypes, there are also masculine stereotypes which play a role in determining what are typical 'male' occupations, such as engineer, police officer, construction worker, truck driver, etc.

Hostile and Benevolent Ideology

Hostile and Benevolent sexism as complementary justifications for gender inequality was found in a 19 nations' study. It is found that benevolent sexism—a subjectively favourable, chivalrous ideology that offers protection and affection to women who embrace conventional roles coexists with hostile sexism, that is, antipathy toward women who are viewed as usurping men's power.[8] It is further pointed out that the favorable communal traits ascribed to women as nurturing, helpful and warm, suit them for domestic roles, whereas men are presumed to possess the traits associated with competence at high-status roles, like—independent, ambitious and competitive. Women's stereotypically communal attributes are also the traits of deference that, when enacted to daily interaction, place a person in a subordinate, less powerful position.[9] Thus, the favourable traits attributed to women may reinforce women's lower status. Jackman (1994), in her persuasive analysis of race, class and gender relations, argued that subordination and affection, far from being mutually exclusive, often go hand in hand.[10] Dominant groups prefer to act warmly toward subordinates, offering them patronizing affection as a reward for "knowing their place" rather than rebelling. Open antagonism is reserved for subordinates who fail to defer or who question existing social inequalities.[11]

In another study participants were asked to evaluate two specific female types, non-traditional (career women) and the traditional (housewives). The study revealed that men's hostile sexism scores uniquely predicted negative attitudes toward career women, whereas their benevolent sexism scores predicted positive attitudes toward housewives.[12]

These results suggest that hostile and benevolent sexism can be simultaneously endorsed because they are directed at different female subtypes. The complementarity of these ideologies stems from how women are split into 'good' and 'bad' types. Women who fulfill conventional gender roles that serve men are placed on a pedestal and rewarded with benevolent/solicitude, whereas women who reject conventional gender roles or attempt to *usurp* male power are rejected and punished with hostile sexism.

Dynamics of Global Forces

Globalisation is accentuated by the increased mobility of capital, technology, skills and human resources. Concern for the adverse effects of trade liberalisation on poverty and income distribution is not confined to humanitarian reasons alone. A key factor underlying this phenomenon has been increasing inequality between unskilled and skilled workers in terms of income and/or employment opportunities.

Major components of global development are:

- Global interdependence in goods and services,
- Widening horizons of transnationals (TNCs),
- Cross-border technology transfers,
- Freer mobility of capital.

Globalization has been a potential source of social inequity. Technological progress has led to the automation of many of the tasks previously undertaken by unskilled workers in the industrialized countries. Studies have shown that in particular, trade openness tends to result in equal income distributions in more skill-intensive countries than in land and capital-intensive countries. Such findings may also emerge from the fact that agriculture is land intensive while manufacturing is skill-intensive.

Trade liberalization would promote growth in income, but would often result in increased income inequality. A vicious cycle would set in from growth: engendered by globalisation (openness); moving over to inequality; and then from inequality to poor growth performance; passing through a high level of political instability and aggregate consumption or a low level of basic education/ health, and trade openness, or all of above; and finally from poor growth to further inequality.

Global Forces in Employment of Women

Globally, most women are crowded into a handful of occupations with little potential for advancement. According to one cross-national study of 25 industrial countries, on the average, women are over-represented in professional, clerical, sales and service occupations, and substantially under-represented in managerial and production jobs.[13]

Global economic restructuring seems to be expanding the number of home workers. Home workers are mostly women and are low paid. According to ILO women make up at least 80 per cent of home workers globally. It is noted by an UN source that the jobs which are held almost exclusively by women are isolated from the organisation, offer minimal opportunities for advancement, and little development of skills through formal or informal learning process.[14] In the garment industry in Delhi, home workers on piece work have been found to earn half the minimum wage.

The proportion of the workforce working part-time increased in the 1980s as against full-time employment. There are more than 50 million part-time workers in the industrialised market economies alone and most of them are women.[15] Global economic restructuring has entailed increasing utilisation of female labour in formal and non-regular employment. The growth of export-oriented industries and the trend towards flexibility in employment may be seen as a one-sided management strategy. Job insecurity reduces job satisfaction, commitment and involvement and is demotivating.[16]

Therefore, public policies are needed to protect part-time

workers and home workers. Social safety nets are necessary not only to protect the losers of the liberalization policies, but also to help implement the liberalization policies themselves and other complementary adjustment programs. Without social harmony and cohesion, those programs would face serious opposition and challenges, and consequently growth will be undermined.

When a society is not well equipped with social safety nets for its people, corporate structural adjustment, for example, becomes a very controversial issue and suffers setbacks due to reactions from labor unions and those most vulnerable to the layoffs.

Recently there has been a number of anti-globalization demonstrations led by international NGOs at international organisations' general assembly meetings, such as those of the IMF and WTO. Demonstrators assert that globalization widens the gap between rich and poor countries. On this issue, the Organisation for Economic Co-operation and Development (OECD) has recently issued a paper stating that globalization would bring benefits to some countries and suffering to others.[17] Thus, generalizing the effect of globalization is difficult, but it should be realized that a certain country or certain stratum within a country suffers from globalization.

Conclusion

From the above discussion on gender based employment, pay and working condition it is clear that global economic restructuring has entailed increasing utilisation of female labour in formal and non-regular employment. It is, therefore, important to note that if *deskilling* and downgrading of jobs is the dominant process of global economic restructuring, then supply-side policies that emphasize education and training will not change the growth in low-skill, low wage jobs, though they may alleviate the plight of some workers at the very bottom. This suggests that the situation calls for changing the course of economic restructuring. Subsequently steps can be taken to eliminate exploitative work practices, enforce the basic ILO conventions, and improve women's labour market positions, including their ability to combine productive and reproductive activities. It is also true that throughout the world women have sought employment in the public sector for its affirmative action policies, generous benefits and implementation of labour codes. The role of governance is immense in this regard. The primary task of Government along with NGOs and civil societies, is to organise various diverse groups and agencies in social safety nets ensuring their full participation and cooperation. Involvement of diverse agencies in the implementation process is an effective alternative. The local government should be the leading agency to coordinate and control various programs.

However, participation by local organisations in the design and implementation process is one sure way to ensure that resources are used effectively, efficiently, equitably, and in keeping with local needs, whether it is watershed, Joint Forest Management (JFM) or Tribal development. Civil societies in order to address corruption, lack of transparency and leakage of funds need to participate as 'Watchdogs' in the entire decision-making process of social safety net design and delivery. They should be trained in best practices and problem-solving through practical hands on exercises.

REFERENCES

1. Anker Richard, 1998, *Gender and Jobs,* ILO, p. 9.
2. Jacobs, J., 1989, "Long-term Trends in Occupational Segregation by Sex", in *American Journal of Sociology* (Chicago), Vol. 95 No. 1, pp. 160-73.
3. Anker, R., 1995, "Labour Market Policies, Vulnerable Groups and Poverty", in H. Figueiredo and Z. Shaheed (eds.), *New Approaches to Poverty Analysis and Policy*-II (Geneva: International Institute for Labour Studies).
4. Mason Oppenheim, K., 1995, *Gender and Demographic Change* (Liege, IUSSP).
5. Mukhopadhyay, Lipi, 2002, "Social Conditioning and Deviant Behaviour", *Indian Journal of Public Administration,* Vol. XLVIII, No. 3.
6. Anker Richard, 1998, *Gender and Jobs,* ILO, p. 23.
7. Glick, P., and Fiske, S.T. (1996), "The Ambivalent Sexism Inventory: Differentiating hostile and benevolent sexism", *Journal of Personality and Social Psychology,* 70, pp. 491-512.
8. Ridgeway, C. (1992), *Gender, Interaction and Inequality,* New York Springer-Verlag.

9. Jackman, M.R. (1994), *The Velvet Glove: Paternalism and Conflict in Gender, Class, and Race Relations*, Berkeley: University of California Press.
10. Glick, P. & Fiske, S.T. (2001), "An Ambivalent Alliance Hostile and Benevolent Sexism as Complementary Justifications for Gender Inequality", *American Psychologist*, 56, Vol. 2, pp. 109-17.
11. Glick, P., Diebold, J., Bailey-Werner, B., & Zhu, L. (1997), "The Two Faces of Adam: Ambivalent Sexism and Polarised Attitudes Toward Women", *Personality and Social Psychology Bulletin, 23*, pp. 1323-34.
12. Charles, Maria (1992), "Cross-National Variation in Occupational Sex Segregation", *American Sociological Review*, Vol. 57, No. 4, August, pp. 483-502. The quote appears on p. 490.
13. Brenton, P., 2000, *Globalisation and Social Exclusion in the EU: Policy Implications*, Working Document No. 159, The Centre for European Policy Studies.
14. Lee Kye Woo and Park Chanyong, 2002, "Globalisation, Growth, Inequality and Social Safety Nets in APEC Economies", *Asian Development Review*, Vol. 19, No. 2, pp. 47-66.
15. UN (1992), *World Investment Report: Transnational Corporation as Engines of Growth*, United Nations, New York, p. 186.
16. Burchell, B., Day, D., Hudson, M., Lapido, D., Mankelow, R., Nolan, J.P. Reed, H., Wiehert, I.C. and Wilkinson, F., 1999, *Job Insecurity and Work Intensification: Flexibility and the Changing Boundaries of Work*, Work and Opportunity Series, No. 11, York: Joseph Rowntree Foundation.
17. Kohl, R., 2001, *Globalisation and Inequality in Southeast Asia*, COM/DEELSA/CD (2001) 11,OECD Development Centre, Paris.

22

Empowerment of Women

Prof. Shiv Raj Singh

Women constitute about 50 per cent of the world population. As per the world economic profile women contribute 50 per cent of food production, make up 30 per cent of the official labour force and utilize 60 per cent of all working hours, but receive 10 per cent of world income and own less than one per cent of the world property.[1] Now-a-days lot of noise is going on regarding the so-called 'empowerment of women'. Empowering women is not a challenge only to developing nations but in developed nations also.

What is Empowerment of Women?

Empowerment, in its simplest form means the manifestation of redistribution of power that challenges patriarchal ideology and the male dominance. It is both a process and the result of the process. It is transformation of the structures or institutions that reinforce and perpetuate gender discrimination. It is a process that enables women to gain access to, and control, material as well as informational resources. The concept of women's empowerment, throughout the world has its roots in women's movement. It is since the mid 1980s that this term became popular in the field of development. In India, it is the Sixth Five Year Plan (1980-85), which can be taken as a landmark for the cause of women.[2] "That society would be highly developed and prosperous where women have their rightful place". The status of women varies enormously from one part of the world to another. However, nowhere do women enjoy equal status with men. The feminist scholars have now started concentrating their attention on empowerment of women, particularly in political arena. The Western feminist scholars have of late felt that unless women seek share in power and extend their role in politics, they cannot be empowered (Stacey M, 1981).[3] The National Commission for Women (NCW) has also expressed its intention to take steps for women's political empowerment. Mohini Giri, the then Chairperson of the N.C.W. in the foreward to the Commission's report for 1997 wrote, "Women's rights and Women's equality cannot be achieved unless women in large number are visible and active. Gandhiji advocated a better place for women in every sphere of life and said, "As long as women of India do not take part in public life there can be no salvation for the country.[4] Subsequently the Constitution of India conferred equal rights and opportunities to men and women in political, social and economic fields. Also a good number of progressive legislations, policies and programmes relating to various aspects of women's life were enacted/undertaken for their upliftment.

Constitutional and Legal Rights of Women in India

The Constitution of India not only grants equality to women but also empowers the State to adopt measures including positive discrimination in favour of women, neutralizing the cumulative socio-economic, educational and political disadvantages faced by them. Article 14 of our Constitution debars discrimination on the ground of sex. The safeguard is meant to protect the rights and interests of women. There is no dearth of statutory provisions, which have been enacted with this aim. Some of the subjects covered by these legislations are equal remuneration, equal opportunity for employment, protection of women's right to property, suppression of immoral traffic, right to medical termination of pregnancy, prohibition of dowry, and child marriage, deterrent punishment for crimes against women including sati.[5] Article 16 guarantees equality of opportunity in Public Employment. Article 39(a), 39(b), 39(e) and 42 of the Directive Principles of State Policy have far reaching implications for provisions of better working conditions and conditions of work for women workers. The state also imposes a fundamental duty on every citizen to denounce practices derogatory to the dignity of women.

To uphold the constitutional mandate, the State has enacted various legislative measures intended to ensure equal rights, to counter social discrimination and various forms of violence and atrocities and to provide support services especially to workingwomen.

Although all laws are not gender specific, the major provisions affect women significantly. Amendments have been periodically carried out to keep pace with emerging demands. They include, among others, the following.[6]

- The Special Marriage Act, 1954.
- The Hindu Marriage Act, 1955.
- The Hindu Succession Act, 1956.
- The Family Courts Act, 1954.
- The Criminal Law (Amendment) Act, 1983.
- The Immoral Traffic (Prevention) Act, 1986.
- The Dowry Prohibition Act, 1961 (amended in 1984 and 1986).
- The Child Marriage Restraint (Amendment) Act, 1976.
- The Equal Remuneration Act, 1976.
- The Medical Termination of Pregnancy Act, 1971.
- The Indecent Representation of Women (Prohibition Act, 1986).

But all these measures have failed to provide a rightful place for women in society because they were not implemented effectively or even sincerely. At present India ranks the 95th position regarding female empowerment in the world.[7]

Political Empowerment

Thus, political empowerment of women is considered as powerful and indispensable weapon for their upliftment and providing them a status equal with men. The Narsimha Rao Government took the first concrete step for empowering women when 73rd and 74th Constitutional Amendment reserving 33 per cent seats for them in rural and urban local bodies were passed. Now the women organizations are demanding reservation of seats for women in legislatures on the pattern of local bodies. These efforts culminated in the introduction of 81st Constitutional Amendment Bill, 1996.

Since then the bill has been tabled many a time in the Parliament but without any result.[8]

While some thinkers believe that political empowerment can change the whole course of women's life in the society, others are of the opinion that mere political empowerment at the level of family and society is equally or even more essential. In fact, the plight of women in Indian society needs to be studied from different angles. It requires multidimensional approach. Women are not intrinsically inferior to men in any matter. In the highest civil service and other competitive examinations, women do much better both qualitatively and also in quantitative percentage terms.[9] But demand for reservation may appear to be an acceptance of inferiority or inability to compete or unwillingness to fight it out. According to one view, reservations are like crutches necessary and useful only for a temporary period of disability. Nobody should like to have a permanent stigma of inability. Even otherwise power does not come from reservation, power will come from education, from developing inner-strength from economic independence and from open competition at the ground level.[10] Women are capable enough to compete and prove themselves more than equal if, they have the opportunity and for that, the first priority is the education of the girl child. For, as Mahatma Gandhi stated: "If you educate a man, you educate only one person. But if you educate a woman, you educate a whole family". The question is, are we thinking of common women of India and their problems? Do we want to help them and ameliorate their miseries and hardships or, are we only looking at the ambitious among them- 'women of influence and power'? The overwhelming majority of Indian women are poor, illiterate and they have neither influence nor power.[11]

Although the year 2001 was declared as Women's Empowerment Year by the international community and since 2002, March 8 will be celebrated as Women's Day every year, this is not sufficient. It requires consistent hard work for changing our attitudes such as men sharing with women the domestic responsibility. Although the National Commission for Women is working hard to protect the women's interest both at domestic level and outside yet concrete steps are required to encourage participation, involvement of women in the day to day life. The primary challenge facing women today, therefore, is to increase their participation so that they get hold of the situation and become actively involved in the process of decision making.[12]

Male domination and gender discrimination in the form of child marriages, dowry demands, wife beating and wife burning, bigamy and polygamy and discrimination in food take, employment, education, health and nutritional facilities are some of the things which need immediate attention as new understanding towards empowerment makes it clear that discriminatory behaviour has to go.[13] One thing must be made clear that by empowering women, the society is not doing any disfavour to the male psyche. Infact, it liberates the men more than it liberates the women.

As far as government efforts are concerned, there is no doubt that major initiatives have been taken over the years to improve the lot of women. But at the same time various steps taken by the Centre as well as the State governments to educate women need constant monitoring. Without education gender equality is unthinkable.[14] A famous Chinese saying goes like this–"If you want to plan for a year plant wheat, if you wish to plan for ten years grow trees but if you want to plan for 100 years educate your women."[15] Education must be imparted to inculcate such values in our children as it would make them consider men and women as equal in every sense of the term. Development of women should be treated as a national movement irrespective of political ideology. Women should not remain passive spectators, they should struggle, they should demand and they should fight for their just cause. It should be remembered that howsoever intelligent doctor may be, howsoever effective his medicine may be, he cannot cure the patient unless the patient himself wants to be cured. This applies to women as well. Women are like "the patients" and indiscrimination, inequality and atrocities are the disease that afflict them. Only when women both individually and collectively, sincerely and genuinely want to get rid of this disease can an abiding remedy be found.[16] One of India's greatest poets, Rabindranath Tagore, expressed the pain and inequity of the situation more than half a century ago, thus, "O Lord Why have you not given women the right to conquer her destiny? Why does she have to wait head bowed, by the roadside, waiting with tired patience, hoping for a miracle in the morrow?"[17]

Conclusion

Women constitute the pivot around whom the family, society, rather the whole humanity moves. Their role in directing and shaping the destiny of the nation is crucial. With the advancement in science and technology the world has moved fast. Women have to assume a dynamic role in the changing context. For their participation in national life, it is necessary that women should occupy positions at the decision making and planning levels. The development of women cannot be achieved in isolation. It needs holistic approach.

Three epoch making events of great historical and political significance have taken place in the 20th century in India. They include the 1942 Quit India Movement under the leadership of Mahatma Gandhi, the revolt against the emergency in 1977 led by Jaya Prakash Narain and the passing of 73rd and 74th Constitutional Amendment Acts, in 1993. The Amendments constitute a watershed for the advancement of Indian women since they ensure that 1/3 of the total elected seats and positions of chairpersons in rural and urban local bodies shall be reserved for women. About one million women are estimated to emerge as leaders at the grass roots level in the rural areas alone. Of these 75,000 are to be chairpersons.[18] As Professor C.E.M. Joad justified, we find that getting employment as the sheet-anchor of economic justice for women is extremely difficult. They beg at the door for employment. Will it not be in the fitness of things to establish exclusive Employment Exchanges for them, the more so as 30 per cent reservation in legislatures for them is on the cards? If this is done, the battle is more than half won. This will draw the attention of all concerned.

REFERENCES

1. Satnam Kaur, *Women in Rural Development*, Mittal Publications, Delhi, p. 3.
2. Shanta Kohli Chandra, 'Women and Empowerment', *The Indian Journal of Public Administration* I, Vol. XLIII, Delhi, July-September, 1997, p. 395.
3. R.K.Verma, Manorma Singh, 'Political Empowerment of Women: Role of Voluntary Organisations', *Vidhan Mala*, Jan.-Dec. 2001 Shimla, p. 91.

4. *The Hindustan Times*, New Delhi, December 12, 2000, p. 10.
5. Surinder Singh, 'Safeguarding Women Rights, Sunday Reading', *The Tribune*, November 6, 1988 (iii).
6. Government of India, *Fourth World Conference on Women*, Beijing, 1995, Ministry of Human Resource Development, New Delhi, March 1996, p. 24.
7. S.S. Chahar, Shashikala, 'Political Empowerment of Women: A Study of Their Representation in Haryana State Legislature 1967-2000', *Vidhan Mala*, Shimla, p. 101.
8. *Ibid.*, pp. 102-03.
9. Subhash C. Kashyap, 'Empowerment of Women Through Reservation', in *Vidhan Mala*, Shimla Jan.-Dec., 2001.
10. *Ibid.*
11. *Ibid.*
12. Shanti Kohli Chandra, *op. cit.*, p. 396.
13. *Ibid.*, p. 397.
14. O.C. Sud, 'Empowerment of Women', *Vidhan Mala*, Shimla, Jan-December, 2001, p. 90.
15. Vidhu Mohan, 'Women and Development: A Psycho-Social Perspective' in R.K. Sapru (ed.), *Women and Development*, Ashish Publishing House, New Delhi, 1989, p. 316.
16. Mamta Kaushal, 'Women Development, Strategies, Challenges and Prospects' in Shiv Raj Singh, P.P.S. Gill, S.S. Chauhan, S.K. Mahajan (eds.), *Public Administration in the New Millennium Challenges & Prospects*, Anamika Publishers, New Delhi, 2003, pp. 306, 308.
17. S.S. Dhaliwal, 'Empowerment of women' in Shiv Raj Singh *et al.* (eds.), *op. cit.*, p. 279.
18. Government of India, *Fourth World Conference on Women*, Beijing, *op. cit.*, p. 2.

23

Women's Empowerment in the Panchayati Raj System: The Case of Orissa

Dr. Sangita Dhal

Prior to 1993,women had very little space in the political system at the grassroots level. With the introduction of the 73rd Amendment Act, 1993, the upsurge in women's power coupled with their increased participation in political activity has undoubtedly affected the grass roots political process. In the light of the fast changing rural socio-political environment, this micro level empirical study was under taken to explore the ongoing transformation in the rural society with increasing participation of women in the political arena. The aim of the research study is to get an insight into the nature, role and extent of participation of the newly elected women Panchayat members in Orissa's rural local self-government.

Introduction

The present paper portrays the findings of an empirical study on the impact of the 73rd Amendment on the rural socio-political environment, and the processes that it has generated in the two sample districts of Jajpur (progressive) and Keonjhar (backward) in the State of Orissa which, despite being a poor and a backward state is at the threshold of transition. With the institution of the Palli Sabha working well Orissa has been a pioneering state in the field of democratic decentralization.[1] The state has also taken concrete steps to ensure gender justice. Orissa is one of the few states, which implemented the proposed one-third reservation of seats for women in panchayat bodies as early as in 1992, when other states were still considering the issue.

Women in Orissa were 'politically dormant' for a long time due to socio-economic constraints that deprived them of equal status and basic human rights to participate in the political processes despite constituting nearly 50 per cent of the population.[2] Women's assertion of their rights and equality is a recent phenomenon that has been guaranteed by the 73rd Amendment. Thus, women's presence in the panchayat bodies has heralded the ascent of more than 30,000 women members to political positions in the length and breadth of rural Orissa, where the traditional mindset is against the participation of women in the government and development processes.

Objectives of the Study

The focal point of our enquiry has been the new panchayati raj system (Post-73rd Constitutaional Amendment), women's role in it, and the changes that have come about in the wake of devolution of power. In specific terms the study seeks to:

- gather a broad picture of the socio-economic conditions (literacy, age, poverty) of the respondents and to determine to what extent these factors affect their performance as women members of the three tier Panchayati Raj Institutions (PRIs),
- to identify the problems/difficulties faced by women representatives of the panchayat bodies,
- to find out the impact, if any, of the progressive or backward nature of the sample area (village, block and district) on the extent and nature of women's participation in the PRIs.

The study hypothesises that women's participation in the PRIs (*i*) will ensure their empowerment on the one hand and on the other, enhance the letter and spirit of grassroot democracy; (*ii*) their meaningful involvement in PRIs will accelerate socio-economic development of and the village, block and district concerned and therefore, the State; and (*iii*) it will enhance their status in the society as equal partners in governance.

Sample of the Study

The study was conducted in two sample districts of Orissa, viz. Jajpur (progressive) and Keonjhar (backward). Field investigation was carried out in two sample blocks-Jajpur (Jajpur district) and Ghatagoan (Keonjhar district). The four sample villages selected are Jahanpur and Chattis Debira from Jajpur block of Jajpur district and the villages of Uperdiha and Balipokhari from Ghatagoan block of Keonjhar district.

Rationale for Selection of the Sample Villages

- There is a marked cultural difference between the four villages. While Jahanpur and Chattisdebira (Jajpur block) reflect the cultural practices of the mainstream Oriya community, Uperdiha and Balipokhari villages (Ghatagaon block) exhibit predominately the tribal culture.
- All four villages reveal different development levels. The pace of development, the level of awareness and number of development programmes implemented, reveal considerable differences from village to village.
- The office of the Sarpanch in the above four village panchayats is reserved for women candidates—Jahanpur for general women candidate, Chattisdebira for Schedule Caste women, Uperdiha for Scheduled Tribe women candidate and Balipokhari for Other Backward Caste women.

Methodology

We adopted the Social Survey Method to collect primary data through field investigations which were carried out in two phases for a fortnight each in October 2000 and December 2000. Individual case studies of the panchayat members were recorded by conducting personal interview and probing into various aspects of their achievements and constraints. The field investigation was conducted by administering a detailed questionnaire and through personal interview. The main tool of data collection was the carefully prepared questionnaire for the various categories of sample respondents who included:

- Women panchayat members of the sample village, block and district;
- Male representatives of the sample village, block and district panchayats;
- General Public from the sample area; and
- Administrative Officials of the sample villages, blocks and districts.

The primary data was collected personally from 100 persons residing in four villages of two blocks of the two sample districts. At the initial stage of establishing rapport, various rounds of formal and informal meetings were held with the different categories of respondents.

Sample Districts: A Comparison

Overall comparison of the two districts shows that Jajpur has an edge over Keonjhar district in terms of socio-economic development, political modernization, literacy level, and availability of infrastructural services.

Table 1.1: Basic Infrastructure Services in the Sample Districts

Name of Districts	*Jajpur*	*Keonjhar*
No. of Primary Schools (Enrolment '000)	1516 (275)	1807 (207)
No. of Secondary Schools (Enrolment '000)	399 (74)	385 (49)
No. of Colleges (Enrolment '000)	50 (27)	47 (20)
Primary Health Centres	54	57
Veterinary Hospitals	19	23
Beds in Hospitals	223	502
No. of Post-offices	302	443
No. of Commercial Banks	82	87
No. of Railway Stations	11	4
per cent of Villages Electrified	91.73	82.14
per cent of Male Literacy Rate (2001 census)	82.69	61.45
per cent of Female Literacy Rate (2001 Census)	72.53	46.71

Source: Districts at a Glance, Directorate of Economics and Statistics, Government of Orissa, 1998-99

Provisional Population Totals, Census of India (Orissa), 2001.

As Table 1.1 shows, of the two sample districts Jajpur occupies a better position in terms of basic infrastructure services and facilities and is therefore more progressive and developed than Keonjhar. This lop-sided development between the two districts can be traced to historical and geo-political factors. The backward inland district of which Keonjhar is a part, had come under the rule of feudal lords (Gadajats) whereas the coastal plains to which Jajpur belongs came under the British administration. The prevalence of two different types of administration in the two regions, contributed to the uneven socio-political and economic development in the state. Thus, Keonjhar district despite having vast natural, forest resources, rich mineral deposits and manpower remains underdeveloped.

A comparative analysis of the social structures of the two districts revealed that factors such as factionalism, use of money and muscle power and role of caste had very little significance in the sample district of Keonjhar as compared to the progressive district of Jajpur. Women in the former district enjoyed a greater sense of freedom to take independent decisions in the panchayat bodies due to the egalitarian culture prevalent in the tribal societies. In the latter (Jaipur) society the status given to women is 'relatively' equal as compared to the women in the coastal districts. Women here share a co-equal status with the male members in the family and are the primary earning members of the family. Further dowry system is non-existent, instead there is the practice of bride-wealth that is made at the time of marriage. They are used to extensive travelling, are more mobile and are visible in the weekly markets. In performing their duties the women members have drawn consistent support of their family members and the local people of the village.

Major Findings from the Field Study

Prior to the 73rd Amendment of the Constitution, participation of women at the panchayat level was marginal in both the sample districts-Jajpur, progressive yet dominated by Scheduled Caste population and Keonjhar, a backward and tribal dominated region. However, taking advantage of the one- third reservation provision, a large number of women candidates from the weaker sections have come into the panchayats now. Three panchayat elections

(1992, 1997, 2002) and the one-third reservation of seats for women have ensured their numerical strength in the rural power structure, and women have been physically there, occupying formal positions of power. However, the study revealed that women did not contest for the non-reserved (open) seats, that is to say, had there been no reservation there would have been no women members in the panchayats.

Earlier (prior to 1993), women were not interested in politics but now after two terms, their participation in the political process has enhanced their political consciousness, awareness and empowerment. As a result they are ready to contest again. All this goes to reveal that the elected women members of the panchayats value their new knowledge and their new sense of freedom and their new political status, as representatives of the people which has relatively improved their social status both at home, and outside.

All this has not only broadened the social base of democracy and widened the extent of Women's participation but also given them the opportunity to articulate and express the views of the marginalized sections and the developmental needs of their community. The newly elected women representatives seemed to be holding some kind of a hope for the weaker sections whose voice was being suppressed till now.

Strengthening Women's Participation in Panchayat Activities

A startling revelation of the study is that the panchayati raj system functioned efficiently in the backward district of Keonjhar when compared with the progressive district of Jajpur. The manner in which the developmental activities has been undertaken indicates a relatively success story of panchayat raj in Keonjhar district. According to the block officials in this district, involving women in the grass roots development process has already started yielding positive results. For instance, the district's (Keonjhar) performance in public health drives has improved significantly since last five years (1997-2001) as compared to earlier such efforts by the administration. This proves that women's participation in the PRIs not merely brings about a qualitative change in their own lives but also improves the functioning of public institutions and thereby accelerates development in their area.

That gram sabha meetings were more popular and better attended in the sample district of Keonjhar (83 per cent) than in the progressive district of Jajpur (28 per cent) indicates that economic backwardness is the true motivator for political participation as demonstrated by the sample district of Keonjhar. In other words, people in the backward region feel that through participation in the social, economic and political processes they may be able to bring about speedy development of their region. The field survey revealed that respondents from Jajpur district were of the opinion that often the gram sabha meetings were devoid of purpose and utility.

Moreover in the sample district of Keonjhar the gram sabhas were playing an active role in approving the Action Plans for socio-economic development including identification of beneficiaries of poverty alleviation programmes and monitoring the utilisation of funds by the Panchayats. The awareness and enthusiasm amongst the elected representatives in the sample gram panchayats here was relatively more and they were keen on holding the panchayat meetings regularly on the scheduled dates.

In this study participation of the sample respondents in the process of governance and development was measured through three parameters:

- Electoral participation (contest, vote, campaign, contribution to the party fund).
- Institutional participation (panchayat meetings, attendance, degree of participation).
- Participation in the decision-making process (formulations of plans, debates, discussion, monitoring, suggestions).

The field study revealed that political participation of women panchayat members was more 'intensive' in voting, attending meetings, and campaigning rather than in organizing party meetings, membership drive etc.

Impact of Socio-Economic Background of Respondents on Participation

The findings also revealed that higher castes women hesitate to play an active role in the political process and generally adopt a 'status-quo' approach. This can be attributed to the impact of feudal political mechanisms and the prevailing social structure. On the other hand, women with lower socio-political background adopt an 'aggressive/persuasive' approach and this can be traced to factors like mobility, greater public exposure, and enthusiasm about their new role and eagerness to do justice to the role that has been assigned to them.

Problems of Women Panchayat Members

During the course of the field study it was found out that many women respondents faced a lot of difficulties during their tenure as panchayat members. Their constraints can be divided under the following heads:

- Socio-economic constraint: caste, gender, and poverty;
- Institutional constraint: lack of power, information, and misuse of fund;
- Constraint at the Gram Panchayat Level: non-cooperation from the male colleagues, manuals are in English, etc.

The study establishes that there are essentially five basic factors that are responsible for better performance by the Elected Women Representatives (EWRs) of the PRIs:

- Personal strength/character
- Mobility
- Minimum educational background
- Training
- Support network system (family, rural youth, officials, male colleagues).

Conclusion and Policy Implications

In the light of the above findings, the following suggestions and policy recommendations can be made. In order to make the gram sabha more vibrant for inculcating community spirit and increase political awareness amongst the masses, it is necessary that elected representatives restore peoples' faith in the gram sabha and should make efforts to encourage their attendance in the gram sabha meetings so that people would be able to voice their views. The agenda of the meetings should be of interest to the bulk of its members and cover a wide range of subjects that vitally affect their day-to-day life.

Last but not the least, it is important that coordination meetings between officials and non-officials should be arranged regularly so that transparency is maintained regarding the development projects that are undertaken by the panchayats. The views and recommendations of the gram sabha should be duly incorporated in the planning process at the block and district levels.

In the final analysis, the study has revealed that majority of the women leaders have exhibited their determination to occupy the public space, however, there are hurdles in the process of empowering women. In order to overcome the hurdles and to make the 'empowerment process' sustainable the EWRs need proper orientation, information, counseling and sensitization continuously through civil society organizations, where the women members get an opportunity to interact with other women members and thereby draw support from their presence.

Thus, working against all odds, facing all kinds of adversities these women representatives at the grassroots level seem to be determined and confident enough to realize the cherished goal of equal partnership in governance, progress and development. It is against the backdrop of poverty and exploitation, one has to appreciate the impact of reservation that has elevated rural women from the position of subjugation to that of dignity and authority. Although their journey has not been smooth and trouble-free, nevertheless, the degree of enthusiasm, and sincerity revealed by the Women Panchayat members holds a bright prospect for a truly participative grassroots democracy in the State. The seeds of empowerment have been sown and now it is the responsibility of the civil society, political leadership and the bureaucratic structure to nurture it to blossom.

REFERENCES

1. Both Palli Sabha and Gram Sabha together act as a forum of social audit and thereby keep a check on the elected panchayat representatives, ensuring transparency and accountability in the political system.

2. S. Panda, "Political Empowerment of Women: Case of Orissa PRIs", *Indian Journal of Public Administration,* Vol. XLV, No. 1, Jan-March 1999.
3. Panchayati Raj Department, *Annual Report,* Government of Orissa, Bhubaneshwar, 2000-2001.
4. G. Palanithurai (ed.), *Empowering People; Issues and Solutions,* New Delhi: Kanishka Publishers, 1996
5. R.N. Das, "Panchayati Raj and Women Participation", *N.K. Chaudhary Center for Development Studies,* Bhubaneswar, 1996.
6. *D.S. Bhuria Committee Report of Seventy-Third Amendment Act in the Fifth Scheduled Areas,* Ministry of Rural Department, Government of India.
7. OSCARD: Participation of Women in Panchayati Raj in Orissa: A Status Report (unpubl. manuscript), Regional Institute of Panchayati Raj and Social Work, Bhubaneswar, September 1993.
8. George Mathew, *Panchayati Raj in India: From Legislation to Movement,* New Delhi: Institute of Social Science, 1994.

24

Article 356 and Centre-State Relations in India

Prof. S.S. Tiwana

The frequent imposition of President's rule in different States under Article 356 of the Constitution by the successive Union Governments for partisan ends during the last fifty three years of its operation, not only surcharged the political climate of the country but also generated national debate on the issue whether Article 356 of the Constitution should be retained or not. There are divergent views for obvious political reasons among political parties on the relevance of Article 356 in the context of fragile and fluid coalition politics in the country at large.

Article 356, it is obvious, was inspired by Sections 93 of the Government of India Act, 1935 which provided that if a Governor of a Province was satisfied that a situation has arisen in which the Government of the Province cannot be carded on in accordance with the provisions of the said Act, he could, by proclamation, assume to himself all or any of the powers vested in or exercisable by a provincial body or authority including the Ministry and the Legislature and to discharge those functions in his discretion. The only exception was that under this section, the Governor could not encroach upon the powers of the High Court. (Section 45 conferred a similar power. upon the Governor-General with respect to the Central Government/Central Legislature). It is alleged that the above two provisions were incorporated in the Government of India Act, 1935 to meet certain purposes and exigencies. The 1935 Act contemplated, for the first time, delegation of certain powers of governance to the Ministries formed by Indian political parties and constitution of Legislatures elected, no doubt, on a restricted franchise. The colonial powers were not inclined to trust these Ministries even with limited powers probably in view of the fact that not only the political parties in India were ambiguous regarding entering the Legislatures and Ministries created under the Act but some of them were also proclaiming that even if they entered the Ministries they would try to break the Governments from within. The said sections therefore provided that if at any time, the Governor or Governor-General felt that the Ministry in the Province or at the Centre was not acting in accordance with the provisions of said Act, he could resume their powers and exercise the same in his discretion. (The provisions of the said Act relating to Central Government were not brought into operation partly because of the onset of World War II.)

Even though Article 356 was patterned upon the controversial Section 93 of the Government of India Act, 1935—with this difference that instead of the Governor, the President is vested with the said power—it was yet thought necessary to have it in view of the problems that the Indian Republic was expected to face soon after Independence.[1] The sociopolitical experience of the farmers of the Constitution made them acutely aware that security of the nation and the stability of its polity could not be taken for granted. The road to democracy was not expected to be smooth. The vast difference in social, economic and political life, and the diversity in languages, race and region were expected to present the nascent Republic with many difficult situations. It is interesting to note that with respect to Union Territories, a provision similar to Article 356 has been incorporated in Section 51 of Government of Union Territories Act, enacted in 1963 and that it was indeed invoked on as many as 13 occasions of the Constituent Assembly. Several members like H.N. Kunzru, H.V. Kamath and others strongly opposed the incorporation of Article 356 (draft Article 278) precisely for the reason that it purported to reincarnate an imperial legacy. However these objections were overruled by Dr. Ambedkar with the argument that no provision of any Constitution is immune from abuse as such and that mere possibility of abuse cannot be a ground for not incorporating it. He stated....

> ".....such articles will never be called into operation and that they would remain a dead letter. If at all they are

> brought into operation, I hope the President, who is endowed with these powers, will take proper precautions before actually suspending the administration of the Provinces.[2]

He further added: "I hope the first thing he will do would be to issue a clear warning to a Province that has erred, that things were not happening in the way in which they were intended to happen in the Constitution."[3]

The emergency provisions of the Constitution were introduced at the fag end of the session in the Constituent Assembly and the debate on them was scanty. Hence there was lack of thorough deliberation on the possible mischief that could be caused by abuse of these powers and the extent of damage that could take place due to wide and vague language of the Article. Further making the proclamation of emergency under Article 356 depending on the subjective satisfaction of the President restricted Judicial review machinery through whom the powers under Article 356 are used is the Governor. No debate took place in the Constituent Assembly on the role of Governor in the context of Article 356.

The Government of India Act, 1935 was not designed to govern any Sovereign Democratic Republic. It was designed and enacted by the British Parliament to pacify the militant demand for self-government in a colony by transferring as little as possible of the governmental powers to the Indian hands. The British Government in fact wanted to retain the control and the whip-hand of the British Parliament through the institutions of the Governor and the Governor-General and provisions like those of Section 93 of the Government of India Act 1935. But State Governments now are elected by the people and these should not be made subordinate to the Central Government.

The Indian Constitution is in the process of acquiring a new structure to suit the emerging political requirements of the country. The framework would be characterized as deconcentrated system with central initiative and decentralized structure. Under this dispensation, the Central Government is not only located at New Delhi but in State capitals as well through the institution of Governors who are appointed by the Centre and hold office at its pleasure.

Since Centre creates the States and appoints the Governors, it becomes incumbent on the part of Centre not only to protect any

State against external aggression and internal disturbance but also ensure that the governance of every State is carried out in accordance with the provisions of the Constitution. So the President is empowered to make a proclamation when he is satisfied that the Government of the State cannot be carried out in accordance with the provisions of the Constitution, based either on the report of the Governor or otherwise. By such proclamation, the President may:

(*a*) assume to himself all or any of the functions of the State or of any other authority except the High Court;
(*b*) declare that the powers of the legislature of the State shall be excercisable by or under the authority of the Parliament.

President can also act independently of the Governor's report, in the case of a situation in which the Government of the State cannot be carried out in accordance with constitutional provisions. But the Governor's report generally forms the basis for President's action.

Dr. B.R.Ambedkar justified the inclusion of the word 'otherwise' in Article 356 on the ground that in emergent situations, the President should come into the field from the very beginning and not after the suppression of the Constitution by the Governor as envisaged under Article 188 of the Draft Constitution. Thus Article 356 empowers the President even to act on his own initiative.

In the State of Rajasthan vs. Union of India case, Justice Bhagwati has also conceded that the inclusion of the word 'otherwise' in Article 356 gave the President very drastic powers which, if misused or abused can destroy the constitutional equilibrium between the Union and the States. He says:

Indeed the usual practice is that the President acts under Article 356(1) of the Constitution only on Governor's report. But use of the words 'or otherwise' in (Article 356) shows that President's satisfaction could be based on other material as well. This feature of our Constitution indicates most strikingly the extent to which inroads have been made by it on the federal principles of government.[4]

It is important to note that certain events which were though inconceivable in constitutional terms, have happened under the shelter of the word 'otherwise' in Article 356. State Governments were dismissed without the report of the Governors not for constitutional breakdown, but to suit the convenience of the party in power at the Centre in 1977, 1980 and again in 1991.

The Central Government dismissed the DMK Government in Tamil Nadu on February 13, 1991 without the report of the then Governor, Sardar Surjit Singh Barnala.[5] The Governor of Bihar Mr. Mohd. Yunus Saleem was dismissed because he had earned the displeasure of the Centre for criticizing the imposition of President's rule in Tamil Nadu in an address to the joint session of the Bihar Legislative Assembly and Council. Sardar Surjit Singh Bamala resigned from the post of Governor in protest against his transfer to Bihar. It is alleged that the then ruling party alliance—the Congress (I) and AIADMK felt that Sardar Surjit Singh Barnala was not suited during Presidents rule in Tamil Nadu following his refusal to send a report on the situation in the State.

Whetfher the Power Under Article 356 can be Limited to Non Compliance with the Directions Given Under Article 365

Article 365 expressly provides that "where any State has failed to comply with, or to give effect to, any directions given in the exercise of the executive power of the Union under any of the provisions of this Constitution, it shall be lawful for the President to hold that a situation has arisen in which the Government of the State cannot be carried on in accordance with the provisions of this Constitution". Article 256 casts an obligation upon the States to so exercise their executive power as to ensure compliance with the laws made by Parliament. Article 257 goes further and states that the executive power of the State shall be so exercised as not to impede or prejudice the exercise of the executive power of the Union and that the executive power of the Union shall extend to giving any appropriate directions to ensure the same. Clauses (2) and (3) of Article 257 empower the Union Government to issue executive directions to State with respect to construction and maintenance of means of communication declared in the direction to be of national importance and with respect to railways. It is debatable whether the Union Government can issue executive directions under any other provision of the Constitution but one thing is beyond doubt - the Union Government cannot issue any executive directions to States to comply with any State laws.

True, a substantial non-compliance with the directions issued under Articles 256 and 257 is bound to attract Article 365 and furnish a ground for taking action under it. But it cannot be argued at the same time that "a situation...in which the Government of the State cannot be carried on in accordance with the provisions of this Constitution" cannot arise in any other way. In other words, violation of the provisions of the Constitution can also occur otherwise than by non-compliance with the laws made by Parliament and without trenching upon the executive power of the Union.

Contrary to the expectations of Dr. B.R. Ambedkar, Article 356 has neither remained a dead letter nor has it been sparingly used. Up to October, 2001, President's rule has been imposed more that 107 times.[6] In short, by such a proclamation the Union would assume control over all functions in the State administration except judicial.

The duration of such a proclamation shall ordinarily be for two months. If, however, the proclamation is issued when the House of the People is dissolved or dissolution takes place during the period of two months, the proclamation would cease to operate on the expiry of 30 days from the date on which the House of the People first, met unless the proclamation is approved by Parliament. The two month proclamation can be extended by a resolution passed by both Houses of Parliament for a period of six months at a time, subject to a maximum duration of three years.[7]

By the Forty Second Constitutional Amendment Act, 1976, the President's satisfaction for making of a proclamation under Article 356 had been made immune from judicial reviews. But the Forty Fourth Constitutional Amendment Act of 1978 has removed that fetter, and so the courts can now intervene if the proclamation is malafide or the reasons disclosed for making the proclamation have no reasonable nexus with the "satisfaction of the President". [8]

The Governors have been given discretionary powers with regard to dismissal of State Government with a view to ensure that States remain subordinate to the Centre. This is evident from B.R.Ambedkar's following reply to M.V.Kamath in the Constituent Assembly.

We do not want to vest the President with any discretionary

power because the Provincial Governments are required to work in subordination to the Centre and, therefore, to see that they do act accordingly, it is the Governor who will reserve certain powers to give the President the opportunity to see that the rules under the Provincial Governments are observed."[9]

But Ambedkar was evasive on the question of discretionary powers to the Governor alone when it was initially being given to the President as well. Perhaps he could not convince the strong provincial lobby in the Constituent Assembly, which stood for state autonomy as a federal framework.

Operational Aspect of Article 356

It needs to be remembered that only the spirit of "cooperative federalism" can preserve the balance between the Union and the States and promote the good of the people and not an attitude of dominance or superiority. Under our constitutional system, no single entity can claim superiority. Sovereignty doesn't lie in any one institution or in any one wing of the government. The power of governance is distributed among several organs and institutions—a sine qua non for good governance. Even assuming that Centre has been given certain dominance over the States, that dominance should be used strictly for the purpose intended, and not for some oblique purposes. An unusual and extraordinary power like the one contained in Article 356 cannot be employed for furthering the prospects of a political party or to destabilize a duly elected government and a duly constituted Legislative Assembly. The consequences of such improper use may not be evident immediately, but may become evident and even irreversible in the long run.

However, over the years, the Centre has not always kept in mind the concept of cooperative federalism or the spirit and which the Article 356 was enacted while dealing with the States and has indeed grossly misused the power under Article 356 on many occasions.

The imposition of President's rule in Bihar on February 12, 1999 has revived the old controversy on the retention or deletion of this love-hate child (Article 356) of the Constitution because Centre loves it and the States hate it.[10] Between 1950–1999 Congress party used or rather misused Article 356 the maximum (90 out of

106 times) and other political parties 16 times for promoting partisan ends. Even in its official reply to Sarkaria Commission on Centre-State relations, the Congress party made it clear that it neither wanted any dilution of Article 356 nor its deletion from the Constitution. Table 1 indicates the frequency of use of Article 356 since the operation of our Constitution.

Table 1: Proclamation of President's Rule in the States

Period	*Frequency*
1950-54	3
1955-59	3
1960-64	2
1965-69	7 (7 cases in 1967-69)
1970-74	19
1975-79	21 (9 cases in 1977)
1980-87	19 (9 cases in 1980)
1988-89	4
1990-99	28
Total	106

On several occasions, State Governments were dismissed even when they enjoyed the majority in the Assembly. These cover instances when provisions of Article 356 were invoked to deal with intra-party problems or for considerations not relevant for the purpose of that article. The proclamation of President's rule in Punjab in June, 1951 and in Andhra Pradesh in January 1973 are instances of the use of Article 356 for sorting out intra-party disputes. The imposition of President's rule in Tamil Nadu in 1976 and in Manipur in 1979 were based on maladministration in these States. On some occasions the State Governments were dismissed without giving them an opportunity to prove their strength on the floor of the House. The very instance of S.R. Bommai, who was the Chief Minister of Kanataka, is proof positive of such abuse. In spite of his asking the Governor to allow him to prove his majority within a very short period, on the floor of the Assembly, the Governor did not give him that opportunity and recommended the dismissal of his Ministry. This action of the Governor naturally invited strong condemnation at the hands of the Supreme Court. In as many as 15 cases, where the Ministry resigned, other claimants were not given a chance to form an alternative Government and have majority support tested in the Legislative Assembly. Proclamation of President's rule in Kerala in March, 1965 and in Uttar Pradesh in October, 1970 are examples of denial of an opportunity to other claimants to form a Government.[11]

In 1977, when Janata Party came to power in the Centre, President's rule was imposed in nine States—Haryana, Punjab, Himachal Pradesh, Uttar Pradesh, Bihar, Orissa, West Bengal, Madhya Pradesh and Rajasthan, after their governments were dismissed and again after the Congress party returned to power in 1980, State Governments and Legislative Assemblies in nine States were dismissed /dissolved respectively. The ground on which they were dismissed is identical in both cases, namely, that the elections to the Lok Sabha have disclosed that people have lost their faith in the political parties which were ruling those states. The argument used in 1977 was that in the aforesaid in nine Congress ruled States, the party has almost been totally rejected by the electorate in the elections to Lok Sabha which showed the disenchantment of the people with the Congress Governments in those States. An identical argument was employed in 1980 against the non-Congress parties.

These figures reveal a sharp rise in the incidence of President's rule from 1967 onwards. During the days of one-party dominance (1950-67), President's Rule was used, as a device to manage the transitional problems and a short spell of this was usually effective in restoring stability in the concerned State. But the situation has changed radically after the Fourth General Elections (1967), bringing a major change in the political environment of India by throwing off the monopolistic control of (the twenty years of uninterrupted) Congress rule in India. The country also witnessed for the first time a multi-party Coalition Government in nine States, the fragmentation of political parties and rise of regional parties. President's Rule in this phase of Coalition Government (1967-72) was imposed in as many as 18 instances, mostly to get rid of the non-Congress Governments by the Congress-led Centre.[12]

Though the Congress party during the Nehru era (did not face any serious electoral threat to its dominant position in the States, the Nehru regime used this constitutional instrument (Article 356) to establish the hegemony of the Congress party. Between 1953 and 1964, the Congress-ruled Centre used Article 356 for five times to dismiss non-Congress State Governments (PEPSU in 1953, Kerala in 1956, Andhra Pradesh in 1954, Kerala again in 1959 and Orissa in 1961) though at that time Nehru was personally opposed to bend the rules of the game, he had to accept. The advice of the Congress bosses who were more inclined to capture political power than to care for the niceties of the Constitution.

However, after the demise of Nehru, politics became an act of crisis management for Indira Gandhi. She made the Congress a centralized and regimented party. Both the democratic culture and value system that had existed within the Congress before the 1967 elections virtually collapsed. In the new Congress fashioned by Indira Gandhi, liberal values eroded and there grew an intolerant view of the opposition parties. Systematic efforts were made to destabilize duly elected non-Congress State Governments. The Indira Gandhi regime (1967-84) used/misused Article 356 as many as 71 times as compared to 11 times during the Nehru-Shastri period. This led to the rapid erosion of India's federal system.[13]

The Congress party during the Rajiv Gandhi era initially did not try to destabilize the non-Congress Governments and refrained from using Article 356 to impose President's rule. But this did not last long and he resorted to the old practice in the face of election reverses in Andhra Pradesh, Karnataka, Punjab, Assam, West Bengal, etc. This was reflected in his reply to the opposition sponsored no-confidence motion against his Government on December 9, 1987. He warned that, "if any State Government was found taking an anti-national posture, he would dismiss it regardless of the majority it enjoyed." The seven non-Congress Chief Ministers at that time felt that his observations went against the true federal spirit. This, however, does not obscure the fact that Rajiv Gandhi's use of Article 356 was minimal-only twice, one in Jammu and Kashmir in 1986 and the other in Punjab in 1987.[14]

The Congress party formed its minority Government in 1991 under the leadership of P.V. Narasimha Rao, when a good number of States were under opposition rule. Political compulsion, combined with the maturity of the leadership prevented the use of Article 356, initially but in the wake of the growing Hindutva communal frenzy unleashed by the BJP/VHP-RSS culminating in the demolition of the Babri Masjid in 1992, the Narasimha Rao led Congress Government dismissed the Madhya Pradesh, Rajasthan and Himachal Pradesh BJP-led Governments on the ground of failure of the law and order administration. Instead of fighting a political and ideological battle, the Congress party took the weapon of President's rule to dismiss these BJP-led Governments, thus adding to its record of using Article 356 for partisan ends. Even the report of the Governors of the three States (Madhya Pradesh, Rajasthan and Himachal Pradesh) created suspicion, because the three Governors submitted identical reports within 24 hours which was something unusual. The Governors, in this case, seem to have acted as a tool of the Centre.[15]

After the submission of Sarkaria Commission Report on Centre-State relations, Article 356 has been used or misused 32 times.[16] It was invoked in (*a*) Assam (November 27, 1990—deterioration of the law and order situation); (*b*) Nagaland (April 2, 1992—fluid party position and deteriorating law and order situation); (*c*) Nagaland (August 7, 1998),' (Karnataka—April 21, 1989) and Meghalaya (October 11, 1991)—these three cases are dealt with by the Supreme Court in S.R. Bommai case and held to be totally unconstitutional and unsupportable; (*d*) Bihar (March 28, 1995—as process of election could not be completed and therefore, to facilitate passage of vote on account by Parliament); and U.P. (1996—no clear majority, in election); and (*e*) Tamil Nadu (January 30, 1988—deadlock due to death of Sri M.G. Ramachandran; (*f*) Mizoram (September 7, 1988—defections reduced the Government to minority); (*g*) Jammu and Kashmir (July 18, 1990 due to militancy); (*h*) Karnataka (October 10, 1990—dissensions in the ruling party—floor-crossing); (*i*) Goa (December 14, 1990—Chief Minister resigned consequent upon his disqualification by High Court—No other Government found viable); (*j*) Tamil Nadu (January 30, 1991—alleged LTTE activities); (*k*) Haryana (April 6, 1991—with disqualification of three MLAS, Government lost majority, Ministry refused to face floor-test and recommended dissolution of House); (*l*) Manipur (January 7, 1992—Government lost majority as a result of resignation of certain members);(*m*) Tripura (March 11, 1993—Government resigned—no alternative viable; (*n*) Manipur (December 31, 1993—1000 persons died in controlling Naga-Kuki clashes and continuing violence), (*o*) U.P. (October 18, 1995—Government lost majority—no viable alternative Government in sight); and (*p*) Gujarat 1996—Government reduced to minority due to defections).[17]

It follows from the facts stated above that more often than not power under Article 356 was exercised wrongly. The Supreme Court judgment which came in *Bommai vs. Union of India* case upheld the ruling given in *State of Rajasthan vs. Union of India* that it was competent for the Court to entertain the petition.[18] In the earlier case, the judgement very much circumscribed the scope of investigation which could be done only if the grounds, taken to be the basis of calling for the action (President's rule), were made known by the Government and are alleged to be malafide, extraneous or irrelevant. In *Bommai vs. Union of India*, the Supreme Court ruled that Article 74(2) did not prohibit the Court from enquiring into the facts which formed the basis of the advice made to the President to declare emergency under Article 356 unless the Government took the plea of secrecy which was granted by the Court.[19] The Court held that it was essential on the 'Part of the Government to defend the action, on the ground of facts contained in the advice, and prove that the impugned action did not suffer from any malafide intention but it was germane to the extra-ordinary conditions existing in the State. It would be binding on the Government to produce in the Court all papers and relevant material forming the basis of the advice.

The judgment rejected the perverse philosophy formulated in *Rajasthan vs. Union of India* that the Union Government could dismiss the State Government to have a better coordination and effective implementation of its socioeconomic policies in the perspective of planned development. Another ground taken was that in a democracy, it was quite legitimate to seek more power through the process of elections. In *Bommai vs. Union of India*, Justice Ahmadi stated, "having noticed the nature of federal structure under the Constitution, the possibility of different political parties ruling at the Centre and in one or more States cannot be ruled out. The Constitution clearly permits it. Therefore, the mere defeat of the ruling party at the Centre cannot by itself entitle the newly elected party which comes to power at the Centre to advise the President to dissolve the Assemblies of those States where the party in power is other than the one in power at the Centre. Even if a different political party came to power at the Centre with a thumping majority, there is no ground to hold that, 'a situation has arisen in which the Government of the State cannot be carried on in accordance with the provision of the Constitution' which is the requirement for the exercise of power under Article 356 of the Constitution. Exercising power under the said provision for dissolving the State Legislative Assemblies solely on the ground of a newly elected political party having come to 'power' at the Centre with a sweeping majority would, to say the least, betray intolerance on the part of the Central Government, clearly basing the exercise of power under Article 356(1) on consideration extraneous to the said provision and therefore legally mala fide".[20]

The result has been that since the said decision, the use of Article 356 has drastically come down. Indeed in the year 1999, when the Union Government recommended to the President to dismiss the State Government in Bihar, the President called upon the Union Government to reconsider the matter in the light of the principles enunciated in the said decision. On a reconsideration of the matter, the Union Government withdrew the proposal. We may also refer to yet another decision where the Governor of U.P. chose to dismiss arbitrarily the State Government without allowing the Government to test its majority on the floor of the House. Following the principles enunciated in *S.R. Bommai vs. Union of India*, the Allahabad High Court restored the dismissed Government to its office (*W. P. 7151 of 1998 disposed of on 23 February, 1998*). This decision was not disturbed by the Supreme Court in appeal though it purported to evolve a peculiar kind of floor-test, namely, both the contenders for the office of Chief Minister were asked to test their strength on the floor of the House. The Chief Minister who was dismissed wrongly by the Governor established his majority and continued in office (*A.I.R. 1998 Supreme Court 1998*).

Need for Amending Article 356

There is a urgent need to amend Article 356 to provide for the following:

(*a*) It should be provided that until both Houses of Parliament approve the proclamation issued under Clause (1) of Article 356, the Legislative Assembly cannot be dissolved or kept in animated suspension. If necessary, it can be kept only under animated suspension.

(*b*) Before issuing the proclamation under Clause (1), the

President/the Union Government should indicate to the State government the matters wherein the State Government is not acting in accordance with the provisions of the Constitution and give it a reasonable opportunity of redressing the situation, unless the situation is such that following the above course would not be in the interest of security of State or defence of the country.

(*c*) Once a proclamation is issued, it should not be permissible to withdraw it and issue another proclamation to the same effect with a view to circumvent the requirement in Clause (3). Even if a proclamation is substituted by another proclamation, the period prescribed in Clause (3) should be calculated from the date of the first proclamation.

(*d*) The proclamation must contain (by way of annexure) the circumstances and the grounds upon which the President is satisfied that a situation has arisen where the Government of the State cannot be carried on in accordance with the provisions of the Constitution. Further, if the Legislative Assembly is sought to be kept under animated suspension or dissolved, reasons for such course of action should also be stated in the appropriate proclamation.

(*e*) Whether a Ministry in a State has lost the confidence of the Legislative Assembly or not, should be decided only on the floor of the Assembly and nowhere else. If necessary, the Union Government should take necessary steps to enable the Legislative Assembly to meet and freely transact its business. The Governors should not be allowed to dismiss the Ministry so long as it enjoys the confidence of the House. The Governor should dismiss the State Government only where a Chief Minister refuses to resign after his Ministry is defeated on a motion of no-confidence or lost its majority support.

Recommendations of Sarkaria Commission on Article 356

In 1983, the Government of India appointed a Commission on Centre-State Relations headed by Justice R.S. Sarkaria to examine and review the existing arrangements of the Centre-State relations in all spheres, and to suggest changes and measures appropriate for the smooth functioning of the Centre Centre-State relations.[21] The Commission after examining various aspects of Centre-State relations in India gave the following recommendations to prevent the misuse of Article 356.

(*a*) Article 356 should be used very sparingly, in extreme cases, as a measure of last resort, when all available alternatives fail to prevent or rectify a breakdown of Constitutional machinery in the State. All attempts should be made to resolve the crisis at the State level before taking recourse to the provisions of Article 356

(*b*) A warning should be issued to the errant State, in specific terms, that it is not carrying on the Government of the State in accordance with the Constitution. Before taking action under Article 356, any explanation received from the State should be taken into account. However, this may not be possible in a situation when not taking immediate action would lead to disastrous consequences.

(*c*) When an 'external aggression' or 'internal disturbance' paralyses the State administration creating a situation drifting towards a potential breakdown of the constitutional machinery of the State, all alternative courses available to the Union for discharging its paramount responsibility under Article 355 should be exhausted to contain the situation.

(*d*) In a situation of political breakdown, the Governor should explore all possibilities of having a Government enjoying majority support in the Assembly. If it is not possible for such a Government to be installed and if fresh elections can be held without avoidable delay, he should ask the outgoing Ministry, if there is one, to continue as a Caretaker Government provided the Ministry was defeated solely on a major policy issue unconnected with any allegations of maladministration or corruption and is agreeable to continue. The Governor should, then, dissolve the Legislative Assembly, leaving the resolution of the constitutional crisis to the electorate. During the interim period, the Caretaker Government should be allowed to function. As a matter of convention, the Caretaker Government should merely carry on the routine work of the Government and desist from taking any major policy decision If the important ingredients described above are absent, it would not be proper for the Governor to dissolve the Assembly and install a Caretaker Government. The Governor should recommend proclamation of President's rule without dissolving the Assembly.

(*e*) Every proclamation should be placed before each House of Parliament at the earliest, in any case before the expiry of the two months period contemplated in Clause (3) of Article 356.

(*f*) The State Legislative Assembly should not be dissolved either by the Governor or the President before the proclamation issued under Article 356 (1) has been laid before Parliament and it has had an opportunity to consider it. Article 356 should be suitably amended to ensure this.

(*g*) Safeguards corresponding, in principle, to Clauses (7) and (8) of Article 352 should be incorporated in Article 356 to enable Parliament to review continuance in force of a proclamation.

(*h*) To make the remedy of Judicial review on the ground of malafides a little more meaningful, it should be provided, through an appropriate amendment, that, notwithstanding anything in Clause (2) of Article 74 of the Constitution, the material facts and grounds on which Article 356(1) is invoked should be made an integral part of the proclamation issued under that Article. This will also make the control of Parliament over the exercise of this power by the Union Executive, more effective.

(*i*) Normally, the President is moved to action under Article 356 on the report of the Governor. The report of the Governor is placed before each House of Parliament. Such a report should be a "speaking document" containing a precise and clear statement of all material facts and grounds on the basis of which the President may satisfy himself as to the existence or otherwise of the situation contemplated in Article 356.

(*j*) The Governor's report, on the basis of which a

proclamation under Article 356 (1) is issued, should be given wide publicity in all the media. Normally, President's rule in a State should be proclaimed on the basis of the Governor's report under Article 356 (1). In Clause (5) of Article 356, the word 'and' occurring between Sub-Clauses (a) and (b) should be substituted by 'or'.[22]

The Srinagar Conclave of Inter-state Council

Also meeting of Inter-State Council was held on August 27-28, 2003 at Srinagar. It reported to have arrived at a consensus inter-alia on preventing the misuse of Article 356. It took a quantum leap forward on evolving path of co-operative federalism.[23] Sarkaria Commission apart, all decisions taken by the Council at Srinagar actually echoed the spirit of the report of the National Commission to Review the Working of the Constitution (NCRWC). The Commission in its report submitted in March 2002 clearly recommended "Article 356 should not be deleted. But it must be used sparingly and only as a remedy of the last resort and after exhausting action under other Article like 256, 257 and 355."

Subhash C. Kashyap held the opinion that Article 356 should be read with Articles 355, 256, 353 and 365. This is usually not done. Insofar as Article 355 speaks of the duty of the Union to ensure that Government of every State is carried on in accordance with the provisions of the Constitution, it is obvious that Article 356 is not the only one to take care of a situation of failure of constitutional machinery. The Union can also act under Article 355 *i.e.* without imposing President's rule in a matter of "external aggression" or "internal disturbance". Article 355 can stand on its own.

Also, the Union Government can issue certain directions under Articles 256, 257 and 353. It is true that Article 356 clearly authorises the President to issue a proclamation imposing President's rule in a State "if he is satisfied that a situation has arisen in which the Government of the State cannot be carried on in accordance with the provisions of this Constitution" but a question may be asked when can the President lawfully hold that such a situation has actually arisen? A very specific and categorical answer is already contained in Article 365 when it says that where a State fails to comply with Union directions (under Articles 256, 257 and others) "it shall be lawful for the President to hold that a situation has arisen in which the Government of the State cannot be carried on in accordance with the provisions of this Constitution".

It is unfortunate that before rushing to issue proclamations under Article 356, no efforts were ever made to ensure that

(*a*) the Union had done all that it could do in discharge of its duty under Article 355;
(*b*) that necessary directions were issued by the Union under Articles 256, 257 etc.;
(*c*) and that the State had "failed to comply with, or give effect to" directions of the Union.[24]

The Inter-State Council has admitted (*i*) that all proclamations under Article 356 were so far issued without taking Article 365 into consideration and (*ii*) that till date, the Union Government had never issued directions under Article 256 and 257 as the mandated pre-conditions for imposition of President's rule under Article 356 read with 365.

Regarding the 'emergency provisions', the Council observed that the safeguards contained in the Bommai judgment, which have already become the law of the land, are adequate to prevent the misuse of the Article 356. The Council directed that 1994 Supreme Court Judgment on in S.R. Bommai case should be incorporated in the Constitution and ask the Centre to move expeditiously in this direction. Having evolved a consensus on controversial Article 356 and 365 along with Article 256 and 257, doors have been opened now for using the forum of the Inter-State Council for discussing larger issues of common and general interest among the States and between the Union and the States.[25]

Conclusion

To conclude, there is a need to review the present disturbing trends developing in the role of Governor. The Constitution must be restored to what its framers intended it to be. Suitable amendments should be made in the Constitution to remove the distortions that have crept in and prevent the abuse of the institution of the Governor in the context of the State relations. It is also suggested that the procedure and method of Governor's appointment should be changed and brought in line with the requirements of the federal-parliamentary system. In addition to it, his discretionary powers, which are unlimited and paradoxical to the parliamentary system should be spelled out and catalogued in articulate terms lest he should have the freedom to act in a lackadaisical way. The suggestions offered above do not go beyond the framework of the Constitution. They do nothing more than to fulfill the clear intent of the farmers of the Constitution. If these are implemented, then the misuse of Article 356 can be prevented.

REFERENCES

1. P.K. Chatterjee, "Retain Article 356 with Suitable Amendments", *Mainstream*, February 21, 1998, p. 17.
2. *Constituent Assembly Debates*, Vol. 9, p. 175.
3. *Ibid.*
4. *State of Rajasthan vs. Union of India*, AIR 1977 SC 1361.
5. *The Hindu*, February 14, 1991, p. 3.
6. *The Tribune*, Chandigarh, August 2, 2002, p. 8.
7. *Constitution of India*, Article 356 Clause (3) and (4).
8. S.K. Jain, "Article 356 and Centre-State Relations", *Mainstream*, April 24, 1993, p. 5.
9. *Constituent Assembly Debates*, Vol. VIII, pp. 473-74.
10. Arun Ghosh, "Article 356 of the Constitution and Bihar Scenario", *Mainstream*, Febuary 20, 1999, p. 3.
11. *A Consultation Paper on Article 356 of the Constitution*, Delhi, National Commission to Review the Constitution, 2000, p. 18.
12. Sandeep Shastri, "Governors and the Federal Polity", *Mainstream*, Delhi, August 13, 1978, p. 8.
13. *Ibid*, p. 9.
14. *Ibid*
15. S.S. Tiwana, "Centre-State Relations in India: A Critique of Governor's Role," *ISDA Journal*, Vol. III, Nos. 3 and 4, Thiruvananthapuram, The Institute for the Study of Developing Areas, September-October and October-December, 1993, pp. 222-39.
16. S.S. Tiwana, "Centre-State Relations in India: A Plea for State Autonomy", *Punjab Journal of Politics*, Vol. XXVII, No. 1, Amritsar, Guru Nanak Dev University, 2002, pp. 1-27.

17. Compiled on the basis of information published in various newspapers.
18. Bommai vs. Union of India, *Judgement Today,* Vol. 2, No. 8, March 21, 1994, SO. 215, pp. 216-24.
19. *Ibid.*
20. *Ibid.*, p. 239.
21. The Sarkaria Commission was formally constituted as per Government of India, Ministry of Home Affairs Notification No. IV/11017/1/83-CSR, June 9, 1983. Subsequently, two more members were inducted, B. Sivaraman was appointed on July 7, 1983 and S.R. Sen on July 27, 1983.
22. *Report of the Commission on Centre-State Relations,* Part-I, Nasik, Government of India Publications, 1988.
23. Satish Misra, "A Move Towards Cooperative Federalism", *The Tribune*, September 6, 2003, p. 13.
24. Subhash C. Kashyap, "There is Consensus on Article 356", *The Tribune,* Chandigarh, September 5, 2003, p. 10.
25. *The Times of India,* Delhi, August 29, 2003, p. 3.

25

Higher Education in India: Policy Issues and Challenges

Dr. Mrs. Yasodha Shanmugasundaram and Dr. Vedagiri Shanmugasundaram

Today we know little about the oldest universities of the world like Nalanda, Taxila and Kancheepuram which produced writers and thinkers of the calibre of Kautilya whose work **Arthasastra** is two thousand years old and **Thirukural**, a Tamil masterpiece authored by the saint-poet Thiruvalluvar is 1,500 years old.

Role of Universities in Development and Nation-Building

The older universities like Oxford and Cambridge in United Kingdom and Sorbonne (f.1253) in France followed the Hamburg tradition evolved from German university system. The university remained aloof from society and this made universities known as the 'ivory towers'. World of knowledge has gone through a sea change in approach, content and method in the last two centuries. The current trend is to place the university as central to society. Social inclusion, wider access, life long learning, new ways of disseminating knowledge are all concepts of higher learning today. Howard Newby, President of the Association of the Chancellors and Principals of United Kingdom, addressing the International Conference on Higher Education for Human Development (New Delhi, Feb. 20-24, 2000) summed up the current status of higher education as—"Not just in case, but just in time, just for you, education".

The Deering Committee which reviewed higher education in the UK in 1997states: "The role of universities is to enable society to maintain an independent understanding of itself and the world".[1] It follows from the above that the present day universities' focus is not the nation but society at large which includes the global world. University teaching crosses national borders. The unique role of the university is as creators of understanding and knowledge. "In a knowledge society many claim the right to help us interpret and understand the world".[2] These claimants are the media, industrial and government research centers and the new breed of corporate universities. All these are not independent of commercial interests. The uniqueness of the university lies in its "individualistic and disinterested nature". understanding implies "going beyond information and knowledge that is acquired with a sense of responsibility not only as generator of knowledge, but also as foundation for action." In short knowledge alone is insufficient. "University education implies an understanding of the nature of knowledge".[3]

At the turn of the third millennium the universities face a major Intellectual challenge to come to grips with its social responsibilities. To be more specific, its capacity to: organize the elements of knowledge and community life necessitates a proper perception of human action.

Changing the working population called the labour into human resource is the essence of development. Therefore through activating the social function of knowledge, the university system, has the major task, of transforming the multitudes in the society as human resources to contribute to the development of the economy and society.[4]

Both advanced and developing countries look at the universities, as "holding the key for the economic revitalization of society"[5] in view of the present day need for specialized knowledge and new skills in the production process. It is expected that universities can train and retrain workers to make them more and more skilled and "generate new knowledge and technology"[6] to accelerate production in the context of increasing local and global competition. It should be mentioned, however, universities should not be pushed into becoming one more element in the market system. This seems to be the trend in American universities. Education-industry linkage is important. But turning education itself into an industry misses the important question of the relationship between knowledge and power and the whole question of morality and society.[7]

From the foregoing discussion we sum up the role and significance of higher education as a major social institution to promote development of the total personality of the student community by inculcating in them commitment to promote the development of alts, science and technology, to develop an indigenous capacity to apply it effectively with emphasis on national problems and contribute to the improvement of entire educational system to serve the community.[8]

Higher Education in India

Higher education in India covers only 7 per cent in the relevant age group. In developed countries this figure stood between 20 per cent and 40 per cent in 1980 and has increased dramatically during the 1990s. These figures are important in the Indian context. In a developing country like India, higher education is an instrument of social change and has the important duty of empowering people. There has been a phenomenal increase in higher education in the last 50 years. Universities have increased tenfold, colleges 15-fold, students 30-fold and teachers about 25-fold. At the turn of the century, there were 300 universities and equivalent institutions, 75,000 colleges with 50 lakh students and 2.5 lakh teachers.

Universities on the western model are of relatively recent origin in India compared with their counterparts in the West. The first three universities were established in 1857 at Calcutta, Madras and Bombay. The Punjab University at Lahore (now in Pakistan) was established in 1882 and the University of Allahabad in 1887. Indian higher education, as it developed in the nineteenth century, was obviously influenced by British models. In spite of its alien character, there was large response to the new system in the metropolitan centers between 1857 and 1992, the number of colleges increased from 21 to 172 and number of students from 4500 to 59,000.

In Macaulay's words, the Indian education system was expected to create "a clan who would be interpreters between us (British) and the millions whom we govern, a class of persons

Indian in blood and colour, but English in tastes, in opinion, in morals and intellect, ...who would be consumers of British goods, provide recruits for the subordinate ranks of East India Company civil service and be loyal to the Raj." It is interesting to note that these very universities served as the springboards of nationalist endeavours for freedom from the British at the turn of the next century. A barrister from Britain, M.K. Gandhi is hailed the Father of the Nation. India became a Republic in 1950.

In Independent India, higher education had to serve objectives quite different from those of the colonial period. The obvious need for building up a self-reliant and growth-oriented economy, an integrated nation and a forward-looking egalitarian society was recognized from the initial stages. Higher education was rightly considered to be the major instrument for effecting the modernization of tradition. The linkage between education and development and the creation of a literate and skilled work force were soon recognized by the educational planners. Expansion of elementary education and strengthening higher education, therefore, came to be simultaneously emphasized.

As the largest democracy in the world, India has also the largest education system as well. Modem higher education is nearly 150 years old. From three pioneer universities of Calcutta, Bombay and Madras, it has now grown into nearly 300 universities with "a vast body of highly skilled academic people equipped with scientific and technological capabilities, robust humanist and philosophical thought and creativity."[9]

A Report of the Ministry of Human Resource Development states the aims of universities in India as follows: Improvement of quality through infrastructure development; Creation of new interdisciplinary oriented university; Curriculum, human resources and research development; and Restructuring of courses to bring relevance to societal needs.

Currently stress is on the generation of new knowledge through research and elimination of obsolete curricula and courses in order to make them relevant to modem times. Knowledge and skills provided to students should reflect the needs of employment market. Self-employment takes a higher point in this approach. The basic aim of education is to promote self confidence and inner strength to face new challenges. The importance of human resource development is recognized both in developing and developed nations because of its contribution to economic growth and the self reliance system further creating and developing scientific technologies for global cooperation and coexistence among the people of the world.

The employment and human resource development orientation of higher education is the need of the present day in the context of India, which is described as a "poor developed country". This description comprehends, "The many sophisticated achievements made by the country in the field of science, technology and other related areas."[10] Still for international comparison, India is an LDC (less developed country) in respect to living conditions, economic growth rate and per capita income. This mixed picture of development is also true of the Indian educational system.[11] Some of the higher education institutions in India and their courses compare well to the best in world. At the same time there are innumerable other institutions whose standards are miserably low.

Problems of Higher Education in India

Indian universities are entering the 21st century with a deep crisis facing them. Obsolescence and the growing irrelevance of the curricula form the core of the crisis. There is widespread disillusionment. Still the century old system of teaching is followed in many universities. The lofty function of the university is the advancement of knowledge by encouragement of original research. Even the performance of its mundane function of the teaching is not satisfactory. We recall the aspiration of Pandit Nehru when he addressed the graduates of Allahabad University in 1947: "Universities in India stood for reason, humanism, tolerance, search for truth and adventure of ideas". Inability to provide competent manpower and high quality research and development support are the bane of universities. A good deal of introspection and dynamic changes are called for to reach the essence of Nehru's vision.

Current problems of the universities are their unmanageable numbers, indifferent teaching methods, outdated examination system, disturbed university campuses, diminishing university autonomy, resource inadequacy, inability to provide competent manpower and high quality research and development support.[12]

Arising from the above, university administration has become a gigantic machine resulting in "enormous waste of time and energy".[13]

Academic politics is taking a heavy toll of academic life in higher education. There is utter lack of professionalism. Materialistic motives are uppermost in educational management. Teachers' apathy and resistance to educational reforms have formed into a vicious circle.[14] Teachers' and students' unions are "more eloquent and militant in matters of pay scale and power but have cared little how to make universities a seeking place for creativity."[15] In short "bureaucratization" and "democratization" have eaten into the vitals of the universities. Intellectuals and scientist, bemoan the plight of the universities. But serious effort is not forth coming to improve the situation.

The University Grants Commission sums up the shortcomings of the university system as follows:

1. The objectives of the universities are not clearly defined in most of the Acts.
2. Lack of adequate authority to the vice-chancellor to discharge his responsibility as the principal Executive and Academic officer.
3. Inadequate decentralization of power to directors of institutes, deans of faculties and heads of departments.
4. Rigidities of the board of studies do not allow introduction of new multi-faculty or inter-faculty courses as also redesign courses.
5. Absence of effective machinery for planning and development, monitoring and accreditation of institutions.
6. Poor financial arrangements and over-dependence on the government leading to infringement of autonomy.
7. Proliferation of universities and colleges, especially for general education, which do not prepare for a career.
8. In view of financial crunch it is suggested that the cost of higher education should be increasingly borne by the consumers themselves instead of looking up to the Government for all the support needed. The fear of

privatization on the one hand and increasing levels of commercialization on the other lead to demoralization and escalating of costs.

9. For a long time, the universities and colleges have been offering too many courses of a general nature, repeating the same curricula over long periods without any appreciation of the changing needs of the society and the economy.
10. Lack of accountability breeds irrelevance and mediocrity. An assessment of the performance of the universities and institutions of higher education must be made in terms of the objectives set forth for them.[16]

It should be noted however, that resource allocation for higher education is not generous even in developed countries. It was already pointed out only 6 per cent of the age group 18-24 are in higher education in India. It was 15 per cent in the UK and 25 per cent in the USA. The same figures for other countries were: Germany 20 per cent, Italy 18 per cent, Japan 21 per cent and Netherlands 22 per cent in 1980s. In USA 2.5 per cent of the GNP is the expenditure of higher education whereas in the LJK it is only 1.1 per cent.[17] Educational planners have been urging the Government of India even as early as 1960 to allocate 6 per cent of the ODP on education. Today it remains at a little over 3 per cent of ODP; this is for entire education. The outcome is obvious. The US is proud that "America is the place where a citizen has the best chance of access to a university. But the British philosophy of higher education was that 'university places should be available to a small percentages of population.'[18] In essence the importance given to the sector of higher education is declining in India as against the case in developing countries. This almost amounts to the dismantling of the higher education system.[19] It is more appropriate to state that funding of higher education is sought to be reduced because quite justifiably starting from primary education, education up to the school level appears to be state propriety. The appalling high rate of illiteracy has to be tackled with great urgency. Resource allocation for higher education from state funds will have to be restrained in increasing degree in future.

Educational Policy In India

The Constitution of India is committed to the ideal of education to all. It set the time limit to reach the goal of universal literacy at 10 years after independence. Woefully none of this was achieved even after 50 years. From the literacy level of 25 per cent for males and 9 per cent for females in 1950,[20] we have moved to the current rate of literacy of 62 per cent (male 64.13 per cent and male 39.29) in 1991. Male-female and urban-rural disparities are persistent. Particularly the dropout rates at school level continues at an alarming rate of 75 per cent at 10th std. Low literacy levels of scheduled caste and scheduled tribes is of great concern. Uneven literacy rates are distributed across the country and across social groups. This defective base of the education pyramid ultimately, results in the low profile of higher education in the country.

As per the recommendation of Radhakrishnan Commission Report (Education Commission Report), the Education Policy of 1968 was adopted. Accordingly, education facilities were expanded and the common structure of education as 10+2+3 has come into vogue (Ten years at high school, two years of higher secondary and three years of graduate course). Yet the general formulation of 1968 policy has not been fully implemented for want of financial support to universities through research projects, sophisticated research facilities and other infrastructural facilities. The educational policy stressed that universities should involve themselves in development issues and become instruments of development in the region concerned.[21]

With regard to girls' and women's education, the national policy on education (1968) envisaged the national system of education to (*i*) play a positive interventionist role in the empowerment of women, (*ii*) contribute towards development of new values through redesigned curricula and textbook, and (*iii*) Women's Studies to be promoted as part of various courses.[22]

It was in this backdrop of low literacy condition at the bottom and a disoriented higher education at the top that the New Education Policy (NEP) was formulated in August 1985 and the Parliament also approved the Programme of Action (POA) in 1986. The Government of India document—*Challenge of Education 1985*—became for basis for the formulation of the National Policy of Education in 1985. The NEP was designed to create a National

System of Education where by all imbalances whereby and disparities are sought to be removed. It brought major changes in education under the Forty Second Constitutional amendment of 1976 which brought higher education from the State List to the Concurrent List. Union and State governments shared thereafter the responsibility of education in all aspects—substantive, administrative and financial. It called for special efforts to bring the educationally disadvantaged viz. SC, ST, minorities, women and handicapped into the educational net. Adult education through functional literacy was made the responsibility of the whole nation.

In the area of elementary education, universal enrolment and retention, along with substantial improvement in the quality of education was envisaged. The non-formal education programme for out of the school children was to be made systematic. The NEP called for an overhaul of the system of planning and management of education. Its concern for the financing of education is noteworthy. It was therefore envisaged that from the Eighth Plan onwards outlay on education should uniformly exceed 6per cent of the National Income.

In sum, the main task of the NEP was to strengthen the base of the education pyramid in order that "those at the top of the pyramid were amongst the best in the world".[23] It stated—'The products of our higher education system have only book learning. They have little capacity for self-study, poor communication skills; a limited world view and practically no sense of responsibility.' The document ends with a cryptic remark that "the whole process of higher education has become warped, disoriented and dysfunctional producing a number of unemployable youth, men and women".

The NEP laid down the following priorities in higher education viz. consolidation and expansion of institutions, development of autonomous colleges and departments, redesigning of courses, training of teachers, strengthening of research, improving efficiency, creation of structures of co-ordination at the state and national levels, mobility, finances, review and monitoring. In respect of most of the above some action has been initiated. But the pace of implementation has been rather slow due to lack of consensus on some important measures such as resource insufficiency, effective monitoring and review mechanism.

In 1989, a Committee reviewed NEP of 1986, and POA with regard to equity, social justice; decentralization of educational rnan4ment, establishment of participatory educational order, inculcation of values indispensable for the creation of an enlightened human society and empowerment of women. In order that the top of the pyramid, higher education, will be the best, the Review Committee gave its recommendations in 1990. This document titled *Towards an Enlightened Society-1990*, made specific recommendations as follows: (*a*) Pressure for opening of new colleges and universities being very intense the government would explore the feasibility of national level statutory mechanism for discouraging non-standard and substandard colleges and universities being started. (*b*) It called for a restructuring of the University Grants Commission. (*c*) The Universities be relieved of the responsibility of holding examination. This has lead to system of autonomous colleges. (*d*) Post graduate education should be supported by adequate research facilities in the concerned subjects. (*e*) with regard to promotion of science and technology, agencies other than the state also must support. Based on the report of Joint Review Committee submitted in 1992 a revised National Education Policy–1992 was approved by the Parliament in May 1992.

The POA of 1992 made certain modification of the POA of 1986. Major outcome of the POA 1992 are the initiating of vocational courses at the degree level, research and studies in emerging and interdisciplinary areas and establishing the National Assessment and Accreditation Council (NAAC) in 1994.[24]

The POA stressed on education as an instrument of empowerment. The meaning of empowerment is spelt out in the POA.[25] The dimensions of empowerment are: (1) Building of positive self-image and self-confidence; (2) Developing ability to think critically; (3) Building up of group cohesion and fostering decision making and action; (4) Ensuring equal participation in bringing about social change and providing the ingredients for economic independence. To sum up, the NEP and POA are the organized policy and instrumental approach respectively to meet the challenges of education.

The need for promoting awareness among the youth for developing and utilizing their full potential for their own betterment and, for national development cannot brook any further delay. In practice we wonder how many of our 'graduates and post-graduates use the skills acquired to achieve their individuality, freedom, self-fulfillment, self-reliance or in short the so much blown up, empowerment'.

Educational Models

Education is the source of knowledge. Universities at the apex of the education system are repositories of knowledge through the varied disciplines in science, humanities and languages. Naturally the specialized knowledge attains the status of power since access to education is limited by social, economic and political factors. To be educated is a privilege and to reach up to higher education is a greater privilege. It gives social status and economic empowerment. Knowledge, therefore, becomes "a positive force in the enhancement of life in society".[26] Knowledge is a double edged weapon. In the absence of moral consciousness of sharing and caring, the same knowledge may become "a source of invidious distinction, oppression and inequality".[27] History is replete with incidents when professionals acted as members of a secret society, keeping the knowledge to themselves without sharing it with ordinary people and particularly the deprived and poor. Robert Dahl remarks that the bargaining strength that is derived from special knowledge, leads to inequalities in resources, strategic positions and is equally a threat to democracy like that arising from inequalities in income and wealth.[28]

In India the distribution of knowledge is highly skewed. Large sections of people are outside the educational system. The male-female gap in literacy and enrolment continues in spite of planned efforts at development. Despite the stark reality of low literacy rate, India is edging into the status of knowledge superpower. The core strength in this respect is in the areas of aerospace, Agri-food, Chemical Process Engineering, Civil and Textile Engineering, Engineering Services, Project Management, System Integration Software, Design of Systems, Intensive Manufacturing, Indigenous Medicine and Entertainment. Natural and human resources of India are responsible for such a strong position. What used to be merely raw material exporters, India is now turning toward value-added products. Information Technology revolution has been highly supportive towards "development of innovative use of multiple technologies with transparent management structure".[29]

India's emergence as knowledge superpower within a decade is a certainty.

The development models of Singapore is an example of such a distinct model. Generation of manpower to the needs of the economy is the responsibility of the educational system. Singapore demonstrated that by introducing computer science at the school level unemployment was brought down to 1per cent. Such streamlining of curricula and fine tuning of students is being taken up in all Asian countries and India in going through educational reform with this perspective.

Human Resource Development And Employment

The concept of university-industry linkage is 'distinct from that of 'education as industry'. The former is to establish a fruitful partnership between university and productive enterprise.[30] Largely the graduates and postgraduates do not have the knowledge and training needed in the job. Industries employing them invariably give on-job training to them. Since the output of the university is the input of industries, a healthy cooperation and interaction between them is essential for the mutual advantage of both sectors. As a social institution education and especially higher education in the present context of knowledge society cannot remain neutral but assume its role as the key component of development. With its potentiality for providing better conditions for life, it is important that science is not divorced from the realm of reality and ethics in particular.

On the realization that human resource is the vital factor in socio-economic development, the Government of India established the Ministry of Human Resource Development in the early eighties. The New Education Policy sums up this approach thus: 'Education is a unique investment in present and future. It should not be possible to further intensify the nation-wide effort in Human Resource Development without the dominant role of education'. Even decades back V.K.R.V. Rao remarked—"Since education is considered an investment leading to economic growth, this is a very good way of getting more funds for education. Many educationists, therefore, started talking of education and economic development to justify the demands for more money for education.[31] For the oft-repeated question—Is education for manpower development or self-fulfillment? The answer is self-fulfillment could be achieved only in an appropriate living condition and therefore manpower development includes within itself self-fulfillment to a large extent.

Teaching, Research and Extension are the three dimensions of higher education institutions Teaching and research find their fruition in the extension dimension where their application can be successfully incorporated towards skill formation, leadership, management and service to community.

Data on unemployment is not readily available with regard to science postgraduates. *The Manpower Profile of Indian Year Book* provides data on unemployment of Engineers. It states that 40 per cent of engineers were unemployed during 1994-95. Keeping in view the G.D.P. growth rate 6.5 1 per cent during 2003-2007, it forecast that 17 per cent of engineers would still be unemployed in 2005.[32] With mushroom growth of self-financed engineering colleges especially in Karnataka and Tamil Nadu, the ratio of unemployed engineers is likely to be higher than the IAMR forecast —above 30 per cent at the least. The above figures are quoted to point out that even the technology based highly professional course like engineering is not able to match the manpower requirements. Then graduates courses which are not quite focussed and of more bookish knowledge have naturally a raw deal in the employment market.[33] Nevertheless, new economic activities could use those footloose technical personnel without dislocating employment market.

Towards the 21st Century: Some Lessons from and to the Rest of the World

Higher education in India is at the cross roads though five decades have passed since its Independence. Its challenges are multifaceted. They are: (*i*) quantitative expansion, (*ii*) linkage between education and employment market, (*iii*) gap between the world of work and knowledge, (*iv*) regional disparities, (*v*) socio-economic basis of educational system, (*vi*) transformation of teaching orientated education into learning oriented education.[34]

Meeting the challenges is a stupendous task before the higher education system, the success of which will depend upon the transformation of the universities as Human Resources for national

Development. The present decline in higher education unless it is reversed will further widen the gap between India and advanced countries.[35]

The President of Romania while addressing the International Conference of University Presidents in Brussels (July 1999) stated that a democratic society is not an abstract society. At the end of the millennium universities should undertake tasks fundamental for the future of mankind: repositioning the man in his distinct role - that of subject as well as an object of social action.[36]

Universities flourish in an atmosphere of freedom and academic autonomy. The principle of separation of finance from management should apply to governments and industries which invest in higher education. In all countries where academic autonomy is respected in theory and practice the social dividend in the nature of better civil society, liberty of thought and belief prevails.

Another area of reform in higher education is student participation. Student evaluation of teaching is feasible in higher education. Accountability is the principle. It may be argued that bias will prevail and the authority of the teachers will be affected. Higher education is a partnership between the taught and teacher.

The basic issue in India is one of attitudinal change on the part of political functionaries who have found illiterate vote banks easier to manage or manipulate than literate citizenry. This is contrary to the concept of democracy, which means rule by the informed citizenry. Illiteracy has resulted in low level of economic development in many countries. Japan's lead in economy is attributed to universal primary education long before Europe attempted it. The role of education will be even greater in the decades to come in the emerging knowledge society. The World Declaration on Education for All (EFA) adopted at the Conference on Education for All which was attended by 155 countries of Jomtien in 1950 under the auspices of the UNDP, UNESCO, UNICEF, stressed the need for expansion of early childhood care, universal access to primary education, improvement in levels of achievement, reduction of adult literacy, expansion of basic education and skill training for the youth, and knowledge of values for better living by individuals and families. These values hold good even to-day.

Indian higher education is in one orbit, nearing high

international standards because of its global links for many centuries. The percolation theory of education is that more higher educated personnel will make universal primary education feasible in terms of supply of teachers. This physical estimate has to be matched by financial and infrastructure resources and motivation for creation of knowledge society, gender equity and respect for freedom of expression and choice of educational streams. All this seems to be in the making. This is the silver line in the otherwise dark cloud—illiteracy, poverty and erosion of democratic values. In the Outline of History, H.G. Wells wrote how human history is a race between education and catastrophe. This is true to day as it was ever before. Higher education is the thinktank of leaders of public opinion, maker of researchers and scholars, teachers of basic and secondary education, and hence in the emerging knowledge society, higher education has priority to an extent never before in earlier epochs of mankind. Education has to be for the good of the individual, society, and the humanity of the present and future.

NOTES

1. *Deering Committee Report*, Ministry of Education, Government of United Kingdom.
2. *Ibid.*
3. John Danial, 'Distance Learning in the Era of Networks', abc Bulletin No. 138, April 1999, pp. 7-8.
4. Emil Constantinescu, 'The 21st Century University: Towards an Ethic of Responsibility', Paper presented at the IAUP Triennial, Brussels, 14-15 July, 1999.
5. Ananta K. Giri, 'Universities and the Horizons of the Future', *University News*, Vol. 13, No. 46, Nov. 13, 1995, p. 1.
6. *Ibid.*, p. 1.
7. *Ibid.*, p. 2.
8. UGC, *Development of Higher Education and Research in Universities*, New Delhi (1980-85).
9. Sacha Joshi and Archana Tomar, 'Initiative for Women Managers in Higher Education', *University News*, 42(9), March 3-9, p. 1. Aims of Universities in India are (Report of MHROD).
10. ANP, Ummerkutty, 'University and Social Transformation in India', *University News*, Monday-July 10, 1995, p. 8.
11. Ashiko Henia, 'Present Higher Education System and Human Resource Development', *International Conference on Higher Education*

for Human Development, New Delhi, Feb. 22-24, 2000 Assn. of Indian Universities, New Delhi in association with the British Council, New Delhi.

12. S.P. Srivastava, 'University Education in India. Current Problems and Future Challenges, *University News*, 37 (18) May 3, 1999, p. 1.
13. Beteille, Andre, *A Career in a Declining Profession*, Minerva, P. 10 and Beteille, Andre, (1992), 'Reclaiming a Public Trust', *Change*, July/August 13-19, 1990.
14. Uberoi, N.K., 'The Fate of Commission and Committees', *Journal of Higher Education*, Vol. 18, No. 13, p. 489.
15. Ananta K. Giri, *op. cit*, p. 7.
16. *Journal of Higher Education*, Vol. 18, No. 44 Autumn 1995, UGC, New Delhi.
17. *International Statistical Comparison in Higher Education*, Department of Education and Science, United Kingdom, 1987.
18. Micheal D. Stephens, (Ed.), *Universities, Education and National Economics*, Rotledge, London, 1989, p. 129.
19. 'Downsizing Higher Education, An Emergent Crisis', *Economic and Political Weekly*, Feb. 15, 2003.
20. Ratna M. Sudarshan, 'Educational Status of Girls and Women', *The Gender Gaps in Basic Education NGO's as Change Agents*, (Ed.), Rekha Wazir, New Delhi, 2000, pp. 39-40.
21. G. Rasool, *National Policy of Education Issues and Developments*, New Delhi, 2001, pp. 203-59.
22. Nirmala Jayaraj, (ed.), 'New Education Policy–Role of Women in Higher Education', in *Higher Education: Vision and Mission for Twenty-First Century*, Madura, 1998, p. 52.
23. *National Education Policy*, 1986.
24. *Commonwealth Universities Year Book 1999*, p. 416.
25. Kirandeep Rajinder Pal Kaen and Hazron K. Mwangi, 'Self fulfillment and International Consciousness in Relation to Achievement of Higher Education Among Women in India', in Power, A.B. (ed.), *Higher Education for Human Development*, AIU, New Delhi, 2000, pp. 133-34.
26. Ananta K. Giri, 'Universities and the Horizons of the Future', *University News*, Nev. 13, 1995.
27. *Ibid.*, p. 3.
28. Dahl, Robert: *Democracy and its Crisis*, Delhi, 1990, p. 333.
29. 'India as a Knowledge Superpower', *Yojana*, Sept. 2002, p. 23.
30. Bellah, Robert *et al.*, *The Good Society*, New York, 1991.
31. Kirandeep and Rajinder Pal Kaur, 'Human Resource Development, Self-fulfillment and International Consciousness in Relation to

Achievement of Higher Education among Women in India'. Paper presented at the *International Conference on Higher Education and Human Development*, New Delhi, 22-24 Feb., 2000.

32. Srivastava J.P. and Rajesh Kumar Kare, 'Growth of Technical Education and Unemployment Pattern', *University News*, 36(50), December 14, 1998, p. 30.
33. *Ibid.*, p. 30.
34. S. Arya, 'Towards Human Excellence in Universities', *University News*, 33 (25), June 19, 1995.
35. 'Downsizing Higher Education–An Emergent Crisis', *Economic and Political Weekly*, Feb. 15, 2003.
36. Emil Constantinescu, President of Romania, 'Twenty-First Century University: Towards an Ethics of Responsibility', *Conference of the International Association of University Presidents*, Brussels, July, 1999.

REFERENCES

Singh, Amrik, "Student Assessment of Teachers' Perspective", *Economic and Political Weekly*, Vol. xxxviii, Nov. 22-28, 2003, pp. 4953-4958.

Tilak, Jandhyala, B.G., No 'Education for all' Yet. Education for All: Review of the book: Is the World on Track? EFA Global Monitoring Report 2002, UNESCO Publishing, Paris 2002 in, *Economic and Political Weekly*, Vol. xxxviii, Nov. 22-28, 2003, pp. 4949-4963.

Shanmugasundaram, Vedagiri (Ed.), *Selected Works of Professor R. Baskaran*, Madras, 2003, Professor R. Baskaran was head of the Department of Politics and Public Administration in the University of Madras from 1947 to 1965. The department established in 1937, is among the earliest to specialize in this subject. Professor Baskaran organized the All India Conference of Political Science in 1950 in the historic Examination Hall situated in Marina Campus of the University of Madras. He was reputed for originality in thought and expression, and though his writings were few, his influence as teacher was great.

Tharu, Susie and Lalita, K: *Women Writing in India: 600 B.C. to Present* (in two volumes), Oxford, 1993.

Lewis, W. Arthur, *The Theory of Economic Growth*, (London, 1955, 1956).

The A.L. Mudaliar Committee Report, *Report of the Secondary Education Commission*, Oct 1952–June 1953, Government of India, 1953.

Sadasivan, D, *The Growth of Public Opinion in the Madras Presidency, 1859-1909*; University of Madras, 1974.

Potter, Robert; Binns, Tony; Elliott, Jeninifer A, and Smith, David, *Geographies of Development*, Longmans, London, 1999.

Hariss, John, Hunter, Janet and Lewis, Colin, *The New Institutional Economics and Third World Development*, Routledge, London, 1995.

Haley, George T; Chin Tiong Tan; Haley, Usha C.V., *New Asian Emperors: The Overseas Chinese, Their Strategies and Competitive Advantages*, Butterworth Heinemann, Oxford, 1998.

Shanmugasundaram, Vedagiri, *Higher Education in the University of Madras*, Madras, 1983.

Streeten, Paul Patrick, *Thinking of Development*, Cambridge University Press, UK, 1995.

Anstey, Vera, *The Economic Development of India*, London, 1929, 1952.

Shanmugasundaram, Yasodha, *Development of the Financial Policy of the Government of India: Influence of the Home Government, 1860-1884*, IASR PRESS, Chennai, 2002.

Balakrishna, R., *The Process of Economic Growth*, Bangalore, 1959.

Rajesvaran, C.D., *British and Russian Socialist Though and Indian Policy*, University of Madras, 1973.

Maran, Murasoli, *State Autonomy*, Madras, 1974.

Index